# TIBETAN YOGA
## AND
# SECRET DOCTRINES

MODERN *GURUS*

Described on pages xviii–xix

# TIBETAN YOGA
## AND
# SECRET DOCTRINES

### OR

Seven Books of Wisdom of the Great Path,
According to the Late Lāma Kazi Dawa-Samdup's
English Rendering

*Arranged and Edited*
*with Introductions and Annotations*
*to serve as a Commentary by*
W. Y. Evans-Wentz

*With Foreword by*
Dr. R. R. Marett

and

*Yogic Commentary by*
Translator-Professor
Chen-Chi Chang

*With a new Foreword by*
Donald S. Lopez, Jr.

OXFORD
UNIVERSITY PRESS
2000

# OXFORD
UNIVERSITY PRESS

Oxford New York

Athens Auckland Bangkok Bogotá Buenos Aires Calcutta
Cape Town Chennai Dar es Salaam Delhi Florence Hong Kong
Istanbul Karachi Kuala Lumpur Madrid Melbourne Mexico City Mumbai
Nairobi Paris São Paulo Singapore Taipei Tokyo Toronto Warsaw

and associated companies in
Berlin Ibadan

First published by Oxford University Press, London, 1935

Second Edition, 1958

First issued as an Oxford University Press paperback, 1967

Published by Oxford University Press, Inc.,
198 Madison Avenue, New York, New York 10016

Oxford is a registered trademark of Oxford University Press

Library of Congress Cataloging-in-Publication Data

Tibetan Yoga and secret doctrines, or, Seven books of wisdom of the Great Path,
according to the late Lama Kazi Dawa-Samdup's English rendering ; arranged and edited
with introductions and annotations to serve as a commentary by W.Y. Evans-Wentz ;
with foreword by R.R. Marett and yogic commentary by translator-professor Chen-Chi
Chang; with a new foreword by Donald S. Lopez, Jr.
    p.cm.
Includes index.
ISBN 0-19-513314-5
    1. Spiritual life—Buddhism. 2. Yoga (Tantric Buddhism). 3. Buddhism—China—Tibet.
I. Title: Tibetan Yoga and secret doctrines. II. Title: Seven books of wisdom of the Great
Path. III. Evans-Wentz, W.Y. (Walter Yeeling), 1878-1965.

BQ7805.T53 2000
294.3'420423—dc21                                                           00-021816

1 3 5 7 9 8 6 4 2

Printed in the United States of America

THIS BOOK

OF

SEVEN BOOKS OF WISDOM

OF THE *YOGA* PATH DIRECT

I DEDICATE

TO THEM THAT SHALL SUCCEED ME

IN THE QUEST ON EARTH

## WISDOM-TEACHINGS AND GOOD-WISHES OF THE ĀDI-BUDDHA SAMANTA-BHADRA

'The Foundation of all is uncreated, uncompounded, independent, beyond mental concept and verbal definition. Neither the term *Sangsāra* nor the term *Nirvāṇa* can be applied to It. To realize It is to attain Buddhahood. Not to realize It is to wander in the *Sangsāra*. . . .

'Not knowing the Foundation, beings aforetime erred. They were overwhelmed by the darkness of unconsciousness, whence sprang ignorance and error. Immersed in error and obscured by ignorance, the "knower" became bewildered and afraid. Then arose the concepts "I" and "Others", together with hatred. When these had grown strong, there was born an unbroken current of *sangsāric* evolution. Then the "five poisons" of the obscuring passions, lust, anger, selfishness, delusion, and jealousy, flourished, and there was produced an interminable chain of evil *karma*.

'The root-source of error among sentient beings is thus unconscious ignorance. And, in virtue of the power of the Good-Wishes of Me, the Ādi-Buddha, may each of them realize the radiant, immaculate mind, innate in every living thing.'

From *The Good-Wishes of the All-Good Buddha Samanta-Bhadra*
(Lāma Kazi Dawa-Samdup's Translation).

# FOREWORD

*Donald S. Lopez, Jr.*

A certain trepidation attends the decision to accept an invitation
to write a foreword to new editions, published in 2000, of the four
books of W. Y. Evans-Wentz: *The Tibetan Book of the Dead, Tibet's
Great Yogī Milarepa, Tibetan Yoga and Secret Doctrines*, and *The Tibetan Book of the Great Liberation*. The four books in their old editions are already burdened with numerous prefaces, commentaries, and introductions, causing one to wonder what another
preface could possibly add. It seems inevitable that the four books
of Evans-Wentz will continue to outlive yet another generation
of commentators, such that anything that a scholar might add
today will only serve as material for a scholar some fifty years
from now, who will demonstrate the biases and misunderstand-
ings of a preface written fifty years ago, a preface that merely offers evidence of the fin de siècle zeitgeist of those who once called
themselves postmoderns.

The four books of Evans-Wentz are surely ground-breaking
works, the first to bring translations of Tibetan Buddhist texts to
the English-speaking public. Evans-Wentz was equally avant
garde in his method, collaborating closely with Tibetan scholars,
a practice that would not become common for another four
decades, after the Tibetan diaspora began in 1959. Yet, for the
scholar of the present day, looking back now more than seventy
years to the publication of the first volume of the series, *The Tibetan Book of the Dead*, in 1927, the Tibetan tetralogy of W. Y.
Evans-Wentz, although a product of our century, seems to have
originated in another age. All four books assume the undifferentiated dichotomy of the materialist West and the mystic East, an
East that holds the secret to the West's redemption. Few of the
concerns of scholars—such as language or culture or history—are
to be found in the books. Instead, the volumes are presented as
repositories of a timeless wisdom preserved by the East, a wisdom

that will someday save the West, ultimately overcoming the duality of the hemispheres to culminate in the Unity of Mankind. This apparently beatific vision has since been shown to be the product of a romantic Orientalism that viewed the traditions of Asia as a natural resource to be extracted and refined for the consumption of the West; the books thus mark a moment in the history of colonialism.

Yet the four books of Evans-Wentz, especially the first, represent an important moment in that history. The products of a chance encounter between a Sikkimese school teacher and an American eccentric traveling in British India in 1919, the books have proved to be among the most durable products of the century's romance of Tibet, radiating their influence far beyond what might be expected from such an unlikely beginning.

Walter Wentz was born in Trenton, New Jersey, in 1878, the son of a German immigrant and an American Quaker. The late nineteenth century was a period of great fascination with spiritualism, the belief that spirits of the dead could be contacted through seances, materialization, automatic writing, and other techniques. Walter took an early interest in the books on spiritualism in his father's library, reading as a teen both *Isis Unveiled* and *The Secret Doctrine* by Madame Blavatsky of the Theosophical Society. These works were to have a profound effect on Walter Wentz. Indeed, it is impossible to appreciate his tetralogy without recognizing his lifelong commitment to Theosophy.

The Theosophical Society had been founded in New York in 1875 by Madame Helena Petrovna Blavatsky, a Russian émigré, and Colonel Henry Steel Olcott, a journalist and veteran of the Union Army during the Civil War. The goals of their Society were "to diffuse among men a knowledge of the laws inherent in the universe; to promulgate the knowledge of the essential unity of all that is, and to determine that this unity is fundamental in nature; to form an active brotherhood among men; to study ancient and modern religion, science, and philosophy; and to investigate the powers innate in man." The Theosophical Society represented one of several responses to Darwin's theory of evolution during the late nineteenth century. Rather than seeking a refuge from science in religion, Blavatsky and Olcott attempted to found a scientific religion, one that accepted the new discoveries in geology and archaeology while proclaiming an ancient and esoteric system of spiritual evolution more sophisticated than Darwin's theory.

Madame Blavatsky claimed to have spent seven years in Tibet as an initiate of a secret order of enlightened masters called the Great White Brotherhood. These masters, whom she called Mahatmas ("great souls"), lived in Tibet but were not themselves Tibetan. In fact, the very presence of the Mahatmas in Tibet was unknown to ordinary Tibetans. These masters had once lived throughout the world, but had congregated in Tibet to escape the onslaught of civilization. The Mahatmas had instructed her in Theosophy, which she also referred to as "Esoteric Buddhism," of which the Buddhism being practiced in Asia, including Tibet, was a corruption.

Throughout her career, she (and later, other members of the society) claimed to be in esoteric communication with the Mahatmas, sometimes through dreams and visions, but most commonly through letters that either materialized in a cabinet in Madame Blavatsky's room or that she transcribed through automatic writing. The Mahatmas' literary output was prodigious, conveying instructions on the most mundane matters of the Society's functions, as well as providing the content of the canonical texts of the Society, such as A. P. Sinnett's *Esoteric Buddhism* (1885) and Madame Blavatsky's *The Secret Doctrine* (1888).

The Theosophical Society enjoyed great popularity in America, Europe, and India (despite repeated scandals and a report by the Society of Psychical Research that denounced Madame Blavatsky as a fraud), playing an important but ambiguous role in the Hindu renaissance in India and the Buddhist renaissance in Sri Lanka (where Henry Olcott was particularly active). Its popularity continued after the death of the founders and into the twentieth century, when Blavatsky's heir, the former British suffragette Annie Besant, selected a young Hindu boy in 1909 as the messiah, the World Teacher, Krishnamurti. He renounced his divine status and broke with the Society in 1930. The death of Besant and other leaders followed soon after and the Society never regained the widespread popularity it once enjoyed, although it remains active, with its international headquarters in Pasadena, California. The Theosophical Society has had a profound effect on the reception of Asian religions, especially Hinduism and Buddhism, in Europe and America during the twentieth century, inspiring, among other works, the Evans-Wentz tetralogy.

Walter Wentz moved to California at the turn of the century, where he joined the American Section of the Theosophical Society in 1901 at its headquarters in Point Loma, headed by Katherine Tingley, who established there the Raja-Yoga School and College, Theosophical University, and the School for the Revival of the Lost Mysteries of Antiquity. At Tingley's urging, Wentz enrolled at Stanford University, where he studied with William James and William Butler Yeats. After graduating, Wentz went to Jesus College at Oxford in 1907, where he studied Celtic folklore. It was there that he added a family name from his mother's side to his surname and became Walter Evans-Wentz. After completing his thesis, later published as *The Fairy Faith in Celtic Countries* (1911), he began a world tour financed by the income he received from rental properties in Florida. He was in Greece when the First World War broke out, and spent most of the war in Egypt.

From Egypt, he traveled to Sri Lanka and then on to India, gaining permission to travel from the British military authorities on the recommendation of a former classmate from Oxford, T. E. Lawrence. Evans-Wentz visited the Theosophical Society headquarters at Adyar and met with Annie Besant. In north India, he studied with various Hindu gurus, especially Swami Satyananda. In 1919 he arrived in the British hill station of Darjeeling on the southern slopes of the Himalayas, where he acquired a worn manuscript of a Tibetan text from a monk (some sources indicate that he acquired it in the bazaar). It was a portion of *The Profound Doctrine of Self-Liberation of the Mind [through Encountering] the Peaceful and Wrathful Deities*, (*Zab chos zhi khro dgongs pa rang grol*) said to have been discovered in the fourteenth century by Karma gling pa (1352–1405). The text is also known as the *Peaceful and Wrathful Deities According to Karmalingpa* or *Kar gling zhi khro* and as the *Bar do thos grol chen mo*, *The Great Liberation in the Intermediate State through Hearing*. Provided with a letter of introduction from the local superintendent of police, Sardar Bahadur Laden La (with whom he would later collaborate on the final volume in his series), Evans-Wentz, who could not read Tibetan, took the text to the English teacher at the Maharaja's Boy's School in Gangtok, named Kazi Dawa Samdup (1868–1922). Dawa Samdup was already acquainted with western enthusiasts of Buddhism, having served as translator for Alexandra David-Neel. She described him in *Magic and Mystery in Tibet*: "Dawasamdup was an occultist and even, in a certain way, a mystic. He sought for secret intercourse with the Dâkinîs and the dreadful gods hoping to gain supernormal powers. Everything that concerned the mysterious world of beings generally invisible strongly attracted him, but the necessity of earning his living made it impossible for him to devote much time to his favourite study.... Drink, a failing frequent among his countrymen, had been the curse of his life.... But, peace to his memory. I do not wish to belittle him. Having acquired real erudition by persevering efforts, he was sympathetic and interesting."[1]

Kazi Dawa Samdup agreed to provide a translation, and over the course of the next two months he met with Evans-Wentz each morning before his school day began. The translations that Kazi Dawa Samdup made for Evans-Wentz would eventually appear in three books: *The Tibetan Book of the Dead* (1927), *Tibetan Yoga and Secret Doctrines* (1935), and *The Tibetan Book of the Great Liberation* (1954). Their time together was brief, however, with Evans-Wentz soon moving back to the ashram of Swami Satyananda to practice yoga. He returned to Gangtok to visit Kazi Dawa Samdup in 1920, shortly before the latter's appointment to the post of Lecturer in Tibetan at the University of Calcutta. This was to be their last meeting; Kazi Dawa Samdup died in 1922. In 1924, Evans-Wentz visited Kazi Dawa Samdup's family in Kalimpong, from whom he received a manuscript translation of the *Rje btsun bka' 'bum* (*The Hundred Thousand Words of the Master*), which Evans-Wentz subsequently edited and published as *Tibet's Great Yogī Milarepa* (1928). Of his relationship with Kazi Dawa Samdup, Evans-Wentz's biographer writes: "The few letters that have survived that they exchanged show a surprisingly distant and formal tone. Even in Dawa Samdup's diaries there is no word to suggest otherwise. There is nothing at all foreshadowing the later declarations that the Lama was the guru of Walter Evans-Wentz, nothing about the 'teachings' the American was supposed to have received."[2]

There is little testimony as to precisely how their collaboration

---

[1] Alexandra David-Neel, *Magic and Mystery in Tibet* (New York: Dover Publications, 1971), pp. 15, 17, 19.

[2] Ken Winkler, *Pilgrim of the Clear Light* (Berkeley, Calif.: Dawnfire Books, 1982), p. 44. The other biographical information on Evans-Wentz here is drawn from Winkler's book. A useful summary is provided by John Myrdhin Reynolds in *Self-Liberation Through Seeing with Naked Awareness* (Barrytown, N.Y.: Station Hill Press, 1989), pp. 71–78.

took place. Kazi Dawa Samdup's English was presumably adequate to the task of producing rough translations. Evans-Wentz describes himself as having served as the lama's "living English dictionary." One can thus assume that much of the terminology derived from Evans-Wentz. And Evans-Wentz provided the lengthy introductions and copious annotations, which together provide the four books with his unmistakable stamp. He did not claim that they were scholarly works; he noted presciently that a critical study of the texts from the perspectives of philology, history, and philosophy was a task for scholars of the future. Instead, he described his works as "anthropological," taking anthropology to mean, "the Knowing, or Knowledge, of Man."

Evans-Wentz made several trips to India in the 1920s and 30s, studying yoga with several prominent neo-Vedantin teachers of the day, including Sri Yukteswar and Ramana Maharshi. He returned to Darjeeling in 1935 and employed two Sikkimese monks to translate another work from the same cycle of texts as the *Bar do thos grol*, entitled *Self-Liberation through Naked Vision Recognizing Awareness* (*Rig pa ngo sprod gcer mthong rang grol*). During the same visit, he received a summary of a famous biography of Padmasambhava, prepared by Sardar Bahadur Laden La, who had introduced him to Kazi Dawa Samdup some sixteen years before. These works would form the last work in the series, *The Tibetan Book of the Great Liberation*, eventually published in 1954.

Evans-Wentz returned to the United States in 1941, and spent the final twenty-three years of his life at the Keystone Hotel in San Diego. He spent his final months at the Self-Realization Fellowship of Swami Yogananda (a disciple of Sri Yukteswar and author of the popular *Autobiography of a Yogi*) in Encinitas, California. Walter Evans-Wentz died in 1965.

Evans-Wentz was apparently never a devotee of Tibetan Buddhism, considering himself instead a practitioner of Hindu yoga. His last contact with a Tibetan teacher seems to have been his collaboration with the two monks at the monastery of Ghoom, near Darjeeling, in 1935. Because his collaboration with Kazi Dawa Samdup was so brief, it is difficult to accept his claim that he was "the recognized disciple" of a Tibetan lama. Indeed, Kazi Dawa Samdup seems only to have been regarded as a "lama" by Evans-Wentz himself. Evans-Wentz remained a Theosophist and wrote for various Theosophical publications throughout the rest of his life. He never learned to read Tibetan; perhaps he did not feel it necessary, almost as if he already knew what the texts must say. And if they did not seem to say that, there was always recourse to their esoteric meaning, something he discusses at length in his introduction to *The Tibetan Book of the Dead*. Still, each of his four books holds an important place in the history of Tibetan Buddhism in the West and they must be regarded as pioneering works, not only in the texts chosen but in the mode of their creation; after the Tibetan diaspora that began in 1959, it became common for Western scholars to consult with Tibetan scholars in their translations of Buddhist texts, just as Evans-Wentz had done decades before.

From the perspective of the modern scholar of Tibetan Buddhism, the four books are fraught with problems: errors in translation, inaccurate dates, misattributions of authorship, misstatements of fact, unjustified flights of interpretation. (Referring to himself in the introduction, Evans-Wentz writes on page 79 of *The Tibetan Book of the Dead*, "The editor himself cannot expect, in a book of this nature, that his own interpretations of controversial problems will meet with universal acceptance; nor can he hope to have escaped all error.") With many decades of hindsight, each of the books seems somehow premature, translations attempted at a time when the requisite scholarly resources were not yet available. Still, Evans-Wentz makes little attempt to place them in their Tibetan literary and religious context. Indeed, there is very little that is "Tibetan" about the books, despite their titles. One wonders whether the adjective carried above all a Theosophical meaning for Evans-Wentz.

There is a certain audacity about the books; Evans-Wentz thought that he understood what he read, reading, as he did, through his bifocals of Theosophy and Hindu Yoga. But if Evans-Wentz had not been so audacious, we would not have had the books and their wide influence; even today, few scholars would feel competent to take on the task of translating and annotating all of the works found in *Tibetan Yoga and Secret Doctrines*, for example, and even if such a book were to be produced, the scholarly apparatus itself would render it esoteric to all but the initiates of Tibetology.

Evans-Wentz had a different, and much larger, audience of initiates in mind for his esoteric wisdom. The four books of Walter

Evans-Wentz are, then, the products of another age, an age when there was little talk of cultural relativism, of radical incommensurability, of historicism, of identity politics, of orientalism, of colonialism, of local histories, or of the late formation of the "world religions." Instead, in these texts, Evans-Wentz finds endless evidence of an ancient and universal wisdom, whose truth is not mediated by language or history or culture, but which is self-evident to all peoples of all races who will seek it. This may strike some as a rather quaint notion in 2000. Yet the books are about to enter their second century in print.

*Tibetan Yoga and Secret Doctrines*, first published in 1935, was intended as the third and final volume of a trilogy. Unlike *The Tibetan Book of the Dead* (1927) and *Tibet's Great Yogi Milarepa* (1928), it is not devoted to the translation and exposition of a single text. Instead, it includes translations of seven texts, produced from the collaboration of Evans-Wentz and Kazi Dawa Samdup in 1919 and 1920. Each of these seven works is worthy of a detailed study; only the most cursory discussion can be provided here.

The first four texts derive from the Kagyu (Bka' brgyud) sect of Tibetan Buddhism, the sect of Marpa and Milarepa. The first of these is a collection of aphorisms by Milarepa's most famous disciple, Sgam po pa (1079–1153), entitled *A Garland of Jewels [of] the Supreme Path (Lam mchog rin po che'i 'phreng ba)*. It has twenty-eight chapters, each containing (with three exceptions) ten admonitions concerning the practice of the Buddhist path: "the ten things to be avoided," "the ten things one must know," etc. (Finding that an aphorism was missing from one of the lists, Evans-Wentz added one of his own to complete it.) Prior to becoming Milarepa's disciple, Sgam po pa had been a monk in the Bka' gdams tradition of Atiśa, and both teachers are praised in the colophon. The text itself does not bear the particular characteristics of any single sect of Tibetan Buddhism, but instead is intended as useful, and easily memorized, advice for anyone undertaking the practice of the Buddhist path. It follows in a long tradition of Indian gnomic verse, which continued in Tibetan among all sects.

This rather prosaic work unexpectedly gives way to a series of esoteric texts, texts that contain advanced tantric instructions that would not normally be imparted without initiation and often

extensive preliminary practice. The first of these (Book II, as
Evans-Wentz calls it) is entitled *Notes on Mahāmudrā* (*Phyag chen
gyi zin bris*) by the great Kagyu scholar Padma dkar po
(1527–1592). "Mahāmudrā," rendered by Evans-Wentz as "The
Great Symbol," might more accurately be translated as "the
Great Seal." The Great Seal is a state of enlightened awareness in
which phenomenal appearance and noumenal emptiness are unified. Like the Great Perfection of the Nyingma, it is considered
to be primordially present. It is not something that is newly created; rather, every moment of consciousness bears its seal. Instead
of emphasizing the attainment of an extraordinary level of consciousness, the Great Seal literature exalts the ordinary state of
mind as both the natural and ultimate state, characterized by lucidity and simplicity. This ordinary mind is contrasted with the
worldly mind. The former, compared to a mirror, reflects reality
exactly as it is, simply and purely, whereas the worldly mind is dis-
torted by its mistaken perception of subject and object as real.
Rather than seeking to destroy this worldly mind as other systems
do, however, in the Great Seal the worldly mind is valued for its
ultimate identity with the ordinary mind; every deluded thought
contains within it the lucidity and simplicity of the ordinary
mind. This identity merely needs to be recognized to bring about
the dawning of wisdom, the realization that a natural purity pervades all existence, including the deluded mind.

Padma dkar po's text provides succinct instructions in the meditative techniques that lead to the realization of the Great Seal.
The main part of the text sets forth the common (in the sense that
they are shared by other systems) and the uncommon (in the
sense that they are unique to *mahāmudrā*) practices. The former
include the standard practices of developing a deep state of concentration, called quiescence (*zhi gnas*), which is then used to develop a realization of emptiness, called insight (*lhag mthong*). The
uncommon practices are also two: the yoga of one taste, which
experiences all phenomena—appearances and the mind—as inseparable, and the uncultivated yoga that identifies the natural
spontaneity of all phenomena as the truth body (*dharmakāya*) of a
buddha.

The third text in *Tibetan Yoga and Secret Doctrines* is also by
Padma dkar po and is entitled *Notes Summarizing the Six Teachings*
(*Chos drug bsdus pa'i zin bris*). It treats the famous "Six Teachings

of Nāropa" (*Nā ro chos drug*), also known in the West as the "Six Yogas of Nāropa." Nāropa is said to have received instruction in the six teachings from the yogin Tilopa. Nāropa conveyed them to Marpa, who transmitted them to Tibet. There are a number of configurations of the six yogas, in most cases involving some combination of inner heat (*gtum mo*), a sexual consort (*karma-mudrā*), illusory body (*sgyu lus*), clear light (*'od gsal*), dream (*mi lam*), bardo, consciousness transference (*'pho ba*), and forceful entry (*grong 'jug*).[3] These various practices seem not to have orig-inated with Nāropa or Tilopa, but rather represent a collection of various tantric teachings that were current in Bengal in the eleventh century. They are all considered highly advanced teach-ings intended to result in the attainment of buddhahood. Within the fourfold tantric division, they are teachings of the completion stage (*rdzogs rim*) of Highest Yoga Tantra (*anuttarayogatantra*).

In Padma dkar po's text translated here, the six teachings are inner heat, illusory body, clear light, dream, bardo, and con-sciousness transference. The foundational practice for the six teachings is the first, the yoga of inner heat, and thus almost half of Padma dkar po's text is devoted to its exposition. Inner heat yoga, at which Milarepa was so adept, is based, as are the other yogas, on a physiology in which winds or subtle energies, serving as the vehicles for consciousness, course through the body via a network of channels. Among these, the most important is the central channel that runs from the genitals upward to the crown of the head. Parallel to the central channel are the right and left channels, which wrap around it at several points, creating con-strictions that prevent wind from moving through the central channel. At these points of constriction, there are also networks of smaller channels which radiate throughout the body. These points are called wheels or chakras. Those located at the crown of the head, throat, heart, and slightly below the navel are empha-sized in inner heat yoga. The practice is a combination of visual-izations and breath exercises that cause the winds to enter into the central channel. Through the generation of heat at the navel chakra, essences called drops at the head, throat, and heart chakras are caused to melt, generating bliss.

[3] For an exposition of the six yogas from the perspective of the Geluk sect, see Tsongkhapa Lobzang Drakpa, *Tsongkhapa's Six Yogas of Naropa*, trans., ed., and intro. by Glenn H. Mullin (Ithaca, N.Y.: Snow Lion Publications, 1996).

The ability to cause the winds to enter the central channel provides the meditator with access to various profound states of consciousness essential to the attainment of buddhahood, most importantly the mind of clear light, the subject of the fourth of the six teachings in Padma dkar po's presentation. It is this most profound state of consciousness that, upon the realization of emptiness, is transformed into the omniscience of a buddha. When the mind of clear light can be identified during the waking state, it is possible to then also gain access to the clear light of sleep, and Padma dkar po offers instructions for both day and night. The third of the six teachings, dream yoga, is dedicated specifically to finding and utilizing the mind of clear light during sleep. In order to reach that point, Padma dkar po provides a series of instructions designed to provide control over dreams. At the conclusion of the practices, the yogin creates an illusory body (the second teaching here), an immortal body made of the most subtle wind and mind that, upon enlightenment, becomes the form body (*rūpakāya*) of a buddha. Prior to that point, there are a series of practices involving the contemplation of both one's own form and then the form of a buddha in a mirror, designed to induce insight into the illusory nature of the body.

The first four of the six teachings are intended to bestow buddhahood in this lifetime. If this is not possible, the last two provide means for doing so after death. The practice of consciousness transference is a technique for forcibly causing one's consciousness to travel up through the central channel, exit from an aperture in the crown of the head, and travel to a pure land, an ideal realm for the achievement of enlightenment. If this is not possible, there is the practice of the bardo, similar to that described in *The Tibetan Book of the Dead*, in which the mind of clear light is identified and buddhahood attained in the intermediate state between death and rebirth. If this is not possible, Padma dkar po provides instructions on how to find an auspicious rebirth.

Book IV includes two more recent texts by Rtogs ldan Śakya śrī (1853–1919) of the Kagyu sect. They are devoted specifically to the practice of consciousness transference, offering more detailed instructions than those found in Padma dkar po's summary version of the six teachings of Nāropa. The first text sets forth the technique for causing the mind to enter the central channel and for causing the aperture at the crown of the head to open, in preparation for sending the consciousness to a pure land at the moment of death. The second text offers instructions to one already skilled in consciousness transference so that he or she will be able to direct the consciousness of one recently deceased into an auspicious realm, ranging for a pure land to an advanced stage on the bodhisattva path.

Book V of *Tibetan Yoga and Secret Doctrine* is devoted to the chöd (*gcod*) ritual, reported by various travelers to Tibet, most notably, Alexandra David-Neel. The text translated here is attributed to 'Jigs med gling pa (1730–1798), a famous discoverer of treasure texts of the Nyingma sect. There is an extensive tradition of *gcod* literature and practice in Tibet, encompassing all sects, including Bon. Regardless of the sect, the practice of *gcod* is most commonly associated with the great Tibetan female yogin, Ma gcig lab sgron (1055–1152?).[4] The *gcod* practitioner is expected to frequent cemeteries and other sites fraught with danger, where he or she will pitch a tent, perform a dance, beat a drum, and blow on a trumpet made from a human thigh bone. This unconventional behavior has led some to speculate that *gcod* is a shamanistic exorcism rite derived from Tibet's pre-Buddhist past. The task of identifying what is and is not authentically "Buddhist" has remained a vexing task for scholars. However, it is quite clear that, according to its traditional history, *gcod* was transmitted from India to Tibet. Regardless of its origins, the ideology of *gcod* is decidedly Buddhist.

The full name of the practice is *bdud kyi gcod yul*, or "the demon to be severed." There is a long tradition in Buddhism of regarding demons as the projections of the desire, hatred, and ignorance that are the root cause of suffering and that must be eliminated on the path to buddhahood. Indeed, according to an Indian enumeration, one's own mind and body are regarded as "the demon of the aggregates" and one of the demons to be eliminated in *gcod* practice is attachment to one's own body. In the *gcod* literature four demons are enumerated: tangible demons, the harmful forces that exist in the external world; intangible demons, the negative mental states resulting from desire, hatred, and ignorance; the demon of delight that takes false

[4] See Jérôme Edou, *Machig Labdrön and the Foundations of Chöd* (Ithaca: Snow Lion Publications, 1996).

pride in the superiority of one's teacher or premature pleasure in the results of one's meditation practice; and the demon of conceit, the belief in self. In keeping with classical Buddhist doctrine, if this last demon can be destroyed through the understanding that there is no self, that the person, and indeed, all phenomena are devoid of any intrinsic nature, then the other three types of demons will also be eliminated. Indeed, the perfection of wisdom literature with its exposition of the doctrine of emptiness is highly revered in the *gcod* tradition as the ultimate means of cutting through the webs of ignorance.

In the *gcod* practice, the meditator imagines his or her consciousness in the form of the goddess Vajrayoginī, abiding in the central channel. She exits from the aperture at the crown of the head, at which point the meditator's body is imagined to collapse. Vajrayoginī cuts off the crown of the skull of the prostrate body, which is immediately transformed into a huge cauldron, into which the body is thrown. The boiling of the body produces an elixir that is offered to all the buddhas, bodhisattvas, and to all sentient beings and spirits, both benevolent and malevolent. These offerings are referred to as the four feasts: the white, variegated, red, and black. The Mahāyāna dyad of wisdom and compassion are represented here. By severing the skull from the body, one cuts attachment to the body, resulting in wisdom. Among the deeds of the bodhisattva is the perfection of giving. Because the body is the object of such great attachment, the gift of the body is often praised as the highest form of the perfection of giving. This compassionate deed produces a great store of merit for the meditator. Indeed, because the practitioner of *gcod* is often a wandering mendicant who has nothing other than his or her own body to offer in order to accumulate the necessary store of merit to progress on the path, *gcod* is sometimes called, "a beggar's collection of merit."

The sixth text in *Tibetan Yoga and Secret Doctrines* is a brief work (reproduced in full facing page 335) entitled *Mode of Being of the Long Hūṃ Endowed with the Five Wisdoms* (*Hūṃ ring po ye she lnga ldan gyi yin lugs*). The mantra *hūṃ* is one of the most prevalent and potent in tantric Buddhism. In the mantra *oṃ āḥ hūṃ*, a white *oṃ* is visualized in the head chakra, a red *āḥ* is visualized at the throat chakra, and a blue *hūṃ* is visualized at the heart chakra. In many tantric meditations, infinite *hūṃs* are emanated from the

heart to fill the universe and are then gathered back into a single
*hūṃ* in the meditator's heart. The entire universe then melts into
emptiness, beginning at the edges and moving inward, until the
body of the meditator, visualized as a buddha, also dissolves, leaving only the letter *hūṃ*. The *hūṃ* then begins to dissolve from the
bottom, until it too disappears into emptiness. In its orthographic
representation, the mantra has five parts, and in the text translated here, each of those parts is made to correspond to one of the
buddha lineages (of Akṣobhaya, Vairocana, Ratnasambhava,
Amitābha, and Amogasiddhi) and to the five wisdoms of a buddha
(the wisdom of the sphere of reality, the mirror-like wisdom, the
wisdom of equality, the wisdom of specific understanding, and the
wisdom of accomplishment).

The seventh and final text is perhaps the most famous of Buddhist sūtras, the *Heart Sūtra*, renowned for its terse exposition of
the doctrine of emptiness. The perfection of wisdom sūtras include texts of varying length, including the *Perfection of Wisdom in
One Hundred Thousand Stanzas* and the *Perfection of Wisdom in
Eight Thousand Stanzas*. The *Heart Sūtra* is considered the quintessence of these longer texts. It is known by heart by Buddhists
throughout Tibet, Korea, China, and Japan and is among the
most commented upon of Buddhist texts.

We must also consider, as always, Evans-Wentz's copious introductions and annotations to these texts. He is typically verbose
here, with many pages where the notes take up more of the page
than the translation. But despite his prolixity, it is a single page of
photographs that most clearly conveys his understanding of the
translations. Facing the title page are six photographs, with the
caption *"Modern Gurus."* Six of the seven are Hindu teachers.
The smallest of the photos in the upper left corner shows Kazi
Dawa Samdup. (It is a cropped version of his photo with Evans-
Wentz that appears as the frontispiece to *The Tibetan Book of the
Dead*.) In his description of the Hindu teachers, Evans-Wentz expresses his personal debt and appreciation to five of the six; the
sixth, Sri Jukteswar (Yukteswar), was the revered guru of Swami
Yogananda, whom Evans-Wentz befriended in California. The
photographs are testimony to an important fact: that despite
Evans-Wentz's rightful fame for bringing Tibetan Buddhism to a
large audience in the West, his own interests lay elsewhere. Although he repeatedly describes, in this book and the others, Kazi

Dawa Samdup as "my guru," he in fact spent very little time with him, and that spent in rather intensive work on the translations. The greater part of Evans-Wentz's time during his visits to India, and the true object of his devotion, was Hindu yoga as it was taught to Western enthusiasts in the early decades of the twentieth century. It is this system that Evans-Wentz seeks to identify with the disparate Tibetan texts translated in the volume. Again, he places photos of yet another of his Hindu gurus, Swami Satyananda, at the beginning of the translation of Padma dkar po's work on *mahāmudrā*. Thus, the longest section of his introduction to the volume is devoted to a discussion of the various forms of Hindu yoga, unaware that they are largely irrelevant to the Tibetan Buddhist practices set forth in the translation. Indeed, for Evans-Wentz, the meaning of the term "yoga" seems to expand until it ultimately encompasses all forms of religious practice—in all cultures and all times—of which he approves: Pythagoreans, the cult of Isis, "the School of Omar Khayyām," Druids, Sufis, Gnostics, Jesuits, and Parsees.

When this view of yoga is combined with his references to Theosophy (he speaks, for example, of "the early dawn of a truly New Science," p. xxvi, and "the secret lore of the Great Sages," p. 50), what results is a universalist view in which Tibet and Tibetan Buddhism are somehow lost, providing little more than instantiations of a larger truth, with Tibetan texts made to speak that truth through Evans-Wentz's careful protection of them behind a wall of introductions and footnotes, providing in many instances a counter narrative of free associations and "yogic" explanations to the text. Despite the prominent role of Tibet in the title of this volume and the others, Tibet in many ways remains here what it was for Madame Blavatsky, a storehouse for occult knowledge. (Indeed, Evans-Wentz uses a passage from her *The Voice of the Silence* as an epigraph for the translation of the first Tibetan text.) With this in mind, the title *Tibetan Yoga and Secret Doctrines* takes on a rather different meaning.

Space does not permit any detailed discussion of the translations themselves. As in the other works, the translations are highly hypostatized, with rampant capitalization and misunderstanding of technical terms. The term *spros bral*, a technical term in Madhyamaka philosophy that means "free of conceptual elaboration," becomes "the Uncreated." Although it is impossible to identify who played what role in the collaboration, one would assume that this style was provided by Evans-Wentz. It appears that the translations were done quickly; he mentions that he and Kazi Dawa Samdup spent one week in July 1919 on the translation of the *mahāmudrā* text in Book II. One must sympathize with Evans-Wentz, being left on his own to introduce and annotate texts that he could not understand. He did not know Tibetan and the scholarship of his day was not always useful; his notes demonstrate that he made considerable effort to consult the available secondary literature. Under such circumstances he was left to make whatever sense of them that he could, and his efforts are not always successful. For example, his long discussion of the Tibetan "mystery play" (289–294), drawn from Waddell, is quite unrelated to the *gcod* text that follows.

His dilemma was exacerbated by the fact that the texts that Kazi Dawa Samdup translated for him in this volume are for the most part of a highly advanced and technical nature. The texts translated in Books II, III, IV, and V are very much of the "don't try this at home" variety. There is thus a certain salvation in the many errors in the translations: they prevent the reader from attempting to put them into practice. For example, in the inner heat practice, one is to visualize what is called a "short *a*." This refers to the vertical stroke that occurs in the Tibetan letter *a*. Visualized in the navel chakra in the central channel, it is this "short a" that bursts into flame, producing the inner heat. Evans-Wentz does not understand this, as is evident from his footnote on page 191.

Looking back on these translations almost a century later, despite all of these difficulties, one can only marvel at the collaborators' choice of such important works and admire their remarkable efforts at bringing them into English. The fact that the works now require retranslation is, in a sense, a testimony to their pioneering work.

# PREFACE TO THE FIRST EDITION

AS in *The Tibetan Book of the Dead* and in *Tibet's Great Yogī Milarepa* so in this book, the third in a threefold series, my aim has been to place on record not only a catena of carefully made translations of texts which are as yet almost unknown in Occidental countries, but also a body of orally transmitted traditions and teachings relating to the texts, which I received from the late Lāma Kazi Dawa-Samdup, who was my Tibetan *guru*.

The present work thus contains much that is new to Western thought, and much that, apart from its value for philosophy and religion, is interesting anthropologically. It should prove to be of the same quality and public appeal as the two volumes of the series which have already been published. Perhaps it may be found to be the most valuable member of the trilogy, inasmuch as it gives the very texts of some of the principal *yogas* and meditations which many of the most illustrious Tibetan and Indian philosophers, including Tilopa, Naropa, Marpa, and Milarepa, employed in attaining Right Knowledge.

This volume is meant at once for the exact scholar and for the general reader. The former will note that the original textual sources, which are sevenfold, are authentic, and that nothing has been incorporated into the texts or presented in the introductions and annotations which has not doctrinal sanction.

The seven chief texts upon which the seven Books, or parts, comprising this volume are based contain teachings and matter dating a long way beyond the time to which the actual manuscripts and block-prints can be referred. A full discussion of this question is contained in the special introductions to the seven Books. The shortened titles of these seven texts, rendered into English, are as follows:

(1) *Gampopa's Supreme Path, called ' The Precious Rosary'*, consisting of twenty-eight categories of *yogic* precepts for the guidance of the disciple;

(2) *The Epitome of the Great Symbol*, a treatise on the practical *yogic* method of realizing *Nirvāṇa*;

(3) *The Epitome of the Six Doctrines*, which are the Psychic-Heat, the Illusory Body, the Dream-State, the Clear Light, the After-Death State, and the Transference of the Consciousness;

(4) *The Transference of the Consciousness*, a *yogic* treatise complementary to the last of the Six Doctrines;

(5) *The Method of Eradicating the Lower Self*, a treatise on the *Yoga* of Non-Ego;

(6) *The Five-Fold Wisdom Attribute of the Long* Hūṃ, a treatise on the *Yoga* of the Five Wisdoms;

(7) *The Essence of the Transcendental Wisdom*, a short *Sūtra* belonging to the *Prajñā-Pāramitā* of the Tibetan canon.

For the benefit of the general reader, I have prefixed to the treatise, in the form of a General Introduction, a brief account of Buddhism, so presented as to contrast with our European conceptions of religion and philosophy, and, to some extent, science. Similarly, in my exposition of the *Yoga* Philosophy, upon which the treatise as a whole is based, I have made use of teachings which have come to me from trustworthy teachers during the course of careful inquiry and research extending over a period of more than fifteen years, spent mostly in the Orient.

In a realm so filled with difficulties for the European mind as this book attempts to explore, it is not to be expected that I have always escaped error. In any event, I trust that readers and critics of this volume will recognize in it, despite any such shortcomings as it may perhaps exhibit, a sincere effort to help, in some small degree, to bring about amongst the peoples of the Western World a better understanding of some of the master minds of Tibet and of India.

Once more in the preface of a printed book, and probably for the last time in this incarnation, I here acknowledge my indebtedness to the late Lāma Kazi Dawa-Samdup, without whose patient toil and guidance neither this treatise nor the two treatises which have prepared the way for it would ever have been written. I also acknowledge my indebtedness to each of my other preceptors and helpers in India and Tibet and throughout the Occident.

In this connexion I cannot omit to record the name of Dr. R. R. Marett, Reader in Social Anthropology in the University of Oxford, and Rector of Exeter College, who has never failed to offer encouragement and sound advice to me, his old pupil, during the past twenty-seven years, that is to say, ever since I came up to Oxford. And now I am further indebted to him for the Foreword to this volume.

I am also very grateful to my good friend and helper, Mr. E. T. Sturdy, translator of *The Nārada Sūtra*, for having read over, both when it was in typewritten form and when it was in proof, the matter contained within these covers, and more particularly for having given attention to the Sanskrit terms and to my exposition of Vedāntic doctrines.

With respect to certain problems relating to the original Tibetan texts, I have been fortunate in having been able to question Dr. F. W. Thomas, Boden Professor of Sanskrit in the University of Oxford.

I owe another debt of like nature to Dr. F. A. M. Spencer, lately Chaplain of Brasenose College, Oxford, and author of a number of works, including *Civilization Remade by Christ*, and *The Theory of Christ's Ethics*, who read the typewritten copy of this volume before it went to the printers, and contributed some constructive criticism concerning certain Christian problems herein touched upon.

To Sir E. Denison Ross, Director of the School of Oriental Studies, University of London, grateful acknowledgement is here made for permission to use his copy of the late Lāma Kazi Dawa-Samdup's rendering of the *Lodan-Gawai-Roltso*.

And I am also indebted to the Bhikkhu Parawehera Vajiranana, attached to the Vidyodaya College, Colombo, Ceylon, at present in England and a candidate for the Degree of Doctor of Philosophy in the University of Cambridge, for having critically examined my exposition of *yogic* practices in relation to Southern Buddhism.

Nor must I forget to thank the many friends who have

voluntarily written to me from the four quarters of the Earth to express appreciation, to offer helpful criticism with respect to my two preceding books, and to convey encouragement for the publication of the present book. Special thanks are due to Madame M. La Fuente, Secretary of *Les Amis du Bouddhisme*, of Paris, for her faithful translation of *The Tibetan Book of the Dead* into French, published as *Livre des Morts Tibétain* (Paris, 1933).

In such manner, then, has this concluding volume of the series been made worthy of presentation to all classes of readers—to those more learned and to those less learned. It is offered to the world as a direct gift from Sages who have advanced far upon the Great Path, known as the Mahāyāna. Their fervent hope, transmitted through their initiated disciple, the translator, and, in turn, through him to the editor, was that the teachings contained within this treatise might meet with sympathetic and careful consideration on the part of the more advanced thinkers of Europe and of the two Americas. They felt, too, that the time had come for a freer exchange of thought between those who devote themselves to investigating and developing the psychic powers innate in man and those who are more concerned with studying the visible phenomena of the external universe. It is only when the West understands the East and the East the West that a culture worthy of the name of civilization will be evolved. In thus coming to realize that it is in reality One Family, humanity will free itself of all such mentally obscuring concepts as are in this epoch concomitant with nationality, race, caste, or creed, and there will dawn a truly New Age.

W. Y. E.-W.

JESUS COLLEGE, OXFORD,
*Midsummer Day*, 1934.

# TABLE OF CONTENTS

# TABLE OF CONTENTS

# BOOK II

## THE *NIRVĀNIC* PATH: THE *YOGA* OF THE GREAT SYMBOL

# BOOK III

## THE PATH OF KNOWLEDGE: THE *YOGA* OF THE SIX DOCTRINES

## BOOK IV

## THE PATH OF TRANSFERENCE: THE *YOGA* OF CONSCIOUSNESS-TRANSFERENCE

## BOOK V

## THE PATH OF THE MYSTIC SACRIFICE: THE *YOGA* OF SUBDUING THE LOWER SELF

## BOOK VI

## THE PATH OF THE FIVE WISDOMS: THE *YOGA* OF THE LONG *HŪṀ*

## BOOK VII

## THE PATH OF THE TRANSCENDENTAL WISDOM: THE *YOGA* OF THE VOIDNESS

# DESCRIPTION OF ILLUSTRATIONS

I. MODERN *GURUS* . . . . . . *Frontispiece*

(1) The late Lāma Kazi Dawa-Samdup, as he appeared in the year 1919, when he was the Head Master of the State School, near Gangtok, Sikkim. In the following year he was appointed Lecturer in Tibetan to the University of Calcutta. (2) The late Srimat Kuladānanda Brahmachāry, of the Jatiababaji Math, Puri. He was one of the most beloved *gurus* of the Madhwāchārya Order, and had many disciples, one of whom is kneeling at his side in reverent obeisance. He was physically remarkable for his beautiful features and luxuriant growth of hair, as the photograph suggests. To him the editor is indebted for a clearer understanding of some of the deeper problems of *yoga*. (3) The late Jagat *Guru* Shankarāchārya Madhusudan Tirtha Swāmi, Head of the Shankarāchārya Math (or Monastery), Puri, founded by the illustrious Shankarāchārya himself. He is seated on the seat of abbotship in his Math. Underneath him is the skin of a royal Bengal tiger. At his right hand stands a brass *kamandalu* (or water-pot) such as is commonly used by mendicants who have made the Great Renunciation ; and, at his left, a bamboo staff, symbolical of the *Brahma-danda* (Staff of Brahmā), represented by the spinal column in man, and, also, indicative of his membership in the *Danda* Order of Brahmin ascetics. He was revered for his remarkable powers of intellect combined with spiritual insight; and to him, too, the editor gratefully acknowledges indebtedness for guidance. (4) The late Vaidyāratna Pandit Maguni Brahma Misra, Teacher of Ayurveda, Government Sanskrit College, Puri. It was on New Year's Day, 1921, that the Viceroy and Governor-General of India, then Lord Chelmsford, conferred upon him the title of Vaidyāratna ('Gem' of Medical Science'), in recognition of his eminent attainments. The editor, who knew him intimately and often enjoyed his hospitality and scholarly assistance, can testify to the saintliness of his character. He was an ideal type of the *guru* who marries and lives as a householder and works in the world as a *karma yogin*. He was of ancient Brahmin lineage ; and was blessed with four sons, all of whom survive him. (5) Swāmi Syamānanda Brahmachāry, of Benares, author of a treatise in English entitled *Truth Revealed*. The editor, when sojourning in the Holy City of the Hindus, in 1918, received from him much help. Swāmi Syamānanda harmoniously combines power of spirituality with power of intellect, and is representative of the *karma yogin* who, although living in the world, has not followed the path of the householder. (6) Srimat Sri Jukteswar Giri, Head of the

Kedar *Āshrama*, Puri.  This venerable *guru* sits yogically postured, on a low wooden seat covered with a leopard skin, outside his *Ashrama*.

## II. THE RAINBOW-ENHALOED SHRINE, SYMBOLICAL OF THE CELESTIAL HIERARCHIES    .    *facing p.* 1

This Shrine stands in the centre of the library of the Pemionche Monastery, Sikkim.  At the base of the rainbow, on the left, is to be seen the protruding end of a large *dorje* (or *lāmaic* sceptre).  On the shelf in front of the Shrine there are seven brass bowls filled with water, which is an offering to the protecting deities; at either end there is a flower-vase, and, next to that on the left, a vessel containing water from which the water in the seven bowls is replenished.  In the background, barely discernible, appear the Sacred Books, some in manuscript, some in block-print form, each carefully wrapped in a cloth and resting in separate pigeon-holes.  The Monastery is built at the end of a high, isolated mountain-spur, overlooking the eternal snows of the Himālayan Ranges, in the Sacred Land of the Gods.

## III. THE GLORIFIED BUDDHA AND THE *GURU* GAMPOPA    .    .    .    .    .    .    .    *facing p.* 57

Photographic reproductions (about three-quarters of the original size) of two water-colours, painted by the late Lāma Kazi Dawa-Samdup.

The Enlightened One is shown sitting in the Buddha-Posture, enthroned on a lunar disk upheld by the stamens and pericarp of a lotus, enhaloed by a rainbow.  His right hand is posed in the ' Earth-touching', or 'Witness-attitude' (Skt. *Bhūshparsha*), in symbol of His having called the Earth to witness His Final Triumph over Evil (personified as the Tempter Māra) when He sat under the Bo-Tree at Buddha-Gayā about to attain Enlightenment.  In his left hand He holds the begging-bowl of the ascetic, symbolical of His world-renunciation.

The *Guru* Gampopa, otherwise known as Dvagpo-Lharje, Milarepa's most spiritually developed disciple, is the compiler of *The Precious Rosary*, contained in Book I.  He is shown in the garb of a Lāma of the Kargyütpa Order, seated, in the Buddha-Posture, on a richly embroidered meditation-cushion, in a preaching-booth.  He holds a Sacred Book, written in Tibetan, whence he is expounding the Doctrine of the Enlightened One—the Ending of Sorrow and the Way of Final Deliverance.

## IV. THE TWO CHIEF *YOGIC* POSTURES    *facing p.* 101

The upper photograph shows Swāmi Satyānanda (see p. 108) sitting in the Buddha-Posture (Skt. *Padmāsana*), and the lower photograph

shows him sitting in the Siddha-Posture (Skt. *Siddhāsana*), at
Birbhaddar, on the Ganges, near Rikhikesh. The Swāmi (clean-
shaven of head and body) sits on a rug superimposed on the skin of
an Indian antelope (see p. 186⁴). In the distant background is to be
seen the grass hut wherein the editor dwelt for a time when at
Birbhaddar enjoying the Swāmi's assistance in the study of things
*yogic*.

### V.  THE DIVINE *ḌĀKINĪ*, VAJRA-YOGINĪ   . *facing p.* 155

A photographic reproduction (original size) of a painting in colours,
on heavy cotton cloth, made on the instructions of the editor, in
Gangtok, Sikkim, by the Tibetan artist Lharipa-Pempa-Tendup-La.
The description of Vajra-Yoginī as given in our text, on pp. 173 to 175,
is in general agreement with this Illustration. In the original painting,
the Goddess, in keeping with her symbolic and esoteric character, is
of a bright ruby-red colour.

### VI.  FOLIOS 1ᵇ, 2ᵃ, 2ᵇ, 3ᵃ OF THE *PHO-WA* MS.  *facing p.* 253

A photographic reproduction (slightly less than one-half of the
original size). The manuscript (written in the headed-letter script
called in Tibetan *Uchen*) was acquired from the Tibetan *yogin* who
supplied the editor with the two manuscripts of Book V when the
editor met him in Darjeeling. (See p. 280.) It is probably not more
than fifty years old, having been copied from an old manuscript
belonging to the *yogin's guru*. The small squares, noticeable on three
of the folios, represent bits of Tibetan paper (like that of all of our
Tibetan manuscripts and block-prints) painted red, and pasted thereon,
by the *yogin* when he was practising *Pho-wa*, in order to emphasize
the passages so marked.

### VII.  FOLIOS 3ᵃ, 3ᵇ, 4ᵃ, 4ᵇ, 5ᵃ OF THE *CHÖD* MS.  *facing p.* 277

A photographic reproduction (about one-half of the original size).
This manuscript (written in the headless-letter script called in Tibetan
*Umed*), like the manuscript described above, is a modern copy of
an old manuscript. A practitioner of the *Chöd* Rite favours small
manuscripts of this character as being more convenient than larger
manuscripts for carrying about secreted in the folds of his robe or
inside his cap.

### VIII.  THE ONE-FOLIO MS. OF THE LONG *HŪM*
*facing p.* 335

A photographic reproduction (about two-thirds of the original size).
At the centre is depicted the Tibetan mystic word-symbol *HŪM* in
its long form. In the original, the acuminated circle tapering in flame
into space is blue ; the crescent is white ; the horizontal line, known

as the 'top-portion', is yellow; the aspirated *Ha* portion beneath, like a figure five, is red; and the remainder of the letter, the silent *Ha* and the vowel-sign, are green. As reference to Book VI will make clear, each of these symbolic parts and colours is esoterically correlated with the symbolism of the Five Dhyānī Buddhas. This manuscript, too, is not very old, having been copied from a *guru*'s manuscript. Its greatly epitomized teachings are suggestive of a Tibetan secret symbol-language, said to be still in use by initiates.

IX. THE *BODHISATTVA*, THE GREAT BEING, ĀRYA
AVALOKITESHVARA . . . . . *facing p.* 343

A photographic reproduction (about one-half of the original size) of a painting in colours, on heavy cotton cloth, also painted for the editor by the Tibetan artist Lharipa-Pempa-Tendup-La, in Gangtok, Sikkim.

Avalokiteshvara, the Divine *Guru* of Book VII, is shown in His symbolical form with four arms and hands, seated in the Buddha-Posture, on a lotus-throne surmounted by a lunar disk, enhaloed by a rainbow. Concerning the significance of the name Avalokiteshvara, see p. 233[2].

# FOREWORD

By R. R. MARETT, M.A., D.Sc., LL.D., F.B.A.,
*Rector of Exeter College, Oxford, and Reader in Social Anthropology in the University of Oxford*

## FROM THE CELTIC FAITH IN FAIRIES TO THE TIBETAN SCIENCE OF *YOGA*

M Y friendship with the author of this work goes back a long way, namely, to the year 1907, when he first came up to Oxford as a post-graduate student from Stanford University in California. It was as a fellow-anthropologist that I came thus to know him ; for his interest lay in exploring the religious experience of mankind in such various forms as may afford the most significant contrasts. His was, moreover, a thoroughly scientific attitude towards his subject, in that he was resolved to find out and set down what others thought and felt to be true without allowing his statement of the facts to be coloured by his private opinions as to what they ought to think and feel. He meant to do his best to look through the window without being baffled by his own reflection in the glass.

Now there is a certain point at which most of us, however dispassionately scientific in intention, are apt to draw a line beyond which, consciously or unconsciously, we refuse to take the other man seriously when he talks what seems to us to be nonsense. Thus, disparaging terms, such as 'primitive credulity', 'confusion of categories', 'prelogical mentality', and so on, come to invade accounts of the unsophisticated mind that to a corresponding extent are falsified; because science has no business to say 'wrong' when it merely means 'different'. Likewise, in dealing with the beliefs of our own peasantry, we may be hardly aware of the implication of relative worthlessness attaching to our use of such a word as ' survival '; though its Latin equivalent *superstitio* might warn us of the danger. Be this as it may, Mr. Evans-Wentz, as he was then—though it was not long before Rennes, the University of that great Breton scholar Anatole Le Braz, conferred on him his first Doctorate—insisted on taking the so-called folk-lore of Europe not at the educated man's valuation, but, so to speak, at its own. He proposed to consider the Celtic faith in fairies, not as a relic of old-world irrationality, but as if there might be some kind of vital truth in it, at least for the Celt. It is to the credit, I think, of the Universities of Rennes and of Oxford that, in due course, they rewarded with degrees one whose judicial impartiality sent him forth to wander up and down Ireland, Scotland, the Isle of Man, Wales, Cornwall, and Brittany, in the hope of tracking down and interviewing the authentic fairy-seer. I believe that such gentry turned out to be few and far between ; nor could any of them help Mr. Evans-Wentz to see a fairy with his own eyes. But fruitful or not, the method at least was sound, and was presently to be tried out in a richer field with substantial gain to positive knowledge. In the West he could but study in the Irish or Breton rustic a bare substratum of primeval paganism, overlaid by a Christianity itself in partial subjection to secular influences ; but in the East there was to be found many an example of the devotee whose religion amounts to a complete philosophy of life, which he does not hesitate as whole-heartedly to put into practice.

From 1911, when the Oxford University Press published *The Fairy-Faith in Celtic Countries*, Dr. Evans-Wentz became a sort of scholar-gipsy, who for the next half-dozen years might be found ranging anywhere between Oxford and the Nearer East, ever bent on gathering impressions of human nature in all its varieties and vagaries. Then in 1917, from Egypt, he repaired to India, the military authorities consenting to admit him on the recommendation of Colonel Lawrence, once his fellow student at Oxford, and always, one might venture to say, a kindred spirit ; and in India, that hotbed of religions, he at length had his chance of getting into touch with all that intense mysticism which pervades every section and grade of the most diversified of the major provinces of humanity. Nor was he slow in making live contact ; for a year later he was taking part in the great Hindu pilgrimage, over the glacier-clad heights of the Himālayas of Kashmir, to the Cave of Amar-Nath, sacred to Shiva, the Lord of the World. The high-priest of the pilgrimage furnished him with a letter of introduction to a learned Brāhmin belonging to one of the temples at Hardwar; and soon he was living as a *sādhu* in a grass hut in the jungles of the Upper Ganges. Already, then, he was being initiated into the science of *yoga*; but his discipleship was not to reap its full reward until he was permitted to enter that carefully protected dependency of the British Empire, Sikkim, whither he afterwards proceeded on an invitation of some years' standing from the ruler Sidkyong Tulku, whom he had known in Oxford, only to find that he had died after a brief reign. A close friend of the late Mahārāja, however, was there to welcome him in the person of the learned Lāma Kazi Dawa-Samdup; and behold our scholar-gipsy transformed into a second Kim, a *chela* sitting at the feet of his *guru* in order that he might partake of his wisdom. This association lasted for some three years—in fact, up to the death of the Lāma, which took place in March 1922. Its fruit is the trilogy of substantial works, based on translations from the Tibetan, and accompanied by an interpretation from within such as demands something even rarer with Western scholars than the ordinary scholarly equipment, namely, a sympathetic insight transcending the prejudices which render the average man antipathetic to any type of unfamiliar experience.

It is not for me, however, here to venture on a valuation of this present book by Dr. Evans-Wentz, whether regarded as a contribution to the history of religion or as an exposition of doctrine. My present concern is simply to testify to the diligence, the ardour, and the veritable abandon, of the search for truth to which my old pupil has given so many of his best years. In fact, I am acquainted with no one who has lived up more sincerely to the principle that to know and so to love Everyman one must seek him Everywhere.

R. R. MARETT.

EXETER COLLEGE, OXFORD,
*June* 7, 1934

# PREFACE TO THE SECOND EDITION

UNDER the best of auspices, this, the second edition of *Tibetan Yoga and Secret Doctrines*, is sent forth to the peoples of the nations. Students of *yoga* and of oriental sciences will discover much of added value in its Yogic Commentary, for which the editor is grateful to Translator-Professor Chen-Chi Chang. Western scientists, especially psychologists and physiologists, will profit greatly, as he suggests, by putting to the test of practical application in their laboratories the various *yogas* which this volume expounds.

Were the Heat *Yoga* to be taught universally in all schools and so become a world-wide practice, there would be no need for central-heating in the dwellings of men, not even in Alaska and Siberia, or throughout arctic and antarctic regions. And, by virtue of a complementary *yoga*, there would be no need for costly expenditures on air-conditioning anywhere in the tropics or during the hot season of the temperate zones. By applying the *Yoga* of the Dream-State and of the *Bardo* and of Transference, mankind would become masters of all states of consciousness, and be able to pass at will from the waking-state to the dream-state, and from the state called life to the state called death, and vice versa, and from one embodiment to another in this world and in other worlds or conditions of existence without any break in continuity of consciousness. Mastery of the *Yoga* of the Clear Light would confer transcendent All-Wisdom, and with it intuitional all-knowledge and all-understanding. By adeptship in the *Yoga* of the Illusory Body, scientists in Europe and the Americas would attain 'right-knowing' of the electronic constitution of the atom, and surpass Einstein in solving the problems relating to gravitation and relativity. By efficiency in such *yoga* as Milarepa, Tibet's master *yogin*, is represented in his Biography as having successfully practised, thus attaining the *yogic* ability to travel through the air in his physical body, transcendent over gravitation, there would be no need of motor vehicles and airplanes, nor of bridges and boats. The Christian *New Testament* itself represents Jesus, the Christos, as having walked on water, like adepts in *yoga* of our own time.

As *The Tibetan Book of the Great Liberation* teaches, the Supreme Magician in *yoga* is Mind. By Mind the Cosmos was shaped. By Mind the Cosmos is sustained in space. By indomitable control of his mind, a supreme master of *yoga* can control all mundane conditionality; he can make, or bring into visible manifestation from the unmanifested, all things that man can make, without wearisome tools and clamorous and noisome factories.

The Occident is, indeed, at the early dawn of an age of a truly New Science. The old science of today, based upon a study of phenomena rather than of noumena, will, like the now obsolete materialism of nineteenth-century physicists, give place to a science, or way of knowing, now called occult not because it is really hidden or inaccessible but because it is transcendent. And it may well be, as Translator-Professor Chen-Chi Chang holds, that this volume will come to be regarded as one of the forerunning treatises of that coming Great Age of a New Science, when, at last, the war-drums shall be stilled and the battle-flags be furled in the Parliament of Man and the Federation of the World.

Then only shall there be throughout all the continents one nation indivisible, one constitution and one law, one flag, one sovereignty, one family of humanity in at-one-ment. Then only shall there be Right Civilization, Right Government, Right Science.

W. Y. E-W.

*San Diego, California*
  Wesak, 1957

# YOGIC COMMENTARY

## By TRANSLATOR-PROFESSOR CHEN-CHI CHANG [1]

IN commenting on this remarkable 'Book of Seven Books of Wisdom of the *Yoga* Path Direct', I shall seek to guide the student to right understanding of the chief *yogas*, which are here set forth for the first time in English translation. Such guidance cannot be anything but suggestive, for the student must himself undertake the Quest and attain the Goal, as the Buddha did, without dependence upon any god or *guru*. My observations will be confined mostly to three of the book's outstanding characteristics, namely its Tantricism, its peculiar *yogas*, and the relationship of its *Mahāmudrā* system to Zen. In conclusion, I shall refer to the scientific significance of the *yogic* practices for psychic researchers and physiologists.

## I. *The Tantricism*

In order to understand Tibetan Tantricism, to which much of the matter of this book relates, it is necessary to realize that the quintessence of Tibetan Tantricism is discernible in the Highest Division of the Esoteric Teaching known as the *Annutara Tantra*. In theory and in practice this paramount doctrine consists of two parts: (1) the Path without Form, or the Path of Liberation, known in Tibetan as the *Tar Lam*; and (2) the Path with Form, or the Tangible Path, known as the *Hdsin Lam*. The Path without Form is the one here represented, in Book II, by the *Nirvāṇic* Path of the Great

---

[1] The Degree (Tib. *Sgra Bsgyur Mkhan-po*: pron. *Cha Gyur Khan-po*), translatable as 'Translator-Professor', was conferred upon Professor Chen-Chi Chang, who was born in China, by his *Guru*, the Living Buddha Kong Ka Lāma, in the Kong Ka Monastery, at Meia Nya, Tibet. It is a special degree or title given to Professor Chen-Chi Chang because of his proficiency in translating into Chinese the Tibetan Buddhist *Sūtras*. The Kong Ka Monastery is of the Kargyütpa School of Milarepa, and, very fittingly, the Professor-Translator is at present rendering Milarepa's collected songs, known as the *Gur-Bum*, or 'One Hundred Thousand Songs', into English, under the sponsorship of the Bollingen Foundation.—W. Y. E-W.

Symbol *Yoga*, the *Mahāmudrā*. The Path with Form is set forth by the more ordinary *yogas*, and is here represented by the Six *Yogas*.

There can be no comprehension of the fundamental teaching, philosophy, and practice of the Tangible Path apart from comprehension of the theory of the Identity of Energy and Consciousness. This theory is dependent upon the most important philosophical interpretation of the basic principles of Tibetan Tantricism, and may be very briefly set forth as follows.

Tantricism views the world as consisting of contrasting antithetical relationships: *Nirvāṇa* and *Sangsāra*, noumenon and phenomenon, potentiality and manifestation, illumination and non-discriminating perception, emptiness and vitality, consciousness and *prāṇa*.[1] Moreover, Tantricism, from the standpoint of ultimate reality, declares that each of these dualities, although apparently antithetical, is inseparably a unity. Accordingly, the disciple, by completely understanding and mastering one member of the duality, automatically understands and masters the other member. Therefore, by realizing that the true nature of Consciousness is Transcendental Wisdom (Skt. *Prajñā*) itself, the *yogin* simultaneously realizes that the essentiality of *prāṇa* is represented by the supramundane vitality, or life essence, of a Buddha.

Basing itself upon this principle, Tibetan Tantricism offers two paths, or types, of *yoga* practice. If the *yogin* practises 'Mind *Yoga*', he automatically practises 'Energy *Yoga*' as well. If the mind be disciplined, transformed, extended, sharpened, illuminated, so also is one's vital energy.

The goal of Buddhism is perfection and enlightenment—to become a Fully Awakened and Fully Energized One, a Buddha, and thus to realize the Threefold Body, the *Tri-*

---

[1] *Prāṇa*, a Sanskrit term, equivalent to the Tibetan term *Rluṅ* and to the Chinese term *Chi*, conveys various meanings: air, breath, energy, wind, vitality, propensity. In an occult sense, as in *yoga*, *prāṇa* refers to a vital essence in the atmospheric air which when absorbed by *yogic* breathing practices, as in *Prāṇayāma Yoga*, recharges the human body with energy, and thereby confers rejuvenation and longevity.

*Kāya*,[1] in completeness. To this mighty end, the aim of the practice is to transmute the normal human consciousness and energy into the Transcendental Wisdom and the Great Vitality. Two methods of transmuting the human nature into the transcendental nature are offered by Tibetan Buddhism. One method lays stress upon 'Practice of Mind' (the Path without Form, or the *Mahāmudrā*). The other method lays stress upon 'Practice of Energy' (the Path with Form, as represented by the Six *Yogas*). By means of different techniques, or approaches in the practice, both methods or paths lead to the same supramundane goal.

The student should not view this Tantric doctrine of the 'Identity of Mind and *Prāna*' merely as theory or philosophy, for it possesses much value in *yogic* practices as well as in spiritual development. Although it is not necessary to expound here all the many aspects of the doctrine, one of the more important of them should receive some attention, namely, 'the reciprocal character of mind and *prāna*', which means that a certain type of mind or mental activity is invariably accompanied by a *prāna* of corresponding character, whether transcendental or mundane. For instance, a particular mood, feeling, or thought is always accompanied, manifested, or reflected by a *prāna* or breathing of corresponding character and rhythm. Thus anger produces not merely an inflamed thought-feeling, but also a harsh and accentuated 'roughness' of breathing. On the other hand, when there is calm concentration on an intellectual problem, the thought and the breathing exhibit a like calmness. When the concentration is in a state of profound thinking, as during an effort to solve a subtle problem, unconsciously the breath is held. When one is in a mood of anger, pride, envy, shame, arrogance, love, lust, and so on, simultaneously there arises the 'air', or *prāna*, of anger, pride, envy, shame, arrogance, love, lust, and so on;

---

[1] The *Tri-Kāya*, the three divine or transcendent bodies—the *Dharma-Kāya*, the *Sambhoga-Kāya*, and the *Nirmāna-Kāya*—assumed by Buddhas and highly advanced *Bodhisattvas* or Divine Incarnations, are more fully explained on pages 10 to 15 of *The Tibetan Book of the Dead*.

and this 'air' can be felt immediately within oneself. In deep *samādhi* no thought arises; so there is no perceptible breathing. At the initial moment of enlightenment, which is also the moment of the total transformation of normal consciousness, the *prāṇa* too undergoes a revolutionary transformation. Accordingly, every mood, thought, and feeling, whether simple, subtle, or complex, is accompanied by a corresponding or reciprocal *prāṇa*.

In the higher states of meditation, the circulation of the blood is slowed down almost to cessation, perceptible breathing ceases, and the *yogin* experiences some degree of illumination, or 'brightness', together with the thoughtfree state of mind. Then not only does a change of consciousness occur, but also a change in the physiological functioning of the body. In the body of a fully enlightened being, the breathing, the pulse, the circulatory and nerve systems are quite different from those of ordinary men. Much evidence in support of this fact is available from Hindu, Tibetan, and Chinese sources.

## II. *The Six Yogas*

The Six *Yogas*, set forth in Book III, teach how the *prāṇa* may thus be employed to transform the *sangsāric* or mundane body's breath, its circulatory system, fluids, and secretions. This physiological transformation of the *sangsāric* body induces a corresponding transformation of the *sangsāric* mind because of the *yogic* identity of consciousness and *prāṇa*, the ultimate result being the transformation of the normal body-mind into the *Tri-Kāya*, or Threefold Body of Buddhahood.

While the exoteric schools of Buddhism, in their later forms, are largely theoretical and philosophical, the emphasis as in all Tantricism is on practice, especially in these Six *Yogas*, which are: (1) the *Yoga* of Heat, (2) the *Yoga* of the Clear Light, (3) the *Yoga* of the Dream-State, (4) the *Yoga* of the Illusory Body, (5) the *Yoga* of the *Bardo* State, and (6) the *Yoga* of Consciousness-transference. The *Yoga* of Heat and the *Yoga* of the Illusory Body are the bases of the other four. It is to the *Yoga* of Heat that the student should give special attention, for this *Yoga* affords realization of the state of the *Dharma-Kāya*. The *Yoga* of the Illusory Body results in realization of the *Sambhoga-Kāya*, and, similarly, each of the supplementary *yogas* has its own specific purpose.

Thus, the *Yoga* of the Dream-State leads to mastery of the states of life and of death, to dominion over the mundane or *sangsāric* state of consciousness, and to realization of the supramundane state. This *yoga* is an extremely important 'touch-stone' for *yogins* wishing to judge or confirm their meditation experiences. The famous Lāma Garma Paoshi is said to have mastered the *Tripiṭaka* in its entirety in one dream.

The *Yoga* of the Clear Light leads to realization of the state of the Transcendental Wisdom, and serves also as a practice supplementary to that of the *Mahāmudrā*. The *Yoga* of the *Bardo* gives mastery of the after-death state; the *Yoga* of Transformation, or Transference, gives mastery of mind energy, so that, after having prepared the right way and right conditions for the mind energy to leave the human body, the successful practitioner may, at will, die peacefully and joyously. The practical application of this last *yoga* is very much in vogue among *yogins* throughout Tibet and China. In China it has been adopted as a special practice by devotees of the Pure Land School. Even if this *yoga* is not completely mastered, but is practised with sincerity, its practitioner will not suffer mental confusion or loss of consciousness when dying.

To the layman, certain aspects of the practice of the Six *Yogas* may appear, at first, mysterious and magical, perhaps even unnatural and repulsive. Such, however, is not the case with the Mind *Yoga*, to which all of them are, in greater or less degree, supplementary, as will be seen by referring to Dr. Evans-Wentz's fourth volume of the Oxford Tibetan Series, *The Tibetan Book of the Great Liberation*.

As a necessary preparation and as a safeguard against untoward effects, the devotee, before embarking upon the practice of any of the Six *Yogas*, must have a sound knowledge of Buddhism and must have practised the 'Four

Preparations', known in Tibetan as the *Snon Hgro Bzi*. He must also have had some experience with advanced stages of *samādhi*. This preparatory or 'Arising *Yoga*', as it is called, develops great strength and power of concentration, ability to retain in visualization a specific image of a Tantric deity without any wavering of the visualization, and ability to visualize the whole of a given *maṇḍala* in a space no larger than the tip of one's finger. Only after such preparation can the serious student advance to the practice of the Six *Yogas*.

Because of the difficulties of preparation and practice, the Kargyütpa and the Nyingmapa Schools have modified the Path with Form and laid emphasis upon the practice of the *Mahāmudrā* instead. Nevertheless, the Six *Yogas* cannot be set aside, and their advantages ought to be noted here. First of all, the Six *Yogas* are productive of more *yogic* power than the *Mahāmudrā* and similar Tantric practices, and provide extraordinary methods whereby the 'Clingings', namely the 'Clinging of Ego' and the 'Clinging of *Dharma*', can be more rapidly overcome. Traditionally, the *Mahāmudrā* has been prescribed as a mild antidote, and the Six *Yogas* as the strong antidote, for Ignorance. The *Mahāmudrā* is not, however, equally effective for all *yogins*, some of whom, after the initial period of development, experience an impediment to further progress, whereupon the *guru* directs them to the Six *Yogas*.

The student should remember that these treatises on the Six *Yogas* are little more than textbooks for *yogins*; they are merely the guide necessary for beginners, for they do not expound in completeness the theory, philosophy, and application. Very essential explanatory matter is set forth by Dr. Evans-Wentz in the excellent footnotes to the texts, and to these footnotes the student should constantly refer.

There are a number of Tibetan commentaries to the texts of these Six *Yogas*. Perhaps the best of them is by Ran Byun Dorje, Garmaba Lamjun the Third, of the Kargyütpa School of Milarepa. It is known as *The Inner Meaning of Tantricism*, which I translated into Chinese some years ago.

Another commentary, *On the Identity of Mind and Prāṇa* (or *Breath*), should be mentioned. The scholarly *Lāmas* of the Sa Skya School produced what is recognized as being one of the outstanding treatises on Tibetan Tantricism. It is called *The Path and the Fruit*. From the School of Padma-Sambhava has come the helpful *Teachings of the Three Yogas*. Tsong-Khapa, founder of the Yellow Sect, now the paramount sect of Buddhism in Tibet, produced two outstanding commentaries on Tibetan Tantric *Yoga*, *The Steps of the Secret Doctrine* and *The Unfoldment of Hidden Meaning*. Tsong-Khapa was a great *Bodhisattva* and a great scholar, but there is some doubt among Tibetans as to whether or not he was an accomplished *yogin*. These *yogic* commentaries of his are, however, highly valued and well known among Mahāyānists.

The *Yoga* of Non-ego, or the *Tchod* Practice, set forth in Book V, is a very popular *yoga* throughout Tibet and Mongolia. In some respects it supplements the Six *Yogas*. It was established and propagated by a remarkable woman philosopher and teacher of *yoga*, Machik-lepdon. This *yogic* system, based upon the *Mahā-Prajñā-Pāramitā Sūtra*, earned for her a high place among Tibetan scholars and practitioners of *yoga*.

After having studied for some years in Tibetan monasteries, I am of the opinion that there are very few scholars or *yogins* who can explain, thoroughly and practically, all the Six *Yogas*. To understand even one of these *yogas*, long practice and long experience are needed ; knowledge or theory alone is not enough.

### III. *Mahāmudrā and Zen*

The *Mahāmudrā* system of *yoga* is somewhat less complex and difficult than the Six *Yogas*, as has already been suggested ; and, in order the better to expound the *Mahāmudrā*'s peculiar characteristics, some comparison will now be made between it and Zen. In their simpler aspects the *Mahāmudrā* and Zen may be intellectualized, but the Six

*Yogas* are concrete practices with clearly defined stages of consciousness and corresponding physiological results, which can be discussed authoritatively only by a *yogin* who has experienced them and charted their effects in his own body and mind. From the scholastic point of view we do not and cannot understand much about this profound aspect of Tibetan and *yogic* Tantricism. It is equally true that one who is merely a scholar and not a practised *yogin* cannot fully understand Buddhism, which is, fundamentally, a system of *yoga* practically applied. In other words, Buddhism is essentially a basis and support for the realization of *Nirvāṇa*, the Ultimate Reality. *Tathatā* ('Thatness') is the Buddhist term to connote this indescribable supramundane attainment. It seems to me that one of the chief reasons for the decline of Buddhism lies in the non-application of its practicable and inner *yogic* teachings, and that this has brought about a dearth of spiritually awakened beings. Among Theravādists not one *Arhant* has appeared for many centuries who was able to explain fully those extremely important subjects of applied Buddhism such as the 'Eight Fundamental *Dhyānas*' and the 'Four Formless *Dhyānas*', the bases of Buddhist meditation, which differentiate the theory and practice of the Buddhist scholar and *yogin* from the theory and practice of the Hindu scholar and *yogin*. No more than incomplete and general descriptions of these *Dhyānas* are available in books. Only those who have had practical experience of these *Dhyānas* are capable of expounding them. How the Eight Fundamental *Dhyānas* affect the breathing, pulse, and bodily secretions is nowhere explained; nor are there complete explanations, even in books, of the various states of consciousness produced by them. The *Abhidharma* and other *Sūtras* of the Theravādists afford some, but quite inadequate, information concerning these fundamentally important *Dhyānas*. In Theravāda Buddhism the theory rather than the practice is apt to predominate; and, were it not for its *yogic* Tantricism, Mahāyāna Buddhism would also be, like Theravāda Buddhism, more theorized about than practically applied. The essence of Buddhism is discoverable in a supramundane realm inaccessible to mundane speculations. Most Buddhists of all Schools glimpse only the rudiments of Buddhist philosophy and grasp only the preparatory and external stages of Buddhist practice.

The expounders of Tibetan *yoga* emphasize that the Path of Form, discussed above, can be dangerous and is more difficult than its companion Path without Form, the *Mahāmudrā*. In modern times, the trend in Tibet has been for devoted *Lāmas* to practise the safer and easier path of the *Mahāmudrā*, the Path of Liberation, rather than the Six *Yogas* of the Path of Form; and understanding and practice of the *Mahāmudrā* is a necessary preparation for any other Tantric *yoga*. There is, for example, a well-known saying in Tibet that Milarepa, the great Tibetan *yogī*, attained Enlightenment through the practice of the Heat *Yoga*. But a study of his Biography and Songs shows that he did not practise this *Yoga* of the Path of Form only, but previously and primarily had practised the *Mahāmudrā*.

In consequence of practical and applied *Mahāyāna*, as found in the *yogic* Tantricism of the *Mahāmudrā* and Zen, and also in the Pure Land School, Buddhism grew and flourished throughout the centuries. But since the aim of the Pure Land School is mainly the attainment of a favourable birth in the Buddha Paradise in order to further the progress of the individual, the essentialities of the practical teaching of Buddhism, namely the applied *Prajñī Pāramitā*, can be found only in Zen and such Tantric *yoga* as is taught by the *Mahāmudrā*. As the historical records prove, these Tantric Schools alone produced great numbers of enlightened beings. Students seriously seeking the Enlightenment of Buddhahood should, accordingly, concentrate their attention upon the teachings of these Schools of the *Mahāmudrā* and Zen.

From my own personal experiences in the study and practice of both Zen and Tantricism, I have discovered that the teachings of Zen and the advanced Tantricism of the *Mahāmudrā* are identical. Any difference discernible is merely the superficial and external one of diversity of style and methods of presentation. The essence is wholly the same. It is, nevertheless, worth while to know where such differences lie and how they arose. To this end, we shall now examine the principles, practices, and styles of the *Mahāmudrā* and Zen as they developed within the *Mahā-yāna*, and begin by examining the three outstanding view-points of Buddhism as a whole.

Firstly, the early *Theravāda*, or Southern School, taught that the way of Enlightenment lay through 'radical abandon-ment'. The *Kleśas*[1] were discarded, the Four Noble Truths were obtained, the Five Aggregates were dissolved, the *Nirvāṇa* of the Non-Residue was reached, *Sangsāra* was annihilated, *Nirvāṇa* realized.

Secondly, the early thought of the Mahāyāna School differed from this approach and placed the emphasis on 'transformation' rather than upon 'abandonment'. Ac-cording to this view, the *Kleśas*, instead of being abandoned, were transformed into *Bodhi*, and thought was transformed by guiding it through *Sangsāra* to *Nirvāṇa*. The Eight Con-sciousnesses were, one by one, elevated to become the Four Wisdoms. The Five Senses were transmuted into the Wis-dom of Accomplishment, while Mind, the Sixth Conscious-ness, became the Wisdom of Infinite Observation. The Seventh Consciousness was transformed into the Wisdom of Equanimity, and the Eighth Consciousness, the *Ālaya* Con-sciousness, became the Great Mirror of Omniscience.

Thirdly, the later thought of the *Mahāyāna* attuned Reali-

---

[1] *Kleśa*, a Sanskrit term, from the verb-root *Kliś*, to suffer, literally meaning 'pain', here refers to that attachment to worldly pleasures, 'good' and 'bad' alike, which is the root cause of mankind's pain and suffering. 'According to Yoga Philosophy there are five *Kleśas*: ignorance, egotism, desire, aversion, and tenacity of worldly existence. According to Buddhism there are ten *Kleśas*: three sins of the body, four of speech, and three of the mind. In order to progress on the spiritual path, it is essential to remove these *Kleśas*.' Cf. Dr. Judith Tyberg, *Sanskrit Keys to the Wisdom Religion* (Point Loma. Calif., 1940), p. 65.—W. Y. E-W.

zation of the principle of Identification and Expansion: the *Kleśas* are *Bodhi*; Consciousness is Wisdom; *Sangsāra* is *Nirvāṇa*. Consciousness is expanded to the final state of Enlightenment. In this later *Mahāyāna* view, Buddhahood is not obtained through destroying the mind's accumulated knowledge, but through direct identification of the limited human consciousness with the infinite Buddha-mind. Thus, when the Buddha was attaining Enlightenment, he observed, 'Strange, indeed, it is, for I see that in reality all creatures are Enlightened, are Buddhas'. Both the *Mahāmudrā* and Zen are founded on this view. As a Zen aphorism expresses it, 'I and all the Buddhas of the past, present, and future breathe through one nostril'. The Sixth Zen Patriarch, Hui-Neng. said:

'The Three Bodies are inherent in one's Essence of Mind,
By the radiation of which the Four *Prajñās* are manifested.
Thus, without closing one's eyes and ears to shut out the external world,
One may attain Buddhahood directly.'

Likewise, the *Do-Ha Mahāmudrā*, by Saraha, teaches:
'No difference existeth between the *Sangsāra* and *Nirvāṇa*;
All manifestations and feelings are identical with the essence of mind.
There being no difference between the sea and its waves,
No difference existeth between Buddhas and other sentient beings.'

Garmapa, another great master of *Mahāmudrā*, taught:
'Although the sentient beings themselves dwell in the realm of Buddhahood,
They fail to realize this, and so they wander, lost in the *Sangsāra*.'

In Tibet there is the following prayer for daily recitation:
'I pray to my *Guru* that I may realize that the self-mind is the *Dharma-Kāya*,
That the self-mind is the *Sambhoga-Kāya*,
That the self-mind is the *Nirmāṇa-Kāya*.'

There are numerous aphoristic expressions or teachings like these in the *Mahāmudrā* School as well as in the Zen School, for both Schools are based upon the doctrine of the identity of the *Sangsāra* and *Nirvāṇa*. The Tibetan term *Sems-Sro*, meaning '[to observe] the nature of mind', synonymous with the inner significance of the term *Mahāmudrā*, indicates the true characteristic of the *Mahāmudrā* system of mind-training. Similarly, the Nyingmapas and Kargyütpas have a *yogic* practice intended to 'point out' the nature of mind, whereby the *guru* illustrates for the disciple how the 'non-existent' or void aspect of mind is to be looked upon as being the *Dharma-Kāya*, the radiant or 'bright aspect' of mind as being the *Sambhoga-Kāya*, and the thought-flowing nature of mind as being the *Nirmāṇa-Kāya*.

Both Zen and the *Mahāmudrā* call their doctrine 'Mind Doctrine', which in Chinese is *Shin-Tsung* and in Tibetan *Sen-Nao-Ba*. Both declare that all teachings, philosophical, religious, or otherwise, are understandable only through knowing the true nature of mind; and, therefore, that by knowing the true nature of mind one knows everything. In contrast to the purely analytical theorizing of the *Yogācārya* School, both Zen and the *Mahāmudrā*, like other Tantric Schools, emphasize *practice*. In this connexion it is of interest to note that although the noble philosophy of the *Yogācārya* itself produced few enlightened beings, those who have reached enlightenment through Zen and the *Mahāmudrā* describe reality in terms quite in accord with the *Yogācārya* point of view and confirm the *Yogācārya*'s analysis.

Thus the *Mahāmudrā* and Zen hold the same initial doctrine concerning the *yogic* grasping of the true nature of mind. The difference between these two Schools lies in their application of this doctrine, which led to somewhat different 'practices' or 'styles', conditioned largely by the originally different environment and history of each School.

From the time of Bodhidharma to Hui-Neng, Chinese Zen largely preserved its Indian character and tradition, and remained very much like the *Mahāmudrā*, which has not changed since its introduction into Tibet from India. But when, after Hui-Neng, there came the division of the Schools, Chinese Zen underwent vast changes, both in style and practice, and the Tsao-Tung School alone retained something of the Indian form. Innovations such as the *koan, mondo*,[1] the Zen dialogue, story, or poem, and the hitting of the disciple by the master, made Zen in its later Chinese period complicated and difficult to understand, especially as theoretical explanations and detailed instructions for the practices were avoided. The master would often reward the disciple with a physical blow rather than a verbal answer. Despite the effectiveness and directness of these Zen methods, the layman could not but feel that Zen is something inexplicable and esoteric. A useful and succinct formula of comparison for Chinese Zen and Tibetan *Mahāmudrā* is that Zen is esoteric *Mahāmudrā* and *Mahāmudrā* is exoteric Zen.

In contradistinction to the *Mahāmudrā*, the later Zen provides no 'map' for its students.[2] They must begin 'in the dark', relying implicitly on the master, and then reach a sudden inner illumination. Offering to the devotee a step-by-step guide to the final goal, the *Mahāmudrā* is closer to the Indian tradition, and easier and safer, although unlike Zen its illumination in the initial stages may not be as sharp, deep, and abrupt or wholly free from conceptualizing.

Unquestionably Zen bestows great power and great freedom—the wished-for liberation. In contrast, there is a danger in the *Mahāmudrā* if the practitioner clings to the one, cosmic, pure consciousness. In the journey to Buddhahood

---

[1] Pronounced *koan* and *mondo* by the Japanese, the original terms, in Chinese being *gon ann* and *wun da*. Traditionally, their application in China is somewhat different from that in the Occident; but, for convenience, the writer employs the Japanese terms, and instead of *Chan* the name Zen, which is familiar to occidental readers.

[2] It may be argued that Chinese Zen also has 'maps' or instructions illustrating the stages to the attainment of Buddhahood, such 'maps' being discoverable in the Ox-herding Pictures, in the Practice of the Four Distinctions of the Lin-Ji School, in the Five Positions of the King and Officers, and so on. But these instructions are too abstruse and inadequate to serve as guides in actual practice.

this oneness must be reduced to the Voidness. Otherwise there cannot be true Liberation. In this view, Buddhism is fundamentally unlike Brahmanism ; for Liberation is attainable only when consciousness is freed from the twofold concept of manifoldness and oneness    Zen has grasped this profound understanding of the Voidness (Skt. *Shūnyatā*), as is indicated by the aphorism, 'All things are reducible to one. To what is the one reducible ? '

A common misconception is that Zen emphasizes only Wisdom (*Prajñā*) and not the Great Compassion (*Karuna*). This is true only of superficial Zen.   A fully enlightened Zen master is also a fully compassionate being.   Similarly, the goal of the *Mahāmudrā* is the Compassion-nature as well as the Wisdom-nature of Enlightenment.   And Enlightenment cannot be one-sided by being merely intellectual.   There must be perfect at-one-ment of Infinite Wisdom and Infinite Compassion.   The words of Garmaba, in the *Vow of Mahāmudrā*, testify to this :

' During the moment of illumination, when I see the original
    face of mind,
A limitless compassion ariseth.
The greater the illumination, the greater is the compassion.
The greater my compassion, the deeper is the wisdom I
    feel.
This unmistakable path of two-in-one is the peerless prac-
    tice of the *Dharma*.'

Parallel to this is the Zen *koan* : 'Before I understood the grand affair (i.e. Enlightenment) I felt as though I had lost my parents.   After I understood the grand affair, I felt as though I had lost my parents.'

Although much more could be added here, our presentation provides a sound basis for understanding the relationship of the *Mahāmudrā* teaching of Tibetan Buddhism to the teaching of the Zen School of Chinese Buddhism.

The instruction concerning the *Mahāmudrā*, or Great Symbol, as set forth by Padma Karpo (or Garbo) in the second book of this volume consists of a standard outline of the practice and resultant stages of the *Mahāmudrā*. For a complementary exposition of the *yoga* of the *Mahāmudrā* the student is advised to study the treatise, attributed to Padma-Sambhava, the Founder of Tibetan *Lāmaism*, concerning the 'Seeing of Mind in its Nakedness' as set forth in Book II of *The Tibetan Book of the Great Liberation*.

#### IV. *Psychological and Physiological Value of these Yogas*

Occidental psychologists and physiologists will discover that the experiences of Hindu, Tibetan, and Taoist *yogins* afford entirely new insight into the psychological and physiological functioning of the human organism during both ordinary and extraordinary states of consciousness. Much of the theorizing of occidental physiology results from the study of *dead* tissue in the dissection of corpses. A scientific method of studying the physiology and psychology of the *living* human body, under varying conditions, from within the nervous system, brain, and viscera, would enrich medical science in the Occident with much essential data which is at present unknown to it. And certain of the practices of *yogins*, particularly those of Tibet and India, do, indeed, afford such a scientific method.

In illustration of this, a friend of mine, after having practised a certain *yoga* for five days, found his body to be illuminated by an inner light of such penetrating quality that he was able to observe the functioning of his brain, heart, and other bodily organs: and at the same time his sensitivity to sound was so keen that he could hear the beat of his heart and pulse, the circulation of his blood, and the more subtle rhythms of his body, which not even the most efficient instruments of the physiologist can detect simultaneously. A master of *yoga* can project his consciousness into each of the various organs and parts of his body, and, independently of them, observe their innermost functionings. In this way, *yoga* can undoubtedly contribute greatly to psychology and physiology in the Occident, and ought therefore to receive scientific attention.

Correlatively, this *yogic* method of research by psychologists and physiologists would be productive of a better understanding of the psychic outcome of Zen Buddhism also, particularly of the experience of illumination, which is invariably accompanied by extraordinary psychological and physiological changes. Traditionally, it has been the policy of Zen not to define or conceptualize such experiences. Nevertheless, as I have found, a knowledge of Tantric *yoga* contributes greatly to an understanding of all aspects of Buddhist enlightenment, including difficult and obscure Zen *koans*.

As a whole, the excellent translations and interpretations set forth in this volume by Dr. Evans-Wentz constitute one of the most original and, in some respects, the most unique contribution made to the Western World in this generation. Quite unlike the more widely known canonical literature of Tibet, which has been translated into Tibetan from non-Tibetan sources, largely Sanskrit, *Tibetan Yoga and Secret Doctrines* is peculiarly a literary and cultural product of Tibet itself. All who are interested in Buddhism, more especially in the practical application of Buddhism by the Sages and Seers of the Land of the Snowy Ranges, will welcome and benefit by this new edition.

*From Photograph by the Editor*

THE RAINBOW-ENHALOED SHRINE, SYMBOLICAL OF THE
CELESTIAL HIERARCHIES

Described on page xix

# GENERAL INTRODUCTION

'O Best of Bhārat's line !—he bowed him low
Before his *Guru*'s feet,—at Kripa's feet,
That Sage all honoured,—saying, "Take my prince;
Teach Parikshita as thou taughtest me."' —
King Yudhishthira, in the *Mahāprasthānika Parva*, or 'Book of the Great
Journey', of the *Mahābhārata*. (Sir Edwin Arnold's Translation.)

## I. The Importance and Original Sources of This Volume

THIS volume contains seven distinct yet intimately related treatises translated from the Tibetan, four in manuscript and three in block-print form, belonging, for the most part, to the Esoteric Lore of the *Mahāyāna*, or 'Great Path'.[1] The first four are of the Kargyütpa School, and present a faithful account of the *yogic* practices which Milarepa, the best known of the Tibetan *yogins*, successfully put to the test of practice, when in hermitage amidst the high snowy solitudes of the Himālayan Ranges. For Milarepa's followers of to-day they still are the Light on the Path leading to Liberation. In the fifth treatise, coming down to us through the School of the 'Old Style Ones', otherwise known as the Ñingmapas, of the Primitive Unreformed Church, more than in any other of the seven, there are elements discernible which very probably had origin in the ancient Bön Faith long prior to the rise of Tibetan Buddhism. The sixth treatise, written in Tibetan on a single illuminated folio, reproduced herein in photographic facsimile as the frontispiece to Book VI, illustrates the character of *Mantra Yoga* and *Yantra Yoga*, common to all Schools of the Mahāyāna of Tibet. The seventh is an epitome of the doctrines of the 'Transcendental Wisdom', known in

---

[1] We have given preference to Sj. Atal Bihari Ghosh's rendering of *Mahāyāna*, of which he says (in *The Tibetan Book of the Dead*, p. 232[1]): '*Mahāyāna* may, and possibly does, mean the "Greater" or "Higher Path" (or "Voyage"), and *Hīnayāna* the "Lesser" or "Lower Path" (or "Voyage"). *Yā* (of *Yāna*) means "to go", and *Yāna* "that by which one goes". Western Orientalists have adopted "Vehicle" as an equivalent of *Yāna*, ... but "Path" is preferable.'

Tibetan as the *S'er-p'yin* and in Sanskrit as the *Prajñā-Pāramitā*, which forms the chief portion of the third division of the *Kanjur*, the Tibetan canon of Northern Buddhism; and is thus representative of the orthodox metaphysics underlying the whole of Lāmaism.

Books I and II are of peculiar interest historically; for, being fundamentally non-Tantric, they help to show that the Kargyütpa School derived some of its chief doctrines from Indian Buddhistic sources quite independently of those called Tantric which were introduced into Tibet by Padma Sambhava, the illustrious founder of the Ñingmapa School. The special introductions prefixed to these two Books will make this clearer. In the other Books, save in Book VII, the principal ritual influence is, by contrast, more or less Tantric. The *Yoga* Philosphy, which is fundamental in all of the Books and gives unity to them when they are assembled in one volume as herein, had, like the Tantricism, sources in India.

Thus, when taken together, these seven treatises, or Books, represent a more or less comprehensive and unified expression of the most important tenets of Mahāyānic Buddhism, some of which in the form herein presented are as yet unknown to the Occident save for a few fragmentary extracts. Therefore, to the student of comparative religion, as to the anthropologist and psychologist, this work offers new fields for study.

Although the number of books concerning Tibetan religions has recently grown, very few of them are little more than journals of travellers, whose principal concern, naturally, is the recording of their experiences of travel and, inevitably, of their own opinions. Sound scholarship, no less in religious than in historical or other problems, must ever depend upon original documents. Personal experiences and opinions vary with the individual and the generation, just as social and moral standards do; but written records are for ever the same. And there is, undoubtedly, great need for just such a catena as this volume presents, of carefully made English renderings, profusely annotated, of some of the most fascinating and highly valued recorded religious teachings of Tibet, the Land of the Snowy Mountains and of *Gurus* and mystic Initiations.

## II. THE COMMENTARY

In order to assist the Occidental reader to grasp the abstruse philosophy of the Tibetan *yogins* and mystics, which is as yet so little understood beyond the confines of Tibet, a comprehensive commentary, comprised in special introductions and copious annotations to each of the seven Books, has been added. The chief source of this commentary is the explanatory teachings privately transmitted from the translator to the editor, supplemented, in some measure, by later research on the part of the editor, both in the Tibetan and Indian aspects of *yoga*, when the learned translator was no longer in this world to elucidate certain problems which arose as the editor reviewed the various texts preparatory to their publication.

## III. SOME MISCONCEPTIONS CONCERNING BUDDHISM

Owing to inadequate knowledge of the Doctrine of the Enlightened One, numerous erroneous opinions concerning it are at present current among European peoples. Unfortunately, too, there has been, on the part of opposing religions, much misrepresentation, some deliberate, some arising from ignorance of the subtle transcendentalism which makes Buddhism more a philosophy than a religion, although it is both.

As a philosophy, and also as a science of life, Buddhism is more comprehensive than any philosophical or scientific system yet developed in the Occident ; for it embraces life in all its multitudinous manifestations throughout innumerable states of existence, from the lowest of sub-human creatures to beings far in evolutionary advance of man. In other words, Buddhism views life as an inseparable whole, beginningless and endless.

### (A) AS TO THE DOCTRINE OF SOUL

It avoids the fallacious reasoning that a thing like the soul, as conceived by popular Christian belief, can, without having existed prior to its expression through a human body, continue to exist after the dissolution of the body, either in a state of felicity or of suffering, for all future time. On the contrary,

Buddhism postulates that what has a beginning in time must inevitably have an ending in time.

According to the Buddha, the belief that the soul (Skt. *ātmā*), as an eternally individualized, unchanging, and indissoluble spiritual essence, is immortal, even though its pre-existence logically be admitted, mentally fetters man and keeps him enslaved to the incessant round of births and deaths. Not until man transcends this belief, in virtue of Right Knowledge, can there come Liberation. And Liberation, or *Nirvāṇa*, is dependent upon transcending the limited human consciousness and attaining supramundane consciousness.

To the great majority of Europeans and Americans, belief in immortality, if it exists at all, is almost wholly founded upon their hereditary predisposition to the animistic theory of soul ; and to them, as is but to be expected, the Buddhist contention, that the theory of an eternally enduring personal self for ever separate from all other selves is untenable, appears to be equivalent to an absolute negation of conscious being.

This problem of soul or non-soul (or, in Sanskrit, *ātmā* or *anātmā*), which is on the whole the most difficult and baffling of all the problems of Buddhist psychology, may perhaps be simplified by having recourse to the following simile :

A man at seventy is not the boy he was at ten, nor was the boy at ten the man he was to be at seventy. Between the two there is, nevertheless, continuity of consciousness. Similarly, the old man is not the child he will be when he is reborn, and yet there is between them a causal nexus although not identity of personality. There is, however, this difference : between the old man and the boy there is normally continuity of memory ; between the child of the new birth and the old man there is, on the contrary, save under exceptional conditions due to *yogic* training prior to death, a more or less complete break in the continuity of memory in the *sangsāric* (or mundane) consciousness, but not in the subconsciousness, which, in our view, represents a microcosmic aspect of the macrocosmic (or supramundane) consciousness.[1]

---

[1] Even as the Moon reflects only a very minute fraction of the light of the Sun, so does the normal consciousness reflect only a very minute fraction of

Thus—as the late Lāma Kazi Dawa-Samdup and other learned Mahāyānists with whom the editor has discussed the problem held—an impersonal principle, this microcosmic representation of the macrocosmic, persists throughout all existences, or states of conditioned being within the *Sangsāra*,[1] but the personal, or soul, or mundane, consciousness, does not. As from youth to old age in this world, so from old age and the moment of death in this world onwards through the after-death state to that of rebirth in this world, there is a causal process, a continuity in perpetual transformations. But the impersonal consciousness-principle is not to be in any way identified with the personality represented by a name, a bodily form, or a *sangsāric* mind ; these are but its illusory creations. It is in itself non-*sangsāric*, being uncreated, unborn, unshaped, beyond human concept or definition ; and, therefore, tran-scending time and space, which have only relative and not absolute existence, it is beginningless and endless. So long as there is ignorance of the True State, and craving for *sangsāric* (or illusory) sensuousness, *sangsāric* mind continues in its cycle of rebirths and redyings. When the ignorance and the craving are overcome by the Great Awakening of Buddhahood and the True State is attained, *sangsāric* mind, that is to say, personal, or soul, consciousness is realized to have, like time and space, merely relative and not absolute existence.

The one supreme aim of the whole of the *Dharma* (or

the subconsciousness, otherwise known as the unconscious, which is the subliminal root of man's illusory being. And also like the moonlight, the ordinary human consciousness is, in the eyes of the unsophisticated man, actual and real in itself, for he is ignorant of its hidden source.

[1] *Sangsāra*, as a transliteration from the Sanskrit, has been preferred by the editor to the more commonly adopted synonymous form, *Saṃsāra*. The noun *Sangsāra* and the adjective *sangsāric*, as employed throughout this volume, imply varying shades of a common root meaning, as the contexts will make clear. Literally, *Sangsāra* means 'going (or faring) on', or continued 'coming-to-be', as in a round of rebirths and redyings. As referring to 'existence', or 'conditioned being' within the phenomenal Universe, *Sangsāra* contrasts with *Nirvāṇa*, which is beyond conditioned being, beyond Nature, across the Ocean of the *Sangsāra*. Sometimes, too, *Sangsāra*, as used herein, implies the material cosmos, or realm of phenomena ; and *sangsāric* implies 'worldly', or 'mundane', or '*karmically*-conditioned', with reference to existence.

Doctrine) is, as the Buddha Himself emphasized, to attain
' Deliverance of the Mind ' :

' And therefore, ye disciples, the gain of the Holy Life is
neither alms, nor honour, nor fame, neither the virtues of the
Order, nor the bliss of *samādhi*, nor clearness of insight, but
the fixed, unalterable Deliverance of the Mind. This, ye
disciples, is the purpose of the Holy Life ; this is its central
core ; this is the goal.' [1]

' Mind ' in this context is to be understood as having reference
to the microcosmic aspect of the macrocosmic mind. And
this ' Deliverance of the Mind ' implies, as has been suggested
above, conquest of Ignorance ; that is to say, transcendence
over all that constitutes the complex content of the mundane
mind (or consciousness), which is merely the illusory reflex of
supramundane mind (or consciousness), or, in the language of
our own texts, of mind in the unborn, unshaped, True State
of *Nirvānic* Enlightenment. Underlying the causal continuity
of the *sangsāric* mind there is thus a supra-*sangsāric* impersonal
principle.

Mundane mind manifests itself as the life-flux of the illusory
five *skandhas* (see p. 356[2]), which constitute conditioned (or
*sangsāric*) being. The life-flux has been likened to a flame fed
by worldly desires. When man ceases to delight in sensuousness, when he has eradicated every worldly ambition, the flame
dies for lack of fuel.

At the first step on the Path, in virtue of *yogic* training,
*Nirvāna* becomes the supramundane object of mundane mind.
As, through right use of a bit of flint and steel and tinder, fire
may be produced, so through right use of the five *skandhas*
*Nirvāna* may be realized. In the *Arhant*, or man made perfect,
the life-flux has reached fruition ; he has freed himself of all
*sangsāric* fetters—greed, hatred, fear, desire, and all wordli-
ness ; he has uprooted all the mundane elements which constitute the very seed of *karmic* existence. So long as the *Arhant*
is incarnate, he retains possession of the five *skandhas*, for
these give him *sangsāric* being. At his final death he relinquishes them for ever, including, as they do, his mundane

[1] Cf. *Majjhima-Nikāya, Mahā-Sāropama Sutta.*

mind (or consciousness). Then he rejoices in Utter Freedom, possessed only of supramundane mind (or consciousness) ; and this truly is the ' Deliverance of the Mind '.

From this aspect, then, Buddhism is fundamentally a system of practically applied *yoga* ; and the Buddha ever teaches of such *yogic* disciplining as will enable ' man ' thus to realize that he is neither the body nor the mental faculties of the body, but that both are merely instruments, whereby he who makes right use of them attains the sublimest of *yogic* accomplishments. Among these many accomplishments, or *siddhi*, the Buddha expounds the *siddhi* of remembering past existences ; [1] of at last transcending all states of conditioned being; and of thus becoming, like the *Arhant,* a Conqueror of the whole *Sangsāra,* with its many mansions of existence, through which, in the words of the Sages of the Mahāyāna, the Conqueror can, if he so wills, ' wander free, as wanders an unbridled lion among mountain ranges ', all the while possessed of unbroken continuity of consciousness.[2] And this figurative language implies that there is no conceivable state of finality like that of an eternal paradise ; that there is no conceivable end of evolution ; that the Cosmos itself is eternally subject to rebirths and redyings, of which the One Mind is the Dreamer, the Source, and the Sustainer.

### (B) AS TO THE DOCTRINE OF *NIRVĀNA*

Although thus denying all possibility of any sort of personal, or soul, immortality in a phenomenal heaven or hell, Buddhism, in its Doctrine of *Nirvāna,* tells of a far greater destiny awaiting humanity ; and perhaps no other Buddhist doctrine has been so much misunderstood as this.

The Sanskrit word *Nirvāna* literally means ' going out ' or ' blowing out ', like the going out of a fire, or like the blowing out of the flame of a candle. It also means ' cooling ', or ' becoming cool ', with respect to sensuous existence. And

---

[1] Cf. the *Lonaphala Vagga,* and the *Brāhmana Vagga, Anguttara-Nikāya* ; also *The Tibetan Book of the Dead,* pp. 40-1.

[2] Cf. the *Samgīti Sutta, Dīgha-Nikāya* ; or *The Tibetan Book of the Dead,* pp. 207-8; also *Tibet's Great* Yogī *Milarepa,* pp. 35-9.

Occidentals who have comprehended no more than these exoteric aspects of its meaning have been responsible for the erroneous opinion, now so widespread, that *Nirvāṇa*, the *Summum Bonum* of Buddhism, is synonymous with total annihilation of being. Rightly understood, *Nirvāṇa* implies the 'going out', or 'cooling', of the Three Fires of Desire, which are Lust, Ill-Will, and Stupidity. When these have been extinguished, or 'become cool', or, esoterically considered, are transmuted into Purity, Good-Will, and Wisdom, thereby dispelling Ignorance (Skt. *Avidyā*), there dawns the Perfect Knowledge of Buddhahood. The great scholars of Buddhist India who supervised the translation from the Sanskrit of the religious lore now embodied in the Tibetan canonical books of the Mahāyāna Scriptures understood this subtle sense of the term *Nirvāṇa*, and translated it into Tibetan as 'The Sorrowless State' (*Mya-ṅan-med*).

To the One Fully Enlightened, or Awakened from the Sleep of Stupidity arising from *sangsāric* (or *karmically*-conditioned) existence, there comes, concomitantly with the giving up of the illusory human body, in the process men call death, the Final Liberation, the severing of the last worldly bond, the 'going out' from the *skandhas* (or final elements of 'becoming'). And this truly is extinction—of *sangsāric* being; it is the *Pari-Nirvāṇa* of a Buddha. Having evolved out of the torpid state of passive development, the human chrysalis thus becomes a Conqueror of Existence. Having discarded, or gone out from, the cocoon woven by *karmic* desire for sensuousness, he has attained Freedom.

Unlike the Semitic Heaven, *Nirvāṇa* is, however, not a final abode of immortal souls; nor is it even a condition of spiritual finality, or absoluteness. It is a State of Perfect Enlightenment, attainable not merely after death, but here on Earth while still incarnate.

*Nirvāṇa* is indescribable, because no concepts of the finite mind can be applied to That which transcends finite mind. Were two Great Sages who had realized *Nirvāṇa* able to meet while in the body there would be between them intuitive and mutual understanding of what *Nirvāṇa* is; but their human

speech would be wholly inadequate to describe *Nirvāna* even
to one another, much less to one who had not realized it.

The Buddha Himself has referred to *Nirvāna* as the
' Unbecome, Unborn, Unmade, Unformed ', whereby ' there is
escape from that which is become, born, made, and formed '.[1]
Thus it is that the Goal of which Gautama has taught, instead
of implying, as its critics have proclaimed, absolute annihilation
of being, really implies a condition of being so transcendent,
and so superior to that implied by the soul theory, that for the
Unenlightened it is utterly beyond human conception. When
man is no longer man ; when man has blown out the flame of
animal desires and transcended personality and the belief in
the permanent existence of an ego or soul, has evolved beyond
the lowly state of humanity, has conquered himself and the
World, has dissipated Ignorance, then will *Nirvāna* be realized
and understood.[2]

## IV. THE INCOMPLETENESS OF THE OCCIDENT'S KNOWLEDGE OF BUDDHISM

When there is taken into account the incompleteness of our
present knowledge of Buddhism, these misconceptions concerning Buddhist doctrines are readily pardonable. It is, in
fact, only within the last fifty years or so that Buddhism has
been under careful examination by Western scholarship. Even
now there exists no complete translation into any Occidental
tongue either of the Pāli canon of the Southern School or of
the Tibetan canon of the Northern School : and each of these
two canons is far more voluminous than the Christian Bible.
Although the Pāli Text Society has done most excellent work
in editing and publishing, in Pāli, standard versions of many
portions of the *Tri-Pitaka*, or ' Three Divisions ', as the three
parts of the Southern Buddhist canon is called, comparatively
few of the texts are available in translations. And European

---

[1] Cf. the Pāli *Udāna* viii. 1. 4, 3. See *The Tibetan Book of the Dead*, p. 68.
[2] As being one of the most authoritative treatises concerning the many
philosophical problems involved in a more detailed examination of the Doctrine
of *Nirvāna*, the student is referred to *The Way of Nirvāna*, by Professor L. de la
Vallee Poussin (Cambridge University Press, 1917).

scholars have done little to advance knowledge of Northern Buddhism beyond indexing, or making outline analyses of, the Tibetan canon, known as the *Kanjur* (*Bhah-hgyur*), ' Translation of the Precepts', and its Commentary, known as the *Tanjur* (*Bstan-hgyur*), 'Translation of the Commentaries', and translating a very few portions of them. The encyclopaedic contents of the Tibetan canon are, therefore, unknown, in any comprehensive detail, outside the monasteries of Tibet, Mongolia, China, Manchuria, and Japan. This is true, too, of the Chinese canon, called the ' Three Treasures' (*San Tsang*).

It is in these fields, more especially in Tibetan, that there awaits to be done enormous research ; and, until this has been completed, it would be unwise to attempt any final summary, historical, philosophical, or religious, based upon published texts or fragmentary translations of the canons.

## V. The Joyous Optimism of Buddhism

Quite apart from sources of information, some sound, some quite unsound, now available in European tongues, enough is known, in virtue of research conducted among learned Buddhists themselves of the two Schools, to make it certain that Buddhism not only parallels Christianity in respect to such ethics as are contained in the Sermon on the Mount, in the Parables of the Gospels, and in the Decalogue, but is more comprehensive. In other words, Christianity, like the Judaism which underlies it, and the Islamic Faith which grew out of both, limits, at least in practice, its moral teachings to man, whereas Buddhism comprises in its Universe-embracing altruism and hope of ultimate deliverance every living thing, sub-human, human, and super-human. Although the Christ Himself has said that not even a sparrow falls to the ground without the Father's notice and that the glory of the Father expresses itself in the lilies of the field,[1] there exists throughout Christendom the irrational belief, so peculiarly Occidental, that immortality is limited to man. Unlike St. Paul, who, in echoing this vulgar belief, believed that God cares not for

---

[1] Cf. *St. Matthew* x. 29; vi. 28; *St. Luke* xii. 27-8.

oxen,[1] Buddhism teaches that all sentient things are inseparably parts of a Whole, and that, consequently, there can be no true blissfulness for any until all attain the Other Shore.

### (A) THE BUDDHA'S DOCTRINE OF DELIVERANCE FOR ALL LIVING THINGS

The ethical incongruity of an eternal Heaven for the elect among human beings and an eternal Hell for the damned finds no place in the Doctrine of the Buddha. So long as there is one being, even the lowliest, immersed in suffering and sorrow, or in Ignorance, there remains one note of disharmony which cannot but affect all beings, since all beings are the One ; and until all are Liberated there cannot possibly be true Bliss for any.

The belief that one part of the Whole can enjoy happiness for eternity while another part eternally suffers misery of the most terrible character conceivable, is quite unthinkable to a Buddhist ; for to him no states of *sangsāric* existence, in heavens, hells, or worlds, are other than *karmic* and, therefore, of but limited duration. In its catholicity, Buddhism, unlike the Semitic Faiths, thus teaches that all living things, in all worlds, hells, or heavens, will ultimately attain to the true spiritual freedom of the *Nirvāṇic* State, beyond all circumscribed and conditioned existences of the *Sangsāra*.

### (B) THE BUDDHA'S WAY TO UNIVERSAL LIBERATION

Like each of the Great Faiths, Buddhism recognizes the unsatisfactory nature of human existence and posits a higher state. But for Buddhism, this higher state, as above suggested, is beyond the range of Nature, beyond personalized existence, beyond all phenomenal paradises and hells. Even as the creatures now breathing the air of the land surfaces of the planet enjoy a relatively higher condition of being than those dwelling in its waters, so, as Buddhism postulates, there are

[1] See 1 *Corinthians* ix. 9. Elsewhere St. Paul presents a less limited outlook on the world and approaches the Buddhist view, as in 1 *Corinthians* 28, and more especially in *Romans* viii. 21-3, where he speaks of the deliverance of the creature (which may, however, refer to man alone) and that 'the whole creation groaneth and travaileth in pain together.'

conditions as much higher above the human as the human is above that of the instinct-governed mammals ; and beyond the highest of *sangsāric* states, known to the Tibetans as '*Og-min* (Skt. *Akanishṭha*), there is *Nirvāṇa*.

Many men there are, as the Tibetan *gurus* teach, who are *karmically* so attached to the state of human existence that they have no desire for any state less sensuous.  Such men are like fish, which, although they be offered the opportunity to evolve out of the water-world to the world of the higher animals exist- ing on the dry land, prefer to remain fish, because they think that there can be no state higher than that they alone know. Again, many men there are who imagine that they would be happy for ever were the Heavenly Kingdom realized on Earth, as it will be in the course of evolutionary progress.  To the Enlightened One, however, no condition of *sangsāric* existence, even if entirely free of illness, old age, and death, can be a final or a completely satisfactory state.  For this reason, Buddhism tells man not to fix his hopes on a worldly Utopia, but first to free himself from the *Karmic* Law of Necessity, and then, having attained the right to enter *Nirvāṇa*, to make the Greater Renunciation of the *Bodhisattva*, not to pass on out of the *Sangsāra* until all its inhabitants, in all states, high and low, and in all kingdoms of existence, are Emancipated, even as the Buddha has been.

All beauty, all goodness, all that makes for the eradication of sorrow and ignorance on Earth, must be devoted to the one Great Consummation.  Then, when the Lords of Compassion shall have spiritually civilized the Earth and made of it a Heaven, there will be revealed to the Pilgrims the Endless Path, which reaches to the Heart of the Universe.  Man, then no longer man, will transcend Nature, and impersonally, yet consciously, in at-one-ment with all the Enlightened Ones, help to fulfil the Law of the Higher Evolution, of which *Nirvāṇa* is but the beginning.

If from the outset of the Occident's contact with the Orient the Doctrine of the Buddha had been presented to the Western World as we now know it really to be, the prevalent popu- lar opinion that Buddhism is both pessimistic and nihilistic could never have been formulated. For, in truth, Buddhism offers such inspiring altruism and such limitless optimism as have never been surpassed, if equalled, in any of the philosophical or religious systems of the world. Moreover, it is the legacy bequeathed to us of this epoch by one of our own fellow men, the princely son of a human father, who claimed no divine prerogatives; and He tells us that neither the believing nor the non-believing in a Supreme Deity, but self-exertion in righteousness and self-directed spiritual evolution, as indicated for us in the Noble Eight-Fold Path, are essential to Liberation. And this, the Way of the Ending of Sorrow, is

' Right Belief, Right Intentions, Right Speech,
Right Actions ; Right Livelihood,
Right Endeavouring, Right-Mindfulness,
Right Concentration.'

Thereby did the Buddha teach that man is the maker and the master of his own fate ; that precisely as man employs life now, so shall man determine his own future in this and in other states of existence. Or, as St. Paul's words echoed six hundred years afterwards, ' Whatsoever a man soweth, that shall he also reap '[1]—a statement which both logically and ethically should imply for present-day Christians, as it did for the Gnostic Christians,[2] and as it does for Buddhists, human reincarnation on Earth, so that where the sowing is the harvesting may be.

Man, according to Buddhism, is under no divine curse, nor is he the bearer of any original sin other than that of his own making.

On Earth, as in a University granting many degrees, man shall continue to matriculate at birth and to enjoy the long vacations afforded by death, as he passes on from lower to higher degrees of attainment until, endowed with the Supreme Degree of Buddahood, he quits Earth's Halls of Learning, prepared to perform his duties in the guidance and government of the Cosmic Whole, of which, in virtue of evolutionary growth

[1] Cf. *Galatians* vi. 7.
[2] Cf. G. R. S. Mead, *Fragments of a Faith Forgotten* (London, 1900), p. 142.

in Right Knowledge, he has become a spiritually conscious part, an Enlightened One.

Many of the texts contained within these covers will serve as commentaries to this suggestive section of our General Introduction concerning the joyous optimism of Buddhism. 'The Ten Great Joyful Realizations', the last of the categories of precepts set forth in Book I, are, in this respect, of particular importance.

## VI. THE WISDOM OF THE MAHĀYĀNA

From this brief exposition of some of the more essential doctrines of the Buddhism common to both the Northern and Southern Schools, we shall now proceed to the more philosophical presentation of these and correlated doctrines of the Mahāyāna as represented by our own texts, in order to guide the reader to right understanding of them.

### (A) THE RELATIONSHIP OF NORTHERN AND SOUTHERN BUDDHISM

We need not, however, be much concerned with the vast and as yet unsolved problem as to whether or not Mahāyānic Buddhism is a philosophical outgrowth of a more primitive Buddhism, as the Southern Buddhists maintain, or really is, as its learned expositors assume, faithfully representative of a higher and, in some respects, an esoteric Buddhism, which the Buddha could not teach until after His disciples had mastered the simpler exoteric teachings, of which the Pāli canon is a faithful record. In the view of these expositors, Northern Buddhism is merely complementary to Southern Buddhism, in much the same manner as the *Upanishads* are complementary to the *Vedas*.

Wherever the truth may lie in this controversial matter— and this remains for scholars of the future to determine—it is certain that the Mahāyāna has given system, together with logical and philosophical continuity, to Buddhism as a whole, as Plato did to the philosophy of Socrates. Furthermore, the Buddhism of the Pāli canon, when divorced from the Mahāyāna, contains many obscure passages and doctrines in great need of elucidation, such as a Great Teacher might reasonably be expected to have offered as a fitting complement of His teachings before having allowed them to go forth to the World.

Inasmuch as all our own texts are based upon the religious lore of Northern Buddhism, we must therein seek interpretation for their more difficult doctrines. In doing so, we must not forget that the Northern, or Mahāyāna, School accepts the Pāli canon of the Southern School as being thoroughly orthodox, but holds that, because it merely suggests and does not contain the more advanced teachings of the Buddha, it is incomplete. In like manner, the more learned of the Gnostic Christians (who were declared 'heretics' by those other Christians that acquiesced in the dogmatic pronouncements of Church Councils) seem to have accepted the Books which now form the canon of the New Testament, but held that there are, in addition, Christian scriptures of an esoteric character which are equally authentic and of more importance. And here, again, the question might be raised, 'Who are the "heretics"?' This problem, too, at least for many outside the Christian fold, is still unsettled, with much to be said in favour of the Gnostic's claim to an esoteric Christianity, which the Councils of the Western Church have repeatedly rejected.[1] As the Gnostic Church of Buddhism, the Mahāyāna, similarly, may or may not be 'heretical', in accordance with whether one be of the Southern or Northern School.

## (B) CONCERNING MIND AND *MĀYĀ*

According to the most authoritative expounders and commentators of these Mahāyānic, or Northern Buddhist, doctrines, such as Ashvaghosha of the first century of our era, Nāgārjuna of the second and third, Asaṅga and Vasubhandu of the fifth, onwards to Hsüan-tsang of the seventh century, Mind (or Consciousness) is the sole reality. Although the Sun is one, yet its rays are many. Similarly, although Mind is one, yet It manifests Itself in the many minds. The Macrocosm is not separable from the Microcosms; neither the One nor the

---

[1] Cf. G. R. S. Mead, *Fragments of a Faith Forgotten* (London, 1900), pp. 13 ff., 122, 148, 153, 605; and C. A. Baynes, *A Coptic Gnostic Treatise* (Cambridge, 1933), p. xxiv.

Many can have any real existence apart from each other. As being the individualized, or personal, aspect which the microcosmic mind (or consciousness) assumes in its own eyes, the ego, or self, or soul, is illusory; it is the unenlightened, or spiritually unawakened, perceiver of phenomena, dependent for its illusory personal character upon its sense of separateness and the interminable stream of sensuous impressions derived from its contact with forms and with the external universe. Thus phenomena give relative existence to the ego as to the world, which erroneously the ego perceives as something outside of or apart from itself. In other words, the ego and the world have no absolute, or true, but merely relative, existence. Therefore, the ego, or soul, is no more real than a reflection of the Moon seen in water; it is a phenomena-composed shadow cast by Reality, but the unenlightened microcosmic mind perceives it as something permanent and self-existing.

The thinking mind, in its unenlightened state, being enveloped in dense mists of appearances, is unable to penetrate the illusion of the *Sangsāra* and see beyond the mists the clear shining Sun of Reality. It mistakes effects for causes, phenomena for noumena. Thus it is that this mirage of representation, which apparently is substantial and real, has no existence in and of itself. It is this Doctrine of Illusion (Skt. *Māyā*) which plays so important a part throughout the whole of the Mahāyānic Philosophy, and in all the texts contained within this volume.

Applied to physics, the Doctrine of *Māyā* implies that matter, although illusorily substantial, is, as our own science already suspects, non-existent save as phenomena, as a manifestation of that primordial energy constituting the electron, whose ultimate source is Mind. Matter is thus a development of thought; and its atomic components and their electronic framework have no real existence of their own any more than have other phenomena, matter being, like all appearances, illusory. The *Sangsāra*, or external universe, is a psychophysical compound of mind; matter, as we see it, being crystallized mental energy, and, consequently, the product of thought.[1]

[1] It is obvious from what Sir James Jeans has set forth in *The New Back-*

## (C) CONCERNING IMPERMANENCE

This is further illustrated by the Buddhistic doctrine of the impermanence of things. One phenomenon instantaneously arises and gives place to another, as one thought gives birth to another. Just as we discern not the passing of cream into butter, so we fail to comprehend the constant flux of all component objects. The densest aspects of matter, like the most subtle invisible gases, are never exactly the same one second after another ; through all alike moves the life-force in its psycho-physical, ever-flowing, ever-structurally modifying pulsation, even as in the body of man. Likewise the ego, or soul, is equally ephemeral, being dependent for its relative existence upon an interminable series of sense impressions, instantaneously arising and passing away, a mere flux of perpetual transformations.

## (D) CONCERNING THE COSMOS AS THOUGHT

The ripples and waves caused by the wind of thought of microcosmic minds on this ever-flowing stream of sensations are the invidualized thoughts, which appear as objects, as materializations of visualizations. In other words, in the Platonic sense, Knowledge, as the Ideals in the Supra-mundane Mind, shows itself in the phenomenal universe. It

*ground of Science* (Cambridge, 1933), pp. 283-4 and 297-8, that Western science has now reached, at least tentatively, substantially the same view concerning reality which the Mahāyānic and other even earlier sages of India reached many centuries ago. Concerning the latest situation in physics, he first shows that ' we have not seen the addition of mind to matter so much as the complete disappearance of matter, at least of the kind out of which the older physics constructed the objective universe'. Then, speaking of present-day science, he adds, ' at the farthest point she has so far reached, much, and possibly all, that was not mental has disappeared, and nothing new has come in that is not mental'. And he says, in this context : ' Our last impression of nature, before we began to take our human spectacles off, was of an ocean of mechanism surrounding us on all sides. As we gradually discard our spectacles, we see mechanical concepts continually giving place to mental. If from the nature of things we cannot discard them entirely, we may conjecture that the effect of doing so would be the total disappearance of matter and mechanism, mind reigning supreme and alone.' It is the master of *yoga* who has succeeded in completely discarding the human spectacles, and, standing apart from them, in *yogic* at-one-ment, has long ago realized ' Mind reigning supreme and alone '.

is the Knowledge which is real, not its reflection in nature. Materialized thought-forms attach themselves one to another, like drops of water in an ocean, and in their totality constitute external nature. Although existing in the form of appearances, as phenomena, the real essence of all things is thought, as noumena, as Mind. Thus Mind is the Cosmos. To the Enlightened One, this apparent duality has no existence, since neither the *Sangsāra* nor *Nirvāṇa* are two things apart from individualism, but merely two aspects of One, which is the All-Knowledge, the All-Wisdom. Hence, as our texts teach, the *Sangsāra* and *Nirvāṇa* are, in this occult sense, said to be inseparable. Duality is present in appearances, but not in essence. Or, as Asanga, in his *Laṃkara Sūtra*, teaches, 'In the transcendent sense there is no distinction between the *Sangsāra* and *Nirvāṇa*.'[1]

### (E) CONCERNING LIBERATION

To realize, by means of *yoga*, the essential nature of all that has both relative and real existence constitutes liberation from Ignorance; it is Buddhahood. All dualistic concepts, all sense of separateness of one microcosmic form from another, or of the Many from the One, must be transcended; personality must be impersonalized; all the circumscribed limitations which constitute self and soul and ego, all sense of I-ness, of mine-ness, must be left behind. Then, in what our texts call the True State, on the Plane of the Ideal, the *yogically* clarified mind ecstatically perceives behind the mists of *Māyā*, behind the mirage of life, behind the Veil of Isis, the Thatness, the Voidness, the Source of Phenomena, the Totality of Knowledge, which is the *Dharma-Kāya*, or 'Divine Body of Truth', of the indescribable At-one-ment of the Buddhas.

Even as the Sun ripens the corn and the fruits of the Earth, so do the Enlightened Ones, by emitting upon the *Sangsāra* the radiances of their all-embracing Love and Compassion, cause the growth and maturity of the *Bodhic* essence which is implanted in all living things. A doctrine

[1] Cf. R. Grousset, *In the Footsteps of the Buddha* (London, 1932), p. 313.

parallel to this seems to have been conveyed in the rites of the Mysteries of Antiquity, in Egypt and in Greece, by the symbolism of the ripened ear of wheat dedicated by the initiate to the Divine Mother, Isis, or Demeter.

### (F) CONCERNING REALITY

Thus it is that in the Quiescent State, induced by such *yoga* as *The Epitome of the Great Symbol* and *The Six Doctrines* expound, the Sage arrives at Right Understanding. He attains to Knowledge in its primordially unmodified aspect ; that is to say, he perceives Reality in its true essence, as Undifferentiated Absoluteness, which is called the Voidness, because separated from all modifications, from all shaping, as the Uncreated, the Unborn. In that ecstatic state, the Sage comprehends the root-nature of things, he sees phenomena from the view-point of noumena ; and for him, therein, in the True State, there is neither the ego, nor the non-ego, neither the *Sangsāra* nor *Nirvāna*, but only Divine At-one-ment. He has reached the Heights beyond appearances, whence he comprehends the fallaciousness of the *sangsāric* belief that the ego and the external universe, or the subject and object, exist apart from one another, or from the One Mind.

*Nirvāna* is, therefore, the liberating of the mind from the *sangsārically*-produced illusions of the human state, the arriving at Right Knowledge, the transcending of personality, or of ego, and the conquest of Life and of the World. Truly, therefore, an Enlightened One is called a Conqueror. In the rapturous words of Asanga, ' Thenceforth his one joy is to bring Enlightenment to all living things.'[1]

### (G) THE ILLUSTRIOUS TEACHERS OF THE MAHĀYĀNA

This brief introductory synopsis of the idealistic philosophy of the Mahāyāna, the ' Great Path ', as we shall discover it throughout our own texts, finds fuller expression in the remarkable treatise entitled *The Awakening of Faith*,[2] by Ashvaghosha, of the first century of our era, and afterwards,

---

[1] Cf. R. Grousset, *op. cit.*, p. 314.
[2] See *The Tibetan Book of the Dead*, pp. 224-32.

during the second and third centuries, in the writings of Nāgārjuna, to whom is attributed the first systematic exoteric exposition of the Doctrine of the Voidness (Skt. *Shūnyatā*). Following Ashvaghosha and Nāgārjuna, there came a long line of illustrious teachers, such as Asaṅga, author of the *Laṃkara Sūtra*, and his brother Vasubandhu, who flourished during the fifth century, and bequeathed to the Mahāyāna an organized system of metaphysics. At the age of 106, Sila-bhadra, then the most revered teacher of philosophy in Nālanda, the famous Buddhist University of India, trans-mitted the Mahāyāna wisdom to his chief disciple Hsüan-tsang, the learned Chinese. It was after Hsüan-tsang had wandered over much of Northern India on pilgrimage, in the footsteps of the Buddha, that he reached Nālanda, in the year 637, and was royally welcomed by Silabhadra, whose *yogic* foresight had already revealed the important part which Hsüan-tsang was destined to play in the dissemination of Buddhism. With mind illuminated, and having in his posses-sion a collection of six hundred Mahāyāna Scriptures in the Sanskrit, Hsüan-tsang returned by the arduous northern overland route to China to proclaim the good tidings of the Holy *Dharma*. And there, in his native land, respected and honoured by the Emperor as by the people, he spent many happy years of a long and pious life in translating the San-skrit manuscripts into Chinese, and in teaching the Doctrine of the Enlightened One. The Light which Hsüan-tsang thus helped to establish throughout the Chinese Empire was soon to spread to Korea and Japan, and from China and India into Tibet, and thence into Mongolia.

Another of the great *gurus* in the Nālanda succession, who came after Silabhadra, was Śāntideva, well known in the Buddhist world of the seventh century. His most important work on behalf of the Faith was to codify, in two treatises, the *Śiksha-Samaccaya* and the *Bodhicaryāvatāra*, the duties and functions of an incarnate *Bodhisattva*, who, according to his view, might be either a monk or a layman. The succession of great teachers of the Mahāyāna School has continued to flourish uninterrupted, in Tibet, Mongolia, and

Japan, and in some of the monastic orders of China; and to-day the succession still continues.[1]

## VII. THE *YOGA* PHILOSOPHY

Inasmuch as each of the seven Books comprising this volume is essentially *yogic* in character, a comprehensive exposition, although in outline, of the *Yoga* Philosophy is included in this General Introduction, for the purpose of assisting the ordinary European and American reader to an intellectual understanding of the various teachings, often profoundly abstruse, which are to follow, and also to amplify our annotations to the texts. In the special introduction to Book II, some consideration will be given to the history of the introduction of the *Yoga* Philosophy, chiefly in its *Mahā-Mudrā* (or 'Great Symbol') form, into Tibet and of its reshaping under Tibetan influences.

### (A) THE MEANINGS OF THE WORD *YOGA*

The word *yoga*, having two recognized Sanskrit roots, has two possible meanings. One meaning is 'to meditate', or 'to go to trance' (as in *Samādhi Yoga*). The other meaning is 'to join'. In the latter sense, the Sanskrit word *yoga* and the English word *yoke* are regarded as having a common root; and this sense of *yoga* seems to be more generally accepted by *yogins* (or *yogīs*), i.e. practitioners of *yoga*, than the former sense. It implies a joining, or yoking, of the unenlightened human nature to the enlightened divine nature in such manner as to allow the higher to guide and transmute the lower. It has also been taken, but less generally, to imply a yoking, or harnessing, or disciplining of the mind itself, by means of mental concentration.

According to the chief authority, Patanjali, in his *Yoga Aphorisms*,[2] which are thought to date from the second or

---

[1] The student desirous of continuing this interesting subject further and in more detail is referred to Nalinaksha Dutt, *Aspects of Mahāyāna Buddhism and Its Relation to Hīnayāna* (London, 1930), and to R. Grousset, *In the Footsteps of the Buddha* (London, 1932). From each of these two works the editor has derived very important guidance.

[2] The editor here acknowledges indebtedness to the excellent English rendering of Patanjali by Prof. J. H. Woods in *The Yoga System of Pātanjali* (Harvard University Press, 1914).

third century B.C. and upon which almost all subsequent
Sanskrit treatises on *yoga* are based, ' Yoga is the restricting
of the fluctuations of mind-stuff.' And, as he continues, 'Then
the seer [that is, the Self] abideth in himself. At other times
[that is, in all other conditions] the Self taketh the same
form as the fluctuations [of mind-stuff].' Or, in other words,
where *yogic* control and discipline are lacking, the Self
identifies itself with the interminable flux of modifications of
the mind ; so that instead of spiritual insight into the true
nature of existence, which is the fruit of *yoga*, there prevails
a condition of mental obscuration called Ignorance (Skt.
*Avidyā*).

### (B) THE AIM AND RESULTS OF *YOGA*

The whole aim of *yoga* is to dissipate this Ignorance and
to guide the *yogin* to what the Buddhists call Right Knowledge ; and, as Patanjali teaches, to attain to Right Knowledge incessant *yogic* practice is essential ' to the end that
[the mind stuff] shall have permanence in the restricted
state '. It is chiefly because of passion, defined by him as
' that which dwelleth upon [sensual] pleasure ', that man is
*karmically* enslaved to the incessant round of deaths and
births.

As the *Udānavarga*, of the Tibetan canonical scriptures,
tells us, ' Whoever hath lived in accordance with this law of
discipline, in gentleness and purity, will, having transcended
deaths and births, put an end to his sorrow.' And, again,
' He who is released from the bonds of the passions, who
hath cast away the body and who hath attained to Wisdom
and gone beyond the realm of illusion, shineth in splendour
as doth the Sun.' [1]

Patanjali goes on to explain how, when the mind is
brought under control and freed from passion, spiritual insight arises, along with knowledge of previous incarnations.
Accordingly, it is only by means of this highest of sciences
called *yoga* that man can come to know himself in the sense
implied by the well-known aphorism of the Greek Mysteries

[1] *Udānavarga*, iv. 35 ; vi. 12. W. W. Rockhill's translation (London, 1883).

and eventually transcend the human state and be yoked to the True State of *Bodhic* Enlightenment. Or it may be said that *yoga* is the practical means whereby the human mind is enabled to realize the illusory character of sense perceptions and objects of the phenomenal world, and, also, of the concept of the self as a thing separable from all other selves. *Yoga* is commonly regarded by its practitioners as the shortest path to the higher evolution of man. The rather misleading criticism, commonly made, that *yoga* leads to nothing more than self-hypnotization, has been considered in the annotations to our texts, on p. 214 *n.*

The devotee's first objective in this science of practically applied religion called *yoga* is to attain such indomitable command of the lower self as will enable him to direct, by power of willing, all the mental processes. A master of *yoga* must possess control over his body as complete as that of an expert driver over a motor-car, in order to direct all its physiological and psychological processes one-pointedly or to inhibit any of them at will, including the beating of the heart. He must be able to make his body immune to each of the elements, including fire, as suggested by the fire-walking ceremony, and to the law of gravitation, as in levitation ; and, with all the activities of the human mentality stilled, be able to direct his higher consciousness to realms of which man, in the normal *yogically*-undisciplined state, has no knowledge.

These and various other powers of a master of *yoga* have been set forth by Rechung, a disciple of Tibet's great *yogin* Milarepa, in his Introduction to Milarepa's *Biography*, as translated from the original Tibetan by the late Lāma Kazi Dawa-Samdup and published by the editor as *Tibet's Great Yogī Milarepa*. To this standard work all readers of our present treatise should refer.

The great *yogin* (or *yogī*), possessed of clairvoyant vision, is said to be able to observe the life of micro-organisms in a way impossible for a scientist with a microscope ; or to study the nature of suns or planets or nebulae the most distant, which no telescope could ever reveal. Being empowered likewise to observe the physiological processes of his own body, he needs no corpse to dissect in order to study physiology. Nor does he practise vivisection in order to test the effects of poisons or drugs or disease germs. Knowing that mind is the creator and controller of the body and of material substances in every combination, medicines and serums are for him unnecessary. He requires no mechanical devices in order to traverse air or water or land, for he tells us that he can quit his gross physical body and visit any part of the Earth or pass beyond the stratosphere to other worlds with a speed greater than that of light. Milarepa is credited with having been able to travel through the air in his fleshly form with the speed of an arrow.[1] Claiming the power of producing food synthetically from the elements of nature (as the Great *Yogin* Jesus is by many believed to have done in feeding the multitude), or raiment, or any illusory object desired, there is for the master of *yoga*, in his own world, no problem of production or distribution, nor any of the thousand social problems which torment the unenlightened populace, who nowadays dream of a utilitarian Utopia governed by technocrats. For him, man's essential purpose in incarnating is not to exploit nature, nor merely to invent machines, nor to make the building of an earthly Paradise the final goal, but to seek first the Kingdom of Divine Power within, whence, without man's inhumanity to man, all things needful to the progress of our race on this planet will flow inexhaustibly; till, in the fullness of time, man will have ceased to be man, having attained the Other Shore beyond all realms of Illusion.

## (C) THE VARIOUS *YOGAS*

Just as there is an infinite variety of personal or sensuous experiences which no one personality can ever wholly know,

[1] Cf. *Tibet's Great* Yogī *Milarepa*, pp. 35-9, 212. Like Rechung in this Biography, Patanjali in the *Yoga Sūtras* (Book III) has described the various super-physical powers which result from mastery of *yoga*. The Buddha, too, in many of the texts of the Buddhist canons has named and commented upon all these and many other accomplishments of Great Masters of *Yoga*, of Whom He was one of the greatest known to history. See, too, our own texts of Book III, §§ 127-34; and, in correlation therewith, *A Search in Secret India* (London, 1934), *passim*, by Paul Brunton.

so there is an infinite variety of spiritual or supersensuous experiences which no one microcosmic entity can ever experience in their completeness. Completeness of Knowledge implies at-one-ment of the parts, and only when the Many become the One can each know the All and the All each.

Therefore, the Path of *Yoga* is not a single path, but a path of many paths, all leading to the One Goal. What the Vedānta proclaims concerning the different Faiths of mankind is applicable also to the various *yogas* : 'As the different streams having their sources in different places all mingle their waters in the great sea, O Lord, similarly the different Faiths which men follow through different tendencies [or temperaments], various though they may appear, crooked or straight, all lead to Thee.'

We shall now proceed to our brief examination of each of the chief *yogas* forming parts, or paths, pertaining to the one system of *yoga*, following the editor's own researches when he was a student living with *yogins* in various parts of India, sometimes in the high Himālayan Ranges on the frontiers of Tibet, sometimes on the upper Ganges in the vicinity of Rikhikesh.

## (1) *Hatha Yoga*

*Hatha*, in *Hatha Yoga*, is popularly held to mean *Health* ; but this meaning is merely secondary. In the *Commentary on the Hatha Yoga Pradīpikā*, by Brahmānanda, the following shloka is given to explain the meaning of *Hatha* (composed of the two letters *Ha* and *tha*) :—

'The letter *Ha* means the Sun [*swara*] ; the letter *tha* [is] said [to mean] the Moon [*swara*].

'By the joining of *Sūrya-Chandra* (the Sun-Moon), *Hatha Yoga* is understood.'

According to this authority, *Hatha* in connexion with *Yoga* means the Sun-*swara* (or Sun-breathing), which refers to breathing *yogically* through the right (or sun) nostril, plus the Moon-*swara* (or Moon-breathing), which refers to breathing *yogically* through the left (or moon) nostril. Taking *yoga* to mean ' to join ', *Hatha Yoga* thus means ' to join together the Sun-breathing and the Moon-breathing', or ' the joining of *Sūrya-Chandra swaras* '. *Ha = Sūrya =* Sun-[breathing] is positive ; *tha = Chandra =* Moon-[breathing] is negative. *Hatha Yoga,* accordingly, primarily refers to the neutralization, by methods of *yoga,* of the process of breathing, for, by the joining of a positive with a negative, neutrality of the two results naturally.

Patanjali, in his chapter on *Prānāyāma,* makes special reference to this neutralization of the two *swaras* ; and in the subsequent chapters of his *Yoga Sūtras* he shows that *Prānāyāma,* or *yogically* induced regulation, or control, of the breathing, should be regarded as being merely preliminary to the higher practices of *yoga.*

The secondary meaning of *Hatha,* namely *Health,* has direct reference to the healthful physical condition produced by *Hatha Yoga* when rightly practised under the guidance of a *guru* who has mastered it.

If *Hatha Yoga* alone be practised successfully and made an end in itself rather than a means to the supreme end of all *yoga* practices, as it commonly is nowadays in India and elsewhere, there results that indomitable control of the physical body and its vitality which many of the great adepts of *yoga* regard as the most salutary preparation for spiritual illumination. Well-authenticated cases are on record of masters of *Hatha Yoga* who have been able to arrest the vital-processes of the body to such a degree as to become like unto one dead. A famous case of this sort, which was made a test case, is that of the Sādhu Haridās, who was buried for four months and afterwards disinterred living, under the careful supervision of the Mahārāja of Lahore, Ranjeet Singh, early in the last century. Over the grave of the Sādhu, who lay therein in a chest sealed by the Mahārāja with the royal seal, barley-seed was sown and grew up, in a place enclosed by a wall and guarded incessantly by armed sentinels. On the day of the interment, the *yogin's* face had been shaven clean, and when he was revived, after the expiration of the four months, his face was as smooth as on the day of his burial.[1] This circumstance of itself is proof that in virtue of mastery of *Hatha Yoga* the vital processes in a human organism can be temporarily suspended. A similar, but far less complete suspension of the vital processes, occurs in the phenomenon of hibernation among certain of the lower animals.

All such results of success in *Hatha Yoga*, although interesting to physiologists, are of themselves purely psychophysical; and, when divorced from the spiritual attainments of the higher *yogas*, become impediments rather than aids on the Path.

It was the various practices associated with *Hatha Yoga*, especially when the *yogin* does not aim to advance beyond them, including bodily mortifications and severe fasting, with which the Buddha experimented at the outset of his spiritual researches, and found inadequate for the gaining of Enlightenment. Nevertheless, as our texts suggest, the various breathing-exercises associated with Tibetan systems of *Hatha Yoga*, are of great value if used aright, that is to say, solely as means to the great end of all *yogas*, which is Emancipation.

Among the Tibetans, and among the Hindus, the neophyte's need of a spiritual preceptor (or *guru*) is always stressed, in order that the neophyte may be led to avoid the many subtle dangers which those incur who unwisely practise any *yoga* unguided. The editor would be remiss in the discharge of his own responsibilities towards the readers of this volume were he not to emphasize this need of a *guru*, especially for the average European or American student of practically applied *yogic* teachings.

## (2) *Laya Yoga* and its Parts

*Laya*, in the term *Laya Yoga*, means ' mind-control '; and *Laya Yoga* is, accordingly, that part of the science of *yoga* concerned chiefly with the *yogic* method of acquiring mastery over the mind, more particularly over the will-power. By

---

[1] Cf. S. A. Vasu, *An Introduction to Yoga Philosophy*, in *The Sacred Books of the Hindus*, vol. xv, pp. 64 ff., Allahabad, 1915.

those Indian *gurus* who regard, as we do, the various *yogas* as being like rounds in one ladder of *yoga*, *Laya Yoga* is taught only after *Prāṇāyāma*, or *Hatha Yoga*, has been mastered, and the disciple, as a direct result, has brought his body under control, is possessed of a disciplined mind and of sound health, and is, therefore, ready to advance.

Under *Laya Yoga* we classify four other *yogas* which, like *Laya Yoga*, depend essentially upon the conscious exercise of the *yogically*-controlled power of mind, as follows :

### (a) *Bhakti Yoga* and *Shakti Yoga*

Psychologically regarded, viewing *yoga* as a unitary whole, *Bhakti Yoga*, or the ' joining ' by means of mentally concentrating on [Divine] Love (Skt. *Bhakti*), results chiefly in one-pointedness of mind. Accordingly, it is classifiable as being a part of *Laya Yoga*.

In certain parts of our texts, wherein the *yogin*, in prayer or devotion, is directed to visualize the *Devatās* or *Gurus* in a mood of profound love and reverence for them, *Bhakti Yoga* is practised.

Likewise, *Shakti Yoga* is a part of *Laya Yoga* inasmuch as it implies the ' joining ' by means of mentally concentrating on [Divine] Power (Skt. *Shakti*), conceived of as being the feminine (or negative) aspect of the Universe-embracing spiritual forces of Cosmic Mind. In this *yoga*, the *Shakti* is commonly personified as a Mother-Goddess. The masculine (or positive) aspect is represented by a personification of the male half of the duality of deity. This dualism has parallel in the subtle Yin-Yang Doctrine of Taoism, as in the corresponding Yum-Yab Doctrine of Lāmaism, the *Yin* (or *Yum*) being the female principle of nature and the *Yang* (or *Yab*) the male principle. There exists similar correspondence between the *Shakti* of the Hindus, the *Sophia* (' Wisdom ') of the Gnostics, and the *Prajñā* (' Wisdom ') of the *Prajñā-Pāramitā*, all three alike being personified as the female aspect of deity.

Whereas in *Bhakti Yoga* one-pointedness of mind is attained through *yogic* concentration on Divine Love as *Bhakti* in *Shakti Yoga* a result *yogically* equivalent comes from *yogic* concentration on Divine Power as *Shakti*. In our texts the Great *Shakti* is Vajra-Yoginī, a Tantric goddess.

### (*b*) *Mantra Yoga* and *Yantra Yoga*

In *Mantra Yoga*, by the expert use of *mantras*, which consist of words or sounds of occult power, and in *Yantra Yoga*, by similar employment of *yantras*, or geometrical diagrams of mystical significance, the *yogin's* aim is to establish telepathic and even more intimate communication with the deities that he invokes to assist him in his *yogic* endeavours. *Mudrā Yoga* (of which some explanation is given in *The Tibetan Book of the Dead*, p. 127) may be regarded as a subdivision of *Yantra Yoga*; for it is dependent upon the *yogic* use of mystic signs (Skt. *mudrā*), which are usually made by posturing the hands or body, and in lesser degree upon mystic symbols more or less of geometrical character.

In our own texts, *Mantra Yoga* and *Yantra Yoga* (chiefly as *Mudrā Yoga*) play a part of considerable importance, as they do in almost all systems of *yoga* which have been shaped in Tibetan environments. As shown in *Tibet's Great* Yogī *Milarepa*, both these *yogas* are employed in the conferring of spiritual power at the time of *lāmāic* initiations. In so far as these two *yogas* are dependent upon *yogic* visualization and, therefore, upon a certain degree of *yogic* control of mind, they, also, like *Bhakti* and *Shakti Yoga*, are to be regarded as specialized parts of *Laya Yoga*.

In the *Śiva Samhitā* (v. 9) of the Hindus, *yoga* is said to be of four kinds, and *Mantra Yoga*, being regarded as the simplest, or easiest to practise, is separated from *Laya Yoga* and placed first in the order of the *yogas*, even in advance of *Hatha Yoga* : ' *Yoga* is of four kinds : first, *Mantra Yoga* ; second, *Hatha Yoga* ; third, *Laya Yoga* ; fourth, *Rāja Yoga*, which discardeth dualism.'

Also in the *Śiva Samhitā* (v. 30), *Nāda Yoga*, which is a form of *Mantra Yoga*, referred to by Patanjali (*Yoga Sūtras*, 35) as that aspect of *yoga* dependent upon mental concentration upon some one of the *vishayas* (sensations) of the body and otherwise known as *Shabda* (Sensation of Sound) *Yoga*, is said to be the best part of *Laya Yoga*. Patanjali explains how, by the aid of any of the bodily sensations such, for example, as the internal sound heard when the ears are stopped with the fingers, which is one kind of *nāda*, or *shabda*, one-pointedness of mind results. And in other Sanskrit works on *yoga* this process is called *Laya Yoga*.

### (c) The Limitations of *Laya Yoga*

*Laya Yoga* is, therefore, to be regarded chiefly as one method of attaining *yogic* control of the human mentality. As such, like *Hatha Yoga*, its right use is merely preparatory. The adept in this *yoga*, also like the adept in *Hatha Yoga*, may induce in himself a state of suspended animation, very often mistakenly regarded by the *yogin* who experiences it as being concomitant with that exalted spiritual illumination which is realized only in the highest *samādhic* trance. If the *yogin* be obsessed by this error, as many of the practitioners of these two lower *yogas* commonly are, he makes no advance on the path of spiritual attainment beyond a certain disciplining and intimate understanding of his own psycho-physical powers. This warning applies to all *yogas* here classified under *Laya Yoga*.

*Laya Yoga*, however, like *Hatha Yoga*, may be of incalculable assistance to *yogins* who by temperament are fitted to profit by it. Great *Yogins* who have practised these *yogas* and attained to Freedom have employed them only as preparatory preliminaries to the higher *yogic* practices.

According to Patanjali (i. 19), those who subordinate or sacrifice their mental powers to nature (i.e. *Prakriti*, or *Shakti*), or to deified men who are deceased (such, for example, as Krishna or Jesus) cause thereby their own return to this world again and again. The aim of the higher *yogas*, which we shall now proceed to consider, is to advance the evolution of man beyond the illusory glamour of *sangsāric*, or worldly, existence, so that *karmic* necessity of rebirth in the human state comes to an end. Then if there be further incarnation on this planet, it comes as a matter of choice, endowed with the exalted consciousness and power derived from having made the Great Conquest; and there is born on Earth one more Guide to lead humanity to the *Nirvāṇic* Goal.

### (3) *Dhyāna Yoga*

*Dhyāna Yoga* is that part of *yoga* dependent upon meditation (Skt. *dhyāna*) leading to mind-control. As such, it stands alone, not being exclusively related to any of the *yogas*, but being an essential practice in all of them. Mastery of *Dhyāna Yoga* is one of the chief essentials for success in the highest of all *yogas*, which is *Samādhi Yoga*.

### (4) *Rāja Yoga* and Its Parts

In the term *Rāja Yoga*, *Rāja* means 'best', or 'royal', or 'highest'. *Rāja Yoga*, therefore, means the best part of *yoga*. It is the 'joining' by the best or royal method. *Rāja Yoga* is the best *yoga* because by means of it the *yogin* attains to self-realization, to knowledge of Reality, in that sense implied by the ancient Greek aphorism Γνῶθι Σεαυτόν ('Know Thyself').

### (a) *Jñāna Yoga*

*Jñāna Yoga* refers to that part of *yoga* dependent upon [Divine] Knowledge (Skt. *Jñāna*); or to the 'joining' by means of *yogic* insight. In other words, self-realization attained by means of *yogically* induced insight into the true nature of existence is the fruit of *Jñāna Yoga*; and thus *Jñāna Yoga* is an essential part of *Rāja Yoga*.

### (b) *Karma Yoga*

In the term *Karma Yoga*, the Sanskrit word *Karma* means 'action', more especially such action as will lead to Emancipation. It, therefore, implies right action, so that *Karma Yoga* is the 'joining' by means of right *yogic* action. Inasmuch as right *yogic* action forms a part of all *yoga* practices, *Karma Yoga*, like *Dhyāna Yoga*, underlies the whole of *yoga*. In the second chapter of the *Bhagavad Gītā*, or 'Song Divine', the great classic of the *Yoga* School, *Karma Yoga* is, accordingly, regarded as inclusive of all *yogas*.

In relation to practitioners of *yoga* who call themselves *karma yogins* in contradistinction to *yogins* pursuing a technique different from theirs, *Karma Yoga*, like *Hatha Yoga* or *Laya Yoga*, may, however, be classified as a specialized part, rather than as the whole, of *yoga*. *Karma Yoga* of this sort is dependent upon renunciation of the fruits of one's actions, in the sense implied by the *Bhagavad Gītā*. It leads to the transcending of personality, or the attaining of selflessness, while working in the world actively, and with fullest energy, as those work who are ambitious in worldly aims, and wholly for the benefit of human kind. This, too, being a royal method, *Karma Yoga* may be regarded as one aspect of *Rāja Yoga*. It is by the lives of such Great Teachers as the Buddha and the Christ that *Karma Yoga* has been ideally exemplified.

## (c) *Kuṇḍalinī Yoga*

To *yogins* who follow the Path of the *Tantras*, it is *Kuṇḍalinī Yoga* which is the Royal Yoga; and with *Kuṇḍalinī Yoga* more than with *Rāja Yoga* in its non-Tantric form most of our texts comprising Books III to VI, being themselves more or less Tantric, are directly concerned. By means of *Shakti Yoga*, the Tantric *yogin* attains discipline of body and mind and then proceeds to the mighty task of awakening the dormant, or innate, powers of divinity within himself, personified as the sleeping Goddess Kuṇḍalinī. One by one the psychic centres, or *chakra*, of his body are brought into functioning activity, as the Goddess awakens in the Root-Support Lotus (Skt. *Mūlādhāra Chakra*) situated in the perineum, at the base of the spinal column, and rises, *chakra* by *chakra*, to meet her *Shakta*, the Lord Shiva, who sits enthroned in the Seventh *Chakra*, in the pericarp of the Thousand-Petalled Lotus (Skt. *Sahasrāra Padma*), in the brain centre. Then, from the mystic union of the *Shakta* and the *Shakti*, is born Enlightenment; and the *yogin* has attained the Goal.[1]

---

[1] All readers who would know more of Tantricism, and of those highly specialized forms of *yoga* which are peculiar to it, should refer to the works of Sir John Woodroffe (published under the pseudonym of Arthur Avalon);

## (d) Samādhi Yoga

In the 'joining' by means of the Quiescent State (Skt. *Samādhi*), the *yogin* transcends personality, and his microcosmic consciousness breaks its fetters and becomes reunited with the Macrocosmic All-Consciousness. This, the Goal of *Yoga*, truly is the transmutation of the limited human nature into the limitless divine nature, the blending or 'yoking' of the lower self with the One Self, of the drop with the Ocean. This supreme result, which European occultists have designated as Illumination and Buddhists *Nirvāṇa*, is attainable, so our Tibetan texts and teachers assure us, by whomsoever shall tread the path of *The Great Symbol*, of Book II, to the very end.

### (D) THE SUMMARY AND CONCLUSION

The various aspects or parts of *yoga* and their general relationship to one another may now be set forth concisely by the following table.

| The Part | Giving Mastery of | and leading to yogic control of |
|---|---|---|
| I. *Hatha Yoga* | breath | physical body and vitality. |
| II. *Laya Yoga* | will | powers of mind. |
| (1) *Bhakti Yoga* | love | powers of divine love. |
| (2) *Shakti Yoga* | energy | energizing forces of Nature. |
| (3) *Mantra Yoga* | sound | powers of sound vibrations. |
| (4) *Yantra Yoga* | form | powers of geometrical form. |
| III. *Dhyāna Yoga* | thought | powers of thought-processes. |
| IV. *Rāja Yoga* | method | powers of discrimination. |
| (1) *Jñāna Yoga* | knowledge | powers of intellect. |
| (2) *Karma Yoga* | activity | powers of action. |
| (3) *Kuṇḍalinī Yoga* | *Kuṇḍalinī* | powers of psychic-nerve force. |
| (4) *Samādhi Yoga* | self | powers of ecstasy. |

There are some other subordinate subdivisions of *yoga* which could be named, but each of them is merely a specialized aspect of some one of the parts of *yoga* here classified.

In so far as *Dhyāna Yoga* is common to all *yogas*, this classification may be reduced to a threefold classification, namely, *Hatha Yoga*, *Laya Yoga*, and *Rāja Yoga*. Each

reference might also be made to *The Tibetan Book of the Dead*, and to *Tibet's Great Yogī Milarepa*, for these two works are based upon *Tantric Yoga* in its peculiarly Tibetan aspects.

leads to the perfecting and the indomitable control of one of the triune aspects of man : the first, to that of the physical man ; the second, to that of the mental man ; and the third, to that of the spiritual man. Viewed thus, as a unitary system divisible into three parts, each part associated with one of the three chief parts of man the microcosm, *yoga* presents itself as being the only complete science of human psychology of which mankind has cognizance. Occidental psychology is far too immature as yet to be regarded as an all-embracing science of man in this sense implied by *yoga*.

Upon making comparative *yogic* study of the seven Books comprised within this volume, the student will discover that each Book is representative of some particular part or parts of the *Yoga* Philosophy as above set forth. Thus, when regarded as a whole, the twenty-eight categories of *yogic* precepts contained in Book I concern all *yogas* in some degree, the emphasis being more especially upon *Laya* and *Jñāna Yoga*. Book II, likewise, treats of the whole of *yoga*, but is essentially a treatise on *Samādhi Yoga*. Book III is based upon various *yogas* : Chapter I being dependent chiefly upon *Hatha Yoga* ; Chapters II to V, upon *Jñāna Yoga* ; and Chapter VI, upon *Kuṇḍalinī Yoga*. Book IV, like Chapter VI of Book III, is especially concerned with *Kuṇḍalinī Yoga* ; Book V, with *Karma Yoga* ; Book VI, with *Yantra* and *Mantra Yoga* ; and Book VII, with *Jñāna Yoga*.

*Yoga*, as a unified whole, may be thought of as an efficient and scientific method of bringing about the development of man's triune nature by means of mental concentration upon the various psycho-physical functions, mental powers, and spiritual forces experienced in and through the human organism. According to the part of *yoga* practised, corresponding advance is made ; but, as the Great *Gurus* tell us, all parts have been necessary in past lives or will be necessary in this life or in future lives for the one who has attained or is destined to attain self-conquest. Thus, in accordance with the disciple's actual development, resulting from *yogic* practices in other lives or in this life, the wise *guru* determines for which *yoga* the disciple is best fitted. And it often happens that no two or more of a *guru*'s disciples are simultaneously practising *yoga* in the same way. Similarly, each reader of this volume will, if he carefully analyses his own mentality, feel a natural affinity for one aspect of its *yogic* teachings rather than for another, and so be inclined to choose such of them as he prefers and then concentrate upon them, or upon any one of them, rather than upon all. And may he ever keep uppermost in his thoughts the *guru*'s warning to the neophyte, to make haste slowly and to act wisely.

## VIII. *YOGA* AND RELIGION

Regarded thus, as the applied psychology of religion, *yoga* is the very tap-root of Hinduism, Buddhism, Jainism, and Taoism. Similarly, if perhaps in less degree, it has nourished the growth of the Faith of the Parsees ; and in the development of the three Semitic Faiths, Judaism, Christianity, and Islam, it has been a very important shaping influence. In its less systematized, and probably degenerate, form, *yoga* plays a part even in some of the magical and animistic cults of the so-called primitive races.[1] Among peoples of higher culture, invocations, exorcisms, masses for the dead or for the living, prayers, *mantric* chants, religious meditations, tellings of beads, methods of attaining spiritual discipline or insight, and all forms of ritual which aim at enabling man to attain to mystic communion with higher than human powers, or liberation from worldly existence, are in varying degrees more or less of the nature of *yoga*.

So far as can be ascertained, the training of the candidate for initiation into the Mysteries of Antiquity was largely *yogic*. Likewise, in the secret societies of uncivilized races of the present day, fasting, both from food and sex indulgence, meditation, penance, purification, and other kinds of practices for the attainment of spiritual discipline are essential for the neophyte to whom there is to be conveyed by solemn initiatory rites the secret doctrines of the tribe.

The history of monasticism in East and West is almost

[1] Cf. R. R. Marett, *Faith, Hope, and Charity in Primitive Religion* (Oxford, 1932), pp. 5-20 ; *Sacraments of Simple Folk* (Oxford, 1933), *passim*.

inseparable from that of *yoga*. When the early Christians, both Gnostic and non-Gnostic, dwelt in the desert and mountain solitudes of Egypt and the Near East as solitary hermits or in communities vowed to the three vows, of poverty, chastity, and obedience, they grafted into the tree of the Christian Faith a form of *yoga* which appears to have had sources both in the monasticism of the ancient Egyptian priests and in that of the early Zoroastrians and Hindus. To-day, more so in the Latin, Greek, Coptic, Armenian, and Abyssinian than in the Anglican or Protestant Churches, *yogic* practices which have had, in at least some degree, this pre-Christian origin are of prime importance. In all monastic orders of Christendom, but more especially in the Jesuit Order, the rules which govern the spiritual training of the monks are based on *yoga*. We find, too, in the fraternities of the Sufis and Dervishes of the Moslem world the same insistence upon *yogic* disciplining of body, mind, and spirit.

It is particularly interesting in this connexion to observe that Sufism, although Islamic in its religious environment, recognizes four stages in the psychic development of the disciple quite like those recognized by the more ancient Hindu and Buddhistic systems. These four stages on the Path of Sufism are: (1) *Hast* (Humanity), in which 'the tenets of Islam and its laws must be faithfully observed' by the neophyte; (2) *Taregut* (Obtaining of Potentiality), in which 'the disciple may lay aside all [exoteric] religious observances and think only on the delights of contemplation'; (3) *Araff*, 'a condition of knowledge akin to inspiration', or *yogic* insight, in which occult powers are developed; and (4) *Hagegut* (Truth), wherein sainthood like that of the *Arhant* is attained. 'All desires, ambitions, and earthly ideas must be cast off, for now the man has become a saint. All four veils are removed and he is free to commune direct with God, the Divine Sun, of whom he is but a spark. The final stage is generally completed in solitude far from the dwellings of man. In the desert or jungle or away in the heights of great mountains the devotee finds peace to contemplate without any outside interruptions.'[1]

[1] Cf. Sirdar Ikbal Ali Shah, *Islamic Sufism* (London, 1933), pp. 31-2.

In all *yogas*, as in those set forth herein in Books II and III, there are corresponding steps on the Path. The first step consists of intellectual comprehension of the teachings as contained in exoteric scriptures. The second step is dependent upon gaining spiritual comprehension of the teachings; or, in other words, upon attaining *yogic* insight into their esoteric significance. The third step consists of glimpses of reality; and the fourth, of full realization. Otherwise stated, there are the sowing of the seed, its germination, the growth, and the fruition. There are also the foundation, the path (or method), and the fruit; or the light, the ignition, and the attainment; as expounded in Book III, Chapter IV, §§ 2, 8.

In the occult symbolism of the Persian poets of the School of Omar Khayyām, as in the mystical eroticism taught in Christian convents, *yoga* appears in its more specialized aspect as *Bhakti Yoga*. So it does, in another form, in the esotericism of the cult of Isis and the child Horus, now metamorphosed into the cult of the Virgin and the child Jesus. One might go on to examine the origin and growth of various other *yogas* in our Western World.

Turning to the past, we find that even among the Druids of Ireland and Britain, monasticism, with its accompanying *yogic* practices, appears to have been established long prior to the time of St. Patrick and St. Columba. Whether it was of indigenous origin, or if by some such agency as the early Phoenicians the Far East through the Near East influenced even these isles beyond the Pillars of Hercules, or there were Atlantean influences such as the ancient Gaelic myths concerning the Western Other World appear to suggest, we shall now probably never be able to decide with historical certainty.

Whatever may have been the origin of Druidism, we are, however, the direct heirs of its more or less *yogic* culture, transmitted to us through our own prehistoric Celtic ancestors. In like manner, we are also indebted to the priests of Odin and Mithras; and, more remotely, to the unknown culture heroes of Aurignacian and Magdalenian man who have left records suggestive of their magical religion painted in the caves of Spain and Southern France.[1] More perceptibly are we the inheritors of the *yogic* legacy of the Egyptians, Greeks, and Romans, handed on through such fraternal orders as the Stoics, the Pythagoreans, and the Neo-Platonists. Much that is best in our art, literature, philosophy, religion, and even science bears witness to this.

In this brief historical review, the aim has been to suggest that *yoga*, when rightly understood, is not, as many in the West assume, something exotic, nor is it necessarily or always magic. In its less developed, or decadent, forms, *yoga* may be regarded as a magical religion; in its more highly developed forms it appears to have evolved to a religious science, in much the same way as, in the eyes of Western scientists, chemistry has evolved from alchemy.

## IX. Buddhistic *Yoga*

Although, as we have said, Buddhism is fundamentally *yogic*, there is need to distinguish Buddhistic from Hindu and other systems of *yoga*. To the occultist, however, the differences are largely a matter of terms and technique and not of essentials.

Thus, to the Hindu, *yoga* implies, as has been set forth philologically above, a joining of the part to the whole, the microcosmic with the macrocosmic, the individualized aspect of consciousness (or mind) with the cosmic or universal aspect, commonly personified as the Supreme Spirit, or Ishvara. Similarly, in Christian and Moslem *yogic* practices, *yoga* implies union with God. Correspondingly, in Buddhistic *yogic* practices the aim is, in the poetical language of *The Light of Asia*, to merge the dew-drop of the individualized aspect of mind with the Shining Sea of the One Mind. Or, otherwise stated, the aim is to transcend all things of the *Sangsāra* (or universe of phenomenal existences) and attain to supramundane consciousness, concomitant with the realization of *Nirvāṇa*.

For the Great *Rishis*, who have illuminated the darkness of

---

[1] Cf. R. R. Marett, *The Threshold of Religion* (London, 1909), pp. 203-20; and W. J. Sollas, *Ancient Hunters* (London, 1924), pp. 397-403, 423.

*sangsāric* mind with the light of the *Upanishads*, or for Patan-jali, no less than for Buddhists of all Schools, the essential purpose of *yoga* is to overcome Ignorance by becoming yoked to, or attaining union with, Knowledge. It is in this sense that Deliverance from Ignorance is as much a doctrine of the Vedānta as it is of Buddhism. And, in our view, it is the same whether one names this Deliverance *Mukti* or *Nirvāṇa*. Indeed, it is the root-doctrine of all the principal faiths of our common humanity that there is innate in man the Light, that the Light shines in the Darkness, and that the Light, in virtue of methods which we call *yogic*, eventually overwhelms the Darkness, so that there remains naught save the Light.

If now we turn to a consideration of the differences as between Northern and Southern Buddhism in the practical application of *yoga*, we find that they are quite sharply defined. The most important, as some of our annotations will point out, are the direct results of corresponding differences which distinguish the two Schools. One of the chief of these is dependent upon the doctrine of the Voidness, which in its complex Mahāyānic form is not favoured by the Southern School. The doctrine itself is, however, as the Mahāyānists point out, foreshadowed in the Pāli canon, as indicated by the *Cula-Suññata* and the *Mahā-Suññata Suttas* of the *Majjhima-Nikāya*, wherein the Theravādin method of meditation upon the Voidness is set forth. The parallel Mahāyānist method is expounded by our own texts in Book VII. Another difference, probably of equal importance, is due to the acceptance by the Northern School and the rejection by the Southern School of much that is classifiable as *Tantric Yoga*; and it is upon *Tantric Yoga* that most of the *yogas* expounded in Books III, IV, V, and VI of this volume are more or less dependent. Then, again, some minor differences have arisen from the greater insistence by the Mahāyāna upon the doctrine that there are superhuman impersonal powers, symbolized by the *Tri-Kāya* (or 'Three Divine Bodies'), which is the esoteric Trinity of the Northern School. Symbolically, the *Tri-Kāya* constitutes—if one may attempt to describe the indescribable—the United Threefold Body of *Bodhic* Essence, which sustains all existences and all *sangsāric* things and makes Deliverance possible for man. It is synonymous with the Thatness of the Vedānta.

From the *Tri-Kāya* there arise and to it return, even as rain-drops arise from and return to the sea, all things constituting the Universe—matter in its various aspects as solids, liquids, gases, energies, and the whole of *sangsāric* mind and conscious-ness. In the *Tri-Kāya* there exist, in a humanly incompre-hensible, impersonalized at-one-ment, all the Buddhas of all the aeons. To the world-pilgrim on the Mahāyānic Path of Deliverance, the *Tri-Kāya* is the transcendent Refuge and Goal.

Another source of difference is the Mahāyānic doctrine, which is complementary to that of the *Tri-Kāya*, concerning *Bodhisattvas*, or beings who have attained *Bodhic* insight into Reality, some of whom are now incarnate on Earth and others, like the coming Buddha Maitreya, are dwelling in heaven-worlds. Although *Bodhisattvas* are not unknown to the Pāli canon, and their existence in heavenly spheres is conceded by the Southern Buddhist, he holds that the Mahāyānist should place more emphasis upon the *Dharma* and less upon prayers and supplications to *Bodhisattvas* in superhuman realms for spiritual guidance. (See p. 213[4].)

The editor believes, however, that the opposition of Thera-vādins of the Southern School to the *Tantric Yoga* of the Mahāyānists, at least in some of its aspects expounded in this volume, may be somewhat modified when, upon unprejudiced examination of the subtle transcendentalism underlying it, they come to comprehend that, after all, the important con-sideration is not so much a matter of methods (providing these be altruistic), or the sort of path traversed by the disciple (providing it be of the ' right-hand '), as it is of the goal which the disciple sets out to reach.

Here again, in a spirit of non-attachment to these differences separating the *yogic* practices of the two Schools, one likes to invoke the Vedāntic simile of the many paths all leading to the One Goal ; or the philosophy of the *Song Divine* uttered by Krishna, the personification of the impersonal Cosmic

Intelligence, that although men in accordance with their various temperaments adopt different methods or paths in *yoga*, all alike, if they be right methods or paths, lead to Deliverance.

Turning now for a moment to view the type of *yoga* common to the Southern School, we find in it no direct invocations to tutelaries, no prayers to superhuman *gurus*, nor any visualizations of Tantric deities such as those which play so important a part in Mahāyānic *yogic* practices. In the *Ratana Sutta*, of the *Khuddaka-Nikāya*, and elsewhere in the Pāli canon, the Buddha is, however, represented as giving instructions to dedicate the merit born of good deeds to *devas* in order to gain their protection ; and in the *Pirit* Ceremony, and in other ceremonies, of Southern Buddhism, the *devas* are invited to accept the merit arising from religious observances—as the *devas* and other classes of invisible beings are in the ritual of the *Chöd* Rite, recorded in our Book V. Furthermore, the meditations, visualizations, and refuges of the Southern School are simpler than those of the Northern School ; and, while not stressing, the Theravādin does take into account, as do our own texts, the classical Buddhistic *Jhānas*, or ecstatic states which result from practising *yoga*.

The visualizations chiefly employed by Southern Buddhists are of ordinary (or non-complex) objects, and much unlike the elaborate visualizations of Tantric *Yoga*. They are very largely confined to the more orthodox objects or subjects of *yogic* meditation, collectively known as those with form (*rūpa*) and those without form (*arūpa*), which are forty in number. They are classified as follows:

   (1) The Ten Artifices, or 'supports', employed in attaining mental fixity, or concentration, namely, earth, water, fire, air, blue, yellow, red, white, space, and consciousness.[1]

---

[1] If, for instance, the element earth be the basis for the concentration, the *yogin* forms a circle, a few inches in diameter, of earth (or clay), preferably of a reddish hue, at a distance of about 3 feet from his meditation-seat, which should be on a higher level than the circle. Then he fixes his gaze upon the circle and concentrates his mind on the element earth while holding to the thought that his own body is composed of earth. After this practice has been performed for a while, the mind attains the state of absorption in the object of

(2) The Ten Impurities of the Human Corpse, the tenth being the human skeleton.

(3) The Ten Meditations: upon the Buddha, the *Dharma*, the *Sangha*, morality, generosity, the *devas*, the breathing-process, death, the living body, and peace.

(4) The Four Limitless States, or Virtues : universal love, pity, joyous sympathy, and quiescence.

(5) The Four Spheres of Formlessness (cf. p. 92 [7]).

(6) And the Meditation upon nutrition, in order to realize the corruptibility and loathsomeness of the body as sustained by food ; and the Meditation upon the four elements (earth, water, fire, air) composing the physical body, in order to realize impersonality.

Complementary to these, there are meditations upon the bodily functions, the sensations, the emotions, the thoughts, the dissolution of all component things, and especially upon the Three Characteristics of Existence, which are, impermanence, sorrow, and non-ego.[1]

There are a number of important canonical texts of the Southern School which specifically treat of such *yogic* meditations. Thus, in the very popular *Mahā-Satipatthāna Sutta* of the *Dīgha-Nikāya*, there are expounded the Four Great Meditations, on the body, the feelings, the mental concepts,

meditation so that the circle will be seen even when the eyes are closed. The practice enables the *yogin* to comprehend the illusory nature of the human body and of all other component things, and thus to realize the state of non-ego, somewhat after the manner set forth in the *Chöd* Rite of our Book V. Similarly, in the Pāli texts and commentaries thereto, explanations are given concerning each of the forty subjects of meditation. In this connexion, the student should refer to the following publications of the Pāli Text Society : the *Anguttara-Nikāya*, translated by E. R. J. Gooneratne; *The Path of Purity*, Part II, a translation, by Pe Maung Tin, of Buddhaghosa's *Visuddhi Magga* ; and the *Manual of a Mystic*, a translation, by F. L. Woodward, of the *Yogāvacāra* treatise.

[1] Having had the privilege of perusing before its publication the forthcoming work by Miss G. Constant Lounsbery, President of *Les Amis du Bouddhisme*, of Paris, entitled *La Méditation Bouddhique: Théorie et Pratique selon l'École du Sud*, I have profited by it, as comparison with this section will show. I find, too, that the results of Miss Lounsbery's researches with respect to *yoga* among the Southern Buddhists of Ceylon support those of my own. All students of the subject will find her treatise of great assistance.

and the *Dharma* (or fundamental principles of Buddhism), similar to those given in our own Book VII. In the *Majjhima-Nikāya*, the *Mahā-Rāhulovāda* and the *Ānapanasati Suttas* treat of contemplation and *yogic* breathing-exercises, much after the manner set forth herein in Book II; the *Anañjasappaya Sutta* treats of meditation on impossibility, *yogic* accomplishments, and Emancipation; the *Kāyagatasati Sutta*, ot meditation on the body; the *Upakkilesa Sutta*, of Right Meditation; and the *Vitakkasanṭhana Sutta*, of the way to meditate in order to dispel evil thoughts by good thoughts. And in the *Khuddaka Nikāya*, meditation is one of the themes of the *Patisambhidā Magga*. Our own texts, as will be seen, afford parallels to most of these *yogas* of the Theravādins.

Among the similar *yogic* practices set forth in this volume, it is with those of the Great Symbol of Book II, which is essentially non-Tantric, that the Theravādin will probably feel most in agreement. Therein the emphasis is, as in much of the *yoga* of the Southern School, upon *yogic* analyses of the mental processes. Correlatively, there is also emphasized in it the importance of meditation upon the breathing-process whereby, as the necessary prerequisites to such analyses, are attained purity of body, rhythm of breath, and calmness of mind. Book V, although largely Tantric and pre-Buddhistic, should interest Buddhists of all Schools because of its teachings concerning non-ego. And, as being dependent upon *yogic* meditations not unlike those which are employed in the Southern School, namely, meditation upon the impermanence, the unsatisfactory nature, and the emptiness of all *sangsāric* things, and upon the non-reality of dualism, or upon the unique oneness of all living things, Book VII ought also to appeal to the Theravādin, despite his traditional antagonism towards much else that is implied in it by the doctrine of the Voidness in its Mahāyānic form upon which the Book is based.

Furthermore, in addition to the various parts of the Pāli canon treating of *yogic* meditation and breathing-exercises mentioned above, there are other important texts in it which tend to show that Southern Buddhism, quite like Northern Buddhism, is, as we have stated, fundamentally a system of applied *yoga*. In this connexion, reference should be made to the following *Suttas* of the *Majjhima Nikāya*: *Anumāna, Ariyapariyesana, Mahā Saccaka, Atthakanāgara, Latukiko-pama*, and the *Mahā Cattarisaka*, which expounds the Eight-Fold Path.

## X. THE PSYCHOLOGY OF THE *YOGIC* VISUALIZATIONS

Although mind-created by the *yogin*, the visualized images of spiritual beings, upon which our texts direct him to concentrate, are not to be regarded by him with indifference. If he merely thinks to himself 'I am creating with my mind', no more than intellectual progress is made. The *yogin* must understand that his practices are not simply mental ; he should regard them ' with exalted regard, veneration, and devotion, looking upon the *Devatās* [i.e. the visualized deities] as real, holy, and divine. They are none the less so because mind-produced, for the mind ultimately is That, and its ideas forms of That.'[1]

The *Devatās* so produced are not, however, to be looked upon as by the unenlightened, that is, as having objective, individualized existence. They are rather to be thought of ' as an artist regards the product of his mind and brush or pencil, with adoration and fondness . . . as the real manifestation of the Deities of the Jambu-dvīpa [i.e. the human world, or the Planet Earth] . . . not only wielding influence in the Jambu-dvīpa, but throughout the whole Universe '.[2] They are the concentrated rays or manifestations of the *Sambhoga-Kāya*, the *Bodhic* Body of Perfect Endowment, the first reflex of the *Dharma-Kāya* (' Divine Body of Truth '), of those Enlightened Ones of the Akanishtha Realm. ' So should one accustom the mind to regard the Divinities as superior beings.'[3] In other words, man as the microcosm cannot separate himself mentally from the Macrocosmic Mind of All.

So, in the text of the *Shrī-Chakra-Sambhāra Tantra*, it is

---

[1] Cf. *Shrī-Chakra-Sambhāra Tantra*, as translated from the Tibetan by Lāma Kazi Dawa-Samdup and edited by Sir John Woodroffe (pseudonym Arthur Avalon), as volume vii of Tantrik Texts (London, 1919), p. 37[3].

[2] Cf. *ibid.*, p. 35[4].          [3] Cf. *ibid.*, p. 37.

said : ' Then, with a view to dispel doubts about the *Devatās*
and the Path, identify the thirty-seven *Devatās*, created by
and meditated upon by the mind, with the thirty-seven
branches of the *Dharma* which leadeth to Buddhahood ; and
these, again, must be thought of as being within the worshipper
himself in the form of the thirty-seven *Devatās*. This practice
is for men of the highest intellect. Men of middling and lower
intelligence should identify the recollection of the body to be
*Khah-do-ma*',[1] otherwise known as the *Ḍākinī* Goddess, or
Vajra-Yoginī, who is to be visualized by the devotee, according
to the descriptions contained in the texts of our Books III
and IV.

' The devotee may doubt whether the *Devatās* are real and
efficacious for the purposes invoked and visualized, and whether
they exist independently of the devotee's mind. Thus, with a
view to dispel such doubts, the *Sādhaka* [i.e. the *yogin*, or
devotee] is enjoined to identify the *Devatās* with the saving
*Dharma* ; so that he may realize the truth that enlightenment
and liberation are to be obtained from himself and by himself
through his own effort and not from any external help or
favour.' [2]

Later on in the same *Tantra* the devotee is admonished thus :
' Having uttered these [*mantras*], let the *Sādhaka* remember
that all these *Devatās* are but symbols representing the various
things that occur on the Path, such as the helpful impulses and
the stages attained by their means. Should doubts arise as to
the divinity of these *Devatās*, one should say " The *Ḍākinī* is
only the recollection of the body ", and remember that the
Deities constitute the Path.' [3]

As the first step on this Path, the *yogin* should deeply
meditate upon the esoteric significance of the *Tri-Kāya*, or
the Three Divine Bodies, through which the Buddha Spirit

---

[1] Cf. *ibid.*, p. 38. *Khah-do-ma* represents the pronunciation of the Tibetan
word *Mkhah-hgro-ma*, meaning, ' Sky-goer', a fairy-like goddess possessing
peculiar occult powers for good or evil, equivalent to the Sanskrit *Ḍākinī*.
The invocation of *Ḍākinīs*, as many of our texts will suggest, plays a part of
some prominence in many of the purely Tantric rituals connected with Tibetan
*yoga*.

[2] *Ibid.*, p. 38[1].                    [3] Cf. *ibid.*, p. 41.

manifests itself, and makes *Bodhic* Enlightenment possible for man immersed in the Ignorance of *sangsāric*, or conditioned, existence. The first of these Three Divine Bodies is the *Dharma-Kāya*, the Divine Body of Truth, the essential formless *Bodhi*, which symbolizes true spiritual experience devoid of all error. The second, the *Sambhoga-Kāya*, symbolizes the reflected Divine Body of Glory, a reflex of the first, in which, in an indescribable superhuman state, exist the *Bodhisattvas* and Buddhas Who have postponed their own final entry into *Nirvāṇa* in order to lead unenlightened beings to Freedom. The third, the *Nirmāṇa-Kāya*, or Divine Body of Incarnation, represents the pure and perfected human form of a Buddha on Earth. Thus, the first of the Three Divine Bodies is the essential ; the second, the reflected ; and the third, the practical aspect whereby the One Wisdom, the One Mind, manifests Itself.

## XI. *Karma* and Rebirth

Every reader of this volume should understand that the teachings concerning *Karma* and Rebirth, which, like the *Yoga* Philosophy. are fundamental in all our texts, are therein nowhere treated as a matter of mere belief; they are regarded as being based upon incontrovertible laws of nature. The Doctrine of *Karma* happens to be scientifically conceivable and, therefore, acceptable, at least intellectually, for the average Occidental, because he has become accustomed to it under its more familiar designation as the law of cause and effect.[1] He, however, like Occidental science, fails to recognize its tremendous psychological implications when applied to the study of man himself. That man and all man's faculties are the result of causes our scientists grant, but save for a very few of the greatest of them, like Huxley and William James,[2] they have not as yet grasped, as the

[1] One of the latest pronouncements concerning this law in relation to relativity has been made by Eddington, as follows: ' Cause and effect are closely bound up with time's arrow; the cause must precede the effect; the relativity of time has not obliterated this order.' Cf. A. S. Eddington, *The Nature of the Physical World* Cambridge, 1928), p. 295.

[2] Cf. T. H. Huxley, *Evolution and Ethics* (London, 1894), pp. 61-2, 95 ; and W. James, *The Varieties of Religious Experiences* (New York, 1902), pp. 521-2.

Oriental thinker has long ago, that man is man and just the kind of man that he is because he is the result of an apparently interminable concatenation of causes with a history which goes back for unknown millions of years. In a biological sense, man is to-day literally the heir of all the ages ; and, as a direct outcome of how he wills and acts now, so shall his future status be in his evolutionary progression here on this planet. If the Oriental sages be right, man has been and will be, in a way as yet unsuspected by our biologists, his own ancestor.

Thus while the Occidental may not question the validity of this law of cause and effect when applied to physics, he does question it when applied universally to psychics. In assuming such an attitude, the Occidental, in the eyes of the Oriental, ceases to be scientific, inasmuch as he fails to see that in any complete science of man the physical cannot be separated from the psychic. The present trend of Western science appears to be, however, quite definitely towards this psycho-physical view of the Oriental, which is dependent upon his postulate that nothing has real existence save Mind.[1]

With respect to rebirth as being an equally Universe-embracing law, the Occidental has no ready-made scientific formula at hand to help him, such as that which he finds in the law of cause and effect with respect to what the Oriental calls *karma*. For this reason he is apt to regard with grave doubt the claim of the master of *yoga* that not only is rebirth scientifically provable by means of *yoga*, but is inseparably correlated with the law of *karma*. In short, it is perfectly true to assert that the Occidental will never understand the teachings of the great sages of the Orient until he realizes in a scientific sense the fundamental and far-reaching import of *karma* and rebirth when looked upon in the Oriental way, as immutable laws governing the whole Cosmos.

---

[1] For instance, Sir James Jeans, in *The Mysterious Universe* (Cambridge, 1931), p. 137, makes the following surmise : ' The old dualism of mind and matter . . . seems likely to disappear, not through matter becoming in any way more shadowy or insubstantial than heretofore, or through mind becoming resolved into a function of the working of mind, but through substantial matter resolving itself into a creation and manifestation of mind.'

In *The Tibetan Book of the Dead* (pp. 39–61) the editor has devoted twenty-two pages to an exposition of the Doctrine of Rebirth, viewed both philosophically and scientifically ; and, in so doing, has set forth the results of his own researches concerning this doctrine. Instead of recapitulating here what has already been published, he prefers to supplement it by emphasizing the great need of a more serious attempt on the part of thinkers and scientists of Europe and of the two Americas to put to the test of Western science this *yogic* doctrine of rebirths and redyings.

As an anthropologist who has dedicated his life to the study of man, the editor, after more than twenty-five years of research, has come to believe that a serious scientific effort to investigate the whence, the why, and the whither of man is of all human endeavours by far the most important. It is herein that East and West, in the fullness of time, shall at last meet in mutual recognition.

Is Occidental man for much longer to be content with the study of the external universe, and not know himself? If, as the editor believes, the Oriental sage is able to direct us of the Occident to a method of attaining scientific understanding of the hidden side of man's nature, are we not unwise in failing to give it unprejudiced scientific examination?

Applied sciences in our portion of the world are, unfortunately, limited to chemistry, economics, mathematics, mechanics, physics, physiology, and the like; and anthropology and psychology as applied sciences in the sense understood in *yoga* are for almost all Occidental scientists mere dreams of impracticable visionaries. We do not believe, however, that this unsound view can long endure.[1]

---

[1] Since this opinion was herein set forth, the editor's attention has been directed to a similar opinion, put on record by Dr. C. D. Broad in *The Mind and its Place in Nature* (London, 1925), p. 666. Admitting the logical possibility of perpetual mental progress of the human race, Dr. Broad suggests that it ‘ depends on our getting an adequate knowledge and control of life and mind before the combination of ignorance on these subjects with knowledge of physics and chemistry wrecks the whole social system. Which of the runners in this very interesting race will win, it is impossible to foretell. But physics and death have a long start over psychology and life.’

## XII. THE EXOTERIC VERSUS THE ESOTERIC TEACHINGS

Not only does our Western science, at present, thus leave us in ignorance concerning the greatest of all human problems, but our Western theology, whose chief concern is with these very problems, has, in large measure, departed from those *yogic* methods of attaining spiritual insight which gave scientific character to Primitive Christianity, more particularly to its Gnostic Schools, now regarded as having been 'heretical'. And that form of purely intellectual, rather than gnostic (i.e. knowing), comprehension of religious teachings, which nowadays leads to the worldly dignity of a doctor of divinity, a bishop, or a pope, has never been regarded by the Wise Men of the East as sufficient to entitle its possessor to become a teacher of religion. Simply to believe a religion to be true, and to give intellectual assent to its creed and dogmatic theology, and not to know it to be true through having tested it by the scientific methods of *yoga*, results in the blind leading the blind, as both the Buddha and the Great Syrian Sage have declared.[1]

Herein is discernible one of the fundamental differences separating religions which are based essentially upon professions of faith and written scriptures declared to be infallible and all-sufficient for mankind's salvation, and the secret doctrines which are dependent upon realization of Truth rather than upon scientifically untested belief.

On the one hand, we see highly organized and in many instances nationally supported and directed churches and priesthoods pledged to promulgate doctrines, dogmatically formulated by church councils, which members are obliged to accept upon pain of excommunication. On the other hand, we see a body of teachings (preserved by secret transmission rather than by bibles) which their masters refuse to have accepted merely intellectually, no conventional or legalized ecclesiastical organization, and no form of faith other than

[1] Cf. 'The Ten Grievous Mistakes [of a Religious Devotee]', aphorisms 4 and 8, pp. 86–7.

that which each man of science must have in the possibility of discovering facts by careful experimentation.

In the Occident, but rarely in the Orient, the mere intellectual acceptance of religion has led to the inhibiting or discouraging of freedom of thought. The rationalistic questioning and scientific testing of that which the orthodox church and priest declare to be true, without knowing whether it be true or not, have been, until quite recently, fraught with serious consequences.

Partly out of distrust of such ecclesiastical tyranny, but more especially for the purpose of preserving arcane knowledge from misuse by the spiritually unfit, the higher or secret teachings, which lie hidden at the root of all the chief world religions, always have been, as they are to-day, transmitted through a select few. The form of this transmission varies, as our texts will explain. Sometimes it is wholly telepathic, sometimes entirely by symbols, often only oral, and never completely by means of written records. A similar system of secret transmission prevailed in all the Mysteries of Antiquity, in Egypt, Greece, and Rome, or wherever the Mysteries were established, as it did amongst the Druids of Gaul, Britain, and Ireland. At the present time it prevails in the occult fraternities of India and Tibet, and elsewhere. Remnants of an ancient occultism exist amongst the aboriginal races of both Americas, of Africa, Melanesia, and Polynesia, in the form of religious secret societies. Some of the more occultly instructed Lāmas and Hindus believe that no people, not even the most degenerate or least cultured, since man has inhabited this planet, have ever been without some fragment of the secret lore of the Great Sages.[1]

The *gurus* themselves tell us that their actual method of transmitting the secret teachings is as ancient as man ; for in no generation as yet have there been amongst the millions of incarnate human beings more than a few who were not en-

---

[1] In connexion with this part of our General Introduction reference should be made to Section II, concerning Symbolism, in the Introduction to *The Tibetan Book of the Dead*, pp. 2-6, particularly to that part of the Section concerned with ' Esoteric ' Buddhism.

amoured of the world, at least in some degree. And it is ever the world-enamoured multitude who are satisfied with belief in, rather than practice and realization of, religion.

## XIII. The Translating and Editing of the Texts

A special introduction precedes each of our seven Books, wherein is given the history of the manuscript or block-print upon which the translation is based. As in the case of *The Tibetan Book of the Dead*, the translating of the present texts was done in Gangtok, Sikkim, by the late Lāma Kazi Dawa-Samdup, assisted by the editor, during the years 1919 and 1920.

On the whole, the rendering has been made as literal as the idiomatic structures of the two languages allow, or as is in keeping with literary English. Not infrequently, however, it was deemed advisable to depart from a strictly word-for-word translation, in order to present in intelligible form the real meaning which a Lāma would derive from certain more or less technically worded phrases. Often, too, it was found necessary to fill out the meanings implied by certain technical or abbreviated terms contained in the Tibetan texts. Every such instance of this, and all interpolations made use of similarly, have been indicated in the translations by square brackets. Furthermore, the numbering of paragraphs and sections of the texts, for the purpose of affording convenience in making references, is also our own addition.

To render one European tongue into another is far easier than to turn into good English highly philosophical Tibetan, which is commonly not merely abstruse in its meanings, but is often symbolical as well. Even to a literate Tibetan layman unacquainted with the ornate and frequently esoteric language of Lāmaism and not well versed in that form of Tantricism which shapes the matter of some of our texts, sound comprehension of their doctrines would be impossible.

The rendering of the phonetic values of the Tibetan language into the phonetic values of the English language is also a task of some difficulty, for as yet no standardized method has been generally adopted by European scholars.

Suggestions have been made in the annotations as to how the transliterated, or anglicized, rather than the original Tibetan forms of the syllabic visualizations which are prescribed by the various texts may be practically applied by the Occidental *yogin* who prefers them.

Had the translator been in our world to read the proofs of this volume, all such errors as may have escaped the editor's carefulness would doubtless have been corrected. The transliterations, too, would have been subject to the translator's revision. As it is, they are, in some instances, probably less technically correct than he would have left them.

Not only our own, but every rendering from the Tibetan into a European language is, in this generation, pioneer in character. Possibly in years to come the translations recorded in this volume may be subject to revision, as has been the case with the first translations of the Bible and of other Sacred Books.

No scholar of this epoch, either in the Orient or in the Occident, was, however, better fitted for the very difficult task of rendering these texts into intelligible English than the late Lāma Kazi Dawa-Samdup. He was an initiate of the mystical Kargyütpa School (whence the greater part of our texts are derived), founded by Marpa and the illustrious *yogin*-poet Milarepa. In addition, he had practical knowledge of the *Yoga* Philosophy, chiefly that form of it developed in the teachings (underlying each of our seven Books) of the *Yogā-cārya* (i.e. ' Contemplative ') School of the Mahā-yāna, into which he had been given special initiation when as a young man he renounced the world and dwelt near his *guru* in hermitage in the mountains of Bhutan. A brief account of the Lāma's unusual career is to be found in *The Tibetan Book of the Dead*, pp. 79–81, and in *Tibet's Great* Yogī *Milarepa*, pp. 24–5. To these two works our present work is complementary and should be studied in connexion with them, more especially with the second, which contains a comprehensive exposition, by Milarepa himself, of *yogic* practices, in virtue of which he is said to have attained to Buddahood in one life-time.

Thus to the late Lāma Kazi Dawa-Samdup each reader of this volume is indebted for the scholarly and sympathetic presentation which it offers of some of the most profound doctrines and secret lore of Tibet. And the editor again formally acknowledges that debt of gratitude and respect which the disciple ever owes to the spiritual preceptor.

## XIV. The Unity and Practical Value of the Texts

The seven Books comprising this volume are arranged in a definite order of sequence. In all Schools of *Yoga* the neo-phyte at the beginning of the Path must know the rules and regulations governing the *yogic* career which he has chosen ; and these are set forth in Book I. In Book II the *yogin* is brought face to face with the great problem of the nature of mind and of reality. If he solves this in accordance with the guidance therein offered to him, he will have attained mastery of his mental-processes, and of himself. Then, endowed with *Bodhic* insight, he can, without danger, attempt the more specialized *yogic* practices expounded in Book III. Of these the most difficult and dangerous is the sixth, namely, the transference of the mundane consciousness ; and this is set forth in more detail in Book IV. In Book V the *yogin* is introduced to a very occult *yogic* method of attaining the mental state of non-ego, or impersonalization, which is largely pre-Buddhistic. None save a very carefully trained and *guru*-guided *yogin* ought ever to attempt this *yoga*. Book VI teaches of the secret doctrine of the Five Wisdoms. And in Book VII the essence of the most transcendental of all Mahā-yānic teachings is set before the *yogin* for profound medita-tion and realization. If it be the *yogin's* good *karma* to progress on the Path up to this point, he will have attained such clear intuitional insight into the true nature of the universe of phenomenal appearances round about him, and of mind, that no longer will he be as are the multitude, for he

will have come out from the Cave of Ignorance into the unclouded Light of Right Knowledge.

Viewed thus, this treatise has unity. Each of its seven
parts is, nevertheless, complete in itself, and can be studied
independently of any other part. This being so, the ordinary
reader will probably be inclined to concentrate his study
upon one or more of the Books rather than upon the treatise
as a whole, in accordance with his mental inclinations. If,
however, he feels fitted to attempt in this incarnation the
very difficult task of treading to the very end the Supreme
Path of the *Bodhisattva*, the seven Books when studied
together should afford him aid of a most valuable and efficient character.

## XV. The New Renaissance and the Masters of Wisdom

Almost imperceptibly for about a century, and more especially within the last fifty years, the higher thought of the
Occident has been profoundly modified by influences distinctly Oriental. The Christianity of the so-called orthodox
tradition itself has felt these fresh spiritual impulses, and as a
result of them, no less than of the revolutionizing effects of
Science, has now come to the most serious crisis in its history.
As the Renaissance of the fourteenth to sixteenth centuries
overwhelmed the Scholastic Philosophy and restored to
Europe the great literature and art of ancient Greece and
prepared the way for the Reformation and the new age of
untrammelled scientific development, so to-day there are
deeply influential ideas, likewise born of the East, which give
promise of a Reformation far more sweeping and thorough
than that which was set in motion by Martin Luther.

It was the feebly reflected Light from the East transmitted
by means of the Platonic and Arab philosophers which
initiated the Rebirth of the Medieval Occident. To-day it
is the strong direct Light of the Orient which is now reshaping the religious life of Europe and of both Americas,
and affecting, in some not unimportant manner, even the

thought of men of science in all Occidental centres of research.

At the meeting of the British Association for the Advancement of Science, in 1933, consideration was given to the scientific probability of the existence of intelligent beings more highly evolved than man ; or, in other words, as we set forth in the Introduction to *Tibet's Great* Yogī *Milarepa* in 1928, to the theory that man does not necessarily represent the end of organic evolution. In similar vein the thought was thrown out to the assembled scientists that there may be unknown states of being wherein transcendent consciousness exists independently of all physical or bodily organisms. Surmises of this character by men of science in the Occident are, of course, rapidly tending to give scientific sanction to the same theories which underlie the whole of our present treatise. It is more than likely that within a few more generations of scientific advance the British Association will welcome to its membership the Wise Men of the East.

Then, in such a glorious New Age of re-established mutual understanding and respect between Orient and Occident, in no small degree will the carefully guarded learning of the master minds of Tibet be found to amplify that of the master minds of India, and help to guide the Western World to a clearer understanding of the old, yet ever new, truths concerning man and man's place in the Universal Scheme, which have constituted since immemorial time the imperishable Light of the East.

It was in like spirit of helpfulness and of personally disinterested desire to be of service to the world that the late Lāma Kazi Dawa-Samdup placed his superior learning and marvellous powers of interpretation at the disposal of the editor and thus made possible the bequeathing of these translations to the peoples of the Occident. Thus, in complement of *The Tibetan Book of the Dead* and of *Tibet's Great* Yogī *Milarepa*, and in fulfilment of the editor's promise given to the translator, his *guru*, many of the most essential and hitherto secret doctrines appertaining to the Great Path of the *Bodhisattvas* are placed on record in this volume and so made available in English form to all who reverence, as the translator and the editor do, the Great Teachers of the Way to *Nirvāṇa*.

It is owing to These Great Ones, Who, like the Buddha, have renounced and conquered the World and the worldly personality, that the life of humanity on Earth has been lifted up out of the Darkness of Ignorance into the Light of Reality and Divine Bliss, and the Path to the Higher Evolution of Man revealed. Indeed, without Them, mankind would be hopelessly imprisoned in the Sensuous, and there would be no avenue of escape from the transitoriness of the *Sangsāra*, with its accompanying sorrow.

*From Water-Colours by the Translator*

THE GLORIFIED BUDDHA AND THE *GURU* GAMPOPA

Described on page xix

# BOOK I

# THE SUPREME PATH OF DISCIPLESHIP: THE PRECEPTS OF THE *GURUS*[1]

## THE INTRODUCTION

### I. THE BOOK'S COMPILER AND HIS FELLOW DISCIPLE

THIS Book is composed of a collection of *yogic* precepts, arranged in twenty-eight categories. It was compiled by Dvagpo-Lharje, the direct apostolic successor of Milarepa (A.D. 1052–1135), and dates from about the middle of the twelfth century of our era.

Dvagpo-Lharje, that is to say, Lharje of the Dvagpo Province, in Eastern Tibet, the place of his birth, is said to have been born in 1077. He died in 1152. As in our texts, he is otherwise known as the Great *Guru* Gampopa. The name Gampopa refers to him as being the reincarnation of King Srong-Tsan-Gampo, the first Buddhist ruler of Tibet, who died in A.D. 650.

Dvagpo-Lharje is also the author of a number of Tibetan treatises concerning the *Mahā-Mudrā* Philosophy and the tenets peculiar to the Kargyütpa School. These, like his work herein presented, are essentially *yogic*. And in the year 1150, just two years before his decease, he founded the Monastery of Ts'ur-lka, which is now the principal seat of the Kargyütpa Order.

The other of Milarepa's two most illustrious disciples was Rechung-Dorje-Tagpa, who wrote the *Biography of Milarepa*, known in the original Tibetan as the *Jetsün Kahbum*, and published in English translation in *Tibet's Great* Yogī

---

[1] The Tibetan manuscript, upon which our translation is based, bears the following title : *RJE-SGAMPO RINPOCHE-HI LAM MCHOG RINPOCHE-HI HPHRENG-WA ZHES-BYA-WA BZHŪGS-SO* (pron. *JE-GAMPO RINPOCHE-YI LAM CHOG RINPOCHE-YI HTEN-WA SHAY-CHA-WA ZHŪ-SO*), meaning, 'Herein Lieth the Venerable Lord Gampopa's Supreme Path, called "The Precious Rosary".' Copious extracts from our own version or from a very similar version of this work were published by Madame A. David-Neel in the Appendix to *Initiations and Initiates in Tibet* (London, 1931), pp. 192–210. Herein is contained a complete rendering, which is the first to be placed on record in an Occidental tongue.

*Milarepa.* This, too, contains many preceptual teachings of the Kargyütpas and can very profitably be studied in connexion with Dvagpo-Lharje's *Precious Rosary.*

Rechung-Dorje-Tagpa, in imitation of his Master, Milarepa, passed the greater part of his life in hermitage ; and, being quite unconcerned with monastic organization, preferred that the apostolic succession, in the line of the Kargyütpa *Gurus,* should pass to Dvagpo-Lharje, as it did, rather than to himself.

## II. THE TRANSMISSION OF THE TEACHINGS

Inasmuch as the essence of the spiritual lore recorded in *The Precious Rosary* is a direct inheritance from the greatest of these *Gurus,* it will be of interest to show briefly the way of its transmission to Dvagpo-Lharje.

The first of the Kargyütpa *Gurus* is Dorje-Chang (Skt. Vajra-Dhāra), the Celestial Buddha, Whom the Kargyütpas regard as the *Ādi,* or ' Primordial ', Buddha. And He, so it is believed, imparted to Tilopa, an Indian *yogin,* the *Mahā-Mudrā* Philosophy, upon which the *yogic* teachings of the Kargyütpa School, like the *yogic* precepts contained in this Book, are chiefly based.

Tilopa, in whom the apostolic succession on Earth thus originated, flourished in India about the middle of the tenth century A.D. ; and was succeeded by Naropa, his favoured disciple. Like the Great *Guru* Padma Sambhava (who founded the Ñingmapa School in Tibet in A.D. 749, whence, as the result of a reform movement, the Kargyütpas separated), Naropa was a professor of philosophy in the celebrated Buddhist University of Nālanda, in north-west India, the principal centre of learning of the epoch. Among Naropa's disciples was Marpa, who, on account of his many translations from the Sanskrit into the Tibetan, came to be known in Tibet, his native land, as Marpa the Translator ; and Marpa became the first of the Tibetan *Gurus* of the Kargyütpa Succession. Milarepa, who was Marpa's chief disciple, succeeded Marpa ; and thence, as we have seen, the apostolic line continued through Dvagpo-Lharje. (See in *Tibet's Great* Yogī

*Milarepa* the frontispiece in colour entitled 'The Great Kar-gyütpa *Gurus*' and the description of the *Gurus* on pages xv to xviii.)

It is chiefly on account of their remarkable practical application of Buddhism by means of practices which are distinctly *yogic*, as Book II, following, will illustrate, that the followers of Marpa and Milarepa are distinguished from all other Tibetan Buddhists. Nowhere among Mahāyānists is there greater—if, indeed, there be as great—insistence upon the *Bodhisattvic* ideal of world renunciation and selfless aeon-long labour looking to the ultimate enlightenment of every sentient being as among the Kargyütpas.

### III. THE TEXTS OF *THE PRECIOUS ROSARY*

Our manuscript of *The Precious Rosary* was copied by the translator from a manuscript in the possession of a wandering *yogin* who passed through Gangtok, Sikkim, some years ago, and accepted for a few days the translator's hospitality.

In keeping with traditional usage, which originated when writing and printing were less common than now, there are still many *yogins* who memorize *The Precious Rosary*. Then, if in their turn they become *gurus*, they may transmit it orally or at least expound it from memory. In addition, each makes his own manuscript copy of these highly prized teachings, either from such oral transmission or, as is nowadays more usual, from the *guru's* manuscript, in order that they may not be forgotten or lost. And, like the translator's *yogin* guest, any Kargyütpa is always glad to loan his copy of *The Precious Rosary* to a pious layman or fellow disciple (such as the translator) for study and transcription.

Although Tibetan block-prints of *The Precious Rosary* are said to exist, neither the translator nor the editor was able, after much search, to procure one for purposes of textual criticism. Manuscript texts, such as ours, are, however, ordinarily faithfully made. As a rule, when compared with one another, they show no more than minor variations in the phrasing of individual precepts or in the order of the precepts forming the categories.

IV.  THE PRECEPTS COMPARED WITH 'ELEGANT SAYINGS'

There are, too, a number of works in Tibetan and Sanskrit consisting of collections of 'Elegant Sayings', which are less purely religious than the Precepts, being more akin to proverbs. One of the most famous of such collections is *The Precious Treasury of Elegant Sayings* (*Subhāshita Ratna Nidhi*) attributed to the Grand Lāma of Saskya, otherwise known as the Saskya Paṇḍita, whom the Chinese Emperor Khubilai Khan, in A.D. 1270, recognized as the Head of the Lāmaist Church. The late Hungarian scholar, Alexander Csoma de Körös, who made a translation of it, gives the full monastic name of this Saskya Pope as Ānanda Dwaja Shrī Bhadra. *The Precious Treasury* was probably compiled while its reputed author was living as a monk in the Saskya Monastery, in the Province of Tsang, Central Tibet.[1]

A few of these 'Elegant Sayings', as revised and reshaped by us from Csoma de Körös's rendering, are here given, as a basis for comparison with the Precepts contained in *The Precious Rosary*:

'A hen, when at rest, produceth much fruit;
A peacock, when it remaineth still, hath a handsome tail;
A gentle horse hath a swift pace;
The quiescence of a holy man is the sign of his being a
    Sage.'                                    (Stanza 20)

'Not to be cheered by praise,
Not to be grieved by blame,
But to know thoroughly one's own virtues or powers
Are the characteristics of an excellent man.'

                                              (Stanza 29)

'In the same place where the Great Lord [Buddha] is pre-
    sent
Who would acknowledge any other man?
When the Sun hath arisen, though there be many bright
    stars in the sky,
Not one of them is visible.'                  (Stanza 33)

---

[1] Cf. A. C. de Körös, *Tibetan Studies* (No. XIV), Calcutta, 1912.

' A foolish man proclaimeth his qualifications ;
A wise man keepeth them secret within himself ;
A straw floateth on the surface of water,
But a precious gem placed upon it sinketh.'

(Stanza 58)

' It is only narrow-minded men that make such distinctions
As " This is our friend, this our enemy " ;
A liberal-minded man showeth affection for all,
For it is uncertain who may yet be of aid to one.'

(Stanza 59)

' An excellent man, like precious metal,
Is in every way invariable ;
A villain, like the beams of a balance,
Is always varying, upwards and downwards.'

(Stanza 74)

' Much talking is a source of danger ;
Silence is the means of avoiding misfortune :
The talkative parrot is shut up in a cage ;
Other birds, which cannot talk, fly about freely.'

(Stanza 118)

' The greatest wealth consisteth in being charitable,
And the greatest happiness in having tranquillity of mind.
Experience is the most beautiful adornment ;
And the best comrade is one that hath no desires.'

(Stanza 134)

' Men of little ability, too,
By depending upon the great, may prosper ;
A drop of water is a little thing,
But when will it dry away if united to a lake ? '

(Stanza 173)

' Hurtful expressions should never be used,
Not even against an enemy ;
For inevitably they will return to one,
Like an echo from a rock.'                    (Stanza 182)

' When about to perform any great work,
Endeavour to have a trustworthy associate ;

If one would burn down a forest,
The aid of a wind is, of course, needed.'    (Stanza 208)

'Meditation without Knowledge,[1] though giving results for
    awhile,
Will, in the end, be devoid of true success;
One may melt gold and silver completely,
But once the fire be gone they grow hard again.'

(Stanza 228)

From a similar collection, entitled *The Staff of Wisdom*
(Tib. *Shes-rab-Sdon-bu*: Skt. *Prajñā-Daṇḍa*), attributed to
Nāgārjuna, the learned expounder of the Mahāyāna, the following 'Elegant Sayings', as translated from the Tibetan
version by Lāma Kazi Dawa-Samdup, are added:

'To him who knoweth the True Nature of things,
What need is there of a teacher?
To him who hath recovered from illness,
What need is there of a physician?
To him who hath crossed the river,
What need is there of a boat?'    (MS. folio 5)

'An astronomer maketh calculations and divinations con-
    cerning the motions of the Moon and the stars,
But he doth not divine that in his own household his own
    womenfolk, being at variance, are misbehaving.'

(MS. folio 7)

'In eating, sleeping, fearing, and copulating, men and beasts
    are alike;
Man excelleth the beast by engaging in religious practices.
So why should a man, if he be without religion, not be
    equal to the beast?'    (MS. folio 8)

'Time is fleeting, learning is vast; no one knoweth the
    duration of one's life:
Therefore use the swan's art of extracting milk from water,
And devote thyself to the Most Precious [Path].'

(MS. folio 13)

---

[1] Or without the guiding teachings of a *guru*.

' Although many stars shine, and that ornament of the Earth,
   the Moon, also shineth,
Yet when the Sun setteth, it becometh night.'

                   (MS. folio 13)

' The science which teacheth arts and handicrafts
Is merely science for the gaining of a living;
But the science which teacheth deliverance from worldly
   existence,
Is not that the true science? '        (MS. folio 15)

' That which one desireth not for oneself,
Do not do unto others.'        (MS. folio 20)

' The foolish are like ripples on water,
For whatsoever they do is quickly effaced;
But the righteous are like carvings upon stone,
For their smallest act is durable.'     (MS. folio 22)

' With the wise and gentle, the contented and the truthful,
Companionship, even in prison, is better than sovereignty
   with the unruly.'       (MS. folio 23)

Other ' Elegant Sayings ', selected from the late Lāma Kazi
Dawa-Samdup's English rendering of *The Ocean of Delight
for the Wise* (Tib. *Lodan-Gawai-Roltso*), are here placed
on record.[1] The translator's Tibetan text, which does not
give the name of the compiler of this collection of maxims, is
contained in a quite recent manuscript made by one of his
pupils in Gangtok either from a block-print or from an older
manuscript.

' The Supreme Path of Altruism is a short-cut,
Leading to the Realm of the Conquerors,—
A track more speedy than that of a racing horse;
The selfish, however, know naught of it.'

                 (Verses 25-8)

---

[1] The original copy of this translation, dated 1908-9, has been placed in the
editor's care by Sir E. Denison Ross, Director of the School of Oriental
Studies, University of London, who, like the editor, in the study of things
Tibetan came into personal relationship in India with the late Lāma Kazi
Dawa-Samdup, the translator.

' Charity produceth the harvest in the next birth.
Chastity is the parents of human happiness.
Patience is an adornment becoming to all.
Industry is the conductor of every personal accomplishment.
*Dhyāna* is the clarifier of a beclouded mind.
Intellect is the weapon which overcometh every enemy.'
(Verses 29-34)

' Gloat not, even though death and misfortune overwhelm
   thine enemies ;
Boast not, even though thou equal Indra [in greatness].'
(Verses 41-2)

' Some there are who turn inside out their whole interior
By means of over-talkativeness.'    (Verses 51-2)

' Be humble and meek if thou would be exalted ;
Praise every one's good qualities if thou would have friends.'
(Verses 66-7)

' Argue not with the self-conceited ;
Vie not with the fortunate ;
Disparage not the vengeful ;
Have no grudge with the powerful.'    (Verses 69-72)

' Relinquish an evil custom even though it be of thy fathers
   and ancestors ;
Adopt a good custom even though it be established among
   thine enemies :
Poison is not to be taken even though offered by one's
   mother ;
But gold is acceptable even from one who is inimical.'
(Verses 73-6)

' Be not too quick to express the desire of thy heart.
Be not short-tempered when engaged in a great work.
Be not jealous of a devotee who is truly religious and pious.
Consult not him who is habituated and hardened to evil-
   doing.'    (Verses 77-80)

' Rogues there are even in religious orders ;
  Poisonous plants grow even on hills of medicinal herbs.'
                                    (Verses 112-13)

' Some there are who marvel not at others removing moun-
    tains,
  But who consider it a heavy task when obliged to carry a
    bit of fleece.'                 (Verses 120-1)

' He who is ever ready to take the credit for any action when
    it hath proved successful
  And is equally ready to throw the blame on others when it
    goeth wrong in the least,
  And who is ever looking for faults in those who are learned
    and righteous,
  Possesseth the nature of a crow.'        (Verses 140-3)

' Preaching religious truths to an unbeliever is like feeding a
    venemous serpent with milk.'       (Verse 146)

' Although a cloth be washed a hundred times,
  How can it be rendered clean and pure
  If it be washed in water which is dirty ? '
                                    (Verses 159-61)

' The unreasoning zeal and narrow-mindedness of an igno-
    ramus merely serveth to lower one's esteem of the per-
    son he trieth to praise.'        (Verse 181)

' The greatest fault to be avoided is Ignorance.
  To overcome the enemy Ignorance, one requireth Wisdom.
  The best method of acquiring Wisdom is unfaltering en-
    deavour.'                        (Verses 186-8)

' He who knoweth the Precepts by heart, but faileth to prac-
    tise them,
  Is like unto one who lighteth a lamp and then shutteth his
    eyes.'                           (Verses 193-4)

' Who can say with certainty that one will live to see the
    morrow ? '                       (Verse 204)

'How can it be just to kill helpless and inoffensive creatures?'

(Verse 214)

These selected 'Elegant Sayings', Proverbs, and Precepts help to suggest the importance and richness of this type of Tibetan literature, which has been much influenced by that of India : and aided by this brief introduction, the reader will now be prepared to profit by the wisdom-lore which has been bequeathed to us by the great Kargyütpa Sages in the Book which follows.

## FROM '*THE VOICE OF THE SILENCE*'[1]

'Give up thy life, if thou would'st live.

\*       \*       \*

The Wise Ones tarry not in pleasure-grounds of senses.

The Wise Ones heed not the sweet-tongued voices of illusion.

\*       \*       \*

If, through the Hall of Wisdom, thou would'st reach the Vale of Bliss, Disciple, close fast thy senses against the great dire heresy of Separateness that weaneth thee from the rest.

\*       \*       \*

The Pupil must regain *the child state he hath lost* ere the first sound can fall upon his ears.

\*       \*       \*

To live to benefit mankind is the first step.   To practise the six glorious virtues is the second.

\*       \*       \*

If Sun thou canst not be, then be the humble planet.

Be humble, if thou would'st attain to Wisdom.   Be humbler still, when Wisdom thou hast mastered.

\*       \*       \*

The Teacher can but point the way.   The Path is one for all ; the means to reach the Goal must vary with the Pilgrims.

\*       \*       \*

Hast thou attuned thy being to Humanity's great pain, O candidate for light?

\*       \*       \*

Compassion speaketh and saith : " Can there be bliss when all that live must suffer?   Shalt thou be saved and hear the whole world cry?"'

[1] Selections from H. P. Blavatsky's English rendering of ' Chosen Fragments from *The Book of the Golden Precepts* ' (London and New York, 1889).

# [THE SUPREME PATH OF DISCIPLESHIP: THE PRECEPTS OF THE *GURUS*]

## [THE OBEISANCE]

Obeisance to the Precious *Guru*!

## [THE FOREWORD]

LET him who desireth deliverance from the fearful and difficult-to-traverse Sea of Successive Existences, by means of the precepts taught by the inspired Kargyütpa Sages, render due homage to these Teachers, whose glory is immaculate, whose virtues are as inexhaustible as the ocean, and whose infinite benevolence embraceth all beings, past, present, and future, throughout the Universe.

For the use of those who share in the quest for Divine Wisdom there follow, recorded in writing, the most highly esteemed precepts, called ' The Supreme Path, the Rosary of Precious Gems ', transmitted to Gampopa, either directly or indirectly, through that Inspired Dynasty of *Gurus*, out of their love for him.

## [THE TWENTY-EIGHT CATEGORIES OF *YOGIC* PRECEPTS]

### I. THE TEN CAUSES OF REGRET

The devotee seeking Liberation and the Omniscience of Buddhahood should first meditate upon these ten things which are causes of regret:

(1) Having obtained the difficult-to-obtain, free, and endowed human body, it would be a cause of regret to fritter life away.

(2) Having obtained this pure and difficult-to-obtain, free, and endowed human body, it would be a cause of regret to die an irreligious and worldly man.

(3) This human life in the *Kali-Yuga* [or Age of Darkness] being so brief and uncertain, it would be a cause of regret to spend it in worldly aims and pursuits.

(4) One's own mind being of the nature of the *Dharma-*

*Kāya*, uncreated, it would be a cause of regret to let it be swallowed up in the morass of the world's illusions.

(5) The holy *guru* being the guide on the Path, it would be a cause of regret to be separated from him before attaining Enlightenment.

(6) Religious faith and vows being the vessel which conveyeth one to Emancipation, it would be a cause of regret were they to be shattered by the force of uncontrolled passions.

(7) The Perfect Wisdom having been found within oneself in virtue of the *guru*'s grace, it would be a cause of regret to dissipate it amidst the jungle of worldliness.

(8) To sell like so much merchandise the Sublime Doctrine of the Sages would be a cause of regret.

(9) Inasmuch as all beings are our kindly parents,[1] it would be a cause of regret to have aversion for and thus disown or abandon any of them.

(10) The prime of youth being the period of development of the body, speech, and mind, it would be a cause of regret to waste it in vulgar indifference.

These are The Ten Causes of Regret.

## II.  THE TEN REQUIREMENTS COME NEXT

(1) Having estimated one's own capabilities, one requireth a sure line of action.

(2) To carry out the commands of a religious preceptor, one requireth confidence and diligence.

(3) To avoid error in choosing a *guru*, the disciple requireth knowledge of his own faults and virtues.

(4) Keenness of intellect and unwavering faith are required to tune in with the mind of the spiritual preceptor.

(5) Unceasing watchfulness and mental alertness, graced with humility, are required to keep the body, speech, and mind unsullied by evil.

(6) Spiritual armour and strength of intellect are required for the fulfilment of one's heart's vows.

---

[1] In the Buddhist, as in the Hindu view, so interminably during inconceivable aeons have evolution and transition and rebirth been going on that all sentient beings have been our parents.  Reference should here be made to a parallel passage and its commentary in *Tibet's Great* Yogī *Milarepa*, p. 203 [1].

(7) Habitual freedom from desire and attachment is necessary if one would be free from bondage.

(8) To acquire the Twofold Merit,[1] born of right motives, right actions, and the altruistic dedication of their results, there is need of unceasing effort.

(9) The mind, imbued with love and compassion in thought and deed, ought ever to be directed to the service of all sentient beings.

(10) Through hearing, understanding, and wisdom, one should so comprehend the nature of all things as not to fall into the error of regarding matter and phenomena as real.

These are The Ten Requirements.

### III. THE TEN THINGS TO BE DONE

(1) Attach thyself to a religious preceptor endowed with spiritual power and complete knowledge.

(2) Seek a delightful solitude endowed with psychic influences as a hermitage.

(3) Seek friends who have beliefs and habits like thine own and in whom thou canst place thy trust.

(4) Keeping in mind the evils of gluttony, use just enough food to keep thee fit during the period of thy retreat.

(5) Study the teachings of the Great Sages of all sects impartially.

(6) Study the beneficent sciences of medicine and astrology, and the profound art of omens.

(7) Adopt such regimen and manner of living as will keep thee in good health.

(8) Adopt such devotional practices as will conduce to thy spiritual development.

(9) Retain such disciples as are firm in faith, meek in spirit, and who appear to be favoured by *karma* in their quest for Divine Wisdom.

(10) Constantly maintain alertness of consciousness in walking, in sitting, in eating, and in sleeping.

These are The Ten Things To Be Done.

---

[1] The Twofold Merit is expounded on p. 97[2].

IV.  THE TEN THINGS TO BE AVOIDED

(1) Avoid a *guru* whose heart is set on acquiring worldly fame and possessions.

(2) Avoid friends and followers who are detrimental to thy peace of mind and spiritual growth.

(3) Avoid hermitages and places of abode where there happen to be many persons who annoy and distract thee.

(4) Avoid gaining thy livelihood by means of deceit and theft.

(5) Avoid such actions as harm thy mind and impede thy spiritual development.

(6) Avoid such acts of levity and thoughtlessness as lower thee in another's esteem.

(7) Avoid useless conduct and actions.

(8) Avoid concealing thine own faults and speaking loudly of those of others.

(9) Avoid such food and habits as disagree with thy health.

(10) Avoid such attachments as are inspired by avarice.

These are The Ten Things To Be Avoided.


V.  THE TEN THINGS NOT TO BE AVOIDED

(1) Ideas, being the radiance of the mind, are not to be avoided.

(2) Thought-forms, being the revelry of Reality, are not to be avoided.

(3) Obscuring passions, being the means of reminding one of Divine Wisdom [which giveth deliverance from them], are not to be avoided [if rightly used to enable one to taste life to the full and thereby reach disillusionment].

(4) Affluence, being the manure and water for spiritual growth, is not to be avoided.

(5) Illness and tribulations, being teachers of piety, are not to be avoided.

(6) Enemies and misfortune, being the means of inclining one to a religious career, are not to be avoided.

(7) That which cometh of itself, being a divine gift, is not to be avoided.

(8) Reason, being in every action the best friend, is not to be avoided.

(9) Such devotional exercises of body and mind as one is capable of performing are not to be avoided.

(10) The thought of helping others, howsoever limited one's ability to help others may be, is not to be avoided.

These are The Ten Things Not To Be Avoided.


## VI.   THE TEN THINGS ONE MUST KNOW

(1) One must know that all visible phenomena, being illusory, are unreal.

(2) One must know that the mind, being without independent existence [apart from the One Mind], is impermanent.

(3) One must know that ideas arise from a concatenation of causes.

(4) One must know that the body and speech, being compounded of the four elements, are transitory.

(5) One must know that the effects of past actions, whence cometh all sorrow, are inevitable.

(6) One must know that sorrow, being the means of convincing one of the need of the religious life, is a *guru*.

(7) One must know that attachment to worldly things maketh material prosperity inimical to spiritual progress.

(8) One must know that misfortune, being the means of leading one to the Doctrine, is also a *guru*.

(9) One must know that no existing thing has an independent existence.

(10) One must know that all things are interdependent.

These are The Ten Things One Must Know.


## VII.   THE TEN THINGS TO BE PRACTISED

(1) One should acquire practical knowledge of the Path by treading it, and not be as are the multitude [who profess, but do not practise, religion].

(2) By quitting one's own country and dwelling in foreign

lands one should acquire practical knowledge of non-attachment.[1]

(3) Having chosen a religious preceptor, separate thyself from egotism and follow his teachings implicitly.

(4) Having acquired mental discipline by hearing and meditating upon religious teachings, boast not of thine attainment, but apply it to the realization of Truth.

(5) Spiritual knowledge having dawned in oneself, neglect it not through slothfulness, but cultivate it with ceaseless vigilance.

(6) Once having experienced spiritual illumination, commune with it in solitude, relinquishing the worldly activities of the multitude.

(7) Having acquired practical knowledge of spiritual things and made the Great Renunciation, permit not the body, speech, or mind to become unruly, but observe the three vows, of poverty, chastity, and obedience.

(8) Having resolved to attain the Highest Goal, abandon selfishness and devote thyself to the service of others.

(9) Having entered upon the mystic *Mantrayānic* Pathway, permit not the body, the speech, or the mind to remain unsanctified, but practise the threefold *maṇḍala*.[2]

---

[1] This implies non-attachment to all worldly possessions, to home and kin, as to the tyranny of social intercourse and custom, which commonly cause the attached to fritter life away in what Milarepa calls the worthless doings of this world. As Milarepa so wisely teaches, ' All worldly pursuits have but the one unavoidable and inevitable end, which is sorrow: acquisitions end in dispersion; buildings, in destruction; meetings, in separation; births, in death.' (See *Tibet's Great* Yogī *Milarepa*, p. 259.) All the Great Sages, in every land and generation, have traversed the Garden of Human Existence, have plucked and eaten of the glamorous vari-coloured fruits of the Tree of Life growing in the midst thereof, and, as a result, have attained world-disillusionment, whereby man first sees that Divine Vision which alone can give to him imperishable contentment both now and in the hour of death. Ecclesiastes, the Jewish Sage, who was once ' king over Israel in Jerusalem ', in language very much like that of Milarepa, tells us, ' I have seen all the works that are done under the sun; and, behold, all is vanity and vexation of spirit.' (*Ecclesiastes* i. 14.)

[2] A *maṇḍala* is a symbolical geometrical diagram wherein deities are invoked. (See *Tibet's Great* Yogī *Milarepa*, p. 132.) The threefold *maṇḍala* is dedicated to the spiritual forces (often personified as Tantric deities) presiding over, or manifesting through, the body, the speech, and the mind of man, as in *Kuṇḍalinī Yoga*.

(10) During the period of youth, frequent not those who cannot direct thee spiritually, but acquire practical knowledge painstakingly at the feet of a learned and pious *guru*.

These are The Ten Things To Be Practised.

### VIII.  THE TEN THINGS TO BE PERSEVERED IN

(1) Novices should persevere in listening to, and meditating upon, religious teachings.

(2) Having had spiritual experience, persevere in meditation and mental concentration.

(3) Persevere in solitude until the mind hath been *yogically* disciplined.

(4) Should thought-processes be difficult to control, persevere in thine efforts to dominate them.

(5) Should there be great drowsiness, persevere in thine efforts to invigorate the intellect [or to control the mind].

(6) Persevere in meditation until thou attainest the imperturbable mental tranquillity of *samādhi*.

(7) Having attained this state of *samādhi*, persevere in prolonging its duration and in causing its recurrence at will.

(8) Should various misfortunes assail thee, persevere in patience of body, speech, and mind.

(9) Should there be great attachment, hankering, or mental weakness, persevere in an effort to eradicate it as soon as it manifesteth itself.

(10) Should benevolence and pity be weak within thee, persevere in directing the mind towards Perfection.

These are The Ten Things To Be Persevered In.

### IX.  THE TEN INCENTIVES

(1) By reflecting upon the difficulty of obtaining an endowed and free human body, mayest thou be incited to adopt the religious career.

(2) By reflecting upon death and the impermanence of life, mayest thou be incited to live piously.

(3) By reflecting upon the irrevocable nature of the results which inevitably arise from actions, mayest thou be incited to avoid impiety and evil.

(4) By reflecting upon the evils of life in the round of successive existences, mayest thou be incited to seek Emancipation.

(5) By reflecting upon the miseries which all sentient beings suffer, mayest thou be incited to attain deliverance therefrom by enlightenment of mind.

(6) By reflecting upon the perversity and illusory nature of the mind of all sentient beings, mayest thou be incited to listen to, and meditate upon, the Doctrine.

(7) By reflecting upon the difficulty of eradicating erroneous concepts, mayest thou be incited to constant meditation [which overcometh them].

(8) By reflecting upon the predominance of evil propensities in this *Kali-Yuga* [or Age of Darkness], mayest thou be incited to seek their antidote [in the Doctrine].

(9) By reflecting upon the multiplicity of misfortunes in this Age of Darkness, mayest thou be incited to perseverance [in the quest for Emancipation].

(10) By reflecting upon the uselessness of aimlessly frittering away thy life, mayest thou be incited to diligence [in the treading of the Path].

These are The Ten Incentives.

## X. THE TEN ERRORS

(1) Weakness of faith combined with strength of intellect are apt to lead to the error of talkativeness.

(2) Strength of faith combined with weakness of intellect are apt to lead to the error of narrow-minded dogmatism.

(3) Great zeal without adequate religious instruction is apt to lead to the error of going to erroneous extremes [or following misleading paths].

(4) Meditation without sufficient preparation through having heard and pondered the Doctrine is apt to lead to the error of losing oneself in the darkness of unconsciousness.[1]

(5) Without practical and adequate understanding of the

---

[1] This refers to that mental chaos or delusion which is the antithesis of the mental discipline acquired by right practice of *yoga* under a wise *guru's* guidance.

Doctrine, one is apt to fall into the error of religious self-conceit.

(6) Unless the mind be trained to selflessness and infinite compassion, one is apt to fall into the error of seeking liberation for self alone.

(7) Unless the mind be disciplined by knowledge of its own immaterial nature, one is apt to fall into the error of diverting all activities along the path of worldliness.

(8) Unless all worldly ambitions be eradicated, one is apt to fall into the error of allowing oneself to be dominated by worldly motives.

(9) By permitting credulous and vulgar admirers to congregate about thee, there is liability of falling into the error of becoming puffed up with worldly pride.

(10) By boasting of one's occult learning and powers, one is liable to fall into the error of proudly exhibiting proficiency in worldly rites.[1]

These are The Ten Errors.

## XI. THE TEN RESEMBLANCES WHEREIN ONE MAY ERR

(1) Desire may be mistaken for faith.

(2) Attachment may be mistaken for benevolence and compassion.

(3) Cessation of thought-processes may be mistaken for the quiescence of infinite mind, which is the true goal.

(4) Sense perceptions [or phenomena] may be mistaken for revelations [or glimpses] of Reality.

(5) A mere glimpse of Reality may be mistaken for complete realization.

(6) Those who outwardly profess, but do not practise, religion may be mistaken for true devotees.

(7) Slaves of passion may be mistaken for masters of *yoga* who have liberated themselves from all conventional laws.

(8) Actions performed in the interest of self may be mistakenly regarded as being altruistic.

---

[1] No true master of the occult sciences ever allows himself to boast or make public exhibition of his *yogic* powers. It is only in secret initiations of disciples, as was the case with Marpa, that they are shown, if at all. (See *Tibet's Great* Yogī *Milarepa*, pp. 132-3, 154-5, 163.)

(9) Deceptive methods may be mistakenly regarded as being prudent.

(10) Charlatans may be mistaken for Sages.

These are The Ten Resemblances Wherein One May Err.

### XII.  THE TEN THINGS WHEREIN ONE ERRETH NOT

(1) In being free from attachment to all objects, and being ordained a *bhikshu* [1] into the Holy Order, forsaking home and entering upon the homeless state, one doth not err.

(2) In revering one's spiritual preceptor one doth not err.

(3) In thoroughly studying the Doctrine, hearing discourses thereon, and reflecting and meditating upon it, one doth not err.

(4) In nourishing lofty aspirations and a lowly demeanour one doth not err.

(5) In entertaining liberal views [as to religion] and yet being firm in observing [formal religious] vows one doth not err.

(6) In having greatness of intellect and smallness of pride one doth not err.

(7) In being wealthy in religious doctrines and diligent in meditating upon them one doth not err.

(8) In having profound religious learning, combined with knowledge of things spiritual and absence of pride, one doth not err.

(9) By passing one's whole life in solitude [and meditation] one doth not err.

(10) In being unselfishly devoted to doing good to others, by means of wise methods, one doth not err.

These are The Ten Things Wherein One Erreth Not.

### XIII.  THE THIRTEEN GRIEVOUS FAILURES

(1) If, after having been born a human being, one give no heed to the Holy Doctrine, one resembleth a man who returneth empty-handed from a land rich in precious gems; and this is a grievous failure.

[1] *Bhikshu* (Skt.) = *Bhikkhu* (Pāli): a member of the *Sangha*, the Buddhist Order of those vowed to the Path of World Renunciation.

(2) If, after having entered the door of the Holy Order, one return to the life of the householder, one resembleth a moth plunging into the flame of a lamp; and this is a grievous failure.

(3) To dwell with a sage and remain in ignorance is to be like a man dying of thirst on the shore of a lake; and this is a grievous failure.

(4) To know the moral precepts and not apply them to the cure of obscuring passions is to be like a diseased man carrying a bag of medicine which he never useth; and this is a grievous failure.

(5) To preach religion and not practise it is to be like a parrot saying a prayer; and this is a grievous failure.

(6) The giving in alms and charity of things obtained by theft, robbery, or deceit, is like lightning striking the surface of water; and this is a grievous failure.[1]

(7) The offering to the deities of meat obtained by killing animate beings is like offering a mother the flesh of her own child;[2] and this is a grievous failure.

(8) To exercise patience for merely selfish ends rather than for doing good to others is to be like a cat exercising patience in order to kill a rat; and this is a grievous failure.

(9) Performing meritorious actions in order merely to attain fame and praise in this world is like bartering the mystic wish-granting gem[3] for a pellet of goat's dung; and this is a grievous failure.

(10) If, after having heard much of the Doctrine, one's nature still be unattuned, one is like a physician with a chronic disease; and this is a grievous failure.

---

[1] According to this simile, lightning in striking water fails of its true purpose, which is to set afire some inflammable object, even as does the giving in alms and charity of things dishonestly acquired.

[2] All living things are inseparably parts of One Whole, so that any injury or suffering inflicted upon the microcosm affects the macrocosm. See pp. 11 and 90[1]. Herein the Kargyütpa Sages prove themselves to be true to the great compassionate doctrine of *ahimsā* (or 'not hurting'), which is stressed by Hinduism, Buddhism, Jainism, Taoism, and Sufism.

[3] The wish-granting gem of Oriental myth, known in Sanskrit as the *Cintāmaṇi*, like Aladdin's magic lamp, grants any desire which its possessor formulates.

(11) To be clever concerning precepts yet ignorant of the spiritual experiences which come from applying them is to be like a rich man who hath lost the key of his treasury ; and this is a grievous failure.

(12) To attempt to explain to others doctrines which one hath not completely mastered oneself is to be like a blind man leading the blind ; and this is a grievous failure.

(13) To hold the experiences resulting from the first stage of meditation to be those of the final stage is to be like a man who mistaketh brass for gold ; and this is a grievous failure.

These are The Thirteen Grievous Failures.

### XIV.  THE FIFTEEN WEAKNESSES

(1) A religious devotee showeth weakness if he allow his mind to be obsessed with worldly thoughts while dwelling in solitude.

(2) A religious devotee who is the head of a monastery showeth weakness if he seek his own interests [rather than those of the brotherhood].

(3) A religious devotee showeth weakness if he be careful in the observance of moral discipline and lacking in moral restraint.

(4) It showeth weakness in one who hath entered upon the Righteous Path to cling to worldly feelings of attraction and repulsion.

(5) It showeth weakness in one who hath renounced worldliness and entered the Holy Order to hanker after acquiring merit.

(6) It showeth weakness in one who hath caught a glimpse of Reality to fail to persevere in *sādhanā* [or *yogic* meditation] till the dawning of Full Enlightenment.

(7) It showeth weakness in one who is a religious devotee to enter upon the Path and then be unable to tread it.

(8) It showeth weakness in one who hath no other occupation than religious devotion to be unable to eradicate from himself unworthy actions.

(9) It showeth weakness in one who hath chosen the

religious career to have hesitancy in entering into close retreat while knowing full well that the food and everything needed would be provided unasked.

(10) A religious devotee who exhibiteth occult powers when practising exorcism or in driving away diseases showeth weakness.

(11) A religious devotee showeth weakness if he barter sacred truths for food and money.

(12) One who is vowed to the religious life showeth weakness if he cunningly praise himself while disparaging others.

(13) A man of religion who preacheth loftily to others and doth not live loftily himself showeth weakness.

(14) One who professeth religion and is unable to live in solitude in his own company and yet knoweth not how to make himself agreeable in the company of others showeth weakness.

(15) The religious devotee showeth weakness if he be not indifferent to comfort and to hardship

These are The Fifteen Weaknesses.

## XV.  THE TWELVE INDISPENSABLE THINGS

(1) It is indispensable to have an intellect endowed with the power of comprehending and applying the Doctrine to one's own needs.

(2) At the very beginning [of one's religious career] it is indispensably necessary to have the most profound aversion for the interminable sequence of repeated deaths and births.

(3) A *guru* capable of guiding thee on the Path of Emancipation is also indispensable.

(4) Diligence combined with fortitude and invulnerability to temptation are indispensable.

(5) Unceasing perseverance in neutralizing the results of evil deeds, by the performance of good deeds, and the fulfilling of the threefold vow, to maintain chastity of body, purity of mind, and control of speech, are indispensable.

(6) A philosophy comprehensive enough to embrace the whole of knowledge is indispensable.

(7) A system of meditation which will produce the power

of concentrating the mind upon anything whatsoever is indispensable.

(8) An art of living which will enable one to utilize each activity [of body, speech, and mind] as an aid on the Path is indispensable.

(9) A method of practising the select teachings which will make them more than mere words is indispensable.

(10) Special instructions [by a wise *guru*] which will enable one to avoid misleading paths, temptations, pitfalls, and dangers are indispensable.

(11) Indomitable faith combined with supreme serenity of mind are indispensable at the moment of death.

(12) As a result of having practically applied the select teachings, the attainment of spiritual powers capable of transmuting the body, the speech, and the mind into their divine essences is indispensable.[1]

These are The Twelve Indispensable Things.

### XVI. THE TEN SIGNS OF A SUPERIOR MAN

(1) To have but little pride and envy is the sign of a superior man.

(2) To have but few desires and satisfaction with simple things is the sign of a superior man.

(3) To be lacking in hypocrisy and deceit is the sign of a superior man.

(4) To regulate one's conduct in accordance with the law of cause and effect as carefully as one guardeth the pupils of one's eyes is the sign of a superior man.

(5) To be faithful to one's engagements and obligations is the sign of a superior man.

(6) To be able to keep alive friendships while one [at the same time] regardeth all beings with impartiality is the sign of a superior man.

---

[1] As a direct result of practically applying the Doctrine, the devotee should attain that spiritual *yogic* power whereby the gross physical body is transmuted into the radiant body of glory, elsewhere in our texts called the 'rainbow body' (see pp. 170, 183ⁿ, 318³, 346); and the erring human speech into the infallible divine speech, and the unenlightened human mind into the supramundane mind, of a Buddha.

(7) To look with pity and without anger upon those who live evilly is the sign of a superior man.

(8) To allow unto others the victory, taking unto oneself the defeat, is the sign of a superior man.

(9) To differ from the multitude in every thought and action is the sign of a superior man.

(10) To observe faithfully and without pride one's vows of chastity and piety is the sign of a superior man.

These are The Ten Signs Of A Superior Man. Their opposites are The Ten Signs Of An Inferior Man.

## XVII. THE TEN USELESS THINGS[1]

(1) Our body being illusory and transitory, it is useless to give over-much attention to it.

(2) Seeing that when we die we must depart empty-handed and on the morrow after our death our corpse is expelled from our own house, it is useless to labour and to suffer privations in order to make for oneself a home in this world.

(3) Seeing that when we die our descendants [if spiritually unenlightened] are unable to render us the least assistance, it is useless for us to bequeath to them worldly [rather than spiritual] riches, even out of love.[2]

---

[1] They are useless in the sense meant by Milarepa when he came to realize that human life ought never to be frittered away in the spiritually profitless doings of this world. (See *Tibet's Great* Yogī *Milarepa*, pp. 176-7, 179-80.) The tenth aphorism of this series having been unintentionally omitted from our Tibetan manuscript by the scribe, we have substituted for it an adaptation of our own, based upon the doctrine of the worthlessness of worldly actions, as thus enunciated by Milarepa, and upon which this category of 'The Ten Useless Things' is based.

These teachings, if practically applied, like those of the Buddha or of the Christ, would result in the cessation of all actions performed selfishly rather than altruistically. The same supreme doctrine of the renunciation of the fruits of action underlies the whole of the *Bhagavad Gītā*.

[2] To fritter away the precious moments of life in heaping up the perishable goods of this world, thinking thereby to benefit oneself and one's family, is unwise. One's time on Earth ought to be given to the winning of those riches which are imperishable and capable of assisting one both in living and in dying. It is the science of accumulating riches of this character which parents should bequeath to their children and not worldly riches which merely intensify and prolong their possessors' slavery to *saṅgsāric* existence. This precept is emphasized by the fifth and sixth precepts which follow.

(4) Seeing that when we die we must go on our way alone and without kinsfolk or friends, it is useless to have devoted time [which ought to have been dedicated to the winning of Enlightenment] to their humouring and obliging, or in showering loving affection upon them.[1]

(5) Seeing that our descendants themselves are subject to death and that whatever worldly goods we may bequeath to them are certain to be lost eventually, it is useless to make bequests of the things of this world.

(6) Seeing that when death cometh one must relinquish even one's own home, it is useless to devote life to the acquisition of worldly things.

(7) Seeing that unfaithfulness to the religious vows will result in one's going to the miserable states of existence, it is useless to have entered the Order if one live not a holy life.

(8) To have heard and thought about the Doctrine and not practised it and acquired spiritual powers to assist thee at the moment of death is useless.

(9) It is useless to have lived, even for a very long time, with a spiritual preceptor if one be lacking in humility and devotion and thus be unable to develop spiritually.

(10) Seeing that all existing and apparent phenomena are ever transient, changing, and unstable, and more especially that the worldly life affordeth neither reality nor permanent gain, it is useless to have devoted oneself to the profitless doings of this world rather than to the seeking of Divine Wisdom.

These are The Ten Useless Things.

### XVIII. THE TEN SELF-IMPOSED TROUBLES

(1) To enter the state of the householder without means of sustenance produceth self-imposed trouble as doth an idiot eating aconite.

---

[1] Time when devoted to kinsfolk and friends should be employed not merely for the sake of showing them proper courtesy and loving affection, but chiefly for the purpose of setting them upon the Path of the Great Deliverance, whereby each living being is realized to be one's relative. All conventional social relationships on the human plane being illusory, it is useless for a *yogin* to dissipate the precious moments of his incarnate existence solely on their account.

(2) To live a thoroughly evil life and disregard the Doctrine produceth self-imposed trouble as doth an insane person jumping over a precipice.

(3) To live hypocritically produceth self-imposed trouble as doth a person who putteth poison in his own food.

(4) To be lacking in firmness of mind and yet attempt to act as the head of a monastery produceth self-imposed trouble as doth a feeble old woman who attempteth to herd cattle.

(5) To devote oneself wholly to selfish ambitions and not to strive for the good of others produceth self-imposed trouble as doth a blind man who alloweth himself to become lost in a desert.

(6) To undertake difficult tasks and not have the ability to perform them produceth self-imposed trouble as doth a man without strength who trieth to carry a heavy load.

(7) To transgress the commandments of the Buddha or of the holy *guru* through pride and self-conceit produceth self-imposed trouble as doth a king who followeth a perverted policy.

(8) To waste one's time loitering about towns and villages instead of devoting it to meditation produceth self-imposed trouble as doth a deer that descendeth to the valley instead of keeping to the fastnesses of the mountains.

(9) To be absorbed in the pursuit of worldly things rather than in nourishing the growth of Divine Wisdom produceth self-imposed trouble as doth an eagle when it breaketh its wing.

(10) Shamelessly to misappropriate offerings which have been dedicated to the *guru* or to the Trinity[1] produceth

---

[1] The Buddhist Trinity is the Buddha, the *Dharma* (or Scriptures), and the *Sangha* (or Priesthood). Neither *gurus* nor priests in a Buddhist or Hindu community have a right to demand any form of payment in return for their performance of religious duties. Their disciples or laymen, however, being in duty bound to provide for their maintenance, make voluntary offerings to them, chiefly in the form of food and clothing, and sometimes in the form of property endowments to their *āshramas*, monasteries, or temples. According to the rule of Buddhist monasticism, no member of the *Sangha* should touch money, but nowadays this rule is not usually observed ; and the offerings commonly include money, often for expenditure in some pious work, such as building a *stūpa*, making manuscript copies of the Scriptures, restoring an image, or to help in the building or repair of a shrine.

self-imposed trouble as doth a child swallowing live coals.[1]

These are The Ten Self-Imposed Troubles.

### XIX. THE TEN THINGS WHEREIN ONE DOETH GOOD TO ONESELF

(1) One doeth good to oneself by abandoning worldly conventions and devoting oneself to the Holy *Dharma*.

(2) One doeth good to oneself by departing from home and kindred and attaching oneself to a *guru* of saintly character.

(3) One doeth good to oneself by relinquishing worldly activities and devoting oneself to the three religious activities,—hearing, reflecting, and meditating [upon the chosen teachings].

(4) One doeth good to oneself by giving up social intercourse and dwelling alone in solitude.

(5) One doeth good to oneself by renouncing desire for luxury and ease and enduring hardship.

(6) One doeth good to oneself by being contented with simple things and free from craving for worldly possessions.

(7) One doeth good to oneself by making and firmly adhering to the resolution not to take advantage of others.

(8) One doeth good to oneself by attaining freedom from hankering after the transitory pleasures of this life and devoting oneself to the realization of the eternal bliss of *Nirvāṇa*.

(9) One doeth good to oneself by abandoning attachment to visible material things [which are transitory and unreal] and attaining knowledge of Reality.

(10) One doeth good to oneself by preventing the three doors to knowledge [the body, the speech, and the mind] from remaining spiritually undisciplined and by acquiring, through right use of them, the Twofold Merit.

These are The Ten Things Wherein One Doeth Good To Oneself.

---

[1] The evil *karma* resulting from the act of impiety is for the devotee as painful spiritually as the swallowing of live coals is for the child physically.

## XX. THE TEN BEST THINGS

(1) For one of little intellect, the best thing is to have faith in the law of cause and effect.

(2) For one of ordinary intellect, the best thing is to recognize, both within and without oneself, the workings of the law of opposites.[1]

(3) For one of superior intellect, the best thing is to have thorough comprehension of the inseparableness of the knower, the object of knowledge, and the act of knowing.[2]

(4) For one of little intellect, the best meditation is complete concentration of mind upon a single object.

(5) For one of ordinary intellect, the best meditation is unbroken concentration of mind upon the two dualistic concepts [of phenomena and noumena, and consciousness and mind].

(6) For one of superior intellect, the best meditation is to remain in mental quiescence, the mind devoid of all thought-processes, knowing that the meditator, the object of meditation, and the act of meditating constitute an inseparable unity.

---

[1] Another rendering, more literal, but rather unintelligible to the reader unaccustomed to the profound thought of Tibetan metaphysicians, might be phrased as follows : 'For one of ordinary intellect [or spiritual insight] the best thing is to recognize the external and internal phenomena [as these are seen] in the four aspects [or unions] of phenomena and noumena'. Such recognition is to be arrived at through *yogic* analysis of phenomena, manifested in or through the cosmos. Such analysis must be based upon the realization that all phenomena, visible and invisible, have their noumenal source in the Cosmic Mind, the origin of all existing things. 'The four aspects [or unions] of phenomena and noumena' are : (1) Phenomena and Voidness (Skt. *Shūnyatā*) ; (2) Clearness and Voidness ; (3) Bliss and Voidness ; (4) Consciousness and Voidness. Upon each of these 'unions' a vast treatise could be written. Here we may briefly state that Phenomena, Clearness, Bliss, and Consciousness represent four aspects of phenomena in opposition to their corresponding noumena, or voidnesses. The *Shūnyatā* (Tib. *Stong-pa-nyid*), the Voidness, the Ultimate Source of all phenomena, being without attributes, or qualities, is humanly inconceivable. In the Mahāyāna philosophy it symbolizes the Absolute, the Thatness of the Vedāntists, the One Reality, which is Mind.

[2] It is usual for the *guru*, somewhat after the manner of the Zen *gurus* of Japan, to put the problem before the *shishya* (or disciple) in the form of a series of interdependent questions such as the following : Is the knower other than the object of knowledge ? Is the object of knowledge other than the act of knowing ? Is the act of knowing other than the knowledge ? Similar series of questions are set forth in *The Epitome of the Great Symbol*, §§ 78, 80, 98, 102.

(7) For one of little intellect, the best religious practice is to live in strict conformity with the law of cause and effect.

(8) For one of ordinary intellect, the best religious practice is to regard all objective things as though they were images seen in a dream or produced by magic.

(9) For one of superior intellect, the best religious practice is to abstain from all worldly desires and actions,[1] [regarding all *sangsāric* things as though they were non-existent].

(10) For those of all three grades of intellect, the best indication of spiritual progress is the gradual diminution of obscuring passions and selfishness.

These are the Ten Best Things.

### XXI. THE TEN GRIEVOUS MISTAKES

(1) For a religious devotee to follow a hypocritical charlatan instead of a *guru* who sincerely practiseth the Doctrine is a grievous mistake.

(2) For a religious devotee to apply himself to vain worldly sciences rather than to seeking the chosen secret teachings of the Great Sages is a grievous mistake.

(3) For a religious devotee to make far-reaching plans as though he were going to establish permanent residence [in this world] instead of living as though each day were the last he had to live is a grievous mistake.

(4) For a religious devotee to preach the Doctrine to the multitude [ere having realized it to be true] instead of meditating upon it [and testing its truth] in solitude is a grievous mistake.

(5) For a religious devotee to be like a miser and hoard up riches instead of dedicating them to religion and charity is a grievous mistake.

(6) For a religious devotee to give way in body, speech, and mind to the shamelessness of debauchery instead of observing carefully the vows [of purity and chastity] is a grievous mistake.

(7) For a religious devotee to spend his life between worldly

---

[1] This is another aspect of or manner of stating the rule of the *karma yogin*, to be free from worldly desires and unattached to the fruits of actions.

hopes and fears instead of gaining understanding of Reality is a grievous mistake.

(8) For a religious devotee to try to reform others instead of reforming himself is a grievous mistake.

(9) For a religious devotee to strive after worldly powers instead of cultivating his own innate spiritual powers is a grievous mistake.

(10) For a religious devotee to be idle and· indifferent instead of persevering when all the circumstances favourable for spiritual advancement are present is a grievous mistake.

These are The Ten Grievous Mistakes.

### XXII.   THE TEN NECESSARY THINGS

(1) At the very outset [of one's religious career] one should have so profound an aversion for the continuous succession of deaths and births [to which all who have not attained Enlightenment are subject] that one will wish to flee from it even as a stag fleeth from captivity.

(2) The next necessary thing is perseverance so great that one regretteth not the losing of one's life [in the quest for Enlightenment], like that of the husbandman who tilleth his fields and regretteth not the tilling even though he die on the morrow.

(3) The third necessary thing is joyfulness of mind like that of a man who hath accomplished a great deed of far-reaching influence.

(4) Again, one should comprehend that, as with a man dangerously wounded by an arrow, there is not a moment of time to be wasted.

(5) One needeth ability to fix the mind on a single thought even as doth a mother who hath lost her only son.

(6) Another necessary thing is to understand that there is no need of doing anything,[1] even as a cowherd whose cattle have been driven off by enemies understandeth that he can do nothing to recover them.

---

[1] The *yogin*'s goal is complete quiescence of body, speech, and mind, in accordance with the ancient *yogic* precept, ' Be quiescent, and know that thou art That '.  The Hebrew Scriptures echo the same teaching in the well-known aphorism, ' Be still, and know that I am God' (*Psalms* xlvi. 10).

(7) It is primarily requisite for one to hunger after the Doctrine even as a hungry man hungereth after good food.

(8) One needeth to be as confident of one's mental ability as doth a strong man of his physical ability to hold fast to a precious gem which he hath found.

(9) One must expose the fallacy of dualism as one doth the falsity of a liar.

(10) One must have confidence in the Thatness [as being the Sole Refuge] even as an exhausted crow far from land hath confidence in the mast of the ship upon which it resteth.

These are The Ten Necessary Things.

### XXIII. THE TEN UNNECESSARY THINGS

(1) If the empty nature of the mind be realized, no longer is it necessary to listen to or to meditate upon religious teachings.[1]

(2) If the unsulliable nature of the intellect be realized, no longer is it necessary to seek absolution of one's sins.[2]

(3) Nor is absolution necessary for one who abideth in the State of Mental Quiescence.

[1] Realization of the empty nature of the mind is attained through *yogic* mastery of the Doctrine of the Voidness, which shows that Mind, the Sole Reality, is the noumenal source of all phenomena; and, that being non-*sangsāric* (i e. not dependent for its existence upon objective appearances, nor even upon thought-forms or thought-processes), it is the Qualityless, the Attributeless, and, therefore, the Vacuous. Once having arrived at this realization, the *yogin* no longer needs to listen to or to meditate upon religious teachings, for these are merely guides to the great goal of *yoga* which he has reached.

[2] According to The Awakening of Faith, by Ashvaghosha, one of the illustrious expounders of the Mahāyāna, 'The mind from the beginning is of a pure nature, but since there is the finite aspect of it which is sullied by finite views, there is the sullied aspect of it. Although there is this defilement, yet the original pure nature is eternally unchanged.' As Ashvaghosha adds, it is only an Enlightened One, Who has realized the unsulliable nature of primordial mind (or intellect), that understands this mystery. (Cf. Timothy Richard's translation of The Awakening of Faith, Shanghai, 1907, p. 13; also the translation made by Professor Teitaro Suzuki, published in Chicago in 1900, pp. 79–80.) So for him who knows that the defilements of the world are, like the world, without any reality, being a part of the Great Illusion, or *Māyā*, what need is there for absolution of sin? Likewise, as the next aphorism teaches, 'for one who abideth in the State of Mental Quiescence', which is the State of Enlightenment, all such illusory concepts of the finite mind as sin and absolution vanish as morning mists do when the Sun has arisen.

(4) For him who hath attained the State of Unalloyed Purity there is no need to meditate upon the Path or upon the methods of treading it, [for he hath arrived at the Goal].

(5) If the unreal [or illusory] nature of cognitions be realized, no need is there to meditate upon the state of non-cognition.[1]

(6) If the non-reality [or illusory nature] of obscuring passions be realized, no need is there to seek their antidote.

(7) If all phenomena be known to be illusory, no need is there to seek or to reject anything.[2]

(8) If sorrow and misfortune be recognized to be blessings, no need is there to seek happiness.

(9) If the unborn [or uncreated] nature of one's own consciousness be realized, no need is there to practise transference of consciousness.[3]

---

[1] Here, again, reference to the Doctrine of the Voidness [of Mind] is essential to right understanding of this aphorism. The State of Non-Cognition, otherwise called the True State [of Mind], is a state of unmodified consciousness, comparable to a calm and infinite ocean. In the modified state of consciousness, inseparable from mind in its microcosmic or finite aspect, this ocean illusorily appears to be ruffled with waves, which are the illusory concepts born of *sangsāric* existence. As Ashvaghosha also tells us in *The Awakening of Faith* (Richard's translation, p. 12), 'We should know that all phenomena are created by the imperfect notions in the finite mind; therefore all existence is like a reflection in a mirror, without substance, only a phantom of the mind. When the finite mind acts, then all kinds of things arise; when the finite mind ceases to act, then all kinds of things cease.' Concomitantly with realization of the True State, wherein mind is quiescent and devoid of the thought-processes and concepts of finite mind, the *yogin* realizes the unreal nature of cognitions, and no longer need he meditate upon the State of Non-Cognition.

[2] For according to the Doctrine of *Māyā* (or Illusion) nothing which has illusory (or phenomenal) existence is real. (See pp. 161–4.)

[3] Consciousness, or mind, being primordially of the Unborn, Uncreated, cannot really be transferred. It is only to consciousness in its finite or microcosmic aspect, as manifested in the *Sangsāra*, or Realm of Illusion, that one may apply the term transference. To the Unborn, in the True State, wherein the *Sangsāra* is transcended, time and space, which belong wholly to the Realm of Illusion, have no existence. How then can the Unborn be transferred, since there is no whence or whither to which It can be related? Having realized this, that the noumenal cannot be treated as the phenomenal, there is no need to practise the transference of consciousness. Book IV, which follows, being devoted wholly to an exposition of the Doctrine of Consciousness-Transference, affords further commentary on this aphorism. (See p. 273, §§ 17–21.)

(10) If only the good of others be sought in all that one doeth, no need is there to seek benefit for oneself.[1]

These are The Ten Unnecessary Things.

### XXIV.  THE TEN MORE PRECIOUS THINGS

(1) One free and well-endowed human life is more precious than myriads of non-human lives in any of the six states of existence.[2]

(2) One Sage is more precious than multitudes of irreligious and worldly-minded persons.

(3) One esoteric truth is more precious than innumerable exoteric doctrines.

(4) One momentary glimpse of Divine Wisdom, born of meditation, is more precious than any amount of knowledge derived from merely listening to and thinking about religious teachings.

(5) The smallest amount of merit dedicated to the good of others is more precious than any amount of merit devoted to one's own good.

(6) To experience but momentarily the *samādhi* wherein all thought-processes are quiescent is more precious than to experience uninterruptedly the *samādhi* wherein thought-processes are still present.[3]

(7) To enjoy a single moment of *Nirvāṇic* bliss is more precious than to enjoy any amount of sensual bliss.

---

[1] Humanity being a unified organism, through which the One Mind finds highest expression on Earth, whatsoever one member of it does to another member of it, be the action good or evil, inevitably affects all members of it. Therefore, in the Christian sense as well, the doing of good to others is the doing of good to oneself.

[2] The six states or regions, of *sangsāric* existence are (1) the *deva*-worlds, (2) the *asura*- (or titan) world, (3) the human-world, (4) the brute-world, (5) the *preta*- (or unhappy ghost) world, and (6) the hell-worlds.

[3] As explained on p. 329[1], there are four states of *dhyāna*, or *samādhi* (profound meditation). The highest of these states is one wherein the *yogin* experiences that ecstatic bliss which is attained by realization of the unmodified condition of primordial mind. This state is designated as the True State, being vacuous of all the *sangsāric* thought-forming processes of the mind in its modified or finite aspect. In the lowest, or first, stage of *samādhi*, wherein complete cessation of these thought-forming processes has not been reached, the *yogin* experiences an incomparably inferior sort of ecstasy, which novices are warned not to mistake for the higher state.

(8) The smallest good deed done unselfishly is more precious than innumerable good deeds done selfishly.

(9) The renunciation of every worldly thing [home, family, friends, property, fame, duration of life, and even health] is more precious than the giving of inconceivably vast worldly wealth in charity.

(10) One lifetime spent in the quest for Enlightenment is more precious than all the lifetimes during an aeon spent in worldly pursuits.

These are The Ten More Precious Things.

### XXV. THE TEN EQUAL THINGS

(1) For him who is sincerely devoted to the religious life, it is the same whether he refrain from worldly activities or not.[1]

(2) For him who hath realized the transcendental nature of mind, it is the same whether he meditate or not.[2]

(3) For him who is freed from attachment to worldly luxuries, it is the same whether he practise asceticism or not.

(4) For him who hath realized Reality, it is the same whether he dwell on an isolated hill-top in solitude or wander hither and thither [as a *bhikṣhu*].

(5) For him who hath attained the mastery of his mind, it is the same whether he partake of the pleasures of the world or not.

(6) For him who is endowed with the fullness of compassion, it is the same whether he practise meditation in solitude or work for the good of others in the midst of society.

(7) For him whose humility and faith [with respect to his *guru*] are unshakable, it is the same whether he dwell with his *guru* or not.

(8) For him who understandeth thoroughly the teachings

---

[1] That is to say, as the *Bhagavad Gītā* teaches, for one who is sincerely devoted to the religious life and is wholly free from attachment to the fruits of his actions in the world, it is the same whether he refrain from worldly activities or not, inasmuch as such disinterestedness produces no *karmic* results.

[2] The goal of *yogic* meditation is to realize that only mind is real, and that the true (or primordial) state of mind is that state of mental quiescence, devoid of all thought-processes, which is experienced in the highest *samādhi*; and, once this goal is attained, meditation has fulfilled its purpose and is no longer necessary.

which he hath received, it is the same whether he meet with good fortune or with bad fortune.

(9) For him who hath given up the worldly life and taken to the practice of the Spiritual Truths, it is the same whether he observe conventional codes of conduct or not.[1]

(10) For him who hath attained the Sublime Wisdom, it is the same whether he be able to exercise miraculous powers or not.

These are The Ten Equal Things.

### XXVI.  THE TEN VIRTUES OF THE HOLY *DHARMA* (OR DOCTRINE)[2]

(1) The fact that there have been made known amongst men the Ten Pious Acts,[3] the Six *Pāramitā*,[4] the various teachings concerning Reality and Perfection, the Four Noble Truths,[5] the Four States of *Dhyāna*,[6] the Four States of Formless Existence,[7] and the Two Mystic

---

[1] In all his relationships with human society, the *yogin* is free to follow conventional usages or not. What the multitude consider moral he may consider immoral, and vice versa. (See Milarepa's song concerning what is shameful and what is not, pp. 226-7, of *Tibet's Great* Yogī *Milarepa*.)

[2] According to the Southern School, the *Dharma* (Pāli : *Dhamma*) implies not merely the Scriptures, but also the study and practice of them for the purpose of attaining *Nirvāṇa* (Pāli : *Nibbāṇa*).

[3] These are the opposites of the Ten Impious Acts. Three are acts of the body, namely, Saving Life, Chastity, and Charity. Four are acts of speech, namely, Truth-telling, Peace-making, Politeness of speech, and Religious discourse. Three are acts of the mind, namely, Benevolence, Good Wishes, and Meekness combined with Faith.

[4] The Six *Pāramitā* (or 'Six Boundless Virtues') are Boundless Charity, Morality, Patience, Industry, Meditation, Wisdom. In the Pali canon ten *Pāramitā* are mentioned : Charity, Morality, Renunciation, Wisdom, Energy (or Industry), Tolerance, Truthfulness, Good-Will, Love, and Equanimity.

[5] The Four Noble Truths taught by the Buddha may be stated as follows : (1) Existence in the *Sangsāra* (the transitory and phenomenal universe) is inseparable from Suffering, or Sorrow. (2) The Cause of Suffering is Desire and Lust for Existence in the *Sangsāra*. (3) The Cessation of Suffering is attained by conquering and eradicating Desire and Lust for Existence in the *Sangsāra*. (4) The Path to the Cessation of Suffering is the Noble Eightfold Path. (See p. 13.)

[6] See p. 329[1].

[7] Literally, 'the Four *Ārūpa* (Formless) Unions'. To be born in any of these worlds, wherein existence is bodiless or formless, is to be united with them. These worlds are the four highest heavens under the sway of the God Brahmā, known as the Higher Brahmaloka ('Realms of Brahmā'). Their names are : (1) *Ākāshānantyāyatana* (Realm wherein consciousness exists in

Paths [1] of spiritual unfoldment and emancipation, showeth the virtue of the Holy *Dharma*.

(2) The fact that there have been evolved in the *Sangsāra* spiritually enlightened princes and Brāhmins [2] amongst men, and the Four Great Guardians, [3] the six orders of *devas* of the

infinite space) ; (2) *Vijñānānantyāyatana* (Realm wherein consciousness exists in the infinite state of consciousness) ; (3) *Ākiñcanyāyatana* (Realm wherein consciousness exists free from the infinite state of consciousness) ; (4) *Naivasaṃjñānā Saṃjñāyatana* (Realm wherein there is neither perception nor non-perception).  These four realms represent four progressive stages in the higher evolutionary process of emptying consciousness of its must subtle *sangsāric* objects, through *yogic* meditation, and thereby attaining higher conditions of *sangsāric* existence preparatory to the attainment of *Nirvāṇa*.  In the first state, consciousness has no object upon which to centre itself save infinite space.  In the second, consciousness transcends infinite space as its object.  In the third, consciousness transcends the second stage and thus becomes free from all thinking or process of thought ; and this is one of the great goals of *yoga*.  In the fourth state, consciousness exists of itself and by itself, without exercising either perception or non-perception, in profoundest *samādhic* quiescence.  These four states of consciousness, which are among the highest attainable within the *Sangsāra*, are reached in *yogic* trance induced by deep meditation.  So transcendent are they that the unwisely directed *yogin* is apt to mistake the realization of them for the realization of *Nirvāṇa*.  (See p. 329[1].)  The Prince Gautama, ere attaining Buddhahood, studied and practised the *yoga* pertaining to the Four States of Formless Existence under two *gurus*, Ārlāra and Uddaka, and relinquished it because he discovered that such *yoga* fails to lead to *Nirvāṇa*.  (Cf. the *Aryaparyesana*, or 'Holy Research', *Sutta*, *Majjhima Nikāya*, i. 164–6.)

[1] According to the Mahāyāna, there is the lower path, leading to the Four States of Formless Existence, and to other heaven worlds, such as that of Sukhāvatī, the Western Paradise of the Dhyānī Buddha Amitābha ; and the higher path, leading to *Nirvāṇa*, whereby the *Sangsāra* is transcended.

[2] Most of the great religious teachers of India have been either of royal descent, like Gautama the Buddha, or of Brahmanical or priestly origin, like Ashvaghosa, Nāgārjuna, Tilopa, and many others who were eminent Buddhists.  Buddhism holds that the historical Buddha, Gautama, is but One of a long succession of Buddhas, and that Gautama merely handed on teachings which have existed since beginningless time.  Accordingly, it is directly due to beings in past aeons having practised these venerable teachings, based as they are upon realizable truths, that there have been evolved enlightened men and gods ; and this fact proves the virtue of these teachings, recorded in the Buddhist Scriptures known as the *Dharma*.

[3] These are the four celestial kings who guard the four quarters of the Universe from the destructive forces of evil, the Four Great Guardians of the *Dharma* and of Humanity.  Dhritarāshthra guards the East, and to him is assigned the symbolic colour white.  Virūdhhaka guards the South, and his symbolic colour is green.  The red guardian of the West is Virūpāksha, and the yellow guardian of the North is Vaishravana.

sensuous paradises,[1] the seventeen orders of gods of the worlds of form,[2] and the four orders of gods of the worlds without form [3] showeth the virtue of the Holy *Dharma*.

(3) The fact that there have arisen in the world those who have entered the Stream, those who will return to birth but once more, those who have passed beyond the need of further birth,[4] and *Arhants*, and Self-Enlightened Buddhas and Omniscient Buddhas,[5] showeth the virtue of the Holy *Dharma*.

[1] The six sensuous paradises, together with the Earth, constitute the Region of Sensuousness (Skt. *Kāmadhātu*), the lowest of the Three Regions (Skt. *Trailokya*) into which the Buddhists divide the cosmos.

[2] These are the deities inhabiting the seventeen heavens of Brahmā which constitute the Region of Form (Skt. *Rupadhātu*), the second of the Three Regions, wherein existence and form are free from sensuousness.

[3] These are the deities inhabiting the four highest Brahmā heavens, wherein existence is not only non-sensuous, but is also formless. These heavens (named above) together with the *Akanishtha* (Tib. 'Og-min) Heaven, the highest *sangsāric* state (see p. 250[2]), constitute the Region of Formlessness (Skt. *Ārūpadhātu*), the third of the Three Regions. Beyond this is the supra-cosmic state, beyond all heavens, hells, and worlds of *sangsāric* existence,—the Unborn, Unmade *Nirvāṇa*. The *Stūpa* (Tib. *Ch'orten*) esoterically symbolizes the Way to *Nirvāṇa* through the Three Regions. (See *Tibet's Great* Yogī *Milarepa*, opposite p. 269.)

[4] These three gradations of human beings correspond to the three steps to *Arhantship* (or Saintship in the Buddhist sense), preparatory to the Full Enlightenment of Buddhahood. 'Entering the Stream' (Skt. *Srotāpatti*), which implies acceptance of the Doctrine of the Buddha, is the first step of the neophyte on the Path to *Nirvāṇa*. 'One who receives birth once more' (Skt. *Sakridāgāmin*) has taken the second step. 'One who will not come back [to birth]' (Skt. *Anāgāmin*), being one who has taken the third step and attained to the state of the *Arhant*, normally would pass on to *Nirvāṇa*. If, however, he takes the vow not to accept *Nirvāṇa* till every sentient being is safely set upon the same Supreme Path that he has trodden, and thus becomes a *Bodhisattva* (or 'Enlightened Being'), he will consciously reassume fleshly embodiment as a Divine Incarnation, a *Nirmāṇakāya*. As a *Bodhisattva*, he may remain within the *Sangsāra* for unknown aeons and so give added strength to the 'Guardian Wall [of Spiritual Power]' which protects all living things and makes possible their Final Emancipation. According to the Pali canon, one who is a *Srota-āpatti* will be reborn at least once, but not more than seven times, in any of the seven states of the *Kāmadhātu*. A *Sakridāgāmin* will assume birth only once more, in one of the *Kāmadhātu*. And an *Anāgāmin* will not be reborn in any of them.

[5] Self-Enlightened (Skt. *Pratyeka*) Buddhas do not teach the Doctrine publicly, but merely do good to those who come into personal contact with Them, whereas Omniscient Buddhas, of Whom was the Buddha Gautama, preach the Doctrine widely, both to gods and to men.

(4) The fact that there are Those who have attained *Bodhic* Enlightenment and are able to return to the world as Divine Incarnations and work for the deliverance of mankind and of all living things till the time of the dissolution of the physical universe showeth the virtue of the Holy *Dharma*.[1]

(5) The fact that there existeth, as an outcome of the all-embracing benevolence of the *Bodhisattvas*, protective spiritual influences which make possible the deliverance of men and of all beings showeth the virtue of the Holy *Dharma*.[2]

(6) The fact that one experienceth even in the unhappy worlds of existence moments of happiness as a direct outcome of having performed little deeds of mercy while in the human world showeth the virtue of the Holy *Dharma*.[3]

(7) The fact that men after having lived evilly should have renounced the worldly life and become saints worthy of the veneration of the world showeth the virtue of the Holy *Dharma*.

(8) The fact that men whose heavy evil *karma* would have condemned them to almost endless suffering after death should have turned to the religious life and attained *Nirvāṇa* showeth the virtue of the Holy *Dharma*.

(9) The fact that by merely having faith in or meditating upon the Doctrine, or by merely donning the robe of the *bhikṣhu*, one becometh worthy of respect and veneration showeth the virtue of the Holy *Dharma*.

---

[1] It is the Holy *Dharma* alone which has revealed to mankind the *Bodhic* Pathway and the supreme teaching that Those who have won the right to freedom from further worldly existence should renounce the right and continue to reincarnate in order that their Divine Wisdom and Experience shall not be lost to the world, but employed to the sublime end of leading all unenlightened beings to the same State of Emancipation.

[2] In having chosen the Path of Infinite Benevolence, the *Bodhisattvas* have projected into the worlds of *sangsāric* existence subtle vibratory influences which protect all living beings and make possible their spiritual progress and ultimate enlightenment, as otherwise explained above. Were there no such inspiring and elevating influences in the world, mankind would be without spiritual guidance and remain enslaved by sensuous delusions and mental darkness.

[3] The Buddhist teaching that the beneficial results of deeds of mercy done in this life assist one even in the unhappy after-death states is proved by experience and so shows the virtue of the Holy *Dharma*.

(10) The fact that one, even after having abandoned all worldly possessions and embraced the religious life and given up the state of the householder and hidden himself in a most secluded hermitage, should still be sought for and supplied with all the necessities of life showeth the virtue of the Holy *Dharma*.

These are The Ten Virtues of The Holy *Dharma*.

### XXVII.  THE TEN FIGURATIVE EXPRESSIONS[1]

(1) As the Foundation Truth cannot be described [but must be realized in *samādhi*], the expression 'Foundation Truth' is merely figurative.[2]

(2) As there is neither any traversing nor any traverser of the Path, the expression 'Path' is merely figurative.[3]

(3) As there is neither any seeing nor any seer of the True State, the expression 'True State' is merely figurative.[4]

(4) As there is neither any meditation nor any meditator of the Pure State, the expression 'Pure State' is merely figurative.[5]

(5) As there is neither any enjoying nor any enjoyer of

---

[1] This category of negations concerning Truth is probably inspired by the canonical *Prajñā-Pāramitā*, upon which the seventh Book of our present volume is based.

[2] The Foundation Truth, which is synonymous with the *Dharma Kāya* (or 'Divine Body of Truth'), is the All-Truth, in its primordial or unmodified aspect. *Yoga*, the Science of Mind (or Truth), consists of three divisions, namely, the Foundation Truth, the Path (or method of attaining realization), and the Fruit (or the realization itself).

[3] 'Path' is merely a metaphor descriptive of the method of realizing spiritual growth or progress.

[4] The True State, realizable in the highest *samādhi*, is, in its microcosmic reflex, a state wherein the mind, unmodified by the process of thought, resembles in its quiescence an ocean unruffled by the least movement of air, as has been similarly stated above. All doors of perception are closed. There is complete oblivion of the material universe of phenomena. The mind attains its own natural condition of absolute tranquillity. The microcosmic mind becomes attuned to the Macrocosmic Mind. Thereby is attained the knowledge that in the True State there are no seeing or seer, that all finite concepts are really non-existent, that all dualities become unities, that there is but the One Reality, Primordial Cosmic Mind.

[5] The Pure State is an intensified aspect of the True State, wherein mind, in its primordial condition, exists unsullied by any predication. In the realizing of it, in the *samādhic* condition, the act of meditating, the meditator, and the thing meditated upon are indistinguishably one.

the Natural Mood, the expression 'Natural Mood' is merely figurative.[1]

(6) As there is neither any vow-keeping nor any vow-keeper, these expressions are merely figurative.

(7) As there is neither any accumulating nor any accumulator of merits, the expression ' Twofold Merit '[2] is merely figurative.

(8) As there is neither any performing nor any performer of actions, the expression ' Twofold Obscuration '[3] is merely figurative.

(9) As there is neither any renunciation nor any renouncer [of worldly existence], the expression ' worldly existence ' is merely figurative.

(10) As there is neither any obtaining nor any obtainer [of results of actions], the expression ' results of actions ' is merely figurative.

These are The Ten Figurative Expressions.[4]

---

[1] The Natural Mood refers to a state of mind, likewise reached in the highest *samādhi*, concomitant with the True State and the Pure State. Therein there is realized that there are really no enjoying or enjoyer, no actions or doer of actions, that all objective things are as unreal as dreams ; and that, therefore, rather than live as do the multitude in the pursuit of illusions, one should choose the Path of the *Bodhisattvas*, the Lords of Compassion, and be a worker for the emancipation of beings *karmically* bound to the Wheel of Ignorance.

[2] This is : Causal Merit, which is the fruit of charitable deeds, and otherwise known as temporal merit; and Resultant Merit, which arises from superabundance of Causal Merit, and otherwise called spiritual merit. (Cf. p. 314³.)

[3] This is : Obscurations of intellect resulting from evil passions; and Obscurations of intellect resulting from wrong belief, such as the belief that there is an immortal personal self, or soul, or the belief that phenomenal appearances are real. (Cf. p. 314³.)

[4] All these aphorisms of negation rest upon the *Bodhic* doctrine that personality is transitory, that personal (or soul) immortality is inconceivable to one who has attained to Right Knowledge. The microcosmic mind, a reflex of the Macrocosmic Mind (which alone is eternal), ceases to be microcosmic, or limited, when immersed in the ecstasy induced by the highest *samādhi*. There is then no personality, no obtainer, no renouncer, no performer of actions, no accumulator of merits, no vow-keeper, no enjoyer of the Natural Mood, no meditator of the Pure State, no seer of the True State, no traverser of the Path; and the whole conceptual or illusory state of mind is obliterated. Human language is essentially a means of enabling man to communicate with man in terms based upon experiences common to all men existing in a sensuous universe ; and the employment of it to describe supersensuous experiences can never be anything more than figurative.

### XXVIII. THE TEN GREAT JOYFUL REALIZATIONS

(1) It is great joy to realize that the mind of all sentient beings is inseparable from the All-Mind.[1]

(2) It is great joy to realize that the Fundamental Reality is qualityless.[2]

(3) It is great joy to realize that in the infinite, thought-transcending Knowledge of Reality all *sangsāric* differentiations are non-existent.[3]

(4) It is great joy to realize that in the state of primordial [or uncreated] mind there existeth no disturbing thought-process.[4]

(5) It is great joy to realize that in the *Dharma-Kāya*, wherein mind and matter are inseparable, there existeth neither any holder of theories nor any support of theories.[5]

(6) It is great joy to realize that in the self-emanated, compassionate *Sambhoga-Kāya* there existeth no birth, death, transition, or any change.[6]

(7) It is great joy to realize that in the self-emanated, divine *Nirmāna-Kāya* there existeth no feeling of duality.[7]

---

[1] Or the *Dharma-Kāya*, the ' Divine Body of Truth', viewed as the All-Mind.

[2] Qualities are purely *sangsāric*, i.e. of the phenomenal universe. To the Fundamental Reality, to the Thatness, no characteristics can be applied. In It all *sangsāric* things, all qualities, all conditions, all dualities, merge in transcendent at-one-ness.

[3] In the Knowledge (or Realization) of Reality all partial or relative truths are recognized as parts of the One Truth, and no differentiations such as lead to the establishing of opposing religions and sects, each perhaps pragmatically in possession of some partial truth, is possible.

[4] Cf. pp. 89[1], 153[2].

[5] To the truth-seeker, whether in the realm of physical or of spiritual science, theories are essential; but once any truth, or fact, has been ascertained, all theories concerning it are useless. Accordingly, in the *Dharma-Kāya*, or State of the Fundamental Truth, no theory is necessary or conceivable; it is the State of Perfect Enlightenment, of the Buddhas in *Nirvāna*.

[6] The *Sambhoga-Kāya*, or ' Divine Body of Perfect Endowment', symbolizes the state of spiritual communion in which all *Bodhisattvas* exist when not incarnate on Earth, similar to that implied by the communion of saints. Like the *Dharma-Kāya*, of which it is the self-emanated primary reflex, the *Sambhoga-Kāya* is a state wherein birth, death, transition, and change are transcended.

[7] The *Nirmāna-Kāya*, or ' Divine Body of Incarnation ', the secondary reflex of the *Dharma-Kāya*, is the Body, or Spiritual State, in which abide all Great

(8) It is great joy to realize that in the *Dharma-Chakra* there existeth no support for the soul doctrine.[1]

(9) It is great joy to realize that in the Divine, Boundless Compassion [of the *Bodhisattvas*] there existeth neither any shortcoming nor any showing of partiality.

(10) It is great joy to realize that the Path to Freedom which all the Buddhas have trodden is ever-existent, ever unchanged, and ever open to those who are ready to enter upon it.

These are The Ten Great Joyful Realizations.

## [THE CONCLUSION]

Herein, above, is contained the essence of the immaculate words of the Great *Gurus*, who were endowed with Divine Wisdom ; and of the Goddess Tārā and other divinities. Among these Great Teachers were the glorious Dīpāṅkara,[2]

Teachers, or *Bodhisattvas*, incarnate on Earth. The *Dharma-Kāya*, being beyond the realm of *sangsāric* sense perceptions, cannot be sensuously perceived. Honoo the mind of the *yogin* when realizing It ceases to exist as finite mind, as something apart from It. In other words, in the state of transcendent *samādhic* ecstasy wherein the *Dharma-Kāya* is realized, finite mind attains to *at-one-ment* with its Source, the *Dharma-Kāya*. Likewise, in the state of the *Nirmāṇa-Kāya*, the Divine and the Sentient, Mind and Matter, Noumena and Phenomena, and all dualities, blend in at-one-ment. And this the *Bodhisattva*, when in the fleshly body, intuitively feels; he knows that neither he himself, nor any sensuous or objective thing, has a separate or independent existence apart from the *Dharma-Kāya*. For a more detailed exposition of this fundamental Mahāyānic doctrine of the ' Three Divine Bodies ' (Skt. *Tri-Kāya*) the student is referred to *The Tibetan Book of the Dead*, pp. 10-15.

[1] The truths proclaimed by the Buddha are symbolized by the *Dharma-Chakra* (the ' Wheel of Truth ') which He set in motion when He first preached the truths to His disciples, in the Deer Park, near Benares. In the time of the Enlightened One, and long before then, the animistic belief in a permanent ego, or self, in an unchanging soul (Skt. *ātmā*), i.e. in personal immortality, was as widespread in India and the Far East as it is in Europe and America now. He denied the validity of this doctrine ; and nowhere in the Buddhist Scriptures, or *Dharma*, of either Southern or Northern Buddhism, is there any support for it.

[2] Dīpāṅkara [Shrī-jñāna], as given in our text, is the Indian name of Atīsha, the first of the Great Reformers of Lāmaism, who was born in Bengal, of the royal family of Gaur, in A.D. 980, and arrived in Tibet in 1038. Having been a professor of philosophy in the Vikramanshīla Monastery, of Magadha, he brought with him to Tibet much fresh learning, chiefly relating to *Yoga* and Tantricism. His chief work, as a reformer, was by enforcing celibacy and a higher priestly morality. Atīsha associated himself with the sect called the Kahdampas, or 'Those Bound by the Ordinances'. Three hundred and fifty

the spiritual father and his successors, who were divinely
appointed for the spreading of the Doctrine in this Northern
Land of Snow ; and the Gracious *Gurus* of the Kahdampa
School.    There were also that King of *Yogins*, Milarepa, to
whom was bequeathed the learning of the Sage Marpa of
Lhobrak and of others ; and the illustrious Saints, Naropa
and Maitripa, of the noble land of India, whose splendour
equalled that of the Sun and Moon ; and the disciples of all these.

Here endeth *The Supreme Path, the Rosary
of Precious Gems.*


## [THE COLOPHON]

This treatise was put into manuscript form by Digom
Sönam Rinchen,[1] who possessed thorough knowledge of the
teachings of the Kahdampas and of the Chagchenpas.[2]

It is commonly believed that the Great *Guru* Gampopa,
[otherwise known as Dvagpo-Lharje], compiled this work,
and that he handed it on with this injunction : ' I entreat those
devotees of generations yet unborn, who will honour my
memory and regret not having met me in person, to study
this, *The Supreme Path, the Rosary of Precious Gems*, and,
also, *The Precious Ornament of Liberation*, along with other
religious treatises.    The result will be equivalent to that of
an actual meeting with me myself.'

May this Book radiate divine virtue ; and may it prove
to be auspicious.

*Mangalam.*[3]

years later, under the second of the Great Reformers, Tsong-Khapa, a territorial
title meaning ' Native of the Onion Country ', the district of his birth, in
Amdo Province, in North-East Tibet near the Chinese frontier, the Kahdampas
became the Gelugpas, or ' Followers of the Virtuous Order ', who now constitute the Established Church of Tibet.

[1] Text : *Hbri-sgom Bsod-nams Rin-chen* (pronounced *Di-gom Sö-nam Rin-
chen*), meaning, ' Meditating One of Precious Merit, of the Cave of the Cow-
Yak '.

[2] These are the followers of the *yogic* teachings contained in the *Chag-chen*
Philosophy, the essence of which forms the subject-matter of Book II of this
volume.

[3] The Tibetan-Sanskrit of the text, literally meaning, ' Blessing ' or ' Happiness ' ; or, in reference to this Book, ' May blessing be upon it '.

THE TWO CHIEF *YOGIC* POSTURES

Described on pages xix–xx

# BOOK II

## THE *NIRVĀṆIC* PATH: THE *YOGA* OF THE GREAT SYMBOL[1]

### THE INTRODUCTION

#### I. THE HISTORY OF THE GREAT SYMBOL TEACHINGS

THERE has probably never been a gift from the East to the West more remarkable for its philosophical and religious history or of more value to the student of the science of mind-control called *yoga* than the present Book. It contains the quintessence of some of the most profound doctrines of Oriental Occultism. These, however, are not obsolete or forgotten doctrines, recovered from the ruins of a culture which has blossomed and died long ago, but doctrines which have been handed down to our own age through an unbroken succession of initiates.

Long before Christianity reached Europe, the teachings now embodied in *The Epitome of the Great Symbol* were being expounded to a chosen few among the learned Brāhmanas and Buddhists of ancient India. According to Tibetan tradition, derived from Indian sources, it is believed that the saintly Buddhist philosopher Saraha (whose exact date, historically speaking, is somewhat uncertain) enunciated the teachings in or about the first century B.C.; that already in his day they were ancient; and that he was thus merely one in a long and illustrious line of *gurus* who uninterruptedly had transmitted the teachings direct from the Great *Rishis*.

Through Saraha's chief disciple, the famous *guru* Nāgārjuna (see pp. 120[3], 344–6) and after him through his dis-

---

[1] The Tibetan block-print, upon which our translation is based, bears the following title : *PHYAG-CHEN GYI ZIN-BRIS BZHUGS-SO* (pronounced, *CHAG-CHEN GYI ZIN-DI ZHŪ-SO*), meaning, ' Herein Lieth the Epitome of the Great Symbol '.  Madame A. David-Neel has also given, in the Appendix to *Initiations and Initiates in Tibet* (pp. 213-20), a brief synopsis of the *Chag-Chen* teachings, of which our present Book II presents the first complete version in a European language.

ciples, it is said that the teachings continued to be transmitted, probably orally. Then in the eleventh century A.D.,
when Marpa, the founder of the Kargyütpa School, went
down to the plains of India from the Land of the Snowy
Ranges, his native Tibet, in search of Divine Wisdom, the
teachings were handed on to him by the learned Indian
Buddhist philosopher Naropa.

Naropa had been initiated into the Great Symbol teachings by Tilopa, who flourished about the middle of the tenth
century. Tilopa, according to Kargyütpa tradition (referred
to above, on p. 58), received the teachings, telepathically,
direct from the Ādi-Buddha, whom the Kargyütpas know as
Dorje-Chang, 'The Holder of the Thunderbolt of the Gods',
a mystical appellation symbolical of divine occult powers.

Inasmuch as the teachings appear to have been already in
existence in India long before the time of Tilopa, it would
probably be more literally correct to interpret this tradition
as really implying that Tilopa was telepathically inspired by
Dorje-Chang, the Divine Patron of the Kargyütpas, to transmit the teachings in such manner as to have them become, as
they did, the foundation teachings of the new succession of
Kargyütpa *Gurus* in Tibet. To this interpretation the late
Lāma Kazi Dawa-Samdup himself was more or less inclined.

The Kargyütpa Line of *Gurus*, of whom Tilopa was thus
the first on Earth and Dorje-Chang the Spiritual Head, has
been described in some historical detail in *Tibet's Great* Yogī
*Milarepa* (pp. 6–8), a work which is one of the best commentaries available in English for practical use in connexion
with our text of *The Epitome of the Great Symbol*. As a
result of having put to the test of practice the Great Symbol
teachings, Milarepa, who was Marpa's successor, attained to
Buddhahood in the course of a single lifetime, as the *Biography* relates ; and to-day he is regarded by Tibetan *yogins*
of all sects as one of the greatest masters of *yoga* known to
history.

According to the Blue Records,[1] one of the most reliable
of Tibetan histories, 'the Upper School' of the Great Symbol

---

[1] Tib. *Tep-ter-ngön-po*, vol. xi, folios 1–3.

Philosophy in Tibet produced three Tibetan versions of *The Great Symbol*, direct from Indian manuscript sources. The first was bequeathed by the teacher Nirupa. The second consists of two parts, the 'upper' and 'lower'. The 'upper' was produced by the Indian Chyagna (Tib. *Phyagna*) when he visited Tibet; the 'lower', by Asū, when he sojourned in the Province of Ü. Another and later translation was made by Nagpo Sherdad of Ngari, a Tibetan who visited India and there met Chyagna.

Atīsha, referred to above (on p. 99[2]) as the earliest of the renovators of Lāmaism, who arrived in Tibet from India in A.D. 1038, was the first teacher in Tibet to emphasize the *yogic* importance of the Great Symbol Philosophy; and we may assume that he himself, like Milarepa early in the following century, was a living exponent of the virtues which are born of its practical application. Dom, another teacher, produced an independent Tibetan version of *The Great Symbol*, but appears to have done little to propagate its doctrines. Marpa produced his own Tibetan version direct from Indian texts, presumably Sanskrit. Other *yogins* who are known to have produced Tibetan versions of *The Great Symbol* are Vairochana-Rakshita, Nirupa, and Rechung, author of Milarepa's *Biography*. Our epitomized and purified version was compiled by Padma-Karpo, during the seventeenth century, after he had compared the numerous and more or less corrupt versions current in the Tibet of his day. Of it he has written, in the Colophon, 'Seeing that unauthorized interpolations, all purporting to be extracts from various portions of the Scriptures [which had crept into the text], were in most cases, unreliable, I, Padma-Karpo, [expurgated them]'.

Thus, from prehistoric times, the teachings which are now crystallized in *The Epitome of the Great Symbol* have been bequeathed, so it is credibly believed, from one generation of *gurus* to another, and thence to our generation.

## II. THE TEXT AND THE TRANSLATION

The text of *The Epitome of the Great Symbol* which we have used in preparing this Book was transmitted in accordance with the ancient and inviolable rule of transmission to the late Lāma Kazi Dawa-Samdup (b. 1868, d. 1922) by his *guru*, the late Hermit-Lāma Norbu of Buxaduar, Bhutan. I, the editor, received it, in turn, from the late Lāma Kazi Dawa-Samdup, my own *guru*, who has herein produced the first translation of it to appear in a European tongue, as he himself said, 'for the benefit of the non-Tibetan peoples of the world'.

As the Colophon relates, the Kashmiri King Zhanphan Zangpo is said to have presented to his *guru*, Padma-Karpo, more than twenty measures of saffron for the compilation of this text and that of *The Six Doctrines*, a complementary system of practical *yoga*, of which an English rendering is contained in Book III, following. Estimating eighty *tolas* to a *seer* and four *seers* to a measure, we find that the King's gift was in excess of 6,400 *tolas* of saffron. At the present time one *tola* of the best saffron is worth about one rupee and a half, so that the kingly gift would to-day be worth more than 9,600 rupees. Taking the rupee to be worth eighteen pence, this sum would equal £720 or about $3,600, at par value.

The text translated by us is an exact copy of the text of *The Epitome of the Great Symbol* as thus prepared for the Kashmiri King, its subsequent history being as follows: During the seventeenth century, Padma-Karpo, or, as his name means, the 'Omniscient White Lotus', went to Bhutan from Tibet and renovated Bhutanese Lāmaism in much the same manner as Atīsha, the teacher from India, renovated the Lāmaism of Tibet six centuries earlier. Padma-Karpo carried with him into Bhutan a duplicate copy of the text of *The Epitome* which he had prepared at the King's command. Then some time afterwards, or about one hundred and fifty years ago as nearly as can be ascertained, Chögyal-Sodnam-Gyaltshan donated one silver coin for the carving of each wooden block of type of the text, 'for the purpose of multiplying the gift of religion', as we learn from the last line of the Colophon.

Our own Tibetan text, in block-print form, is a copy

printed from these same blocks. It consists of seven large folios of two pages each, including the title-page ; and for each page one block of carved type was employed. Thus, for the making of the blocks, fourteen silver coins were given by the pious donor.

These block-types lay in the State Monastery of Bhutan, at Punakha, the capital. Then, shortly after the time when our copy was printed off from them, they, together with the printing-house containing them, were destroyed by a conflagration resulting from a Bhutanese civil war.

How our text came into the possession of the translator is best told in his own words: ' From December, 1887, until October, 1893, I was stationed at Buxaduar, in Bhutan, near the frontier of India, as interpreter to the British Government ; and it was there, during the first part of that period, that I encountered my *guru*. He was commonly known as the Hermit *Guru* Norbu (Tib. *Slob-dpon-Mtshams-pa-Nor-bu*, pronounced, *Lob-on-Tsham-pa-Nor-bu*), Norbu itself meaning " Gem ". The name which he received at the time of his initiation was " [He of] Good Fame " (Tib. *Snyan-grags-bzang-po* : pronounced *Nyam-da-zang-po*).

' Shortly after he had accepted me as his *shiṣhya*, I received from him the teachings contained in *The Epitome of the Great Symbol*, with appropriate initiation and guiding instructions.

' He then possessed three block-print copies of *The Epitome*. One of these, which he gave to me upon my parting from him in 1893, was lost. Very probably it was carried away without my permission from Gangtok, whither at the beginning of 1906 I was called, by the then Mahārāja of Sikkim, to the head-mastership of the Bhutia Boarding School, a Sikkimese State institution, in which post I have since remained. In February, 1916, I visited my *guru* to pay him my respects and to obtain from him spiritual authority and assistance to translate for Sir John Woodroffe (pseudonym Arthur Avalon, editor of *Tantrik Texts*) the *Dēmchog Tantra*.[1]

---

[1] This translation was made and published in volume vii of Tantrik Texts, edited by Arthur Avalon, London and Calcutta, 1919.

At the same time I also obtained from him permission to translate *The Epitome of the Great Symbol* and other similar *yogic* treatises, which, like *The Epitome*, are considered too precious and sacred to give out to the world without authoritative sanction. In granting this permission, he said to me, "There are very few amongst the upgrowing generation of our own people who will care to strive earnestly for spiritual development. Therefore it seems to me that these sublime truths will make more appeal to truth-seekers in Europe and in America."

'That was the last talk I had with my *guru*. Eight months later, at the age of about 78 years, in October 1916, he passed out of our world ripe in knowledge.

'When the visit neared its end and I was about to take final leave of my *guru* he gave to me, as a farewell gift, his own copy of *The Epitome*, knowing that I had lost the copy which he had given to me previously. Strange to relate, this copy also disappeared. The third and last of the copies of *The Epitome* my *guru* had presented to one of his disciples living in Buxaduar ; and the copy whence our translation has been made is this very copy, which I obtained from the disciple by post. So far as I am aware, there is no other copy in existence, not even in Bhūtan.

'A few words concerning the life of my *guru* may prove to be interesting. He was by birth a native of Bhutan, descended of an old and respected family long known for its ardent support of the Faith of the Buddha. His maternal uncle was abbot of the State Monastery of Bhutan, to which institution the block-type of *The Epitome of the Great Symbol* belonged. As a boy, he was dedicated to the Buddhist priesthood by his parents ; and his uncle, the abbot, becoming his *guru*, he passed his novitiate and received his education within that monastery.

'Not only did he become the rightful heir to his uncle's worldly possessions, but was also entitled to assume the abbotship of the monastery at the death of his uncle-*guru*. In the Bhutan of his day communal strife being so common that even the legal and religious rights of Buddhist priests were often violated by selfish laymen, it happened that Norbu's right to inherit his uncle's property was disputed by certain worldly minded head-men of Punakha. In order that the monastery wherein his boyhood and early manhood had been passed might not suffer by reason of a prolongation of the dispute, Norbu left it, renouncing all the property and also the abbotship, and went into hermitage near Buxaduar, where I found him and took him as my *guru*.

'Norbu was a life-long *brahmachārin* (i.e. he had kept inviolate the monastic vow of chastity) and a fully ordained *bhikṣhu* (i.e. a Buddhist priest, or monk, who has renounced the world in order to devote himself to the service of humanity, with no fixed habitation, and dependent upon charity for maintenance). He was of kindly and strong personality and fervent faith, whose eyes had seen beyond the limits of normal human vision. By his death I have been left without a *guru*.'

After the late Lāma Kazi Dawa-Samdup and myself had completed the translation of the *Bardo Thödol* (published as *The Tibetan Book of the Dead*, Oxford University Press, 1927) and other Tibetan works while we were together in Gangtok, Sikkhim, he introduced me to the teachings of *The Great Symbol* and suggested the translation of its *Epitome*, our actual text. We began the translation on the 23rd of July 1919, and completed the first draft of it, rather rapidly for such a difficult task, on the 31st of the same month. When the whole was finished, after subsequent revision, the Lāma, as translator and teacher, addressed to me this statement, which I recorded in writing :

'I had hoped on more than one occasion to translate this text of *The Epitome of the Great Symbol*, but the sublime nature of the subject-matter, together with my lack of knowledge of the phraseology of European and modern philosophy, which is essential for the production of an intelligible English rendering, deterred me. My earnest desire thus remained unfulfilled until now, when, through your aid, it has been realized. Therefore do I rejoice at having been able to carry out the injunctions of my *guru* to transmit this precious teaching to the world—especially to the educated and thinking men and women of Europe and America.'

### III. THE CHARACTER OF THE GREAT SYMBOL TEACHINGS

The Great Symbol, known in Tibetan as the *Ch'ag-ch'en*,[1] equivalent to the Sanskrit *Mahā-Mudrā* ('Great *Mudrā*', or 'Great Attitude', or, as the translator preferred, in its correlation with the Tibetan, 'Great Symbol'), is the written guide to the method of attaining, by means of *yoga*, such mental concentration, or one-pointedness of mind (Skt. *ekāgrata*), as brings about mystical insight into the real nature of existence. It is also called 'The Middle Path' (Tib. *Ümai-Lam*), since it avoids the two extremes which the Buddha in all his teachings opposes, the extreme of ascetical mortification of the body on the one hand and of worldliness, or licentiousness, on the other. By following the *yogic* teachings conveyed by *The Epitome of the Great Symbol*, one sets oneself consciously upon the Path whose Goal is *Nirvaṇā*—Emancipation from the thraldom of the Wheel of Nature, from the interminable round of deaths and births.

These teachings, as conveyed by our text, having been handed down for many generations in Tibetan, both orally and in manuscript, have been more or less influenced by Tibetan Buddhism. Their fundamentally *yogic* character is, however, unchanged, as comparison with similar systems of *yoga* still being taught by *gurus* in India will show.

Swāmi Satyānanda, himself a practising *yogin*, and the head of a small school of *yoga* situated on the Ganges, at Birbhaddar, near Rikhikesh, United Provinces, India, has, at my request, critically examined our translation; and, although he is inclined to disagree with certain of the non-essential details of the Great Symbol system, considers it, in its essentials, as of more than ordinary value. He says of it, 'It describes three chief methods of training the mind : (1) by means of visualization, (2) by use of the *Dorje* Recitation to control the breathing,

---

[1] Tib. *Phyag-rgya-ch'en-po*, usually contracted to *Phyag-ch'en*, pronounced *ch'ag-ch'en*.

and (3) by separating the mind from the link of the breathing through using the process of pot-shaping the body.

'I cannot but state that *The Epitome of the Great Symbol* is the only work known to me which offers just this sort of *yogic* instruction. Had I seen the work before writing my *Anubhūta Yoga Sādhan* (Calcutta, 1916) much of the time spent by me in discovering the genuine method of *Prānāyāma* (i.e. *yogic* control of the *prāna*, by means of *yogically* regulating the breathing or vitality of the human body) would have been saved.'

As the Swāmi also rightly observes, our text assumes that the *Yoga* of the Great Symbol will be practised only under the personal guidance of a competent *guru*. Accordingly, some details of instruction are omitted from the text, the *guru* being expected to supply them. This, too, is, in large measure, true of all systems of *yoga* which have been reduced to writing, Patanjali's *Yoga Sūtras* being a classic example. No manual of *yoga* is ever intended to be anything more than a summarized outline of teachings which were originally oral. More often than not it is merely a series of suggestive notes dictated by a *guru* to his *shishya* (or disciple) for the *shishya's* private guidance at such times as the *guru's* personal attention cannot be expected, as for instance, when the *shishya* (otherwise known as the *chela*) has temporarily gone into solitary retreat for purposes of practically applying the instructions.

The Swāmi ends his criticism as follows: 'This treatise deserves the attention of all who are unable to practise *yoga* in the regular way. Its theoretical portion, concerning tranquillity of mind, should be highly useful to them. It matters little whether one practises immobility of body and immobility of speech or not, or whether one's mind be separated from the link of the breathing or not ; one can easily follow the process of tranquillizing the mind, and this process, if conscientiously followed, alone is sufficient to bestow upon its practitioner an unimaginable peace, that peace which passes all mundane understanding.'

### IV.  THE LINE OF THE *GURUS*

The Indian, or parent, Line of the *Gurus* of the Great Symbol teachings, which, in the Obeisance of our text, is called the White Dynasty [or Line], can be, as we have observed, traditionally traced from the first century B.C. to the time of Marpa, who established the Tibetan branch of it during the latter half of the eleventh century A.D.  There is, therefore, an unbroken history of the doctrine, in one form or another, for about two thousand years.  According to the traditional lore of the Kargyütpas, this history also extends backward into the pre-Christian era for unknown centuries.

Marpa, the first of the Tibetan *Gurus* of the Line, is said to have passed eighteen years as a *shishya* in India, and to have consulted about one hundred learned Indian philosophers. His Tibetan version of *The Great Symbol* must, therefore, have been based upon the most authoritative text procurable in his time.

Whether the Indian Line of the *Gurus* of the Great Symbol School survived the foreign invasions and resultant social and religious upheavals which intervened between the days of Marpa's sojourn in India and our own epoch we have been unable to determine.  It may well be that the text of *The Great Symbol* has become lost in the land of its origin, like so many other Indian texts, and survives only in Tibetan translations.

The Tibetan branch of the White Line of *Gurus* is, philosophically considered, distinct from all other Tibetan Lines or Schools ; it is commonly known as the *Kargyütpa*, which means, 'Followers of the Apostolic Succession'.  From the time of Marpa till to-day the Great Symbol mode of mystical insight (Tib. *Ta-wa*) has been fundamental in Kargyütpa philosophy and systems of ascetic practices.

Milarepa, the successor of Marpa, was a wandering ascetic, who lived for many years as a hermit in rock caverns amidst the most unfrequented solitudes of the high snow-clad mountains of Tibet, where, through mastery of the *yoga* of *The Great Symbol*, he developed supernormal powers of a most wonderful sort, as told in his *Biography*. To Milarepa, the saintly and successful mystic, more than to Marpa, the scholar-transmitter of Indian lore, the Kargyütpas owe their origin as a sect of practical *yogins* which is to-day still flourishing.

In addition to his two most prominent disciples, Dvagpo-Lharje and Rechung, Milarepa is reputed to have developed eight other disciples to adeptship in *yoga* ; 108 others to mastery of the science of generating vital-heat (Tib. *Tŭmmō*), so that clad in only a cotton cloth, the dress of all Kargyütpa *yogins*, they were immune to the severe cold of the Tibetan winter ; and to have set numerous other disciples, male and female, on the Path of *Bodhic* Enlightenment. In Rechung's words, ' By the virtue of his mighty grace and good wishes, he left behind him saintly disciples as numerous as the stars in the sky. The number of those who were never to return to *sangsāric* [or worldly] existence was like the grains of sand on the Earth. Of male and female who had entered the Path, there were countless numbers.' [1]

Dvagpo-Lharje, as already shown above, in Book I, became Milarepa's successor and the third of the human *gurus* of the Kargyütpa Line. Thence the Line of the White *Gurus* continued until, twenty-fourth in direct succession from Marpa, there came the *Guru* Padma-Karpo, the author of our text of *The Epitome of the Great Symbol*. It is by his initiatory name, ' The Gem Possessing Power of [Divine] Speech ' (Tib. *Ngag-Dvang-Nor-bu*, pronounced *Ngag-Wang-Nor-bu*), that Padma-Karpo is better known in the records of the Kargyütpa Hierarchy.

As Head of the Hierarchy of the White Line of *Gurus*, otherwise known as the Kargyütpa Line, Padma-Karpo undoubtedly enjoyed access to the various Tibetan manuscript texts of *The Great Symbol*, together with their emendations and commentaries, which had accumulated during the course of the six centuries since the days of Marpa. Therefrom, as the Colophon of our text makes known, Padma-Karpo, at the wish of his royal disciple, the Kashmiri King, extracted

[1] Cf. *Tibet's Great Yogi Milarepa*, p. 304.

the essentials and compiled *The Epitome of the Great Symbol* exactly as we have it.

According to reliable traditions, the King went to Padma-Karpo as a pilgrim, and renouncing both his kingdom and the world, even as did the Royal Prince Siddhartha Who became the Buddha Gautama, was accepted by Padma-Karpo as a *shishya* on probation. After the kingly ascetic had passed a number of years in study and *yogic* practice under the *Guru*, he returned to Kashmir as a Buddhist monk, and seems to have established there a Kashmiri hierarchy of the White Line. The late Lāma Kazi Dawa-Samdup was of opinion that possibly there may be some account of such a Kashmiri Line in records preserved in the Himis Monastery in Ladāk, this monastery having historical relationship with the Kargyütpa School through the dissenting sects of Kargyütpas which grew up in Bhutan.

Following our text, the place of Padma-Karpo's *yogic* retreat was in the southernmost part of Tibet near the frontiers of what is now the State of Bhutan. There, too, the King probably made his valuable gift of more than twenty measures of saffron, brought, no doubt, from Kashmir, the Land of Saffron.

To-day, Padma-Karpo is the chief authority concerning the Tantric lore of the Kargyütpa School. His writings comprise standard works on astrology, medicine, grammar, history, rituals, art, philosophy, metaphysics, and occultism. He is credited with having compiled and edited some fifty-two to fifty-eight volumes. He was also a noted poet, and his mystical rhapsodies are well known throughout Bhutan, being published in a popular work called *The Rosary of Divine Hymns* (Tib. *Rdo-rje-glu-Hpreng*, pronounced *Do-rje-lu-Hteng*). He was a contemporary of the Fifth Dalai Lāma, who died in the year 1680.[1]

In the time of Padma-Karpo, the small Himālayan kingdom of Bhutan was a land even less known than Tibet. Its indigenous inhabitants were in a low cultural condition and much given to brigandage and intestine strife. Then, towards the end of the seventeenth century, there came into Bhutan,

[1] Cf. Sir Charles Bell, *Tibet Past and Present* (London, 1924), p. 37.

from the Ralung Monastery of Tibet, a succeeding *guru* of the White Line who was destined to continue and bring to a successful issue the spiritual purification initiated by Padma-Karpo. It is said that his remarkable sanctity shone like a sun in the midst of darkness. In virtue of his unusual religious powers, he gained such ascendancy over the Bhutanese that they gladly accepted him as their first *Dharma Rāja*, or Divine King, and he became known to them as [He of] the Victorious Power of Speech, The Irresistible Destroyer of Illusion (Tib. *Ngag-dvang-Rnam-rgyal-Bdud-hjoms-Rdo-rje*, pronounced *Ngag-wang-Nam-gyal-Dü-jum-Do-rje*). Through him, in turn, and thence onwards to the Hermit *Guru* Norbu, the teachings of *The Great Symbol* continued to be fostered and handed on.

Such, then, is the interesting history of *The Great Symbol*, and of our *Epitome* of it, and of the White Line of *Gurus*, whence these teachings have been transmitted to us. It was the earnest desire of the translator that all who read this Book sympathetically may thereby be assisted, even though but little, to partake of the spiritual inheritance which it offers, to enter the Path, and, ultimately, to reach the Supreme Goal.

## WORDS OF THE BUDDHA FROM THE PĀLI CANON

'As in the Great Ocean, O disciples, there is but one taste, the taste of salt, so, O disciple, in the doctrine which I preach unto you, there is but one taste, the taste of Deliverance.

*    *    *

'This people, who differentiate themselves, having attained existence, sunk in existence, praise in existence.

*    *    *

'Behold this variegated world, sunk in ignorance, full of pleasure-loving beings unemancipated.

*    *    *

'Should a man not exert himself on every occasion, not exist for another, not live for the sake of others, truly, he doth not live the holy life.

*    *    *

'The Wheel is broken; the Desireless is attained.
The river-bed is dry; no water floweth;
No more the broken wheel will roll.
This is the end of Sorrow.'
From the *Udāna*
(Maj.-Gen. D. M. Strong's Translation.)

# [THE *NIRVĀṆIC* PATH: THE *YOGA* OF THE GREAT SYMBOL]

## [THE OBEISANCE]

(1) Obeisance to the Precious White Dynasty [of *Gurus*]!

## [THE FOREWORD]

(2) Herein, in the expounding of this Guide, called ' The *Yoga* of the Simultaneously-born Great Symbol ',[1] intended for setting the ordinary continuity of the Knower face to face with the pure Divine Wisdom,[2] are the preliminary instructions, the essential subject-matter, and the conclusion.

## [PART I: THE PRELIMINARY INSTRUCTIONS]

(3) The preliminary instructions are both temporal and spiritual.

(4) The temporal instructions, which come first, are made clear elsewhere.[3]

---

[1] When, in virtue of having practised *yogic* meditation, there has been established communion between the human mind and the divine mind, or between the normal human consciousness and the supernormal cosmic consciousness, man attains to true understanding of himself. He realizes intuitively that the Knower, and all objects of knowledge, or all knowing, are inseparably a unity; and simultaneously with this realization there is born the Great Symbol, which occultly signifies this spiritual illumination. Like a philosopher's stone, the Great Symbol purges from the mind the dross of Ignorance (*Avidyā*); and the human is transmuted into the divine by the spiritual alchemy of *yoga*.

[2] Our present text is called a ' Guide ', for it directs the religious pilgrim on the Path leading to complete *Nirvāṇic* Enlightenment and Emancipation. Not until the lower self has been absorbed into the higher self can the illusion of personality be broken, and not until then can the continuity of the Knower be realized as having no beginning and no ending, as being eternally in at-one-ness with the All-Knowledge. It is thus that the human is raised to the divine and set face to face with the pure Divine Wisdom.

[3] The temporal instructions are those conveyed by sermons intended to direct laymen to the higher way of life. Once the decision is reached to take the first step on the Path, the disciple no longer has need of the temporal or exoteric instructions, and he begins to acquire those which are spiritual, or, in relation to the unenlightened multitude who are mentally unable to understand them, esoteric.

## [*THE REFUGE, THE RESOLUTION, AND THE COMMUNION WITH THE* GURUS]

(5) In the spiritual instructions, which come next, the initial steps are to begin with the Refuge and the Resolution and to lead up to the Communion with the *Gurus*.[1]

## [*THE SEVEN BODILY POSTURES*[2]]

(6) Then, as hath been written in *The Realizing of Vairochana*,[3]

---

[1] This part of the instructions may be adjusted, if necessary, to the religious inclinations of the disciple. A Hindu *yogin*, for instance, would probably substitute for the Buddhistic ritual, herein implied, a similar ritual from his own sect, or else use none at all, as did a Brāhmin *yogin* at Rikhikesh, on the Upper Ganges, from whom I received some *yogic* guidance. Being the most noble historic example of One Who gained the Supreme Victory, the Buddha Gautama is rightly regarded by Buddhists as the Refuge and Guide, in Whom the disciple at the beginning of the Path, which He Himself trod, should repose faith. For the neophyte, faith is the first essential. Without faith that there is a Goal which can be attained, the initial step on the Path would be impossible. Therefore, the preliminary rule is that the neophyte must, at the very beginning of the spiritual journey, give appropriate form to the expression of this faith. In conforming to this rule, the Buddhist of Tibet employs a fivefold ritual, as follows :

(*a*) The Refuge in its long Tibetan form. The first and essential part of it, which resembles the short Triple Refuge of the Southern Buddhist, runs thus :

‘ Through the intercession of the *Guru*, we (i.e. all beings) go for refuge to the Buddha.

We go for refuge to the Buddha’s Doctrine.

We go for refuge to the Assembly of the Lāmas.’

(*b*) The Resolution in its shortened form : ‘ I resolve to become a Buddha in order that I may be enabled to aid all sentient beings to attain to Buddhahood.’

(*c*) The Meditation on the Dhyānī Buddha Vajra-Sattva (Tib. Dorje-Sempa) ; and the Recitation of the *Mantra of One Hundred Syllables*, for the expiation of evil *karma*.

(*d*) The Offering up of the Universe in mystic sacrifice ; which, in this connexion, signifies the renunciation of the world and of the *Sangsāra* as a whole.

(*e*) The communion with the *Gurus*, by visualizing the *Gurus* as being seated in *yogic* posture and in a perpendicular line, one directly above the other, the human *guru* hovering over the disciple’s head, and the others in their due order of apostolic succession, with the celestial *guru*, Vajra-Dhara (Tib. Dorje-chang), topmost.  (See pp. 266 [1], 274-6.)

[2] In Sanskrit these are known as *āsanas*. They cut off, or short-circuit, certain bodily forces or currents, and thus greatly assist in practising *yoga*. They also make the body pliant and capable of great endurance, eliminate undesirable physical conditions, cure illnesses, and calm the functioning organs and the mind.

[3] Text : *Rnam-snang-ngön-byang* (pronounced : *Nam-nang-ngön-jang*), the

'Straighten the body and assume the *Dorje*-Posture; [1]
One-pointedness of mind is [the path leading to] the
Great Symbol.'

(7) [Accordingly], place the feet in the Buddha-Posture.[2]
Place the hands level and equipoised below the navel.[3]
Straighten the spinal column. Throw out the diaphragm.[4]
Bend the neck to the shape of a hook, the chin just pressing
against the Adam's apple.[5] Place the tongue upward against
the roof of the mouth.[6]

title of a Tibetan treatise on *yoga*, intended to guide to the realization that all
phenomena are illusory. Vairochana (Tib. Nampar-nangzad) is the Dhyānī
Buddha of the Centre. (See p. 339 [1].) He here symbolizes the *Dharma-Dhātu*,
or Fundamental Wisdom. By putting oneself into spiritual communion with
Vairochana, the true nature of existence is realizable. (Cf. p. 212 [2].)

[1] The *dorje* is the *lāmaic* sceptre; and the *Dorje*-Posture (or *Āsana*) is a
posture of equilibrium, both mentally and physically, symbolized by the *dorje*'s
equipoise.

[2] Lit., 'Place the feet in the posture of the *dorje*', i.e. the cross-legged
posture in which the Buddha is commonly imaged, called by the Hindus the
lotus-posture (Skt. *Padmāsana*). (See Illustration facing p. 101.)

[3] In this posture, which is the posture of meditation, the hands are held open,
with the palms upward and horizontal, just below the level of the navel, the
middle finger of one hand touching that of the other hand at the tip and the
thumbs folded at the base of the index fingers.

[4] Or, 'Throw the breast forward, with the shoulders backward'.

[5] Lit., 'the knot', i.e. the 'Adam's apple'.

[6] Swāmi Satyānanda, who is referred to in the Introduction, considers this
passage incomplete in its directions. He writes, in criticism of it : 'The tongue
should really be placed, not against the roof of the mouth, but be turned upward
in such manner that the tip shall reach the hook-like formations at the beginning
of the internal nostril openings and by pressing against them plug the openings.
This practice is known as *Khechari Mudrā*. Without it the *yogin* cannot realize
the tranquil state at the time of practising *āsana*; but until the beginner has
made certain progress in *yoga*, the *Khechari Mudrā* is not to be employed.' To
practise the *Khechari Mudrā*, the tongue itself must first be trained; and, in
most cases, gradually lengthened. The lengthening is brought about by massag-
ing and stretching the tongue. It is also usually necessary for most *yogins* who
wish to practise this *Mudrā* to sever, little by little, over a period of months,
the membrane on the tongue's lower surface which holds the tongue at the
centre, known as the *fraenum linguae*. *Yogins*, by this means, like animals
which hibernate by closing their internal nostril openings with their tongue,
acquire the power of suspending the vital processes of the body. This results
in conservation of energy and longevity, but of itself is not conducive to
spiritual advancement. The *yogic* short-circuiting of the purely physical and
animal functions of the body should be made use of only as an aid to the conquest of the lower self.

(8) Ordinarily the intellect is controlled by the senses. It is the sight which chiefly controlleth it. [Therefore], without winking the eyes, or moving, focus the gaze to the distance of about five and one-half feet.[1]

(9) These [i.e. the seven postures described above] are called the Seven Methods of Vairochana [i.e. the seven means of understanding psycho-physical processes]. They constitute the fivefold method of inducing deep meditation by physical means.[2]

## [*THE EFFECTS OF THE SEVEN BODILY POSTURES*]

(10) The crossed-leg posture regulateth the inspiration.[3] The posture of equilibrium equalizeth the vital-heat of the body.[4] The straightening of the spinal column together with the expanding of the diaphragm regulate the nervous fluid pervading the body.[5] The bending of the neck regulateth the expiration.[6] The placing of the tongue against the roof of the mouth together with the focusing of the gaze cause the vital-force[7] to enter into the median-nerve.[8]

(11) The five 'airs' thus having been made to enter into the median-nerve, the other function-controlling 'airs'[9] also enter into it, and there dawneth the Wisdom of Non-Cogni-

---

[1] Lit., 'to the distance of a yoke'. The yoke being an Indian measure based on the width of a yoke for a pair of oxen, the distance is thus approximately five and one-half feet.

[2] The paragraph which follows expounds this fivefold method; and paragraph 11, following, expounds the result attained.

[3] Lit., ' the downward-moving air'.

[4] Lit., 'the warmth-equalizing air'.

[5] Lit., ' the air called the pervader'.

[6] Lit., 'the upward-moving air'.

[7] Lit., 'the life-holding air'. In each of these five references, 'air' refers to a function-controlling energy of the body, for which there is no exact equivalent in the language of European physiology. In Sanskrit it is known as *prāna*. (See *The Tibetan Book of the Dead*, pp. 214-15.)

[8] This is the principal channel for the influx of the vital-force. It extends through the centre of the spinal column. Subsidiary psychic-nerves branch off from it and distribute to each of the psychic-centres (Skt. *chakra*) the vital, or *prānic*, force, upon which all psycho-physical processes ultimately depend. (See *ibid.*, pp. 215-17.)

[9] These are such as control the processes of digestion, secretion, circulation, transmission of mental impulses, sensations, &c. (See *ibid.*, p. 215.)

tion, otherwise known as bodily tranquillity, or immobility of body, or the body abiding in its natural state.[1]

### [*THE TRANQUILLITY OF SPEECH*]

(12) The observing of silence, after having cast out the dead breath [of expiration], is called the tranquillity or immobility of speech, or the speech abiding in its natural state.

(13) Think not of the past. Think not of the future. Think not that thou art actually engaged in meditation. Regard not the Void as being Nothingness.[2]

(14) At this stage do not attempt to analyse any of the impressions felt by the five senses, saying, 'It is ; it is not.'[3] But at least for a little while observe unbroken meditation, keeping the body as calm as that of a sleeping babe, and the mind in its natural state [i.e. free of all thought-processes].

### [*THE TRANQUILLITY OF MIND*]

(15) It hath been said,

' By entirely refraining from forming thoughts and mental visualizations,

By maintaining the bodily calmness of a sleeping babe,

And endeavouring meekly and zealously to follow the *guru*'s authorized teachings

There will undoubtedly arise the Simultaneously-born State.'[4]

(16) Tilopa hath said,

' Do not imagine, do not think, do not analyse,

Do not meditate, do not reflect ;

Keep the mind in its natural state.'

---

[1] The natural state of the body, as of all things, is a state of perfect tranquillity.

[2] The Void (Tib. *Tong-pa-nyid*; Skt. *Shūnyatā*) is not the void of nothingness, but the Thatness, the Norm of Being, the Cause and Origin of all that constitutes finiteness. Since It cannot be described in terms of phenomenal or *sangsāric* experience, the unenlightened alone regard It as being nothingness.

[3] The *Bodhic* Path is the ' Middle Path ', devoid of such extremes of positiveness and negativeness as these two assertions imply. (Cf. p. 143[1].)

[4] This is the realization aimed at by the practice of the Great Symbol *Yoga*, as shown above.

(17) The Master of Doctrines, the Lunar Radiant Youth,[1] hath said,

'Undistractedness is the Path followed by all the Buddhas.'

(18) This is what is called mental tranquillity, immobility of mind, or the mind abiding in its natural state.[2]

## [*THE FOUR RECOLLECTIONS*]

(19) Nāgārjuna [3] hath said,

'O mighty one,[4] The Four Recollections [5]
Having been shown to be unmistakably the sole Path
traversed by the Buddhas,[6]

[1] These titles, as contained in our text, refer to Gampopa, otherwise known as Dvagpo-Lharje, Milarepa's chief disciple and immediate spiritual successor, the compiler of the precepts forming the subject-matter of Book I, above.

[2] Lit., 'abiding in its own place'. Undistractedness implies perfect tranquillity of body, speech, and mind ; the body, speech, and mind, according to this *yoga*, being inseparably interdependent. In this connexion it should be noted that the word *naldjor* (*rnal-byor*), the Tibetan equivalent of the Sanskrit word *yoga*, unlike the word *yoga*, does not signify 'union', but 'complete mental tranquillity', and, therefore, 'mastery in contemplation'.

[3] According to *lāmaic* tradition, Nāgārjuna is believed to have been born during the first century B.C., or about four centuries after the *Pari-Nirvāna* of the Buddha ; and to have lived for six hundred years. His work in the world extended into the second and third centuries A.D. Thereafter he is said to have gone into a secret retreat in Southern India, whence he spiritually directed, as a *guru*, his beloved friend and patron, the Indian King to whom the advice contained in the verses which follow was originally given. Nāgārjuna was the first great exponent of the Mādhyamika Philosophy, which profoundly influenced Tibetan Buddhism and was finally crystallized in the great canonical work of Northern Buddhism known as the *Prajñā-Pāramitā*. (See Book VII.)

[4] Nāgārjuna is addressing the Indian Buddhist King, Vikramāditya (Udyana), known in Tibetan as Dechöd-Zangpo, with a view to impressing upon him the importance of keeping the mind fixed upon 'The Four Recollections' (comparable to 'The Four *Smritis*' of the Hindus), which may be classified as recollection of the need of mastery (1) of the body, (2) of the senses, and (3) of the mind, and (4) of the need of maintaining incessant watchfulness over these means of action, called 'the doors of action'.

[5] Lit., 'the recollection of the knowledge of the body', with reference to 'The Four Recollections'.

[6] Lit., 'Those Who have passed on to Happiness' : Tib. *Bde-gshe-gs* (pron. *De-shay*) : Skt. *Sūgata*.

Do thou maintain zealous watchfulness over them at all
times;
Through carelessness herein, all spiritual efforts become
fruitless.'

(20) The mental state of this recollecting is undistractedness. It hath been defined in the *Abhidharma*[1] thus: 'Recollecting is the non-forgetting of things with which one hath
been familiar.'

[Here endeth Part I: the Preliminary Instructions.]

## (21) PART II: THE ESSENTIAL SUBJECT-
MATTER

This hath two parts: the Ordinary Practices [or Teach-
ings], and the Extra-ordinary Practices.[2]

### [*THE ORDINARY PRACTICES*]

(22) The first, the Practice of the Ordinary [Teachings],
also hath two parts:

Seeking Experience of the State of Quiescence [of Body,
Speech, and Mind], which is the aim of meditation, through
practising the *Yoga* of One-pointedness;[3]

Analysing the Essential Nature of the 'Moving' and the
'Non-Moving',[4] through practising the *Yoga* of the Uncreated,[5]
and thus realizing supramundane consciousness.[6]

---

[1] In Pāli, *Abidhamma*. (See p. 343.)

[2] The goal of the ordinary practices is spiritual blissfulness within the
*Sangsāra*, in heaven worlds. The goal of the extra-ordinary practices is
*Nirvāṇa*, beyond all heavens, worlds, and states of *sangsāric* existence.

[3] Text: *Rtse-gchig* (pronounced *Tse-chig*): Skt. *Ekāgrata*, meaning 'One-
pointedness [of mind]', with reference to intense mental concentration upon
a single object or thought. (Cf. p. 329[1].)

[4] The 'Non-Moving' is the Supramundane Mind, the Spectator of the
phenomena of nature, which are the 'Moving', or the Transitory. As will be
seen later on in this treatise, the 'Moving' is represented by thoughts which
arise and vanish.

[5] Text: *Sprös-bral* (pron. *Tö-dal*), meaning, 'separate from creation', i.e.
the Uncreated, or *Nirvāṇa*, as contrasted with the *Sangsāra*, or universe of
matter and phenomena. The *Yoga* of the Uncreated is the method of realizing
the Uncreated *Nirvāṇa*.

[6] Or, in other words, the *Nirvāṇic*, or Supra-*sangsāric* Consciousness.

[THE FIRST OF THE ORDINARY PRACTICES: THE *YOGA*
OF ONE-POINTEDNESS]

(23) The first of these two parts, namely, Seeking Experience of the State of Quiescence, which is the aim of meditation, through practising the *Yoga* of One-pointedness, may be practised either with or without an object [upon which to concentrate]. If an object be used, it may be a breathing or a non-breathing object.

### [THE USE OF NON-BREATHING OBJECTS]

(24) Two classes of non-breathing objects are prescribed: Ordinary Objects, like a small ball or a small bit of wood;[1] Holy Objects, like [symbolizations of] the bodily form, the speech [or word], and the mind [or thought] of the Buddha.

### [THE CONCENTRATING UPON A SMALL BALL OR BIT OF WOOD]

(25) The method of using those of the former class, namely, an ordinary object like a small ball or a small bit of wood, now followeth.

(26) Place a small ball, or a small bit of wood,[2] in front of thee as an object upon which to concentrate thy thought. Do not permit the 'Knower'[3] either to stray from or attempt to identify itself with it; but fix thy gaze upon the object one-pointedly.

(27) Meditate upon thy *guru* as being [seated] upon the crown of thy head.[4] Regard him as being, in reality, the Buddha. Pray to him, using the *Manam-khama*[5] Prayer.

---

[1] The ball may be of any substance, wood, bone, metal, clay, glass, or crystal; and the bit of wood may be of any shape.

[2] Very often this is a common stick, set up by placing a sharpened end of it in the ground of the cave or place of meditation.

[3] Text: *Shes-pa* (pron. *She-pa*): 'Mind', 'Knower', i.e. the mind in its knowing, or cognizing, functions.

[4] On the crown of the head, just at the junction of the parietal bones of the skull, is situated the 'Aperture of Brahma (Skt. *Brahmarandhra*)', whence, according to *yogic* teachings, the consciousness-principle normally goes out of the body, either permanently at death, or temporarily in *samādhic* trance. The visualization of the *guru* as being seated upon the crown of the head thus has esoteric significance for the *yogin*. (See p. 266[1].)

[5] Text: *Ma-nam-mkhah-ma* (pron. *Ma-nam-kha-ma*). This has reference to mothers being as infinite in number as are the heavens in expanse. Mothers

[And add this request to thy prayer]: 'Vouchsafe me Thy "gift-waves" that I may attain the highest boon of the Great Symbol'.[1]

(28) Then, having prayed for the boon-conferring 'gift-waves', absorb them into thyself. Think that thy mind is blended with the Divine Mind [of the *Gurus*].[2] And remain in that state of [mental] at-one-ment as long as possible.

(29) Whatever experiences the mind hath from moment to moment report to the *guru* [at regular intervals], and continue meditating.

(30) If oppressed [with drowsiness], steady the gaze, meditating in a place from which a vast expanse of country may be seen. If the mind be sluggish, also make use of this method [to freshen it], and discipline it with undistracted concentration.[3] If the mind be restless [or wandering], sit

are so regarded because of the belief that every sentient being has been a mother at some time in the course of the innumerable cycles of rebirths and redyings (See p. 60[1].) The Prayer itself is as follows:

'We, Mothers, equalling in infinity of number the heavens in infinity of expanse, all sentient beings,
Seek refuge in the *Guru*, the Buddha as the *Dharma-Kāya*;
We seek refuge in the *Guru* as the *Sambhoga-Kāya*;
We seek refuge in the *Guru*, the gracious *Nirmāṇa-Kāya*;
We seek refuge in the Buddha, the Precious One.
May the mind of all sentient beings be turned towards the Doctrine,
And may the religious career of each of them be crowned with success;
May errors on the Path be dispelled,
And the errors themselves be transmuted into Wisdom.'
The 'Three Divine Bodies' constitute three stages in the spiritual evolution from the human state to the divine states. (See p. 46.)

[1] The 'gift-waves' are waves of psychic energy, which stimulate spiritual development and greatly assist the aspirant seeking *Nirvāṇic* Enlightenment, the highest boon of the *yogic* practices of the Great Symbol. These 'gift-waves' are sent forth telepathically from the *Gurus*, some of whom exist on Earth, others in the superhuman realms. It is the granting of these 'gift-waves', otherwise known as the 'conferring of power', which constitutes the true spiritual initiation.

[2] The disciple must reach at-one-ment, both with his human *guru* and, through him, with the superhuman *Gurus* of the apostolic succession, in order to tread the Path safely and successfully. The human mind must be purified with the spirituality of the Teachers and mystically united with the All-Mind, or All-Consciousness, in order to attain the Great Goal.

[3] Prolonged meditation may cause tiredness of body and mind, leading to drowsiness and sluggishness. By way of diversion, and to overcome these hindrances, the *yogin* is here directed to go to a place like an isolated hill-top,

within the hermitage, lower the gaze, and make [bodily and
mental] relaxation the chief aim [for the time being].

### [THE CONCENTRATING UPON THE BODILY FORM : THE SPEECH AND THE MIND OF THE BUDDHA]

(31) The representations employed for the second class of
non-breathing objects, namely, symbolizations of the bodily
form, of the speech, and of the mind of the Buddha : for
the bodily form, an image [of the Buddha] ; for the speech,
syllables ; for the mind, a seed-like form [or a dot].[1]

(32) In making use of the first of these objects, the bodily
form, one may have either a metallic [or other] image or
a picture [of the Buddha]. Or [one may employ] a visualization of the Buddha's bodily form, yellow like unto burnished
gold, beautified with all the signs and graces [of spiritual
perfection], enhaloed in radiance, and robed in the three robes
of the Order, thought of as being ever present in front of
thee.[2]

(33) In making use of the second of these objects, a
syllable, as symbolizing the principle of speech [of the
Buddha], visualize in front of thee an image of a lunar disk
about the size of a finger-nail and upon it the syllable *HŪṂ*,
as finely depicted as a hair.[3]

whence, by looking out over an extensive landscape, the gaze becomes
steadied and the mind freshened, so that he can continue meditating.

[1] Text : *thiglē* (pron. *tiglē*) : Skt. *bīja* : 'seed, dot, point', or ' drop '.

[2] The form of the Buddha as shown in the Illustration facing p. 57 may be
used as the basis for this visualization.

[3] The lunar disk symbolizes the gradual dispelling of the gloom of Ignorance
(*Avidyā*), as the disk of the waxing moon gradually dispels the gloom of night.

Ordinarily, the *HŪṂ* symbolizes the mind-principle, but it is here made

the symbol of the speech-principle, which is usually *ĀH* , because this
exercise in visualization is merely elementary. (Cf. p. 267.) *HŪṂ* signifies
' It is ' or ' It exists '. Here, as in most instances throughout our texts where
syllabic visualizations are prescribed, the Occidental student whose aim is
practical application of these *yogic* teachings, under wise guidance, may employ
the transliterated forms rather than the original Tibetan forms. Appropriate
mental concentration is the essential thing ; and this can be attained, with
right results, by employing, in accordance with the instructions, either of the
two forms of the syllables. It is of importance, however, to correlate with
the transliterated forms their correct phonetic values as *mantric* sounds.

(34) In making use of the third of these objects, a seed-like form, as symbolizing the mind [of the Buddha], visualize a seed, oval in shape like an egg, about the size of a pea, emitting rays of light, and marvellous to behold, and mentally concentrate upon it.[1]

### [THE USE OF BREATHING OBJECTS]

(35) In the second method [of attaining mental concentration], by using breathing objects, there are employed the *Dorje* Recitation,[2] and the ' Pot-shaped '.[3]

#### [THE CONCENTRATING UPON THE *DORJE* RECITATION]

(36) The first procedure, in employing the *Dorje* Recitation, is:

While maintaining bodily and mental tranquillity, concencentrate the mind upon each inhalation and exhalation of breath to the exclusion of all else. Count [inaudibly] from one and two up to twenty-one thousand six hundred breathings. This will enable one to attain expertness in knowledge of the number of exhalations and inhalations [per day].[4]

---

[1] This seed (*tiglé*) is said to have its Tibetan prototype in the pearl-like excrescences found in the ashes of the funeral-pyre after the cremation of a Great *Yogin*. (See *The Tibetan Book of the Dead*, p. 133.) These are considered the material proof of there having been manifested through the fleshly form the Divine Force of *Bodhic* Mind, or of the *Dharma-Kāya* reflected through its two reflexes, the *Sambhoga-Kāya* and the *Nirmāṇa-Kāya*. Accordingly, the visualization is to be as if glorified with divine radiance.

[2] Text: *Rdo-rje-hi-bzlas-pa* (pron. *Do-rje-yi-day-pa*): Skt. *Vajra Japa*: ' *Dorje* (or Mystic) Recitation', which is an inaudible counting of the breathings, as the directions which follow make clear.

[3] Text: *Bum-chan*, with reference to the Tibetan *yogic* practice of causing the abdomen to take the shape of an earthen pot, as our text later on explains.

[4] Tibetans who dwell in the highlands of Tibet, say, from 12,000 to 15,000 feet above sea-level, have a much greater lung capacity than the ordinary European. As the air of high altitudes contains proportionally less oxygen than the air of low altitudes, such Tibetans inhale a greater volume of air than we do in order to absorb sufficient oxygen. Nature has adjusted them to their environment. A test would need to be made to determine whether the number of their breathings in any given period of time is normally greater or less than ours. In any event, the Tibetan *gurus* assume, like the Hindu *gurus*, that under normal conditions there should be about 21,600 breathings (one breathing being counted as one inhalation plus one exhalation) per day of 24 hours, 900 per hour, and 15 per minute. The purpose of the counting of the breathings is to make the breathing regular and rhythmic, to the end of *yogically* attuning the body.

(37) Next, take note of when the breathing beginneth [so many seconds after the exhalation] and in what manner the breath entereth. And consider whether the breath entereth at more than one part of the body.

(38) In virtue of these practices, the mind followeth the entrance and exit of the breath [and, like the breathing, becometh rhythmically attuned]. Thus doth one become well acquainted with the nature of the process of breathing.[1]

(39) Then, keeping the mind concentrated upon the breathing-process, observe how the breath passeth from the tip of the nose [through the nostril openings] to the bottom of the lungs, how it originateth [or cometh in], and how long it is retained [before being exhaled].[2]

(40) By this practice, one cometh to know, just as they really are, the colours, the duration, and the retention-period of each breathing.[3]

(41) Then, by observing the condition of the five fundamental elements [in the body, namely, earth, water, fire, air, and ether], each by itself, unblended with another, the increase or decrease of the number of inhalations and exhalations is to be noted.[4]

---

[1] The Tibetan disciple does not ordinarily have a very clear understanding of just how the breathing-process is carried on, and so he is set the task of analysing it.

[2] It is well for the student to remember that, according to *yoga*, the life-giving part of air inhaled is not chiefly the oxygen, which is absorbed into the blood through the functioning of the lungs, but the *prāna*, which has been referred to above as being essential to all psycho-physical activities of the body.

[3] The incoming air of the inhalation being pure and transparent, its colour is said to be pure; the outgoing air of the exhalation, being impure and non-transparent, its colour is said to be impure.

[4] Ordinary reflection will lead one to recognize, in the constitution and functioning of the various bodily organs, and in the manifestations and focusing of the *prānic* and other life-forces in the body, the play of the five elements. The purely physical constituents represent the element earth ; the bodily fluids, the element water ; the animal heat, the element fire ; the gaseous parts, the element air ; and the more subtle psychic (or *prānic*) vitality, the element ether. In this practice, the *yogin* must be vividly conscious of the circulation of the blood and *prāna*, of the functioning of each bodily organ, and of the arising and disappearing of each thought. Even from the elementary practices, which up to this point have been expounded, the Occidental reader will recognize that *yoga* is a science requiring for its mastery not merely greatness of mind and of spirit, but, also, profound knowledge of the body, to the end that all parts and functions of the human organism may be wisely controlled and rightly used.

(42) Now, by visualizing each expiration as the syllable *A ŪM* [or *ŌM*], white in colour, and each inspiration as the syllable *HŪM*, blue in colour, and the retention period [of the breathing] as the syllable *ĂH*, red in colour, one cometh to know, [intuitively, or without mental process], the time required for each part of the breathing-process.[1]

### [THE CONCENTRATING UPON THE 'POT-SHAPED']

(43) Next, in employing the 'Pot-shaped', the procedure is to expel completely the dead air from within, making three efforts in expelling it. Inhale gently the outer air through the nostrils. Draw up into the 'Pot-shaped' the air inhaled and retain it so as long as possible.

(44) In virtue of these practices, that thing called mind,—so difficult to control, because of its inability normally to function apart from the breathing-process which causeth it to shift constantly from one thought to another,—is disciplined, and becometh freed from this dependence on the breath.[2]

---

[1] Even as the heart or lungs function without conscious effort, so must the *yogic* timing of the breathing be made to go on automatically. Up to the end of paragraph 40, as above, the teachings concern preliminary, or less thorough methods. all of which, however, are necessary to prepare the beginner for this advanced process. Herein *A ŪM* 〰 is the symbol of the Spiritual Power of the Buddha. Its whiteness symbolizes purity. Thus, by being transmuted into the mystic sound *A ŪM*, and made pure, the expiration is sent forth into the world psychically charged with influences making for compassion and good. Similarly, so the Tibetans commonly believe, diseases are cured and evil *karma* absolved by the breathing in of the air exhaled by a Great *Yogin*. The *HŪM* 〰, the symbol of the embodiment of the life-force of Divine Beings, like Buddhas and *Bodhisattvas*, is to be visualized as being the life-force of the Buddha Gautama. When the inspiration, transmuted into the syllable *HŪM*, has ended, and while there is the retention period, the *HŪM* is to be transformed into the syllable *ĂH* 〰, symbolical of the vocal-principle, or speech, of the Buddha, as Universal Divine Sound or Vibration. Then whatever words be spoken by the *yogin* will convey, to whomsoever hears them, spiritual benefit and the power of truth. The blue of the *HŪM*, like the blue of the infinite expanse of the sky, symbolizes constancy and eternity ; and the red of the *ĂH*, Divine Love.

[2] This passage in the original Tibetan is quite abstruse. The sense of it may be otherwise stated as follows : The normal duration of a thought equals the

[THE CONCENTRATING WITHOUT USING OBJECTS]

(45) In employing the second method of concentrating the mind, namely, that in which no objects are used, there are three processes : the instantaneous cutting off of a thought at the root the very moment, as in a flash, it ariseth ; the leaving unshaped whatever concept or idea appeareth ; and the art of letting the mind assume its natural condition [of absolute quiescence, unmoved by the disturbing process of thought].[1]

[THE INHIBITING OF THE THOUGHT-PROCESS]

(46) The cutting-off of a thought at the root the very moment, as in a flash, it ariseth, is practised as followeth :

In meditating, in the manner above explained, one findeth that, because of the mind responding to stimuli, thoughts crop up continuously. Knowing that the birth of even a single idea should be prevented, one must try to inhibit this continuous cropping up of thoughts, by exercise of mental alertness. Thus, as soon as a thought sprouteth, try to chop it down, root and all, and continue meditating.

(47) By prolonging, during the meditation, the period of time in which the effort is made to prevent the arising of thoughts, one finally cometh to be aware of thoughts following close on the heels of one another so numerous that they seem interminable. This is the recognizing of thoughts, which equalleth the knowing of the enemy.[2]  It is called ' The First Resting Place ', the first stage of mental quiescence attained ;

duration of one breathing. Concomitant with the change of breath there is change of thought. But when the very difficult task of disciplining the mind is accomplished, by successful application of these practices, this dependence of mind on breath is overcome. However much one tries to retain a thought unchanged, the change of breath normally induces some change, however slight it may be, in the thought ; or an entirely new thought may displace it. The purpose of these exercises is to train the mind to function independently of the breathings, and thereby not be affected by thought-processes. Concepts arise in the mind because of stimuli. Remove or neutralize the stimuli and thought-processes cease, and the mind attains the Natural State. There is a good deal in the *Upanishads* concerning this interdependence of mind and breath.

[1] Briefly stated, these three processes are : instantaneous stopping of thought; allowing ideas to roam at will, unrestricted ; and letting the mind rest, in perfect tranquillity.

[2] The enemy for the *yogin* is unruly thoughts.

and the *yogin* then looketh on, mentally unperturbed, at the interminable flow of thoughts as though he were tranquilly resting on the shore of a river watching the water flow past.[1]

(48) Once the mind attaineth the tranquil state, for even the briefest moment,[2] it understandeth the arising and the cessation of thoughts. This understanding maketh one to feel as though thoughts were becoming more and more numerous, but, really, thoughts are always arising, and there is neither increase nor decrease of them. Thoughts are born instantaneously. That which is apart from and capable of immediately arresting this birth of thoughts is the Reality.[3]

### [THE NON-REACTING TO THOUGHTS]

(49) In the next practice, the leaving unshaped whatever concept or idea appeareth, the procedure is to be indifferent to the thought, allowing it to do as it liketh, neither falling under its influence, nor attempting to impede it.[4] Let the mind act as its shepherd [or watchman]; and go on meditating.

---

[1] To convey the real meaning intended, a free and amplified rendering has been necessary here. The passage might be rendered literally thus: 'It is called "The First Resting Place", comparable to the shore of a river past which the water floweth.' In other words, if the *yogin* is successful up to this point, he will have attained to freedom from the mental tyranny of the thought-process and be ready for the still greater tasks ahead of him on the *Nirvāṇic* Path.

[2] Hindu *yogins* describe this (the briefest measure of time of which they conceive) as equal to the time which elapses between the cutting through of the first and the second of three hundred banana leaves, piled one upon another, when, at a single stroke, a sword cuts through all of them.

[3] Text: *Chös-nyid* (pron. *Chö-nyid*). The Reality is not the human mind, but that which takes cognizance of the ever-flowing current of thought. Only in the True State is Reality realizable; and therein, if the *yogin* be attuned to Reality, to the Noumenal Source, the arising of thoughts can be prevented, just as when one, in control of a switch, is able to turn on or off an electric current.

[4] This is diametrically opposed to the process contained in the passages above, numbered 46 to 48. There exists, however, no incongruity for one familiar with preliminary *yogic* practices, all of which are chiefly means to the end of disciplining the mind, somewhat as the study of Latin often is for the schoolboy. By the former practice, the *yogin* comes to realize that thought-forming is as natural as breathing, and can no more be stopped, while the body is biologically normal and the mind active, than can any other of the processes concomitant with incarnate existence. The latter practice, now being considered, leads to the true goal, where the Knower, enjoying supramundane consciousness, stands aside and looks on, without attachment, at the mechanical flow of the thoughts.

Thereby thoughts will cease to arise and the mind will attain the state of passive tranquillity and one-pointedness.

(50) Again, thoughts are apt to have motion, like that of a meteorite [flashing across the heavens instantaneously yet unbrokenly].[1]

(51) By meditating as before, the duration of the state of quiescence is prolonged. This is called 'The Middle State of Quiescence', likened [in its unperturbed tranquillity] to a calm flowing river.

(52) The practice of keeping the mind in that relaxed condition precipitateth the sediment in the mind.[2]

(53) The Master of Doctrines,[3] hath said,

'If the mind be left relaxed, it attaineth tranquillity ;
If water be left undisturbed, it attaineth clearness.'

(54) And the Great Lord of *Yogins* [Milarepa] hath said,

'When the mind is left in the primordial, unmodified condi-
    tion, Knowledge dawneth ;
When this condition is maintained, comparable in its calm-
    ness to the flow of a calm river, Knowledge in its
    completeness is attained.
Wholly abandon all directing and shaping of thoughts ;
Ever maintain quiescence of mind, O *yogin*.'

(55) The Great Saraha hath summarized the essence of the teachings concerning this dual process, which is concomitant with meditation, in the following verses :

'When bound [or unrelaxed], the mind trieth to wander in
    each of the ten directions ;
When freed, it remaineth firm and motionless.
I have come to understand that it is a stubborn thing like
    a camel.'

---

[1] Text : *Khyur-khyur*, an onomatopoeic term expressing motion as of a meteorite flashing across the heavens, or as of an arrow in passage through the air, or as of a line of smoke driven by a gentle breeze.

[2] The sediment is the thoughts, as the quotation which follows, in amplifica-tion, shows.

[3] The text does not contain the proper name of this Sage ; but he was either Gampopa or Tsong-Khapa, both of whom were eminent apostles of the White Dynasty of *Gurus* whence, as indicated by the Obeisance, our treatise originates. (See pp. 57, 100[n].)

[The Art of Attaining the Natural State of the Mind]

(56) The third process, the art of letting the mind assume its natural condition, consisteth of four parts.

[*The Metaphor of the Spinning of the Brāhmanical Thread*]

(57) The first part concerneth maintaining evenness of mind, as carefully as evenness is maintained in the spinning of a Brāhmanical thread.[1] The thread must be spun neither too tightly nor too loosely, but evenly. Likewise, in meditating, one must not strain the mind too much; otherwise loss of control over the thoughts will ensue.[2]

(58) Through too much laxity, one falleth into slothfulness. Therefore one must meditate evenly.

(59) At the outset, the beginner is apt to strain his mind through using the Instantaneous Chopping-down Process.[3] But when fatigued with this process, relax by [changing over to that of] letting the thoughts roam at will.[4]

(60) This method of alternating the tensing with the relaxing process, which is employed in our School, hath now been considered. And the tensing and relaxing of the mind, being like the tensing and relaxing during the spinning of a Brāhmanical thread, hath come to be called 'Keeping the mind in condition like that of the spinning of a Brāhmanical thread.'

[*The Metaphor of the Sundering of a Straw-Rope*]

(61) The second part, called the art of keeping the mind as sundered from thoughts as one portion of a straw-rope, when snapped, is sundered from the other portion, is dependent upon indomitable resolve to maintain undistracted alertness. For the previous attempts at inhibiting thoughts have created thoughts.[5]

---

[1] The Brāhmanical thread, which the Brāhmin wears as a symbol of his caste, should be spun, according to tradition, by a virgin and with the greatest care; for, if it be broken in the spinning, misfortune will result. Saraha (cf. p. 101) was a Brāhmin by birth, and this accounts for his use of the simile.

[2] The thoughts must be kept under control, with the consciousness, like a shepherd, watching over them.

[3] See paragraph 46, above.         [4] See paragraph 49, above.

[5] Heretofore the efforts made to stop the arising of thoughts, or to control them, or not to control them, have inevitably created other thoughts. Now

(62) Because the above-described processes of inhibiting thoughts have not been employed without using the cognizing faculty and thus creating fresh thoughts, the meditation hath been marred.[1]

(63) The abandoning of both the cognizing faculty and the cognizer, and the allowing the mind to rest in the passive tranquil state, is known as the art of keeping the mind sundered from all mental functioning and exertion, the process of the sundering being compared to the snapping of a straw-rope.

[*The Metaphor of the mentally alert Child*]

(64) The third part is called ' Keeping the mind like that of a little child looking [with intensest mental alertness] at [the frescoes on] a temple '.

(65) By tying the elephant of the mind to the pillar of the cognizing faculty and the cognizer, each of the vital-airs is kept in its own channel.[2]

(66) Through the effects produced by this practice there come smoke-like or ethereal shapes, and ecstatic bliss whereby one almost swooneth.[3]

the aim is to reach a higher stage of tranquillity. Each straw of the straw-rope represents a thought. The rope represents the continuity of the thought-process, which, like the rope itself, is to be broken.

[1] The *yogin* is now told, as he ought already to have discovered, that he is not far progressed after all ; the Goal is still far off. Nevertheless, as he will come to learn, his *yogic* practices have been as necessary to his development as muscular exercises are in the development of an athlete.

[2] The mind in its perverse and stubborn aspect has been compared previously to a camel. Here, looked at as being cumbersome and unwieldy, it is compared to an elephant. In the body resides the vital-force (Skt. *prāṇa*) divided into ten vital-airs (Skt. *vāyu*). *Vāyu* being derived from the root *vā*, ' to breathe ' or ' to blow ', refers to the motive power of *prāṇa*. These *vāyu*, composed of negative *prāṇa*, control the bodily functions ; and thus each has its own place and duty. Health, essential for the *yogin*, depends upon keeping each vital-air normal, or in its own channel of operation. (See *The Tibetan Book of the Dead*, pp. 214-15.)

[3] These results are due to the ' vital-airs ' finding their way into the median-nerve (Skt. *sushumṇā-nāḍī*), which is the chief channel for the flow of the psychic forces, whose conducting agents are the *vāyu*. Apart from this psycho-physical cause there is a spiritual cause which parallels it, namely, the *yogin*'s first faint glimpses of the state of mind unmodified by thought-processes. In the Occident this ecstatic condition is known as Illumination. It is the first fruit of

(67) In experiencing the non-cognizing state of body and mind and having a feeling as if floating in the air, whatever visions or apparitional appearances may arise, are neither to be held on to through showing liking for them nor inhibited through dislike. Hence this non-holding on to and non-inhibiting of any vision hath been called 'Keeping the mind like that of a little child looking [with intensest mental alertness] at [the frescoes on] a temple '.[1]

*[The Metaphor of the Indifference of an Elephant]*

(68) The fourth part concerneth keeping the mind in the state which hath been likened to that of an elephant when pricked with thorns.[2]

(69) When cognitions arise while the mind is quiescent, consciousness of them is concomitant with their arising. The 'Preventer' [i.e. the consciousness *yogically* trained to that intense alertness above described, which controlleth thoughts] and the thing to be prevented [i.e. the process of thought-formation], having been brought face to face, one thought is prevented from giving way to another thought.[3]

(70) Because the 'Preventer' hath come of itself without

perfected meditation. While experiencing it, the *yogin* is ecstatically overwhelmed with intense mental quiescence, born of an intuitive sense of at-one-ment with Nature and the Source of Nature. No longer is he human, but divine; he is attuned to the True State. His next aim must be to acquire the *yogic* ability to enter this state at will and to remain in it for longer and longer periods. His ultimate aim must be to enter it permanently at death; or else choose the Higher Path of the *Bodhisattva* and renounce his Freedom in order that through his guidance other beings may likewise be freed.

[1] The child looking first at one fresco and then at another, without attachment to any, all the while maintains the most intense mental alertness, not knowing what sort of a picture he will see next; and it is this sort of expectant, but unattached, mental alertness which the *yogin* must exercise at the present stage of his progress.

[2] This process consists in keeping the 'Knower' wholly unresponsive to the stimuli of the incessant arising and passing away of thoughts, just as an elephant, because of its thick hide, is not responsive to the stimuli of being pricked with thorns.

[3] Upon attaining mental quiescence, the apperception, or consciousness, which then acts subconsciously, or in an automatic manner, like that of the pulsation of the heart, rises up simultaneously, or concomitantly, with the birth of a thought. As a result, the thought is arrested in its development, and prevented from transmuting itself into another thought.

one's needing laboriously to seek it, this condition is called
' Being in the state wherein the unbroken current of consciousness functioneth automatically '.

(71) The art of keeping the mind in that state wherein
there is neither inhibition of nor reaction to thoughts, when
thoughts are perceived, hath been compared to the state of
indifference which an elephant showeth when pricked with
thorns, and it hath been named accordingly.[1]

[THE FINAL STATE OF QUIESCENCE]

(72) This [condition] hath been designated as the final
state of quiescence, and likened [in its calmness] to an ocean
without a wave.

(73) Although while thus quiescent there is cognition of
the [mental] motion [of thoughts arising and vanishing], nevertheless, the mind having attained its own condition of rest or
calmness and being indifferent to the motion, the state is
called ' The state wherein falleth the partition separating
motion from rest '.[2]

(74) Thereby one realizeth one-pointedness of mind.

(75) That which recognizeth the ' Moving ' and the ' Non-
Moving ' [or motion and rest, as being one and inseparable],
is called, when It be rightly understood, ' The All-Discriminating Wisdom, or the Supramundane Intellect.'[3]

[1] This *yogic* art may be defined as supreme spiritual indifference to the
physical and mental effects of stimuli. It is one of the first steps whereby
*sangsāric* illusions are made neutral, in order that the True State may be
realized. Such realization, however, is not the final goal; ultimately there must
be realized that both the *Sangsāra* (or the Created) and *Nirvāna* (or the Non-
Created) are, in the last analysis of the *Bodhic* Illuminated Mind, inseparably
One. In other words, the state of thought and the state of non-thought are but
the two extremes of a duality, which, when the *Yoga* of the Great Symbol has
been mastered, will be seen as a unity.

[2] The *yogin* is now being prepared, as the remainder of the treatise shows,
to attain to the great realization that all dualities are but negative and positive
aspects of unities, of which motion and rest are one.

[3] The mind in man is inseparable from the All-Mind. The object of *yoga* is
to bring about the joining, or at-one-ment, of the human and divine aspects of
mind. This can only be accomplished when mind is freed from the illusions of
*sangsāric* existence and comes to know its If. The All-Discriminating Wisdom
is the Wisdom of the *Bodhic* (or Supramundane) Consciousness (or Intellect) of
the *Nirvānic* State, whence comes the divine power of knowing each thing
separately, yet all things as one. (Cf. p. 232, § 37.)

(76) As the *Elegant Sūtra* [1] saith,

'The stage now reached, in virtue of the body and mind having acquired excellent training by these practices, is called "The Stage of Reflection and Analysis".'

[THE SECOND OF THE ORDINARY PRACTICES :
THE *YOGA* OF THE UNCREATED]

(77) The second part of the Ordinary Practices,—the Analysing of the Essential Nature of the 'Moving' and the 'Non-Moving', through practising the *Yoga* of the Uncreated, and thus realizing supramundane consciousness,—hath three divisions: the Analysing of the 'Moving' and the 'Non-Moving'; the Realizing of the Supramundane Consciousness; the Meditating upon the *Yoga* of the Uncreated.

[THE ANALYSING OF THE 'MOVING' AND THE 'NON-MOVING']

(78) In the first practice, the Analysing of the 'Moving' and the 'Non-Moving', the following analytical processes are required :—

With the Intellect of the All-Discriminating Wisdom, born of the quiescent state of non-cognition [or the indifference to the arising and vanishing of thoughts], one observeth :—

What the real nature of the 'Non-Moving' [or mind] is when it is motionless ;

How it remaineth motionless ;

How it moveth from the state of motionlessness ;

When moving whether it maintain its tranquillity of motionlessness ;

Whether it move any at all while maintaining the state of motionlessness ;

Whether the 'Moving' is other than the 'Non-Moving' ;

What the real nature of the 'Moving' [or thought] is ;

and, finally,

How the 'Moving' becometh the 'Non-Moving'.[2]

---

[1] Text: *Mdo-sde-rgyan* (pron. *Do-de-gyan*). This *Sūtra* is so called because of its elegant rhetorical and literary style.

[2] These abstruse problems resemble the strange conundrums which are set the neophyte in the Zen Schools of Japan. Apart from their usage as mental exercises, they serve to awaken transcendental intelligence.

(79) One cometh to know that neither is the 'Moving' other than the 'Non-Moving', nor the 'Non-Moving' other than the 'Moving'.

(80) If the real nature of the 'Moving' and the 'Non-Moving' be not discovered by these analyses, one is to observe:—

Whether the Intellect, which is looking on, is other than the 'Moving' and the 'Non-Moving';

Or whether it is the very self of the 'Moving' and the Non-Moving'.

(81) Upon analysing, with the eyes of the Self-Knowing Intellect, one discovereth nothing; the observer and the thing observed are found to be inseparable.

(82) And because the real nature of this inseparableness cannot be cognized, the stage thus attained is called 'The goal beyond mind.' It is also called 'The goal beyond all theories.'[1]

---

[1] To the True State, wherein even the Ultimate Duality, the *Sansgāra* and *Nirvāna*, is realized to be an Inseparable Unity, no concepts of the intellectual world can be applied. It is also beyond all dogmas and theories. This teaching is synonymous with the occultly abstruse teaching contained in the *Prajñā Pāramitā*: '*Shūnyatā* (the Formless, the Non-Material) is naught other than form, nor is matter separate from *Shūnyatā.*' As Occidental physicists have already discovered, there is a certain stage reached in the analysis of matter when matter dissolves into electrons and these into electrical energy. And, no doubt, eventually they will arrive at proof of the ancient postulate of *yoga*, that matter and mind are but the dual aspects of a unity. Likewise, in biology, it has been found that there is no line of demarcation separating the animal from the vegetable kingdom; for there are lowly life-forms, having characteristics common to both kingdoms, which botanists classify as plants and zoologists as animals. Again, in chemistry, a stage may be attained where all chemical compounds become transmutable into the one uncompounded mother-element. Similarly, the *yogin*, in his psycho-physical researches into the nature of mind, finds that it is neither this nor that, neither phenomena nor noumena, but both. No one of the various aspects of mind or of mental activity can be said to be separate from one another; they form a unity, just as do all the various manifestations of life and matter. The *guru* will say to the disciple. 'The flame of a lamp gives light, and heat, and consumes oil. Are the flame, the light, the heat, and the consuming of the oil four separate or separable things?' Step by step the disciple is thus led to the realization that similarly all the innumerable aspects of the mind and intellect are but rays of the One Mind and Intellect. This attainment is not, however, of finality, but merely of knowledge of mind in its microscopic character. Not until the finite

(83) The Lord of Conquerors [1] hath said,

'Mind-made goals, however noble, end in disillusionment,

And the mind-transcending Thatness cannot thus be called a goal; [2]

E'er inseparable the thing that sees is from the thing that's seen;

'Tis by the *guru's* kindly guidance that this truth disciples glean.'

(84) That method of analysing [as above described] hath been referred to by the Pandit Shāntideva [3] thus :—

'While holding fast to the *samādhic* state [of perfected quiescence],

Without in any way being distracted even for the briefest moment,

And exercising the analytical powers of mind,

Each mental process is to be examined separately.'

(85) Of the metaphor of fire and fuel, In the *Sūtra* entitled *Kasyapa's Questioning*,[4] it is written,

'By the rubbing of one stick against another, fire is produced;

By the applying of that fire, both sticks are burnt up.

Similarly, the Super-Intellect is born of the union of the "Moving" and the "Non-Moving";

And by That, to which they give birth, both are consumed.'

(86) This introspective analysis, conducted by the Super-

mind becomes the Infinite Mind, and 'the dewdrop slips into the Shining Sea', in the state of the Supramundane Consciousness, is the *Nirvāṇic* Goal reached.

[1] Text: *Rgyal-vahi-dvang po* (pron. *Gyal-wai-wang-po*) : Skt. *Jinendra*. This title refers to one of the Tibetan masters of the Great Symbol Yoga.

[2] Text: *lta-va* (pron. *ta-wa*) : Skt. *drishti*: 'culmination', 'destination of vision', hence, 'goal'. The Thatness being beyond the cognizance of the *sangsāric* mind, no *sangsāric* mind-made attributes can be attached to It. Goals which the *sangsāric* mind conceives cannot lead beyond the *Sangsāra*, and must, therefore, if attained, result in disillusionment. The quest is for the non-*sangsāric Nirvāṇa*, which, being supramundane, cannot, in fact, be called a goal, for it is a realization of what already is.

[3] Text: *Zhi-va-lha* (pron. *Shi-wa-lha*) : Skt. *Shāntideva*, meaning, 'Peaceful' and 'Divine One', an Indian exponent of the Great Symbol Philosophy.

[4] Text: *Höd-srungs-kyis-zhüs-pahi-mdo* (pron. *Wö-sung-kyi-shü-pai-do*) : Skt. *Kāshyapa-paripricchā Sūtra*.

Intellect, is known as 'The Analytical Meditation of the Hermit'. It is not like the analytical meditation of the intellectualist, for the intellectualist's analysis is external [or dependent upon sensuous experiences].[1]

[THE REALIZING OF THE SUPRAMUNDANE CONSCIOUSNESS]

(87) The second practice, the realizing of the Supramundane Consciousness, is thus :—

Whatever thoughts, or concepts, or obscuring [or disturbing] passions arise are neither to be abandoned nor allowed to control one ; they are to be allowed to arise without one's trying to direct [or shape] them. If one do no more than merely to recognize them as soon as they arise,[2] and persist in so doing, they will come to be realized [or to dawn] in their true [or void] form through not being abandoned.[3]

(88) By that method, all things which may seem to be obstacles to spiritual growth can be made use of as aids on the Path. And, therefore, the method is called 'The utilizing of obstacles as aids on the Path'.[4]

---

[1] Or, in other words, the hermit *yogin* is independent of book-learning in making his analysis ; he seeks knowledge from within himself. The intellectualist, on the contrary, measures experience in terms of the sensuous, or external, world, because he has never known the spiritual inner life. Hence, the intellectualist's meditation is called external, in contradistinction to the hermit's internal meditation. In this connexion, Milarepa says, 'I have never valued or studied the mere sophistry of word-knowledge set down in books. . . . [This leadeth] but to mental confusion and not to such practice as bringeth actual realization of Truth.' (Cf. *Tibet's Great* Yogī *Milarepa*, p. 245.)

[2] Here, too, as previously directed, the *yogin* is to look on at the thoughts or passions without being in the least influenced by them. Although detached from them, as a spectator is from the actors on a stage, the detachment must be the *yogic* detachment of indifference.

[3] A shepherd, conscious of his indomitable control over his sheep and lambs, may look on at the playfulness of his flock without in any way being attached to or influenced by the playfulness, and without shaping or directing it. And although he may allow them to wander at will while they graze, he never loses sight of or abandons them.

[4] Although the underlying idea herein is much akin to that of the Christian who regards trials and tribulations as aids to spiritual living, it is more complex, being *yogic*. The *guru* can be imagined as expounding it somewhat as follows: 'A traveller is walking along a narrow foot-path at night. Suddenly he stops and jumps aside terror-stricken, crying out, "A cobra! a cobra!" Regaining confidence, he grasps his bamboo staff firmly, strikes a light, and sees a coil of

(89) This art of attaining Liberation by merely recognizing the thoughts, whereby one acquireth understanding of the inseparable nature of the abandoner [i.e. the mind] and of the thing to be abandoned [i.e. the thought], is called ' The Essence of the Practice of the Sublime Path ', or ' The Reverse Method of Meditation '.

(90) After having attained Liberation, there cometh infinite compassion for all those sentient beings who have not as yet recognized the true nature of their own mind.[1]

(91) Although one's time should be fully devoted to practising mental dedication of body, speech, and mind to the good of all sentient beings, nevertheless, seeing that in virtue of the above intellectual processes belief in the reality of things hath been corrected, one cannot be adversely influenced [by

rope lying in the way. " Ah ! " he says, " that is just what I need as a girdle " ; and he picks it up and winds it around his waist and goes on, ashamed of his ignorance.' What was ignorantly called a cobra, is found to be, when seen in the light of right understanding, not only harmless, but quite useful. Similarly is it with all the processes of the finite mind. Seen in the darkness of *Avidyā* (Ignorance of Right Knowledge), that which really is both harmless and use-ful appears to be just the opposite. When *sangsāric* thoughts, and passions born of these thoughts, are transmuted by the alchemy of the Great Symbol, they merge, in at-one-ment, with the *Dharma-Kāya* Mind. The *yogin*, when the realization comes, knows that thoughts instead of being inimical, as he took them to be at first, are, as phenomena, existing things which are inseparably related to the thoughts of the Universal Mind. Then, by a retrospective and reversive process, the *yogin*, exercising the *yogic* indifference of non-attachment to all phenomena, his whole body and mind relaxed, in the state of the perfected quiescence of the highest *samādhi*, allows the interminable flow of thoughts to go on unimpededly, or naturally. As he does so, the thoughts automatically assume a rhythmic vibration, in tune with the vibration of the Thoughts of the Infinite Mind, of which the cosmic creation is the phenomenal fruit. Thus, the *yogin* utilizes as aids on the Path the thoughts which appeared to be obstacles. So is it with all other obstacles, for in the last analysis of the Perfected Sage, all conceivable things of Nature (of the *Sangsāra*), whether they be invisible thoughts or their embodiment as objective forms, are products of the One Mind. The paragraph which follows is in furthur elucidation of this.

[1] Up to this stage, the progression has been from the limited, personal worldly mind (or consciousness) to the unlimited impersonal cosmic mind (or consciousness). Now comes the reversive method. The *yogin* from the im-partial, impersonal, disinterested standpoint of the cosmic mind, analyses mind in its human aspect. The macrocosmic measures the microcosmic. Then arises great compassion for all sentient beings who have not realized the true nature of their limited and delusion-creating mind.

such apparently egotistical dedication], just as one cannot be affected harmfully by taking charmed poison.[1]

(92) Through taking into consideration this sort of practice [of seemingly egotistical dedication], there hath been formulated the prayer, of which the first verse is,

'Whatever dawneth on the Path may I neither abandon nor adopt.'[2]

### [THE MEDITATING UPON THE *YOGA* OF THE UNCREATED]

(93) The third practice, the Meditating upon the *Yoga* of the Uncreated, hath three divisions : the Analysing from the Standpoint of the Three Times [the Past, the Present, and the Future] ; the Analysing from the Standpoint of Substance and Non-substance [or of Matter and Non-matter] ; the Analysing from the Standpoint of Singleness and Plurality [or of the One and the Many].

---

[1] Should the dedication be visualized as an action born of the personal self, there would arise the erroneous concept of self as a separate entity. The truth that all living creatures are inseparably one must be held to indomitably. The contrary belief is the poison to be avoided, and the right belief is the charm or antidote for the poison. The dedication must be regarded as the natural thing to do, without thought of self. Apart from this philosophical view, we may here note that there is a peculiar practice in *Hatha Yoga* whereby poisons of all sorts can be taken internally without ill effect. Such poisons are said to be charmed, i.e. infused by psychic forces which neutralize their destructive character and transmute them into non-poisons, by a sort of mental, or *yogic*, alchemy. (See *Tibet's Great* Yogī *Milarepa*, p. 249.)

[2] The full prayer to the Divine *Gurus* is as follows :—

'Whatever dawneth on the Path may I neither abandon nor adopt.
But vouchsafe thy "gift-waves", O *Gurus*, that the phenomenal and existent
May be realized as the Three Principles of the Cosmic Whole.'

The 'gift-waves', as elsewhere explained, are the helpful spiritual, or psychic, influences telepathically conveyed, as in initiations, from *Gurus* in divine and *Bodhisattvic* realms to disciples on Earth. The Three Principles of the Cosmic Whole (Tib. *Skū-gsum*,—pron. *Kū-sum* : Skt. *Tri-Kāya*) are the three aspects of the Body of Truth, the *Dharma-Kāya*. (See p. 98[6-7].) From the viewpoint implied by this prayer, they may be expounded as follows : (*a*) the Universal Body, the unified expression of all form, from the body of the lowliest sentient creature up to the glorified body of a Buddha, Who has reached the end of all *sangsāric* evolution ; (*b*) the Universal Speech, the unified expression of sound, from the simplest elemental sound in nature up to the divine speech of Buddhas ; (*c*) the Universal Mind, the unified expression of mind, from the lowest instinctive function or reaction to stimuli, in the most elementary of living things, up to the completely unfolded mind, or consciousness, of a Fully Enlightened One.

[THE MEDITATIONS UPON PAST, PRESENT, AND FUTURE TIME]

(94) The first, the Analysing from the Standpoint of the Three Times, is [according to the following meditations] :—

The past thought hath vanished ;

The future thought, being as yet unborn, hath not come into existence ;

The present thought cannot be fixed [or identified] as being the present.[1]

(95) By carrying on observations [or meditations] in this manner, the character of all [*sangsāric*] things cometh to be realized as like that of the Three Times.[2]

(96) All things have no existence in themselves ; it is the mind which giveth them being.[3]

[THE NON-REALITY OF BIRTH, DEATH, AND TIME]

(97) The realization that birth, death, and time [4] have no existence in themselves, hath been referred to by Saraha thus :—

‘ Birth in matter having been made neutral like the sky,

---

[1] The present thought has but a momentary existence ; no sooner is it born than it passes away. It cannot, therefore, be fixed, or identified as being present ; it is, in fact, inseparable from both the future, whence it arose as the present, and the past, into which it vanishes. The purpose of this meditation is to cause the *yogin* to realize that past, future, and present are, also, an inseparable unity, and that the *sangsāric* view of time is erroneous, time itself being, like all other *sangsāric* things or concepts, illusory.

[2] All things perceived by the unenlightened mind are seen only in their illusory, or unreal, aspect ; but by the successful *yogin* they are realized, in their true state, as being inseparably parts of the Universal Whole. As the next paragraph explains, things have this illusory existence because the mind gives them being and characteristics.

[3] A more literal rendering is, ‘ All things have no existence apart from the mind which holdeth them to be existing.’ In other words, all *sangsāric* things have no existence apart from the Supramundane Mind. The cosmos is but the materialization of the thoughts of the One Mind ; to the Hindu it is the Dream of Brahma. It is but of the stuff of which dreams are made. To produce in the *yogin* the Supreme Awakening from this *Sangsāric* Dream is the aim of the Great Symbol teachings, as of all true *yoga*.

[4] Or, as an alternative rendering, ‘ birth, cessation, and duration ’. Herein we learn that the great minds of the Orient have long ago anticipated relativity ; that birth, death, and time exist only in relation to the mind which perceives them as existing.

What remaineth to be born when matter hath been left
 aside ! [1]

The natural state from beginningless time hath been the
 Unborn State ;

To-day is this truth realized, by its having been demonstrated by my *guru*, the protector.'

The meditative analysis is to be carried on in accordance
with this reference [by Saraha].

[THE MEDITATIONS UPON MIND AND MATTER]

(98) The second method, the Analysing from the Standpoint of Substance and Non-substance, is according to the following meditations :—

Is one's mind a thing which ' Is ', as being composed of
 matter ; or is it a thing which ' Is not ', as not being composed of matter ?

If material, of what material substance is it ?

If an objective thing, of what shape and colour is it ?

If a cognizing faculty, is it merely an ephemeral thing
 like a thought ?

If non-material, how doth it assume various aspects ?

And who made it ?

(99) If the mind were a material thing, one would be able,
after having meditated upon it in this manner, to regard it as
something substantial. But from the standpoint of the observation of the Super-Intellect, it is found to be something
which cannot be called anything ; so one is unable to classify
it as being a thing composed of matter. As being the subject
of analysis for the Super-Intellect, neither can it be classified

---

[1] The sky is here figuratively regarded as being neither this nor that, as having no *sangsāric* characteristics such as finite mind attributes to sensuous
objects ; it is, therefore, neutral. The *sangsāric* concept that there is a thing
called matter, having been left aside by the enlightened *yogin*, as being illusory
and only relatively true in connexion with the unenlightened who regard it as
a reality, birth, too, which cannot occur without material form, is left aside, or
transmuted into neutrality like that of the undifferentiated sky. The stage is
thus reached in which all such concepts as birth, death, and time are found to
be purely *sangsāric*, or non-existent in or of themselves.

as being non-material nor as being non-existent. Accordingly, since it is neither a material thing nor a non-material thing, it cannot be placed at either of two extremes; and, therefore, this method is called 'The Middle Path'.[1]

(100) This accepted conviction [or truth] hath not been arrived at merely by the processes of deduction and induction, but essentially because of the *guru*'s teachings, which have made one to see the Priceless Gem lying unnoticed within one's reach. Therefore have these teachings been [also] called 'The Great Truth'.[2]

(101) It hath been said,

'He into whose heart the *guru*'s teachings have entered,
Is like unto one who hath been made to see a treasure lying unnoticed within his reach.'[3]

---

[1] Text: *Dvumahi-Lam* (pron. *Ümai-Lam*): Skt. *Mādhyamika-Marga*: Middle (or Central) Path. The Madhyamika School of Buddhism is itself known as the 'Middle Path'; it avoids the two extremes of 'It is' and 'It is not'. In the *Nidāna Sanyutta* xv, *Sanyutta-Nikāya*, of the Pāli canon, it is said: '"Every thing is" is one extreme, "Every thing is not" is the other extreme. The Tathāgata, avoiding these two extremes, teacheth the Doctrine of the Middle Path.'

[2] Here a summing up may be made, after the *guru*'s own fashion :—
Who is the Spectator? It is the Super-Intellect, the Supramundane Consciousness.
Upon what does It look? Upon the tranquil and the non-tranquil, the 'non-moving' and the 'moving'.
Whence did the Super-Intellect arise? From the One Mind, wherein all minds are in at-one-ment.
What is the Mind? It is not a visible, substantial thing; to It no concepts of the finite mind can apply. It is beyond characterization, being Unborn, Unmade; It is Reality. Not even the Buddhas, Who have realized It, have seen It, or perceived It with any of the senses. It is non-existent, because It is the Basis and the Stay of both the *Sangsāra* (embodied existence in the realm of the Six Worlds of sentient life) and *Nirvāṇa* (existence in the state of Perfect Enlightenment, or Buddhahood). It is not a separable thing; It is not a compound thing. It is a Transcendent Unity; and that Unity is realizable on the 'Middle Path', through practice of the *guru*'s teachings as recorded herein.

[3] The mind within oneself, which is the source of all true wealth, remains unknown to those enamoured of the worldly life. Man does not know himself; and, enslaved by Ignorance (*Avidyā*), he passes on unceasingly from one state of illusory existence to another. Through the *guru*'s teachings, the Way to Freedom is found; long has the Treasure been unnoticed. The *guru* reveals the Treasure, the Priceless Gem; and the faithful disciple puts aside the things of the world, and, entering the Path, attains the *Nirvāṇic* Goal.

[THE MEDITATIONS UPON THE ONE AS THE MANY]

(102) The third method, the Analysing from the Stand-point of Singleness and Plurality, is according to the following meditations :—

Is the mind a single thing ?

Or is it a plural thing ?

If it be a single thing, how doth it come to be such, seeing that it manifesteth itself variously ?

If it be a number of things, how can it be so, since all of them must necessarily be inseparably one in their true nature ? [1]

(103) Observing thus, one findeth the mind not to be a number of things ; and, as it is free of the extremes [of single-ness and plurality], it is called 'The Great Symbol', that which doth not abide in absolute rest [or finality].[2]

---

[1] Mind, as man knows it, is a complex compound of various sensations, or feelings, perceptions, or cognitions, reasonings, memory, consciousness. If such aspects of the mind, or mentality, be separate or separable things from man's point of view, they are, nevertheless, from the *Bodhic* point of view known in reality to be of the nature of the Void, and thus an inseparable unity in relation to the One Mind. In other words, the microcosmic mind is but a reflex of the Macrocosmic Mind, in which all things are in at-one-ment.

[2] Text : *rabtu-mi-gnas-pa* (pron. *rabtu-mi-na-pa*) : 'not abiding in absolute rest [in the blissful state of *Nirvāṇa*]'. The state symbolized by the Great Symbol is, according to the School of the Middle Path (Tib. *Ūma-pa* ; Skt. *Mādhyamika*), equivalent to the highest state of Reality, the *Shūnyatā*, or Voidness. This School asserts that the *Shūnyatā* is neither a state of non-entity, or nihilism, nor a state of individualized being, but something apart from both states, a condition of existence indescribable in any known terms of language ; for language is dependent upon concepts derived from experiences in a sensuous universe, and Reality is non-sensuous. The *Gurus* of the Great Symbol School accept these fundamental *Mādhyamika* tenets. They, accordingly, teach that *Nirvāṇa* is not to be regarded as a final state, wherein its realizer selfishly abides in absolute rest and bliss. That is to say, *Nirvāṇa* is not a state to be realized for one's own good alone, but for the sake of the greater good which will accrue to every sentient thing merely in virtue of a realization of It. Thus it is that in Tibet all aspirants for the Divine Wisdom, for the Full Enlighten-ment known as *Nirvāṇa*, take the vow to attain the state of the *Bodhisattva*, or Great Teacher. The vow implies that the *Nirvāṇic* State will not be finally entered, by the one taking the vow, until all beings, from the lowest in sub-human kingdoms on this and every other planet to the highest of unenlightened gods in the many heaven-worlds, and the most fallen of dwellers in hell-worlds are safely led across the Ocean of the *Sangsāra* to the Other Shore. Southern Buddhists are inclined to regard *Nirvāṇa*, at least when attained by *Pratyeka*

(104) In the quiescent state of *samādhi*, for the *yogin* who thus attaineth realization, the All-Discriminating Wisdom of the Transcendental Intellect alone dawneth, and nothing else. Therefore, the Great Symbol, the Reality, is called 'That which is devoid of characteristics'.

### [THE REALIZING OF REALITY]

(105) As a result of these meditations, all attachment to the belief in the reality of things is purged away, and everything appeareth illusory, like magically-produced phantasmagoria.

(106) That being so, it hath been said,

'In front of me and behind me, and in the ten directions,
Wheresoever I look, I see only the Thatness ;
To-day, O Protector [or *Guru*] the illusion hath been broken.
Henceforth I shall ask nothing of any one.'

### [*THE EXTRA-ORDINARY PRACTICES*]

(107) The second part of Part II, the Extra-Ordinary Practices, consisteth of two parts: the *Yoga* of Transmuting all Phenomena and Mind, which are inseparable, into At-one-ment [or Unity] ; and the *Yoga* of Non-Meditation,[1] whereby all things are transmuted into the *Dharma-Kāya*, by the Simultaneously-born Immaculate Mind [or Great Symbol].

### [THE FIRST OF THE EXTRA-ORDINARY PRACTICES: THE *YOGA* OF TRANSMUTING ALL PHENOMENA AND MIND INTO AT-ONE-MENT.]

(108) First cometh the practice of the *Yoga* of Transmuting all Phenomena and Mind, which are inseparable, into At-one-ment [or Unity]:—

(or Non-teaching) Buddhas, as a state of finality. Mahāyānists, however, say that *Nirvāna* is a state of mind reached as a result of evolutionary spiritual unfoldment, and that It cannot, therefore, be regarded as a final state, inasmuch as evolution has no conceivable ending, being an eternal progression.

[1] Text *sgom-med-kyi-rnal-hbyor* (pron. *gom-med-kyi-nal-jor*) : '*yoga* of non-meditation', with reference to a higher stage of *yoga* in which there is what may be called a transmutation of meditation, concomitant with a state of transcendental consciousness aroused by meditation. Once this state of intuitive insight is attained, meditation, which is merely a means of attaining it, is unnecessary ; just as a traveller who has reached port no longer needs the ship which carried him there.

By means of the simile of sleep and dreams, recognize all phenomena to be mind. By means of the simile of water and ice, recognize noumena and phenomena to be a unity. By means of the simile of water and waves, transmute all things to the one common state of at-one-ment.

[THE MEDITATION UPON SLEEP AND DREAMS]

(1c9) Of these three, the first, the Recognizing of all Phenomena to be Mind, by means of the simile of sleep and dreams, is according to the following meditation :—

Whatever be seen during sleep is not something apart from mind.

Similarly, all phenomena of the waking-state are but the dream-content of the Sleep of Obscuring Ignorance.[1] Apart from the mind [which giveth them illusory being] they have no existence.

(110) By allowing the relaxed mind to rest upon whatever ideas [or visions] arise, all external phenomena and one's own mind [with all its internal phenomena] are realized as being inseparable, one from another; and are transmuted into at-one-ment.

(111) The Lord of *Yogins* [Milarepa], hath said,

' The dream dreamt last night,

Wherein phenomena and mind were seen as one,

Was a teacher; didst thou not [O disciple] so understand it ?'

(112) It hath also been said,

' Transmute the Three Regions,[2] omitting from them nothing,

Into the essence of the One Great Passion, [Universe-embracing Love Divine].'[3]

---

[1] Man, immersed in the *Sangsāra*, is wise only in sensations, in knowledge derived from experiences in a sensuous universe. All his worldly learning is, in fact, unreal; and, by its egotistical character, obscures the True Wisdom. It is for this reason that *yogins* call it *Avidyā*, ' Ignorance [of Truth]'; in which state the unenlightened multitude exist as in a feverish nightmare, knowing naught of the Path leading to the Supreme Awakening into Freedom.

[2] These are the Three Regions into which the Buddhists divide the Cosmos, to accord with the three conditions of *sangsāric* existence, as described above, on p. 94[1–3].

[3] The transmutation is a mystical process dependent upon exalted *yogically-*

## [THE MEDITATION ON WATER AND ICE]

(113) The second practice, the Identifying of Phenomena as Noumena, by means of the simile of water and ice, is according to the following meditation :

Since all phenomena [or phenomenally appearing things] which arise present no reality in themselves, they are said to be of the noumena.[1] Though not formed into anything, yet they give shape to everything. Thus it is that phenomena and noumena are ever in union,[2] and said to be of one nature. They are, for example, like ice and water [two aspects of a single thing].

(114) By that means, one cometh to know that the three dualities, Bliss and the Voidness, the Clear Light and the Voidness, Wisdom and the Voidness,[3] are unities ;[4] and this is

induced visualization. Its purpose is to aid the *yogin*, both mentally and spiritually, to realization of the complete selflessness of the *Bodhisattvic* state, to which he aspires. The *yogin* when practising it is directed by the *guru* somewhat as follows : ' The Cosmos, as the Three Regions, is to be visualized as being a duality in unity. Visualize the energizing aspect of the Cosmos as being the Divine Father (Tib. *Yab*) and the intellectual aspect of the Cosmos as being the Divine Mother (Tib. *Yum*). Think of them as being in union (Tib. *Yab-Yum*), and inseparably one. Realization of this divine at-one-ment is the Goal, the Great Symbol.'

At the stage now reached by the *yogin*, the Great Symbol teachings might be summarized for him by the *guru* thus : ' By realizing the True State, beyond life and death, beyond transitoriness and sorrow, wherein mind and matter, phenomena and noumena, and all dualities are known to be inseparably a unity, one attaineth the bliss of Perfect Enlightenment. In virtue of having realized the True State, there ariseth, in the one of *Bodhisattvic* mind, an overwhelming, compassionate love for all sentient beings yet immersed in Ignorance (*Avidyā*), and the desire to lift them up to the Light of Truth.' Accordingly, knowledge of the One Great Universe-Embracing Passion, Love Divine, is born of having entered the *Bodhisattvic* Path of the Higher Evolution.

[1] In other words, they are of the Voidness regarded as the noumenal background or Source of the physical universe of phenomena.

[2] Nothing in the whole range of Mahāyānic symbolism has been more misunderstood by Europeans than the images of the Divine Father-Mother (Tib. *Yab-Yum*) in sexual union, which symbolize this unity of phenomena and noumena, as they do the unity of all dualities, including the highest duality conceivable, namely, that of the *Saṅgsāra* and *Nirvāṇa*.

[3] In each duality the Voidness typifies the Noumenal Source whence arise all spiritual experiences, even the highest. The Bliss is the Bliss of Enlightenment ; the Clear Light, the Inner Illumination ; the Wisdom, the Divine Wisdom.

[4] Or ' are in union ', as symbolized by the corresponding *yab-yum* imagery.

called ' The Realization of the At-one-ment of all Spiritual
Experiences '.

(115) It hath been said,

' If one hath fully understood, all things are the Thatness;
None will discover anything other than the Thatness.
What is read is the Thatness, what is memorized is the
    Thatness,
And what is meditated upon is also the Thatness.'

[THE MEDITATION UPON WATER AND WAVES]

(116) The third process, the Transmuting of all Things to
the One Common State of At-one-ment, by means of the
simile of water and waves, is according to the following meditation :

As waves are produced from water itself, so, in like
manner, is to be understood how all things are the offspring
of the mind, which, in its own nature, is Voidness.

(117) Saraha hath said,
        ' Since all things are born of the mind,
        Therefore is the mind itself the *guru*.' [1]

(118) This teaching is called ' The One Truth pervading
the Realm of Truth ' ; [2] and, therefore, known as the Oneness
manifesting itself in the Many. The *yogin* who hath mastered
it, realizeth the Voidness in every state [of consciousness], as
the fruit of Knowledge.

[THE SECOND OF THE EXTRA-ORDINARY PRACTICES :
    THE *YOGA* OF NON-MEDITATION]

(119) Next cometh the practice of the *Yoga* of Non-Meditation, whereby all things are transmuted into the *Dharma-Kāya*

---

[1] It is a fundamental tenet of the Buddhism of all Schools that the human
*guru* is merely a guide, as was the Great *Guru*, Gautama the Buddha. Each
aspirant for *Nirvānic* Enlightenment must be a law unto himself; he himself,
not the *guru*, must tread the Path. One must eat one's food for oneself; and,
as the Buddha taught, each pilgrim on the Great Pilgrimage must really be his
own light and his own refuge. *Nirvāna* is to be realized not by the proxy of a
*guru*, but by the *yogin* himself.

[2] Or the *Dharma-Dhātu* (Tib. *Chōs-kyi-dvyings*—pron. *Chō-kyi-ing*) literally
meaning, the ' Seed (or Potentiality) of Truth '.

[or Body of Truth] by the Simultaneously-born Immaculate Mind [or Great Symbol]:

When the Ignorance which was to be overcome hath been dispersed, the effort to overcome it ceaseth, and the Path cometh to an end and the Journey is completed.

The Journeying having ceased, there is no place beyond the ending of the Path to explore ; and one obtaineth the Supreme Boon of the Great Symbol, the Unabiding State of *Nirvāṇa*.[1]

[*THE SUMMARY OF THE TEACHINGS*]

(120) In the complete versions of *The Transmutation*,[2] [Naropa quoteth his illustrious *guru*, Tilopa, thus]:

[1] Text : *Mignas-pahi-mya-ngan-las-hdas-pa* (pron. *Minay-pai-mya-ngan-lay-day-pa*) : *Mignas-pahi* = 'non-abiding'; *mya-ngan-las-hdas-pa* = ' passing beyond sorrow', which is the accepted Tibetan rendering of the Sanskrit word *Nirvāṇa*. The Path through the *Sangsāra* ends upon the realizing of *Nirvāṇa*. There is no *place* beyond *Nirvāna* to explore, for *Nirvāna* is not a place, but a state of mind. There is, however, according to Mahāyānic Buddhism, as already stated, unending evolutionary progression ; so that *Nirvāṇa* is to be regarded as a Spiritual Rest-House on the Highway through Eternity. For the Fully Enlightened Ones, no line of demarcation exists between the *Sangsāra* and *Nirvāṇa*. They live in both states, and for Them neither state is an abiding or fixed state. Were *Nirvāṇa* an abiding state, that is to say, a state of finality, like the Heaven of the Semitic Faiths, no further evolutionary progress would be possible beyond It.

The Great Ones and the *Bodhisattvas*, as explained above (on p. 144[2]), renounce their right to pass on to a still Higher Evolution and remain within the Cosmos for the good of all sentient beings. It is these *Bodhic* Forces, thus active in the Cosmos, which, little by little, during the ages, modify the harshness of unenlightened Nature: and, by their All-Embracing Love and Compassion, lead mankind, step by step, towards a perfected social order on Earth. We can visualize a time in the infinity of the future when these Forces will have neutralized the sorrowful struggle for existence, will have conquered Evil and transmuted it into Good, will have dissipated Ignorance with the Light of Divine Wisdom, and so transformed the Cosmos that the *Sangsāra* and *Nirvāṇa* really will be in At-one-ment. Then will every living thing have attained the Goal of the Great Symbol. Then will the Journey through the Cosmos be ended for ever ; and the Path of the Higher Evolution be entered and lead to a Goal utterly beyond the conception of finite mind.

[2] This refers to a treatise, in Tibetan, concerning the *yogic* method of transmuting the body and transferring it, along with the principle of consciousness, to other planes of existence. The full title of the treatise is, *The Lord Naropa's Transcendental Doctrine called ' The Great Chariot for entering upon the Sublime Path, the Guide to Transmutation and Transference'*. Our quotation from it describes the state of the Perfected *Yogin* who has mastered the *Yoga* of the

' All hail! this is the Wisdom of the Intellect of him who
knoweth himself;
It is indescribable by use of speech, and is not an object of
the mind.
I, Tilopa, have [beyond this] nothing [further] to reveal.
' Act so as to know thyself by means of symbols in thine own
mind,[1]
Without imagining, without deliberating, without analysing,
Without meditating, without introspecting; keeping the
mind in its natural state.'

Herein, in these verses, is contained the essence of all that
hath gone before.

[Here endeth Part II: the Essential Subject Matter.]

## [PART III: THE CONCLUSION]

(121) Part III, the Conclusion, consisteth of recognizing
the Great Symbol, and setting oneself face to face with It;[2]
analysing the impediments [or obstacles] and errors [or
strayings away from the Truth] while treading the Path;
differentiating experiences, and practical knowledge [or con-
victions resulting from *yogic* practices] from theoretical knowledge [or mere mental understanding of verbal definitions].

### [*RECOGNIZING THE GREAT SYMBOL; AND THE FOUR* YOGIC *ATTAINMENTS*]

(122) In the first, recognizing the Great Symbol, and setting

Great Symbol. Books III and IV, which follow, present the essence of this
Doctrine by Naropa in relation to the transference of the principle of consciousness.

[1] This refers to those teachings that are conveyed wholly by means of
symbols and into which the *yogin* presumably has been initiated, so that, therefore, they have become a part of his mental content. Even in Islamic Sufism
there developed a similar method of instruction: ' In the beginning, says the
mystic *Khaja*, the doctrine of *Tasawwuf* was taught by signs, as even now the
occult part of it is similarly dealt with. The adepts could talk with each other
by signs without uttering a word.' (Cf. Sirdar Ikbal Ali Shah, *Islamic Sufism*,
London, 1933, p. 20.) And *Tasawwuf*, which consists firstly of hearing and observing the teachings of the *Shariat*, or canon of Islam, and secondly of meditating upon them, corresponds to the first two steps in Buddhistic *yoga*, namely,
hearing the *Dharma*, and pondering it.

[2] That is to say, there must be not only mental understanding, or recognition,
of the teachings, but actual transcendental realizing of them.

oneself face to face with It, the process is [fourfold] : to attain the state of quiescence ; [1] to utilize the experiences on the Path ; to differentiate the various experiences, and the degree of fervour, and the stages reached on the Path ; [2] to possess knowledge of having realized the fruits of any of these attainments.

These constitute the four classes of *yogic* attainment.

## [*ANALYSING THE IMPEDIMENTS AND ERRORS WHILE TREADING THE PATH*]

(123) In the second, analysing the impediments [3] and errors while treading the Path, the process is thus :

The impediments arising from phenomena becoming inimical [or mentally disturbing or confusing] are cleared away by the knowledge of the oneness of phenomena and mind. The impediments arising from thoughts becoming inimical are cleared away by the knowledge of the oneness of thoughts and the Body of Truth [or *Dharma-Kāya*].[4] The impediments arising from noumena becoming inimical are cleared away by the knowledge of the oneness of noumena and phenomena.

(124) The three errors arising from over-fondness for the

---

[1] Lit. 'To establish the foundation'. It is upon the state of quiescence, as upon a foundation, that the *yogin* must build.

[2] At a certain stage in the *yogic* practices, the *yogin* experiences four complementary degrees of fervency called, 'Warmth', 'Climax', 'Fortitude', and the 'Best of Truth'. The first degree, the 'Warmth', is so called because it is likened unto a fire which consumes the vulgar notions concerning phenomena and mind, and thus aids the *yogin* to realize Truth. It is concomitant with experiencing the first glimpses of Reality. The second degree, the 'Climax', is the climax of the glimpses, preceding the fuller dawning of Reality. The Light of Truth dissipates the Darkness of the Night of Ignorance. After this stage, no doubt or uncertainty concerning the Path, now illuminated with Divine Wisdom, can arise. Then, with 'Fortitude', the pilgrim goes onward till he reaches the 'Best of Truth', *Nirvāṇa*.

[3] Impediments are impediments only when the mind holds them to be impediments. It is only when the unenlightened mind of the neophyte regards a thing as an impediment to be got rid of that the thing becomes inimical to peace of body and mind.

[4] In realizing the Body (or State) of Truth, the True State, or Reality, the intuitive conviction is attained that the arising and vanishing of thoughts is a natural process, in tune with the rhythmic law of all things, and, as such, is inseparable from the One Body of Truth, in which everything mystically merges in divine at-one-ment.

quiescence born of meditation[1] are to be overcome [or avoided]
by the directing of one's spiritual development towards the
state wherein is experienced the Transcendental Vision.[2]

(125) There are four states in which one can go astray on
the Path :

The going astray in the state of the Voidness is overcome
by meditating upon the Voidness as being Compassion.[3] The
going astray in the state of sealing [4] [the mind to further
ingress of truth] is overcome by realizing the True Nature of
things as they are. The going astray in the state of the
' Preventer ' [trying to prevent the arising of thoughts] is overcome by realizing the inseparable union of the ' Preventer ' and
that which the ' Preventer ' trieth to prevent [5] The going astray

---

[1] The three errors are : over-fondness for analysing thoughts and thought-
processes; over-fondness for reflecting upon the analysis; and over-fondness
for the quiescent state of mind. (See p. 329[1].) Any of these conditions. when
the *yogin* grows habituated and attached to it, prevents further progress on
the Path. There are some *yogins* who become so over-fond of the quiescent
state of mind, particularly those practising *Hatha Yoga*, that unless safeguarded
by a wise *guru* they make no effort to advance beyond it, and not infrequently
develop the delusion that they have attained the Goal. So, for these reasons,
it becomes the duty of the *guru* not only to expound the teaching, but to
impress upon the disciple that the Path has many pitfalls, and that many misleading will-o'-the-wisps of the senses are certain to be seen thereon ere the
end be attained.

[2] That is, Reality. wherein, unlike when in the state of *dhyāna,* or meditation, no error exists or can arise.

[3] This going astray in the state of the Voidness arises from egotistical
thoughts such as, ' *I* shall never come back to human birth again ; *I* am living
on Earth for the last time ; *I* shall quit *sangsāric* existence for ever ; *I* have
reached the Goal ; *I* have realized *Nirvāna.*' Not until all self-consciousness be
eradicated, be transmuted into selflessness, into All-Embracing Altruism so
overwhelmingly selfless that no thought of self be left, can there be attunement
with the *Bodhisattvic* State, which is the Goal of the Great Symbol.

[4] Text : *rgyas-hdebs* (pron. *gyay-deb*) = ' sealing ', ' putting the seal to ',
with reference to the very serious error of egotistical dogmatism, or the
delusion that one's attainments and understanding are complete and infallible.
This closing of the doors of the mind to fresh truth automatically stops further
spiritual growth. It is called the *cul-de-sac* of the *pandit,* or intellectualist, and
has ever proved to be the great failing of ecclesiastical organizations, and the
cause of the decay of religions based upon scriptures accepted as presenting
truth in its completeness and finality.

[5] At the outset, the disciple was directed to try to prevent the arising of
thoughts, and came to realize that not only can thoughts not be inhibited, but
that efforts to do so merely produce more thoughts. The next step was to

on the Path itself is overcome by realizing the Simultaneously-born Great Symbol [1] and attaining Liberation.

### [DIFFERENTIATING EXPERIENCES AND PRACTICAL FROM THEORETICAL KNOWLEDGE]

(126) In the third, differentiating experiences and practical from theoretical knowledge, the process is thus :

Intellectual comprehension of the True State of the mind, by having heard and pondered concerning it, is theoretical knowledge. To understand it in terms of Oneness is Experience.[2] Actual mastery of it up to the Uncreated is Conviction.[3] But the term Complete Knowledge is not amiss when applied to its Complete Realization.

[Here endeth the text of *The Epitome of the Great Symbol*.]

### [THE COLOPHON]

[Now follows, on the second half of the seventh and last folio of our block-print, the following interesting story concerning the origin of the text.]

cease all efforts at inhibiting them. To remain in the state of the 'Preventer' is to be like a boy remaining in the kindergarten when he ought to have advanced to a higher form.

[1] The Simultaneously-born Great Symbol may be defined also as the ever-existent state of the Primordial and Immaculate Mind, which, when realized, confers Liberation. Of this state, the normal human mind is oblivious. Once Liberation be attained, errors on the Path cease. There is, nevertheless, in some *yogins*, a strong inclination to review, or retrace, the steps on the Path after the Goal is won. This is due to a peculiar fondness for the *yogic* exercises themselves. It is overcome by ever abiding in the State of Freedom.

[2] This implies *yogic* realization that the microcosmic mind in its natural, or true, condition is an unsullied, undisturbed, ever-flowing stream of consciousness, non-created and indestructible, arising from and returning to the Primordial One Mind.

[3] By having experienced the transcendent state, wherein dawns, in the inner consciousness, the realization that there is the Goal, ere the Goal has been attained, the *yogin* arrives at as complete a conviction concerning the existence of the Goal as one who sees the dawning of the day, ere the Sun has arisen, does concerning the existence of the Sun. In other words, long before the final attainment of the Goal, which is the Uncreated, *Nirvāṇa*, the faithful disciple arrives at absolute certainty that there is the Uncreated and that It is attainable.

The King of Zangkar,[1] named Zhanphan Zangpo,[2] having desired that the text of this treatise on *The Great Symbol*, and also that on *The Six Doctrines*,[3] be put into standardized compilations, presented more than twenty measures of saffron [to me, the compiler, who was his *guru*, named Padma-Karpo]. Seeing that unauthorized interpolations, purporting to be extracts from various portions of the Scriptures [which had crept into the text], were, in most instances, unreliable, I, Padma-Karpo [expurgated them]: and [as a result of my labours] hereby hand this Book on for the benefit of future devotees. I compiled it while living in the essence of devotional practices, in the southern mountains of Karchu,[4] at the place known as Essence of Perfection.[5]

May it prove to be auspiciously beneficial.

[Finally, at the end of the Colophon, this further comment is added]:

In order to multiply the gift of religion, Chögyal-Sodnam-Gyaltshan [6] donated one silver coin for the carving of each block-type [of this Book].[7]

[Here the Book endeth.]

---

[1] Text: *Zangs-dkar* (pron. *Zang-kar*). (Cf. p. 251³.)

[2] Text: *Gzhan-phan Bzang-po* (pron. *Zhan-phan Zang-po*), meaning, 'The Good Helper of Others', is probably the Tibetan rendering of a proper name originally in Sanskrit.

[3] Book III, following, contains the translation of *The Six Doctrines*, as compiled by the Bhikshu Padma-Karpo.

[4] Text: *Mkar-chu* (pron. *Kar-chu*). This range of mountains is in the southern part of Tibet, due south of Lhassa, and adjoining the eastern corner of Bhutan, in the district of Lhobrag Tsangpo, through which flows the river of the same name.

[5] Text: *Byang-chub-snying-po* (pron. *Chan-chub-nying-po*), meaning 'Essence of Perfection'. This appears to be the name of a hermitage or else of a small isolated place apart from villages. (Cf. p. 251.)

[6] Text: *Chös-rgyal-bsod-nams-rgyal-mtshan* (pron. *Chö-gyal-sod-nam-gyal-tshan*), meaning, 'Righteous King, the Banner of Good Fortune', is probably the honorific name of some noble and pious layman.

[7] There being seven folios of the block-print, each measuring nineteen and one-half inches in length and four inches in width, and a printed page to each side of a folio, or fourteen printed pages in all, fourteen blocks of type were carved, in wood; so that the pious nobleman donated fourteen silver coins.

THE DIVINE *ḌĀKINĪ*, VAJRA-YOGINĪ

Described on page xx

# BOOK III

## THE PATH OF KNOWLEDGE: THE *YOGA* OF THE SIX DOCTRINES[1]

### THE INTRODUCTION

#### I. THE FOUR CLASSES OF *TANTRAS*

THE matter of this Book, and of Book IV which follows, is in large measure Tantric, particularly that part of it concerned with visualizations and meditations. And in this connexion it is of importance for the student of history and of religious origins to know that the Lāmas recognize four chief classes of *yogic Tantras*, which may be briefly described as follows : (1) *Tantras* expository of the Thatness, or Ultimate Truth, and (2) of the Occult, or Mystic, Sciences ; (3) the *Yoginī*, or *Shakti*, *Tantras* ; and (4) the *Kālachakra Tantras*.

According to *lāmaic* tradition, the first class had origin 'in the east' (which probably refers to eastern Bengal) in the time of King Rab-sal (Rab-gsal), who is believed to have flourished before the beginning of the Christian era. The second class arose through Nāgārjuna and his followers during the second and third century of the Christian era, 'in the south' (which refers to Southern India). The third class, to which this Book and Book IV are related, is traceable to a learned teacher called Lawapa, of Urgyan (or Odyana), the ancient name of a region now comprised within the territory of Afghanistan, 'in the west' of India. It was Padma Sambhava, also of Urgyan, who first introduced and popularized among the Tibetans this class of *Tantras*. Padma Sambhava, otherwise known by his followers as *Guru* Rinpoch'e, the 'Precious *Guru*', is credited with having had eight Indian

---

[1] The Tibetan block-print, upon which our translation is based, bears the following title : *CHŌS DRUG BSDŌS-PAHI ZIN-BRIS BZHŪGS-SO* (pron. *CHÖ DUG DÜ-PAI ZIN-DI ZHÜ-SO*), meaning, 'Herein Lieth the Epitome of the Abridged Six Doctrines'.

*gurus* belonging to eight different Schools of Buddhism. Out
of the various teachings thus received he is believed to have
formulated the eclectic system of thought, now popularly
known in Tibet as that of the 'Red Caps', who constitute
the primitive Ñingmapa School. Concerning this system,
European scholars know very little from original sources; for
the contents and exact character of its Scriptures are as yet
mostly unknown outside Ñingmapa monasteries. So here, too,
there exists an almost virgin field for research, which should
produce material of great value to the history of Buddhism.
The fourth class, consisting of the *Kālachakra Tantras*, is
said to have originated 'in the north', in Shambala, and to
have been introduced into India about A.D. 600.

Although the distinctly Tantric elements contained herein, in
the texts of Books III and IV, are a legacy from the 'Precious
*Guru*', the treatises themselves are a compilation of the Kargyütpa School, which separated from the 'Old Style Ones'
as a result of a reform movement initiated by Marpa and
Milarepa in the twelfth century and is to-day flourishing
independently—like the Khadampa School, now transformed
into the Established Church of Tibetan Buddhism. The Introduction to *Tibet's Great* Yogī *Milarepa* treats of the dis-
tinguishing characteristics of the Kargyütpa School and of
the doctrines peculiar to the Kargyütpas.

Whereas in the preceding treatise all the teachings are
directed to the supreme end of arriving at Right Knowledge
concerning the real nature of mind and of the universe of
phenomena, in the present treatise the technique of the *Yoga*
Philosophy, more especially of that Tantric form of it called
in India *Kuṇḍalinī Yoga*, is made applicable to the following
Six Doctrines, more or less peculiarly Tibetan.

## II.  THE DOCTRINE OF THE PSYCHIC-HEAT

The first of these is known to the Tibetans as *Tūmmō*, signi-
fying a peculiar bodily heat, or warmth of a psycho-physical
character, generated by *yogic* means. According to the secret
lore, the word *Tūmmō* refers to a method of extracting *prāṇa*,
from the inexhaustible *prāṇic* reservoir in Nature, and storing

it in the human-body battery and then employing it to transmute the generative fluid into a subtle fiery energy whereby a psycho-physical heat is produced internally and made to circulate through the nerve-channels of the psychic nervous system.

This system, invisible to all save those possessed of clairvoyant vision, is the psychic counterpart of the physical nervous system. Its nerve-channels are called in Tibetan *tsas* and in Sanskrit *nāḍi*. Of these there are three of primary importance: the Median-Nerve (Tib. *Ūma-tsa*: Skt. *Sushumṇā-naḍī*), extending through the centre of the spinal column; the Right-Nerve (Tib. *Roma-tsa*: Skt. *Pingalā-nāḍī*); and the Left-Nerve (Tib. *Kyangma-tsa*: Skt. *Idā-nāḍī*). The last two, like two serpents, are said to coil round the Median-Nerve to the right and to the left. Connected with these three there are numerous subsidiary psychic-nerves by which the psycho-nervous energy (Tib. *Shugs*: Skt. *prāṇa*) is carried to each psychic nerve-centre (Tib. *khorlo*: Skt. *chakra*) and therein stored and thence distributed to every organ and part of the body. The system is described in more detail in *The Tibetan Book of the Dead*, pp. 214–16.

According to our text, in practising the art of *Tūmmō*, the *yogin* must employ very elaborate visualizations, meditations, postures, breathings, directing of thought, training of the psychic-nerve system, and physical exercises. Our annotations are sufficiently numerous and detailed to serve as a commentary and to afford the student some practical guidance. But, as the Tibetan *gurus* emphasize, it is highly desirable for the neophyte, prior to beginning the practice of *Tūmmō*, to obtain preliminary initiation and personal guidance from a master of the art.

A lengthy probationary period is usually necessary before the *yogin* can arrive at any assurance of success. At the outset, he must accustom himself to the minimum of clothing and avoid, as far as possible, resort to fire for warming the body. It is by their never wearing furs or woollen garments or seeking artificial external heat that the masters of the art are recognized. The *yogin* must also observe the strictest

sexual continence, for it is chiefly upon the *yogically* transmuted sex energy that proficiency in *Tūmmō* depends.

The actual practising must not be done inside or near the
dwelling of a householder, but preferably in some place of
hermitage, such as a remote mountain cave, far removed from
localities where the air is made impure by smoke or the auric
emanations of towns or villages. A *yogin* aiming at mastery
of the art may remain in such solitary hermitage for a very
long time and see no human being save the *guru*, who will
appear at intervals to direct the *yogin*'s progress. The beginner is advised to perform the *yogic* exercises in the
early morning before sunrise, when Nature and the Earth's
magnetic currents are apt to be the least disturbed. Once
the art is mastered, it can be practised anywhere and at any
time.

As progress is made in this science of *yogically* conserving
and directing the physical, mental, and psychic energy of the
human organism, the hermit *yogin* gradually develops the
psycho-physical warmth. The subtle fiery energy, accompanied by a pleasant warmth, begins to pervade every atom
of his body, and, little by little, he acquires the *yogic* power
of enduring, with comfort, the most extreme cold, clad only in
a single cotton cloth, or even entirely nude. Reference to this
is made in *Tibet's Great* Yogī *Milarepa*, p. 170:

    ' The warming breath of angels wear,
      As thy raiment pure and soft.'

When the probationary training ends and the neophyte feels
confident of success, the *guru* not infrequently tests him to
judge of the degree of proficiency attained. The following
account of such a testing is given by Madame David-Neel,[1]
whose interesting researches and experiences in the Orient,
especially with respect to Tibetan mystics, parallel in many
ways the editor's own:

' Upon a frosty winter night, those who think themselves
capable of victoriously enduring the test are led to the shore
of a river or lake. If all the streams are frozen in the region,

[1] Cf. A. David-Neel, *With Mystics and Magicians in Tibet* (London, 1931),
pp. 227–9.

a hole is made in the ice. A moonlight night, with a hard wind blowing, is chosen. Such nights are not rare in Tibet during the winter months.

'The neophytes sit on the ground, cross-legged and naked. Sheets are dipped in the icy water. Each man wraps himself in one of them and must dry it on his body. As soon as the sheet has become dry, it is again dipped in the water and placed on the novice's body to be dried as before. The operation goes on in that way until daybreak. Then he who has dried the largest number of sheets is acknowledged the winner of the competition.'

The size of the sheet varies. Some sheets are quite small, being little larger than the ordinary face towels; others are as big as large shawls. The rule requires that the *yogin* must have dried at least three of the wet sheets in order to be entitled to wear the insignia of proficiency in *Tümmō*, namely, the single white cotton shirt or robe, on account of which he comes to be called, in Tibetan, a *Repa*, meaning 'Cotton-Clad One'. Mila-repa, the great Tibetan *Yogin*, as his name, meaning 'Mila, the Cotton-Clad One', indicates, mastered the art of *Tümmō* under the guidance of his *guru* Marpa. Eight of Milarepa's advanced disciples, as stated in the first chapter of Milarepa's *Biography*, were also *Repas*. Other *Repas* are named in the appendix to the *Biography*.[1]

In addition to the drying of wet sheets on the *yogin*'s body, another test, to ascertain the degree of warmth which the *yogin* can generate, consists in making him sit naked in the snow, the quantity of snow melted under and round about him indicating his proficiency.

That there are at the present time adepts of *Tümmō* in hermitage in Tibet, many of whom, being followers of Milarepa, are of the Order of Cotton-Clad Ones, is undoubtedly true. More than one European has occasionally caught glimpses of such ascetics, and well-authenticated accounts of their immunity to the arctic-like temperatures of the Tibetan winter are current throughout the high Himālayan countries.

Being a part of *Hatha Yoga*, *Tümmō* appears to be known

[1] Cf. *Tibet's Great* Yogī *Milarepa*, pp. 41, 305.

also to Hindus. I recall that during the summer of 1918 I had as travelling companions for a few weeks a group of naked Hindu ascetics, who had come, as I had, direct from the torrid plains of India. We met in Srinagar. Thence, in the midst of a moving throng of thousands of pilgrims from all parts of India, of both sexes and of many castes, we set out *en route* to the glacier-clad heights of the Himālayas of Kashmir, on the age-hallowed pilgrimage to the Cave of Amar-Nath, wherein the holy of holies is a natural *lingam* (phallus) of ice, sacred to Shiva, the Lord of the World.[1] A certain number of the ascetics donned no clothing, not so much as a loin-cloth, even when we had attained an altitude of ten thousand feet above sea-level, where the nights were freezingly cold and the glaciers and snowy peaks breathed down upon us their icy breath. A few of the ascetics, even when the glaciers were being traversed, were still unclad and remained so during the whole pilgrimage. Others, shortly before, or when the Cave was reached, wrapped about themselves thin cotton garments; whilst the least adept used blankets in which they had been carrying their meagre food supply.

At that time, I knew nothing of the Tibetan art of generating the extraordinary bodily warmth. Consequently I did not question these Hindu ascetics as to their remarkable *yogic* hardihood, attributing it to their being, as no doubt some of them were, masters of *Hatha Yoga*, which confers immunity to extremes of cold and also of heat.

At Rikhikesh, on the Ganges, I once witnessed a demonstration of the *yogic* immunity to extreme heat. A naked *yogin* at midday in the hot season sat on the shimmering sands of the river-shore surrounded by four glowing fires of heaped-up wood and dried cow-dung within only a few feet of his naked body, each fire being in one of the four cardinal directions. The unclouded midsummer sun, directly over his

---

[1] Shiva, as the personification of the forces in nature making for destruction, is the Lord of Regeneration, and so his symbol is the phallus, or male organ of generation, as it was of Osiris, the Egyptian deity associated with human fertility.

uncovered head, constituted the fifth fire in the *yoga*, called the *Pancha-Dhūni* (' Five-Fires'), which he was practising. Similar feats, proving *yogic* immunity from heat and from fire itself, have been witnessed and attested by Europeans, not only in India and Ceylon, but throughout the South Sea Islands and elsewhere, in connexion with the fire-walking ceremony. And in some of the *Tovil* (Devil-Dancing) Ceremonies of Ceylon fire is trodden upon and grasped by the devil-dancers without harm, in virtue of the use of *mantras* called ' fire-cooling *mantras*' (Sinhalese, *gini-sisil*).

### III. THE DOCTRINE OF THE ILLUSORY BODY

The Doctrine of the Illusory Body, the second of the Six Doctrines, represents a Tibetan adaptation from Indian sources of the Doctrine of *Māyā*, which is a most fundamental doctrine in all Schools of Buddhism as in the Vedāntic School of Hinduism.

The Doctrine of *Māyā* asserts that the whole world and cosmic creation, subjective and objective, is illusory, and that mind is the sole reality. The objects of our senses, our bodily apparatus, our mental cognitions, inferences, generalizations, and deductions are but phantasmagoria. Though men of science classify and give fanciful Latin and Greek names to the various forms of matter, organic and inorganic, matter itself has no true existence. Colour and sound, and all things seen by the eyes or perceived by the sensory organs, as well as space and dimension, are equally fallacious phenomena.

*Māyā* is the Magic Veil, ever worn by Nature, the Great Mother Isis, which veils Reality. It is by *yoga* alone that the Veil can be rent asunder and man led to self-knowledge and self-conquest, whereby Illusion is transcended. Ultimate Truth is illusorily ever associated with Error ; but, like an alchemist of things spiritual, the master of *yoga* separates the dross, which is Ignorance, from the gold, which is Right Knowledge. Thus, by dominating Nature, he is liberated from enslavement to Appearances.

Professor Shāstrī has shown, in his scholarly examination

of the Doctrine of *Māyā*,[1] that the germs of the doctrine already existed in the later stage of Vedic civilization; and that, in the course of its long evolutionary history, the word *māyā* itself, in different grammatical forms, has connoted various but fundamentally interrelated concepts.

Primitively, *māyā* denoted a form of intelligence, energy, power (*shakti*), and deception. It chiefly implied a mysterious will-power, whereby Brahman wills, and as *māyā*, form is realized. As denoting deception, *māyā* refers to that magical glamour of appearances which causes the unenlightened percipient of them to conceive multiplicity and duality as being real. As the supreme magician, *māyā* produces the great cosmic illusion, the universe of phenomena.

The fundamental meaning of the word *māyā*, derived from the root *mā*, is 'to measure'. Hence *māyā* is that illusive projection of the Cosmos whereby the immeasurable Brahman appears as if measured. From the same root is further derived the meaning of 'to build', and this leads to the concept of the phenomenal universe being the magical structure built by Brahman, or, in the Mahāyāna sense, by Mind.

As an outgrowth of the earlier Vedic age, the Doctrine of *Māyā* is traceable throughout the *Brāhmanas* and the *Upanishads*, where its meaning is chiefly 'illusion', till, in the time of Shankara, this meaning became fixed. Historically speaking, *māyā* has commonly been viewed from two chief aspects: (1) 'As the principle of creation—*māyā* as a cause—corresponding to the sense of *shakti* (wondrous power); or (2) As the phenomenal creation itself—*māyā* as an effect—corresponding to the sense of "illusion", "appearance", etc.'[2]

That the microcosmic mind is not different or really separate from the Macrocosmic Mind has been aptly illustrated by the thinkers of India: Air in a sealed jar, as they explain, is not different from the outer air surrounding the jar, for once the jar is broken the confined air becomes the unconfined;

---

[1] Cf. Prabha Dutt Shāstrī, *The Doctrine of Māyā* (London, 1911). A similar but less comprehensive, survey was previously made by L. N. Apte in his work also entitled *The Doctrine of Māyā*, published in Bombay in 1896.

[2] Cf. P. D. Shāstrī, *op. cit.*, p. 31.

and, similarly, by breaking the Vessel of *Māyā*, the micro-cosmic mind becomes what it ever has been and ever will be, the Macrocosmic.

Primordial Mind, whence *māyā* arises, is ever unborn and unconditioned; It transcends its own creations. The Lord Krishna, in the *Bhagavad Gītā*, declares that with a single portion of His Essence He created the visible universe and yet ever remains apart from it.

Worlds and universes are mind-made; they are of the stuff of which dreams are shaped. It is their illusiveness which is *māyā*. Things, appearances, are what mind makes them to be. Apart from mind they have no existence. When, by means of *yoga*, the microcosmic aspect of mind is swept clear of the mists and the mirages of conditioned being, it sees itself as the One, emancipated from all *māyāvic* delusions, from all con-cepts of multiplicity and of dualism, from all the magical deceptions of Nature.

As wonderful power, or essential energy, in the form of heat, light, and electronic motion; as the mighty vibratory Dance of Life, as Nature, from whose Womb creatures come forth into Delusion, *māyā* is the Great Shakti, the Mother of Creation, containing in Herself the Primeval Germ, or Egg, the Universe-embracing Collective Thought-Form of Father Mind, realized, through illusory matter, as Appearances. Through innumerable myriads of forms, through innumerable myriads of eyes and sense-organs of creatures, through in-numerable myriads of microcosms, Mind knows Itself to be the Dreamer of *Māyā's* Kingdom. But until the Mirage of Being is scattered by Bodhic-Enlightenment, the Many know not the One.

The Doctrine of *Māyā* is the philosophical basis for the related doctrine of the One illusorily perceived as the Many, of the Macrocosm as the totality of all microcosms. In Greek thought, this was summed up in the axiom of Xenophanes, 'All is One'. Parmenides later taught concerning the unique unity of being and thought. Plato, like his great disciple Plotinus, arrived at substantially the same conclusion in the Doctrine of Ideas. Kant, too, probably influenced by the

Platonic School, similarly postulated that the world has no metaphysical, but purely an empirical, or apparitional, existence. Schopenhauer gratefully acknowledges indebtedness to the *Upanishads* for the formulation of his parallel deductions. On the assumption that the Universe has a relative existence, in relation to Mind whence it arose, the theory of Relativity represents a modern restating, in terms of Western science, of the age-old Doctrine of *Māyā*.

Thus, in the meaning conveyed by the Doctrine of *Māyā*, the illusory body, the *māyāvi-rūpa* of Hindu Philosophy, is, like the whole Cosmos, of which it is a part, merely an appearance, a transitory thought-form, like every object in Nature. Like the Earth and the Universe, whence it sprang, it has a relative, but not a real existence. As an appearance, which is comparable to a magical illusion, the illusory body of man is no more than an emanation of Mind, in the sense implied by the Tibetan term *tulku*, referring to the physical manifestation of the *Nirmāṇa-Kāya* ('Body of Divine Incarnation'). It is merely the *māyāvic* product of the will to live, the offspring of desire, the *sangsāric* sheath of mind.

### IV. THE DOCTRINE OF THE DREAM-STATE

The Doctrine of Dreams, which follows, further illustrates the Doctrine of *Māyā*. It shows that even as all sensuous experiences of the waking-state are illusory, equally illusory are all sensuous experiences of the dream-state; these two states forming the two poles of human consciousness. In other words, Nature as a whole is the Dream of the One Mind; and until man conquers Nature, and thereby transcends *māyā*, he will remain asleep, dreaming the Dream of Ignorance. Whether in this world, or in any after-death state, all *sangsāric*, or *karmically*, conditioned experiences, are but dreams.

Only when one awakes from sleep is the illusory character of a dream realized; only when the dreamer of the Dream of Ignorance awakes, in the unconditioned, sleepless, dreamless, True State, can the illusory character of the *Sangsāra* be comprehended.

We speak of the dream-state as being unreal and the waking-state as being real. Strictly speaking, however, both states are unreal, for they depend upon the same order of objective and sensuous perceptions, those of the dream-world merely being internal and those of the waking-world external. The mind alone is the cognizer of sensuous impressions, and the mind makes no real distinction between these, whether they be internally or externally cognized. In the mind, as in a mirror, both the internal and the external sense objects are reflected, and apart from mind have no existence, being, as the Doctrine of *Māyā* teaches, merely appearances.

By a careful analytical study of dreams and psychological experimentation on himself as the subject, the *yogin* at last comes actually thus to realize, and not merely to believe, that the total content of the waking-state as well as of the dream-state is, in fact, illusory phenomena.

As a spider spins from the substance of its own body a web and then draws the web back again into itself, so the All-Mind, personified by the Hindus as Brahmā, evolves the Cosmic Creation from Itself and again absorbs it. The Web of Brahmā is the *māyā* into which sentient beings fall and are held in *sangsāric* bondage; it is the Wheel of Life to which they are bound by *karma*; the Promethean Rock to which humanity is chained, a prey to the Eagles of Desire.

Brahmā sleeps and wakes. When He sleeps, His Dream is the Cosmic Creation. When He wakes, His Dream ends. His Dream-State is the *Sangsāra*; His Waking-State, *Nirvāṇa*. In the All-Mind both the Created and the Uncreated, the *Sangsāra* and *Nirvāṇa*, have origin; and in the All-Mind's Supreme Comprehension both are in at-one-ment.[1]

[1] How nearly our own Western science has reached a view parallel to this of the Wise Men of the East will be seen in what Sir James Jeans has put on record in *The Universe Around Us* (Cambridge, 1933), on pp. 294 and 354-5. He speaks of reducing ' the whole of nature to a mental concept, since the texture of nature is nothing but the texture of the space-time continuum '. Then he propounds the following view: ' All this makes it clear that the present matter of the universe cannot have existed for ever; indeed, we can probably assign an upper limit to its age of, say, some such round number as two-hundred million million years. .... The universe now becomes a finite picture whose dimensions are a certain amount of space and a certain amount

The whole purpose of the Doctrine of Dreams is to stimulate the *yogin* to arise from the Sleep of Delusion, from the Nightmare of Existence, to break the shackles in which *māyā* thus has held him prisoner throughout the aeons, and so attain spiritual peace and joy of Freedom, even as did the Fully Awakened One, Gautama the Buddha.

### V. THE DOCTRINE OF THE CLEAR LIGHT

The Clear Light, in its primal aspect, symbolizes the unconditioned, pure *Nirvāṇic* Consciousness, the transcendent, Supramundane Consciousness of a Fully Awakened One. It is a Mystic Radiance of the *Dharma-Kāya*, of the *Nirvāṇic* Consciousness free of all *sangsāric* or conditioned obscuration. It cannot be described ; It can only be known ; and to know It is to know the Thatness of all things. As being colourless, or without qualities, It is the Clear Light ; as being without limitations, It is All-Pervading Intelligence ; as being unknowable in terms of *sangsāric* consciousness, and without form, It is the Formless Void.

The Clear Light is momentarily experienced by all human beings at the moment of death ; by masters of *yoga* it is experienced in the highest states of *samādhi* at will, and unceasingly by Buddhas. The conscious realizing of the Clear Light, while still incarnate, is synonymous with the attainment of Buddhahood. Much more difficult is it to realize the Clear Light after the process called death, as *The Tibetan Book of the Dead* teaches. Hence, as in Books I and II, above, the *guru* urges the neophyte not to throw away the rare opportunity offered by human birth to win the Great Treasure.

of time ; the protons and electrons are the streaks of paint which define the picture against its space-time background. Travelling as far back in time as we can brings us not to the creation of the picture but to its edge ; the creation of the picture lies as much outside the picture as the artist is outside the canvas. On this view, discussing the creation of the universe in terms of time and space is like trying to discover the artist and the action of painting by going to the edge of the picture. This brings us very near to those philosophical systems which regard the universe as a thought in the mind of its Creator.'

In words vibrant with the spiritual insight and greatness of one of the Masters of Tibetan Wisdom, the Clear Light is referred to thus :

' Difficult is it to attain Knowledge of the Formless. Equally difficult is the acquiring of emancipation from *karma* and re-birth, and the realizing of the Clear Light, bright as the com-bined radiance of a gem, of fire, of the Moon, and of the Sun. From the Clear Light its kindred lights, shining in the Dark-ness, are born. From them cometh the radiance and warmth of the light of the Sun. From the light of the Sun cometh the light of the Moon ; and from the Moon, the embodiment of coolness, cometh the All-Pervading Radiance of Wisdom. Thus, the fundamental Voidness, which illuminateth the phe-nomenal objects of Nature, maketh visible all the World Systems.' [1]

### VI.  THE DOCTRINE OF THE AFTER-DEATH STATE

The fifth of the Six Doctrines, the Doctrine of the *Bardo*, or Intermediate State, following death and preceding birth, is an epitomized version of the *Bardo-Thödol* (' Liberation by Hearing while on the After-Death Plane '), comprised in two books in the original, and translated and expounded in detail in *The Tibetan Book of the Dead*.

The reader will observe that the Doctrine of *Bardo* as herein presented is complementary both to the Doctrine of the Clear Light and to the preceding doctrines concerning *Māyā* ; for it views the after-death state as being merely a prolonged dream-state following and dependent upon the equally illusory state called the living-state.

As *The Tibetan Book of the Dead* continually emphasizes, unless the dying person possesses, as a result of having suc-cessfully practised *yoga* while incarnate, the *yogic* power to hold fast to the after-death condition in which the Clear Light dawns, he mentally sinks downward, stage by stage, and the Clear Light of Reality fades from his consciousness. Then

---

[1] As translated by the late Lāma Kazi Dawa-Samdup, from a Tibetan treatise known as *Bsre-hpho* (pron. *Se-pho*), meaning, ' Blending and Transform-ing ', folios 60–1.   Further reference is made to this treatise on p. 230 [3].

for him comes the second death, the after-death death, and he begins to experience the true *Bardo*.

Therein, even more deeply immersed in the hallucinatory delusions arising from *māyā* than he was in the living (or waking) state, he remains for such period of time as his *karma* determines. Thence, when the hour strikes, he enters the womb and begins life anew, still enslaved to passions and dominated by Ignorance.

If, on the other hand, the dying person be one who while living had acquired proficiency in *yoga*, then, by a supreme effort of will, when about to expire, he enters into the highest *samādhic* trance, in transcendent communion with the Clear Light, and his death takes place without break in continuity of consciousness. Thus, unlike the unenlightened, he transcends the swooning into unconsciousness, which normally accompanies the separation of the principle of consciousness from the earth-plane body at the moment of death. No master of *yoga* ever dies in the normal manner, unless, perchance, he be killed suddenly and unexpectedly; he merely relinquishes the physical form which he has come to recognize as no more than a garment to be put on or off as desired, in full consciousness while immersed in the ecstatic condition of mind wherein the Clear Light ever shines. The *Bodhisattva* knowingly enters upon the Path of Rebirth at the auspicious moment; and, being of the Fourth Order of Initiates, 'cometh into existence in the mother's womb knowingly, remaineth in it knowingly, and cometh out from it knowingly', as the Buddha teaches.[1]

This mighty accomplishment of wandering at will, with ever unbroken continuity of consciousness, through all states of illusory being, with microcosmic mind attuned to and in divine at-one-ment with the Macrocosmic Mind, is the Goal of the *Dharma*. The Conqueror of *Māyā* becomes a master of life and death, a Light in the Darkness, a Guide to the Bewildered, a Freer of the Enslaved. In the transcendent language of the Great Path, the *Mahāyāna*, no longer is there for Him any distinction between the *Sangsāra* and *Nirvāna*.[2]

---

[1] Cf. the *Samgīti Sūtta, Dīgha-Nikāya*, of the Pali canon.
[2] It is this theme which underlies the whole of Book V, following.

Like an unbridled lion roaming free among the mountain ranges, He roams at will through the Existences.[1]

According to the esoteric symbology of the Tibetan *gurus*, the process of death is compared to that of a lamp dying for lack of oil. By similar symbolism, they explain esoterically the various apparitional phenomena, such as the radiances, sounds, and forms, perceived by the one when dying and in the after-death state.

Rationally considered, as *The Tibetan Book of the Dead* teaches, all apparitional visions seen by the deceased are purely illusory, being nothing more than the hallucinatory embodiments of the thought-forms arising from the mental content of the percipient, as a direct result of the psychic stimuli produced by the death-process reacting upon the mind. In other words, as an outcome of death, intellectual impulses assume personified form in the after-death dream-state.

Correspondingly, during the process of rebirth, which is the reverse of death, occur parallel phenomena perceived in reversed order. There exists in Tibetan a very vast literature, to which our present text belongs, concerning both the discarding and the assuming of a human body ; and also much matter descriptive of the prenatal state, while the consciousness is overshadowing and directing the growth of the embryo in the womb.

## VII. THE DOCTRINE OF CONSCIOUSNESS-TRANSFERENCE

The last of the Six Doctrines, which concerns the art of transferring the consciousness (Tib. *rnampar-shes-pa*—pron. *nampar-she-pa* : Skt. *vijñāna-skandha*), is called in Tibetan *Pho-wa* ; and *Pho-wa* is one of the most jealously guarded of the secret *yogic* practices of Tibet, as of India, more especially with respect to its practical application by the *yogin* while still incarnate. The Introduction to Book IV, which follows, will make this clear. In our present text, the art is expounded chiefly for the benefit of the *yogin* himself. The second half of the longer version of the *Pho-wa*, in Book IV, expounds the doctrine in its ritual aspect, as applicable by the priestly

[1] Cf. *Tibet's Great Yogī, Milarepa*, p. 35.

officiant on behalf of a person about to die or recently deceased. It is preferable, therefore, that our two texts of the *Pho-wa* be studied together.

Success in the transferring of the principle of consciousness is dependent upon proficiency in *Kuṇḍalinī Yoga*. In the *Jetsün-Kahbum*, the process itself is ' likened to a bird flying out of an open skylight ',[1] the skylight being the Aperture of Brahma, situated on the crown of the head at the sagittal suture where the two parietal bones articulate, opened by means of the *yogic* practice of *Pho-wa*. The bird flying out of it is the consciousness-principle taking its departure from the body, either permanently at death or temporarily during the *yogin*'s exercise of the art. It is through mastery of *Pho-wa* that the Great *Yogin* transcends normal processes by voluntarily relinquishing his old, outworn body and taking a new body, without suffering any break in the continuity of his consciousness. In the esoteric sense implied by the Christian initiate St. Paul, the grave thus loses its sting and death its victory ; and the Great *Yogin* becomes truly the Conqueror, both of Death and of Life.

[1] Cf. *Tibet's Great* Yogi, *Milarepa*, p. 155.

# [THE PATH OF KNOWLEDGE: THE *YOGA* OF THE SIX DOCTRINES]

## [THE OBEISANCE]

(1) Obeisance at the feet of the Holy, Glorious *Gurus*!

## [THE FOREWORD]

(2) The Explaining of this Guide to the wonderful method of making pre-eminently clear the automatic production of the Wisdom of the Simultaneously-born,[1] by means of controlling the mind and breath, which are correlative with the sublime human body,[2] consisteth of two parts; the Tradition of the Succession of *Gurus*; and the Teachings handed down by that Succession.

(3) Of these two, the first is in accordance with the Prayer of the Succession.[3]

(4) The second, the Teachings which have been handed down by that Succession, are twofold: the Systematic Teaching, according to the *Tantras*; and the Ear-Whispered Teachings, which appertain to the Order of *Gurus* who convey their instructions telepathically.[4]

---

[1] The True Wisdom is born in the devotee simultaneously with the *Bodhic* recognition of the unreality of all states and conditions of phenomenal, or *sangsāric*, existence. See p. 115[1].

[2] Text: *Rdo-rje-hi-lüs* (pron. *Do-rje-yi-lü*): Skt. *Vajra-Kāya*: 'Sublime Body', with reference to a beautiful, well-proportioned, and healthy human body. If the devotee possesses a diseased, infirm, or impure body, he must first perfect it by special *yogic* practices. By Tibetan, as by Indian, *gurus*, it is commonly held that *Hatha-Yoga* ('Health-Yoga'), whereby bodily diseases, infirmities, and impurities are eliminated, is the first preparatory step on the Path to Enlightenment. The Buddha Gautama is credited with having been born in a body endowed with all physical and spiritual beauties and perfections and, as He ascertained, by experimenting with *Hatha-Yoga* and *yogic* bodily mortification, all such practices were for Him unnecessary.

[3] One form of this Prayer is contained in the text of Book IV, p. 262.

[4] The Systematic, or Methodical, Teachings are those formulated into texts to be studied by the disciple under the *guru*'s personal guidance. Those which are Ear-whispered, that is, Esoteric, are never committed, in detailed completeness, to writing. By means of what our text calls 'gift-waves', or 'psychic emanations', that is, telepathy, the secret teachings are transmitted from the Divine *Gurus* in the Heaven Worlds direct to the human *gurus* of the Succession incarnate on Earth. (See p. 123[1], above.) The human *gurus*, in turn,

(5) Herein is explained the Ear-Whispered Teachings, which appertain to the Order of *Gurus* who convey their instructions telepathically.

(6) These teachings are in two parts: those which are preparatory, and those which constitute this treatise.

(7) The first, the preparatory, are to be found elsewhere.[1]

(8) The second, those which constitute this treatise, consist of the Psychic-Heat, the Illusory Body, Dreams, the Clear Light, the Intermediate State, and the Transference.[2]

## [CHAPTER I: THE DOCTRINE OF THE PSYCHIC-HEAT]

(9) The first, the Psychic-Heat, consisteth of three parts: the Preliminaries; the Fundamental Practices; and the Practical Application.

transmit these secret teachings to specially selected disciples. Our text, being based upon the 'Ear-Whispered' Teachings, is, therefore, purposely undetailed. Very often it is little more than a series of phrases, arranged in incomplete sentences, which to the uninitiated reader may sometimes appear meaningless or else enigmatic (as they are often intended to be), but which to the initiated disciple suggest the teachings in their entirety. Epitomized treatises of this character, like the *Yoga Sūtras* of Patanjali, are comparable to summaries of a professor's lectures. The *guru* is expected to explain the enigmatical passages and to amplify the texts by verbal commentary.

[1] The preparatory teachings are the ordinary exoteric teachings which prepare the neophyte for the preliminary steps on the Path leading to Initiation. As they are available in numerous popular religious treatises, and in Scriptures, upon which, like most exoteric teachings, they are based, our text merely mentions them. It is true, of course, that, when published, the hitherto 'esoteric' and 'ear-whispered' teachings of our own text will be, in large measure, also exoteric.

[2] The Tibetan of the text for these six occult doctrines is as follows: (1) *Gtūm-mō* (pron. *Tūm-mō*), meaning, 'Psychic (or Vital, or Secret) Heat (or Warmth)', which is the necessary driving force for the devotee seeking spiritual development, and the means for the solitary hermit, in the very severe cold of the snowy ranges of Tibet, to be comfortable without fire; (2) *Sgyu-lüs* (pron. *Gyu-lü*), meaning, 'Illusory Body' (or 'Illusoriness of the Body'), whereby is realized the transitory and illusory nature of one's own body and of all component things; (3) *Rmi-lam* (pron. *Mi-lam*), meaning, 'Dreams', whereby is realized that even as dream experiences are unreal, so are all waking experiences; (4) *Höd-gsal* (pron. *Öd-sal*), meaning 'Clear Light', the visual state when experiencing Reality; (5) *Bar-do* (pron. *Bar-do*), meaning, 'Intermediate State', with reference to the state of existence intervening between death and rebirth; and (6) *Pho-va* (pron. *Pho-wa*), 'Transference [of the Consciousness]', as in *yoga*.

## [*PART I: THE FIVE PRELIMINARY EXERCISES*]

(10) The first, the Preliminaries, consisteth of five exercises: Visualizing the Physical [or External] Body as being Vacuous; Visualizing the Psychic [or Internal] Nerve-System as being Vacuous; Visualizing the Protective Circle; the Training of the Psychic Nerve-Paths; and the Conferring of the 'Gift-Waves' upon the Psychic Nerve-Centres.

### [PRELIMINARY EXERCISE I: VISUALIZING THE PHYSICAL BODY AS BEING VACUOUS][1]

(11) In the first of the preliminary exercises, Visualizing the Physical Body as being Vacuous, proceed according to the practices which now follow.

(12) At the outset, say the Prayer leading up to the communion with the Divine *Guru*.[2]

(13) Then imagine thyself to be the Divine Devotee Vajra-Yoginī,[3] red of colour; as effulgent as the radiance of a ruby;[4] having one face, two hands, and three eyes;[5] the right hand

---

[1] This *yogic* exercise of visualizing the physical body and then its psychic nerve-system as being internally vacuous is, as will be seen, chiefly preparatory to the realization that the human organism, like all things in Nature, is wholly vacuous and illusory.

[2] One form of this Prayer is given on p. 262. (Cf. pp. 116[1] and 182-4.)

[3] Text: *Rdo-rje-rnal-hbyor-ma* (pron. *Do-rje-nal-jor-ma*): Skt. *Vajra-Yoginī*: 'Divine Yoginī' (or Devotee), a Tantric personification of spiritual energy and *Bodhic* Intellect. When visualized and through practice of *yoga* realized as such, the Goddess confers upon the *yogin* success in *Siddhi* ('miraculous Accomplishment'). The Illustration facing p. 155, above, depicts the mystic form of the Goddess in accordance with the textual description which now follows.

[4] The colour and effulgence symbolize the Radiance of Wisdom which consumes or dispels Ignorance (Skt. *Avidyā*), or the belief that appearances, or even the personality, or ego (itself a mental conglomerate dependent wholly upon a sensuous universe), are real. The Truth, as personified in *Vajra-Yoginī*, which disperses the Gloom of Ignorance, is that Reality is non-*sangsāric*, beyond all such concepts of the ego as are by the ego's very nature limited to earths, universes, heavens, hells, and sentient beings; It is the Unborn, Uncreated, called *Nirvāṇa*.

[5] The third eye, situated in the forehead at the junction of the eye-brows, as depicted on images of the Buddha, is the Eye of *Bodhic* Insight. In man, in its latent or undeveloped condition, it is physiologically represented by the pineal gland, which, when *yogically* developed, is said to become the seat of clairvoyant vision.

holding aloft a brilliantly gleaming curved knife and flourishing it high overhead, cutting off completely all mentally disturbing thought-processes;[1] the left hand holding against her breast a human skull filled with blood;[2] giving satisfaction with her inexhaustible bliss;[3] with a tiara of five dried human skulls on her head;[4] wearing a necklace of fifty blood-dripping human heads;[5] her adornments, five of the Six Symbolic Adornments, the cemetery-dust ointment being lacking;[6] holding, in the bend of her arm, the long staff, symbolizing the Divine Father, the *Heruka*;[7] nude, and in the full bloom

---

[1] By the discriminating power born of *yoga*, as by a keen knife, unruliness of mind is dominated, or cut off, *yoga* being, as defined by Patanjali (*Yoga Sūtras*, i. 2), 'the suppression of the transformations of the thinking principles', or 'the restraint of mental modifications'.

[2] The human skull filled with blood symbolizes renunciation of the world, in virtue of which the Goddess bestows success in *yogic* practices.

[3] This refers to the ecstatic bliss attained by this *yoga* in its character as *Kuṇḍalinī Yoga*.

[4] The tiara of human skulls denotes that the highest degree of spiritual discernment, to be attained by meditation on the Goddess, is unattainable without renunciation of the world.

[5] These heads are to be visualized as having been freshly severed from human bodies. They signify that in the devotee (of whom Vajra-Yoginī is the divine personification) there must be complete and irretrievable severance from the *Sangsāra* (as the Round of Deaths and Births), and that through the power thereby conferred upon the devotee by the mystic Goddess, there is won *Bodhic* memory, which can never be lost, of the undesirability of *sangsāric* existence. Thus, all desire to re-enter the *Sangsāra*, except as a *Bodhisattva* to work for the salvation of unenlightened beings, is for ever extinguished, even as life has been extinguished in the decapitated bodies. Each of the fifty heads is symbolized by one of the fifty phonetic visualizations set forth on p. 180, following.

[6] The five of the Six Symbolic Adornments of *Vajra-Yoginī* are : (1) the tiara of human skulls, (2) the necklace of human heads, (3) the armlets and wristlets, (4) the anklets, and (5) the breastplate Mirror of Karma, held in place by double strings of human-bone beads extending over the shoulders and thence downwards to and around the waist. These adornments are interpreted in *Tibet's Great* Yogī *Milarepa*, pp. xv–xvii. The sixth of the adornments, the cemetery-dust ointment, which is lacking, is so called because it is made of dust collected in a cemetery, or place of cremation, and rubbed over the whole of the body. This *yogic* ointment symbolizes utter renunciation of the world and conquest over fear of death ; and is thus like the ashes with which Indian *yogins* anoint themselves. The Six Symbolic Adornments denote the Six *Pāramitā* ('Boundless Virtues') which are necessary for the attaining of Buddhahood. (See pp. 92[4], 352.)

[7] The *Heruka* is the *yogic* personification of the male, or positive, aspect of the Enlightening Power ; his consort, Vajra-Yoginī, is the personification of its

of virginity, at the sixteenth year of her age ;[1] dancing, with
the right leg bent and foot uplifted, and the left foot treading
upon the breast of a prostrate human form ;[2] and Flames of
Wisdom forming a halo about her.[3]

(14) [Visualize her as being thyself], externally in the shape
of a deity, and internally altogether vacuous like the inside
of an empty sheath, transparent and uncloudedly radiant ;
vacuous even to the finger-tips, like an empty tent of red silk,
or like a filmy tube distended with breath.[4]

(15) At the outset, let the visualization be about the size
of thine own body ; then, as big as a house ; then, as big as
a hill ; and, finally, vast enough to contain the Universe.
Then concentrate thy mind upon it.

(16) Next, gradually reduce it, little by little, to the size of
a sesamum seed,[5] and then to the size of a very greatly
reduced sesamum seed, still having all the limbs and parts
sharply defined.  Upon this, too, concentrate thy mind.[6]

female, or negative, aspect. The long staff, symbolizing the Heruka, indicates
that the Divine Pair are in union, for the two aspects of the Enlightening
Power, or Truth, are inseparably One. (See p. 147[2-4], above.)

[1] The Divine Mother is nude ; for, like the Divine Father, she is one of the
*Herukas*, ' the Unclad ', being ' naked ' to all things of the *Sangsāra*, of which
she has divested herself. And, being unsullied by the world, she is depicted in
the flower of virginity, like a beautiful maiden of sixteen.

[2] The treading under foot of a human form symbolizes the treading under foot
of all things of the *Sangsāra*—of Ignorance, and Illusion ; for of these is Form
the product.

[3] The Flames, or Radiances, of Wisdom, constituting the aura of the Goddess,
dispel, from the Path, the Gloom of Ignorance, and all Uncertainty or Error ;
for the Flames are the direct outcome of *yoga*, or meditation on the Saving
Truths, which consume, like mystic flames, all Wrong Knowledge.

[4] Each of these similes has *yogic* significance, which will become clear as the
teachings are unfolded.

[5] The sesamum (Skt. *til*) seed is small like a mustard seed. Our text here
contains *til* untranslated, as a bit of internal evidence of these teachings having
originated in India.

[6] These exercises are for habituating the mind of the *yogin* to the two
extremes of size—the maximum and the minimum, the universal and the
infinitesimal, the unlimited and the limited, preparatory to the realization of the
Many as the One, or of the One as the Many. It has, too, as will be observed
in the following section, special value in connexion with exercising and
strengthening the channels of the psychic and *prāṇic* forces of the body.

[PRELIMINARY EXERCISE 2: VISUALIZING THE PSYCHIC
NERVE-SYSTEM AS BEING VACUOUS]

(17) In the second of the preliminary exercises, Visualizing
the Psychic Nerve-System as being Vacuous, proceed according to the practices which now follow.

(18) As extending through the centre of thy body [from
the perineum to the Aperture of Brahma on the crown of the
head],[1] thy body visualized as being the body of the Divine
Yoginī, of normal size, imagine the median-nerve as possessing
the following four characteristics: redness like that of a solu-
tion of lac,[2] brightness like that of the flame of a sesamum-
oil lamp, straightness like that of the inner core of the plantain
plant,[3] and hollowness like that of a hollow tube of paper.
Let this visualization be about the size of a medium-sized
arrow-reed.

(19) Then, when that hath been done, expand the visualization to the size of a staff, then to the size of a pillar, then to
the size of a house, then to the size of a hill, and, finally, make
it vast enough to contain the Universe.

(20) Meditate upon the median-nerve as pervading every
part of the visualized body, even to the tips of the fingers.[4]

(21) When the visualization is the size of a sesamum seed,
meditate upon the median-nerve pervading it as being in
thickness the one-hundredth part of the diameter of a hair
[and hollow].

(22) It hath been said,

'Create [or visualize] vacuity in that which is not clearly
defined [because so minute];

---

[1] This is the highway for the circulation of the psychic forces of the human
body. (See pp. 157, 170.)

[2] A dark red resin used in Oriental countries for making a brilliant red dye.

[3] A tropical plant allied to the banana, which contains a straight inner core,
comparable to the median-nerve at the centre of the spinal column.

[4] But the median-nerve does not really pervade the body thus. This meditation exercise is for the purpose of helping the beginner in *yoga* to recognize
the vacuity, or unsubstantiality, and, thereby, the unreality, of all component
things, including the human form, each existing thing, alike, being the product
of transitory phenomena.

Create vacuity in that which cannot be caught hold of [by the eye, because invisible];

Create vacuity in that which doth not rest [or is transitory].'[1]

## [PRELIMINARY EXERCISE 3: VISUALIZING THE PROTECTIVE CIRCLE]

(23) In the third of the preliminary exercises, Visualizing [or Meditating upon] the Protective Circle, there are three parts: the Art of Posturing the Body; the Art of Breathing; and the Art of Directing Thought [or Mental Imagery].[2]

(24) The first of these three, the art of posturing the body, consisteth of the seven methods of making manifest all [psycho-physical] processes [or things].[3]

(25) In the Art of Breathing, one is to exhale the dead air thrice, then to press down the inhalation [to the very bottom of the lungs], then to raise the diaphragm a little so as to make the distended chest conform to the shape of a closed vessel [like an earthen pot] and to hold it thus as long as possible.[4]

[1] The first process of creating, or visualizing, vacuity has reference to material substance in its most minute organic aspects, barely visible to the human eye unaided by a microscope; the second, to matter in its invisible forms; the third, to the smallest particle of time mentally conceivable (cf. p. 129 [2]).

[2] These three arts, namely, the *yogic* posturing of the body (Skt. *āsana*), the *yogic* disciplining and right directing of the breathing-process (Skt. *prāṇā-yāma*), and the *yogic* mastery of the thought-process (Skt. *dhāraṇā*) arouse in the *yogin* psychic virtues which shield him from worldly distractions and undesirable influences, and bestow upon him soundness of physical, mental, and spiritual health. Therefore they are called the 'Protective Circle', as will be seen more clearly at the end of this section.

[3] In *The Epitome of the Great Symbol*, §§ 6-9, above, these seven methods are called the 'Seven Methods of Vairochana'. At this point in the present treatise their expounding has been left to the *guru*; but later on they are set forth herein in connexion with the Fundamental Practices, in §§ 49-50.

[4] Comparison should here be made with the same process as given in *The Epitome of the Great Symbol*, § 43, and designated as the employing of the 'Pot-shaped'. This forming of the air-distended chest into a shape like that of an earthen pot is done by drawing in the diaphragm and contracting the lower abdominal muscles. As in the Great Symbol practice, the 'Pot-shaped' is employed as an object upon which to fix the gaze when engaged in *yogic* meditation.

(26) In the Art of Directing Thought [or Mental Imagery], one is to imagine, when the expiration is going out, that innumerable five-coloured rays are issuing from each of the hair-pores of the body and radiating over the whole world and filling it with their five-coloured radiances, and that when the inspiration is coming in they are re-entering the body through the hair-pores and filling the body.

(27) Each of these [two complementary exercises] is to be performed seven times.[1]

(28) Then imagine that each of the rays is changed into the syllable *HŪM*,[2] vari-coloured ; and that while the expiration is going out the world is being filled with these *HŪMS*, and that when the inspiration is coming in, that one's body is being filled with them.   Do this seven times.

(29) Next imagine that the *HŪMS* are changed into Wrathful Deities,[3] each having one face and two hands ;[4] the right hand held aloft, flourishing overhead a *dorje* ;[5] the left hand held in a menacing posture against the heart ;[6] the right leg bent and the left leg held tense ;[7] of very angry and fierce mien and of five colours,[8] none of them larger than a sesamum seed.

---

[1] These exercises are commonly employed in order to attain the power of transferring thought, as in telepathy, and visualizations or pictures, as in television ; both of which arts have long been known to masters of the occult sciences of the Orient and made use of without the costly and cumbrous physical apparatus of European scientists.

[2] See p. 127 [1].

[3] These Deities are wrathful in appearance because they symbolize the protective spiritual power of good which ever threatens evil. Exoterically, their menacing attitude is interpreted as meaning 'Beware !' to evil elementals ; and, esoterically, as 'Ever present !' to the disciple whom they protect.

[4] In other aspects, these deities, like many of the Hindu deities, are imaged as having many hands and faces.

[5] The *dorje* here symbolizes almighty power. It also has correspondence with the curved knife which Vajra-Yoginī similarly flourishes overhead.

[6] This posture indicates that thoughts, which are believed to originate in the heart psychic-centre, must be controlled, so that evil or destructive thoughts cannot arise ; hence the menacing attitude, which indicates opposition to undesirable influences.

[7] This posture of firmness signifies the immutability of the deities' protective influence over the disciple.

[8] These five colours correspond (as throughout *The Tibetan Book of the Dead*) to the colours assigned to the Five Elements, namely, Blue (Ether),

(30) As the expiration is going out, think of them as going out with it and filling the world.

(31) As the inspiration is being drawn in, and held, imagine them as coming in with it and filling the body.

(32) Perform these two complementary exercises seven times each, making, in all [with the above], twenty-one exercises.[1]

(33) Then think that each of the hair-pores of thy body is filled with one of these Wrathful Deities, with his face turned outwards, and that all of them taken together constitute a coat of mail which thou art wearing.[2]

Green (Air), Red (Fire), White (Water), and Yellow (Earth). In our text here, they symbolize the five vital (or life-sustaining) elements of nature in their primordial (or pure) form.

[1] In the outbreathing process there is actually a subtle force (the psychic, or *prāṇic* force) going out, as the *yogin* will come to understand. Although at this stage he may regard his exercises as being merely exercises in visualization, they are, nevertheless, intended to build up round about him a 'protective circle', or psychic barrier, which elementals and other invisible beings of an inimical sort cannot pass. Likewise, with each *yogically*-directed inspiration, the subtle force is drawn into the body and stored in the centres, or lotuses, of the psychic-nerve system to provide for the *yogin*'s internal protection. Such a 'protective circle', within and without, is essential to success in all *yogas*. The visualized deities are here merely personifications of this 'protective circle', which is established and controlled by consciously directed thought-forms.

[2] Little by little the neophyte has been led up to this stage where he is now directed to establish the 'protective circle', metaphorically described as being like a coat of mail. Thoughts being things, the *yogin*, by use of visualization *yogically* directed, causes his mentally-created images of protecting deities to assume concrete form on the fourth dimensional, or psychic, plane. And, although the offspring of mind, they afford him genuine protection; for a thought-form thus *yogically* charged with psychically potent forces of good can ward off a correspondingly powerful thought-form or entity of evil. The *gurus* maintain that a 'protective circle' of this character is essential at the very outset of *yoga* practices, in order that the *yogin* may be immune, as far as possible, to all the many strange dangers and errors which ever threaten the treader of the Path. When the functioning of certain normally dormant faculties is brought about by the practising of *yoga*, they are likely to be misused, either intentionally, as in black magic, or else through ignorance. The *guru*'s keen watchfulness must never be relaxed while the pupil is in this critical period of training. The 'protective circle', like a guardian angel placed on never-ceasing guard over the thoughts and actions of the neophyte, acts the part of a lieutenant of the *guru*. But apart from all this psychology, the *yogin* must be ever aware that the practical aim of his present training is to attain

## [PRELIMINARY EXERCISE 4: TRAINING THE PSYCHIC NERVE-PATHS]

(34) In the fourth of the preliminary exercises, the Training of the Psychic Nerve-Paths [or Nerve-Channels], proceed according to the practices which now follow.

(35) Visualize, to the right of the median-nerve, the psychic-nerve of the right side of the body, and, to the left, the psychic-nerve of the left side of the body, each extending from the tip of the nose up to and over the brain [thence round the sides of the head and down the sides of the body], the lower termination being at the base of the generative organ [i.e. in the perineum].

(36) Visualize both these nerves as being hollow; and in the left-side one these letters:

> *A, Ā; I, Ī; U, Ū; RI, RĪ; LI, LĪ; E, EĪ; O, OŪ; ANG, Ā;*[1]

(37) And in the right-side one these letters:

> *KA, KHA, GA, GHA, NGA; CHA, CHHA, JA, JHA, NYA; TA, THA, DA, DHA, NA* [hard, as dentals];
>
> *TA, THA, DA, DHA, NA* [soft, as palatals]; *PA, PHA, BA, BHA, MA; YA, RA, LA, VA; SHA, KSHA, SA, HA, KSHYA.*[2]

proficiency in the art of generating the Psychic-Heat; and that each of the visualizations so far practised has direct bearing upon this psycho-physical accomplishment.

[1] These sixteen vowel-symbols, used in the visualization exercise, are pronounced as follows: *A* like the *u* in *but*, *ā* as in *father*, *i* as in *it*, *ī* like *ee* in *seen*, *u* as in *put*, *ū* like *oo* in *boon*, *ri* as in *rim*, *rī* like *ree* in *reel*, *li* as in *lit*, *lī* as *lee*, *e* as in *elm*, *eī* like *ai* in *aim*, *o* as in *on*, *oū* as in *out*, *ang* like *ung* in *hung*, and *ā* as in *ah*. In *Tantras* in Sanskrit, wherein there are similar visualizations, the sixteen vowel-symbols are given as follows: *a, ā; i, ī; u, ū; ri, rī; lri, lrī; e, ai; o, 'au; am, ah.* (Cf. Arthur Avalon, *Tantrik Texts*, vii, p. 16, London, 1919.)

[2] These thirty-four consonantal-symbols with the sixteen vowel-symbols comprise the Tibetan phonetic equivalents of the Sanskrit alphabet, upon which the Tibetan alphabet is based. The last five appear in Sanskrit Tantric works as *Sa, Sha, Sha* (Hard), *Ha, Ksha*. (Cf. Arthur Avalon, *op. cit.*, p. 16.) According to Hindu tradition, the letters of the Sanskrit alphabet were first revealed by Brahmā, the Creator, to Ganesha, the God of Learning, and by Ganesha imparted to mankind. Owing to this divine origin, the sounds of

(38) Visualize the outline of these letters to be as fine as the fibre of a lotus; and all of them as being red of colour and arranged in a perpendicular line, one above the other. Then, as the expiration goeth out, meditate upon these letters as going out with it, one after another; and, as the inspiration cometh in, as coming in with it, but entering the body through the orifice of the generative organ.

(39) Continue the meditation, concentrating the mind upon this rosary of letters, each thus following the other like fairy-fires, and keep up the twofold breathing process [i.e. breathing through the right and left nostril alternately].

(40) These practices, being like the making of a water-course prior to the bringing of the water, constitute a very important art.[1]

[PRELIMINARY EXERCISE 5: CONFERRING THE 'GIFT-WAVES' UPON THE PSYCHIC NERVE-CENTRES.]

(41) In the fifth of the preliminary exercises, the Conferring of the 'Gift-Waves' upon the Psychic Nerve-Centres, proceed according to the practices which now follow.

(42) Visualize at the heart-centre of the median-nerve,[2]

these letters when properly intoned in *mantras*, or words of power, are said to convey celestial psychic influences, in the form of 'gift-waves' of grace. All these phonetic visualizations taken together number fifty; and they are symbolized by the fifty blood-dripping human heads which form the mystic necklace of the Great Shakti, the Divine Mother, Vajra-Yoginī.

The relationship between form and sound is well known to Tibetan, as to Hindu, masters of the occult sciences. (See *The Tibetan Book of the Dead*, pp. 220-2.) In the text before us, the psychic power which the disciple is now being taught to develop and direct will, eventually, be realized by him in its esoteric correspondence with *mantric* sound. Marpa, for example, demonstrated to his disciple, Milarepa, the secret correlation between sound, form, and colour, and the *yogic* method of materializing the deities. (See *Tibet's Great Yogī, Milarepa*, p. 163.) Milarepa is credited with similar powers. Thus, long before the rise of physical sciences in Europe, Indian, and, in turn, Tibetan, *yogins* seem to have recognized the fundamental law of vibrations, and to have applied it in a manner as yet hardly suspected by Europeans. In this connexion, however, it is worth noting that there are many references to these sorts of *yogic* accomplishments in the very ancient Finnish Epic of *Kaleva-lā*.

[1] The water-course which these preliminary exercises are intended to open up, i.e. set into functioning activity, is the psychic nerve-paths. When the water-course is made, the water, i.e. the psychic, or *prāṇic*, force, consciously controlled, flows through it.

[2] This heart-centre is the *Anāhata-chakra*. (Cf. p. 191, § 68.)

which is to be the size of a medium-sized straw, the root-
*guru*[1] [in *yogic* sitting posture]; and over his head, [likewise
in *yogic* sitting posture], one above the head of another in
a perpendicular line, the Succession of *Gurus* of these Six
Doctrines.

(43) Meditate upon the *Gurus* as being thus carefully
arranged [in order of precedence, the Supreme *Guru*, Vajra-
Dhāra, uppermost, and thy human *guru* lowermost], like a
rosary of very small pearls.

(44) Then pray unto Them with the Prayer Formula of the
Six Doctrines:[2]

'Vouchsafe your "gift-waves",[3] O *Gurus*, that the Four
  Powers may be conferred upon my mind.
Vouchsafe your "gift-waves" that all things visible and
  existing may dawn upon me in the form of deities.
Vouchsafe your "gift-waves" that the vital-force may enter
  into the median-nerve.
Vouchsafe your "gift-waves" that the ecstatic warmth of
  the psychic-heat may blaze up.
Vouchsafe your "gift-waves" that the impure illusory body
  may be transmuted ;
Vouchsafe your "gift-waves" that the pure illusory body
  may dawn.[4]

---

[1] The root-*guru* is here the disciple's human *guru*, the lowermost in the
visualization of the *gurus* which follows. He is so called because in him the
disciple, like a tree, finds root support and nutriment to grow spiritually ; and
it is through the root-*guru* that the divine link, between man and the superhuman Teachers, is kept unbroken. In other contexts the root-*guru* is the
supreme *Guru*, Vajra-Dhāra (as on pp. 266-7) of whom the human *guru* is the
representative on Earth.

[2] This Prayer Formula is merely mentioned in the Tibetan text, for the *guru*
is expected to impart it to the *yogin*. The translation of it which follows has
been incorporated into our English text from a rare manuscript containing
esoteric teachings. The translator acquired the manuscript when he was
undergoing his *yogic* novitiate in Bhutan.

[3] As explained above (on p. 123[1]), these 'gift-waves' are helpful psychic
and spiritual influences which the Divine *Gurus* radiate or broadcast. The
Christian, in like manner, prays for heavenly grace and guidance.

[4] Up to this point, the six verses of the Prayer symbolize for the *yogin*, as
the *guru* privately explains, a gradual spiritual development. In the first verse,
the conferring of the Four Powers, i.e. the *yogic* powers of right use of the

Vouchsafe your "gift-waves" that the illusory visions of dreams may be dispelled.[1]

Vouchsafe your "gift-waves" that the Clear Light may be recognized as being within me.[2]

Vouchsafe your "gift-waves" that the pure Paradises may be attained through consciousness-transference.[3]

Vouchsafe your "gift-waves" that Buddhahood may be attained in this very life-time.

Vouchsafe your "gift-waves" that the Highest Boon, *Nirvāṇa*, may be attained.'[4]

(45) Or else pray thus:

'Vouchsafe, O *Gurus*, your "gift-waves" that all phenomenal appearances shall dawn upon me as Psychic-Heat.

---

body, of the speech, of the mind, and of the divine nature, symbolizes the sowing of the seed. The second verse symbolizes the rain and the sun and the seasons arousing the dormancy of the seed; the third verse, the sprouting of the seed; the fourth, the growth; the fifth, the blossoming; and the sixth, the fruit.

The impure illusory body is the gross physical body undisciplined by *yoga*; the pure illusory body is the visualized body. The transmutation refers to the *yogic* transmutation of the gross physical body, whereby (as Milarepa is shown in his *Biography* to have done) the perfected *yogin* may quit Earth-plane existence without experiencing the phenomena of death or loss of body, after the manner of the Jewish Prophet Elijah, of whom it is reported (in 2 *Kings* ii. 11) that as he was about to be taken up into Heaven in a whirlwind there appeared before him a chariot of fire, the symbol of the radiant glory of the transmuted form.

[1] That is, *yogically* comprehended as being unreal, as will be made clear in the Doctrine of Dreams, which follows.

[2] Or, 'of the self', which may be compared with the Gnostic teaching of St. John that 'the light shineth in darkness; and the darkness comprehended it not. . . . *That* was the true Light, which lighteth every man that cometh into the world'. (*St. John*, i. 5-9.)

[3] The yogic method of transferring the human consciousness from one *sangsāric* plane of existence to another is set forth in the last of the Six Doctrines. The pure Paradises are the four highest of the Brahmā heavens, through which the master of *yoga* passes on to *Nirvāṇa*. (See p. 92 [7].)

[4] These last five verses of the Prayer represent, as the *guru* again privately instructs the *yogin*, a gradual transitional unfoldment from the lowly human plane to the divine plane of the Supreme Awakening. By realizing that the so-called waking-state is as unreal as the so-called dream-state, the *yogin* attains to communion with the Clear Light within himself, and, in virtue of its guidance, eventually attains the Highest Boon.

Vouchsafe your "gift-waves" that all phenomenal appearances shall dawn upon me as Illusion.[1]

Vouchsafe your "gift-waves" that all phenomenal appearances shall dawn upon me as the Clear Light.

Vouchsafe your "gift-waves" that all phenomenal appearances shall dawn upon me as the *Tri-Kāya*.[2]

Vouchsafe your "gift-waves" that I may be transferred
higher and higher.

Vouchsafe your "gift-waves" that I may be empowered to
attain the Highest Goal.'[3]

(46) Then, having so prayed, visualize all the *Gurus* of the
Succession as merging themselves into the body of the Root-
*Guru*; and, then, that the Root-*Guru* mergeth into the
Essence of Inexhaustible Bliss, and that it filleth thy whole
body.

[Here endeth Part I : The Five Preliminary Exercises.]

## [*PART II: THE THREE FUNDAMENTAL PRACTICES*]

(47) The Second Part of the Psychic-Heat Doctrine, the
Fundamental Practices, consisteth of three practices: Producing Psychic-Heat; Psychic-Heat Experiences; and Transcendental Psychic-Heat.

### [FUNDAMENTAL PRACTICE 1 : PRODUCING PSYCHIC-HEAT]

(48) In the first practice, Producing Psychic-Heat, there
are : the Art of Posturing the Body ; the Art of the Calm [or
Soft] and Violent [or Forced] Breathing ; and the Art of the
Meditative Mental Imagery.

#### [THE ART OF POSTURING THE BODY]

(49) The first, the Art of Posturing the Body, is, quoting
the principal text, as followeth :

' Place the body in the Buddha-Posture.  Make the verte-

---

[1] This has reference to the phenomenon of Nature as being illusory or like
a magically-produced phantasmagoria, and thus devoid of reality. The *yogin*
must be aware of the illusoriness of this illusion when it dawns.

[2] The 'Three Bodies', or Reality.  (See p. 98[7].)

[3] This Prayer is contained in our Tibetan text, and may be used instead of
the longer Prayer preceding it.

brae of the spinal column straight like unto a pile of
metallic coins, one coin on top of another. Throw out the
diaphragm to its full extent. Hide the oesophagus well [by
letting the chin touch it]. Place the tongue against the
roof of the mouth.[1] Place the hands just below the navel,
with the bends of the wrists pressing against the thighs in
the posture of equilibrium.[2] Without changing the angle
of vision [which is naturally adopted when these postures
have been assumed] or the flow of the thought-current, link
the thought-process with the breathing-process and forcibly
control the mind.[3]

‘The Buddha-Posture affordeth the means whereby one
realizeth complete enlightenment [or Buddhahood]. One
may also sit with the legs crossed in the *Siddha*-Posture.’[4]

(50) These quoted directions may be otherwise stated as
followeth:

Sit in the Buddha-Posture with the right leg crossed over

---

[1] See p. 117[6].

[2] See p. 117[3].

[3] Within the time-period of one inhalation and exhalation the mind normally
changes its thought-formations; and here in our text the forcible control means
that the mind must be forcibly controlled during the time required for each
breathing-process, which is the linking of the thought-process with the
breathing-process. Beyond this time-period of one breathing, the thought-
process cannot be restrained, as the *yogin* will come to understand. Herein,
again, as taught in *The Epitome of the Great Symbol*, the thought-process and
the breathing-process are found to be interdependent, and the control of the
latter gives control over the former. When the breathing has been rhythmically
regulated, the arising and passing away of thoughts will be found to have
become attuned to its rhythm.

[4] In the Buddha-Posture (Skt. *Buddhāsana*), also called by Tibetans the
*Dorje*-Posture (Skt. *Vajrāsana*), the legs are so crossed that the feet rest upon
the upper portion of the thighs, the soles turned upward, the right leg on the
outside. In the *Siddha*-Posture (Skt. *Siddhāsana*), which is easier to assume
and more commonly employed to-day by practising *yogins* in India, the legs
are crossed in such manner that the left heel presses against the region of the
perineum and the right foot rests upon and in the fold of the left leg. These
two are the most favoured among the numerous postures, or *āsanas*, described
in Sanskrit works on *Yoga*. As here suggested in our text, these two postures
may be used alternately. The illustrations opposite p. 101, above, show a Hindu
*yogin* practising them. Either is said to be efficacious in helping the *yogin* to
control the various vital and *prāṇic* currents of the body to the great end of
attaining Liberation.

the left.[1] Place the hands in the equilibrium posture just below the navel, with the bend of the wrists [pressed against the thighs] bracing the upper part of the body. Make the spinal column straight, like unto a perpendicular pile of Chinese brass coins.[2] Expand the diaphragm to its maximum fullness. Let the chin press against the oesophagus. Place the tongue against the roof of the mouth, and fix the sight on the tip of the nose or else on the horizon, [or sky], straight in front of thee.

In all else do as above directed ; but now, [as an alteration], sit with the legs crossed in *Siddhāsana*. And have a meditation-band, measuring, when twice doubled, about the circumference of one's head ; and arrange it under the knees and encircling the body, [making it fast and secure], so as to support the body.[3] Also have a meditation-cushion, about one cubit, [i.e. 18 to 22 inches] square, four fingers thick, and well stuffed.[4]

[1] This amplification of the quoted directions is necessary, because, as can be observed in Tibetan images of various Buddhas seated in the Buddha-Posture, the right leg is crossed over the left, whereas in the similar *āsana* of the Hindus called *Buddha-Padmāsana*, the left leg is crossed over the right.

[2] These coins are made with a hole through the centre so that they can be strung together like beads on a string. Each coin represents one of the vertebrae strung on the spinal cord, through the hollow of which extends the median-nerve.

[3] The meditation-band is placed so as to encircle the body, i.e. across (or under) the shoulders (or round the neck) and the legs in their *yogic* posture. It is so used to prevent the legs losing their posture when the *yogin* enters into deep meditation and no longer has consciousness of the body. By making the band longer or shorter, the *yogin* may adjust it to suit his bodily conformation, or, if it will not keep in place otherwise, he may tie it to his body.

[4] The more conservative Indian *yogins* follow the ancient rule that a *yogin* when meditating should sit upon a mat of *kusa*-grass. They claim that such a mat, when placed on the bare ground of their place of meditation, neutralizes, or in some way changes, the character of the magnetism emanating from the earth. Others employ a regular meditation-cushion, made of any sort of soft material, save material derived from animal bodies, special exception being made in favour of tiger and leopard skins with the hair on them, the tiger and leopard being, as they were in Ancient Egypt, sacred to the gods. It is here worth noting that on walls of many an old temple along the Nile the chief priests are depicted wearing leopard skins. Often in India I have come across a solitary *yogin* wearing a leopard (or, rarely, a tiger) skin, in the manner of an Egyptian priest. The skin is the symbol of Shiva, the deity specially associated with *yoga* ; and the *yogin* makes excellent use of it ; for it serves as

[THE ART OF THE CALM AND FORCED BREATHING]

(51) The second part of the practice of Producing Psychic-Heat hath the two divisions: the Calm [or Soft] Breathing, and the Violent [or Forced] Breathing.

[*The Calm Breathing*]

(52) The first, the Calm Breathing, consisteth of two practices: the Preliminary Practice of Nine Bellows-like Blowings, and the Fundamental Practice of the Four Combined Breathings.

(53) The former, the Preliminary Practice of Nine Bellows-like Blowings, consisteth of breathing thrice [through the right nostril only] while the head is being slowly turned from right to left; then, while the head is being slowly turned from left to right, breathing thrice [through the left nostril only]; then breathing thrice straight in front of one [through both nostrils], the head stationary; these breathings to be in such a soft and gentle manner as to be imperceptible; next, using stronger breathings, thrice [in these same three directions and manners]; next with the twisting and blowing sort of breathing, thrice [in these same three directions and manners].

(54) These practices are nine in all, thrice repeated.[1]

covering for his body by day, as his sleeping-rug at night, and as a cushion when he meditates. The skin of the Indian antelope is also permissible. In place of *kusa*-grass (which flourishes chiefly in the jungles of India, especially along the Ganges), the Tibetans employ various soft materials as filling for their kind of meditation-cushion. The fine quill-like hair of the Tibetan musk-deer (a species of antelope), which is very costly, is preferred.

[1] These practices will appear more comprehensible if listed as follows:
Three gentle breathings from right to left through the right nostril,
Three gentle breathings from left to right through the left nostril,
Three gentle breathings straight in front through both nostrils.

Three stronger breathings from right to left through the right nostril,
Three stronger breathings from left to right through the left nostril,
Three stronger breathings straight in front through both nostrils.

Three twisting and blowing breathings from right to left through the right nostril,
Three twisting and blowing breathings from left to right through the left nostril,
Three twisting and blowing breathings straight in front through both nostrils.
These comprise in all twenty-seven breathings, or nine breathing-practices

(55) Of the latter of the two practices of the Calm Breathing, namely, the Fundamental Practice of the Four Combined Breathings, it hath been said:

'Bend the neck to conform to the shape of an iron hook,
Expand the chest to conform to the shape of an earthern pot,
Tie the breath into a bow-knot,[1]
And shoot the breath forth like an arrow.'

(56) It hath also been said:

'Inbreathing, and filling, and equalizing,
And shooting the breath out, are the four practices.
Without understanding of these four combinations,
There is danger of changing their virtue into harm.'

(57) Explanations of the above quotations now follow.

(58) The drawing in of the breath through both nostrils from a distance of about sixteen fingers in front of one, without any sound, is called 'inbreathing'.

(59) Pressing the air of the inspiration down to the very bottom of the lungs and then contracting the diaphragm so as to raise the thorax, thereby making the chest conform to the shape of an earthern pot and holding it thus, is called the 'filling'.

(60) When no longer able to retain this pot-like shape, draw in short breaths, pressing the inhaled air to the right and left so as to equalize the lung expansion. This is called the 'equalizing'.

(61) When one feeleth incapable of continuing this equalizing, then through both nostrils, gently at the beginning and end and with greater force in the middle of the process, the flinging of the breath outward is the 'shooting the breath forth like an arrow'.

---

thrice repeated. In the twisting and blowing breathings, the stomach is to be churned with a rotary motion through muscular action, the trunk of the body twisted about concomitantly with this churning; and the breathing-process made strong, so that the lungs are completely emptied, and then filled to their full capacity, with each expiration and inspiration.

[1] The two sides of the contracted diaphragm combined with the compression at the navel, as in the forming of the 'Pot-shaped', constitute the 'bow-knot'.

[*The Violent Breathing*]

(62) The second part of the second practice of Producing Psychic-Heat, namely, the Violent Breathing, consisteth of five practices: the Art of the Bellows-like Blowings of the Breathing, to prevent the rebounding of the air;[1] the Art of Inbreathing to cause the air to enter into all its natural channels; the Art of Maximum Lung Expansion to control the breathing [in the producing of the psychic-force]; the Art of Gaining Complete Mastery over the Breathing, to cause the psychic-force [extracted from the inbreathed air] to enter into the capillaries of the psychic-nerves; and the Art of Relaxing the Breathing, to bring about a mingling of the external and internal psychic-force.[2]

[THE ART OF THE MEDITATIVE MENTAL IMAGERY]

(63) The third part of the practice of Producing Psychic-Heat, namely, the Art of the Meditative Mental Imagery, hath three divisions: External Psychic-Heat; Internal Psychic-Heat; and Secret [or Hidden] Psychic-Heat.

---

[1] The process here indicated consists of expelling the air of the exhalation forcibly, as in the bellows simile above, so that the lungs are completely emptied to the very bottom, and then of refilling the lungs completely to the very bottom by slowly drawing in the inspiration. This prevents the common tendency to take in fresh air in short breaths as soon as the exhalation is completed, which process is known as 'the rebounding of the air'. The present exercise is intended for making the inhalation complete and deep. Some of the ancient *Rishis* held that each man's life is dependent upon a *karmically* fixed number of breathings, and that if the duration of the time required for one inhalation and expiration be prolonged by practice of *yoga*, the man's life itself would be prolonged correspondingly.

[2] In the first of these five practices the aim is prevention of the ' rebounding of the air' ; in the second, to make the resultant deep-breathing a matter of habit ; in the third, the applying of this deep-breathing so as to produce psychic-force; in the fourth, the actual producing of the psychic-force; and in the fifth, the extracting of the psychic-force from the air inhaled and storing it in the psychic-centres, or *chakra*. The psychic-force so stored is called internal psychic-force, and that extracted and not yet stored, is called the external, as will be seen from the passages which follow. To carry out these practices successfully there must be concentration of mind upon the purpose of each practice and upon the final end to which they are all directed. The *yogin* must also be fully aware that the atmosphere is the great reservoir of psychic-force, and that this must be taken in and transmuted into bodily vital-force in virtue of the breathing-practices.

### [*External Psychic-Heat*]

(64) Of the first, the External Psychic-Heat, it hath been said :

 ' Meditate upon the illusory body
 Of the instantaneously-produced tutelary deity.' [1]

(65) In other words, create a vivid mental image of the vacuous body of Vajra-Yoginī the size of a normal human body, as before described.

### [*Internal Psychic-Heat*]

(66) Of the second, the Internal Psychic-Heat, it hath been said :

 ' Meditate upon the four wheels ;
 Each shaped like an umbrella,
 Or like the wheel of a chariot.' [2]

(67) In other words, visualize at the centre of the vacuous, filmy body, the vacuous median-nerve, the vacuousness symbolizing Reality in its true nature [as Voidness] ; its colour red, symbolical of Bliss ; transparently bright, because its psychic functioning dissipateth the obscurations of Ignorance ; and in its perpendicular straightness symbolical of the trunk of the Tree of Life.[3] Visualize it, endowed with these four characteristics,[4] as extending from the Aperture of Brahma,

---

[1] The visualization of Vajra-Yoginī, which is instantaneously produced, is purely illusory, being without any reality apart from the mind which gives it being. The External Psychic-Heat is so called because externally, by making use of the visualized deity, a factory for the production of the psychic-heat is set up. The atmospheric air is the raw material whence the psychic-heat, or psychic-force, is extracted. By the *yogically*-directed breathing-process, the psychic-force is made to enter into the median-nerve and its capillaries and stored in the centres, or *chakra*, of the psychic-nerve system. When thus stored it is known as the Internal Psychic-Heat. The visualization of the illusory form of Vajra-Yoginī is merely a preliminary step, leading to the building of the factory.

[2] As the text itself proceeds to explain, these four wheels are the four chief *chakra*, or centres, of the psychic-nerve system.

[3] The median-nerve as the chief of the psychic-nerves with its so-called Root-Support, the first of the psychic-centres, the *Mūlādhāra*, situated in the perineum, is the trunk of the tree of man's psychic life, whence the *yogin* plucks the Fruit of Liberation.

[4] Namely, perpendicularity, transparent brightness, redness, and vacuity.

[on the crown of the head], to a place [i.e. the *Mūlādhāra-chakra*] four fingers below the navel; its two ends flat and even ; and to the right and left of it, the right and left psychic-nerves, [i.e. the *pingalā-nāḍī* and the *iḍā-nāḍī*], like the intestines of a lean sheep, extending over the top of the brain and thence down to the front of the face, and there ending in the two nasal apertures. Visualize the lower end of these two subsidiary nerves as entering into the lower end of the median-nerve with a complete circular turn like that of the bottom of the letter *cha* (ཚ).

(68) From the place, [the *Sahasrāra-chakra*], wherein these three psychic-nerves meet, on the crown of the head, [at the Aperture of Brahma, imagine thirty-two subsidiary psychic-nerves radiating downward. Imagine sixteen radiating upward from the throat psychic-centre, [the *Visuddha-chakra*]. Imagine eight radiating downward from the heart psychic-centre, [the *Anāhata-chakra*]. Imagine sixty-four radiating upward from the navel psychic-centre, [the *Maṇipūra-chakra*]. Each group of these subsidiary nerves is to be visualized as appearing like the ribs of a parasol, or like the spokes in the wheel of a chariot, of which the connecting parts are the median-nerve and the right and left psychic-nerves.[1]

(69) In these ways carry on the meditation.

### [*Secret Psychic-Heat*]

(70) Of the third, the Secret Psychic-Heat, it hath been said :

'In the use of the one-half of the letter *A*,[2]
As the object upon which to meditate,
Lieth the art of producing the Psychic-Heat.'

(71) Accordingly, visualize at the point where the right and

---

[1] In this simile, the two upper psychic-centres are the two convex sides of the one wheel, and the two lower psychic-centres are the two convex sides of the other wheel of the chariot, of which the axle and the body is the median-nerve running through the middle of the four centres ; and the right and left psychic-nerves are like the tongue or shafts. This simile is not perfect, but merely approximate.

[2] The first half of the Tibetan letter *A* is known to Tibetan *yogis* and mystics, who made use of it in visualization, as the 'short-*A*'. The full form is ཨཱ ; the half-*A* is ཨ.

left psychic-nerves meet with the median-nerve, four fingers below the navel, the half-*A*, in hair-like outline, floating, and half a finger in height, of reddish brown colour, hot to the touch, undulating and emitting like a cord moved by the wind the sound of 'Phem! Phem!'[1]

(72) Then clearly visualize a letter *HAM*,[2] white of colour, inside the median-nerve at the crown of the head, [within the Thousand-Petalled Lotus], and as if it were about to drop nectar.

(73) Thereupon, by drawing in breath, the vital-force entereth into the right and left psychic-nerves.

(74) These expand, as if distended with air; and thence the vital-force passeth into the median-nerve and, striking against the hair-like short-*A* [or half-*A*], filleth it out into its fully shaped red form.

(75) While the 'filling' and the 'equalizing' are thus going on, concentrate thy mind upon the processes.

(76) While exhaling, imagine that the breath is going out

---

[1] In this context, the 'Phem! Phem!' also represents the sound made by a burning taper. Four fingers below the navel psychic-centre is the hidden abode of the sleeping Goddess Kuṇḍalinī, the personification of the Serpent Power, or the latent mystic fire-force of the body. The short-*A* is symbolical of this feminine occult power; and the object of the present visualization is to arouse the sleeping Goddess into psychic activity. In this exercise there are four kinds of visualization : (*a*) of form (the short-*A*); (*b*) of colour (reddish brown); (*c*) of touch (the hot to the touch); and (*d*) of motion (the undulating).

[2] This is the Tibetan letter-symbol for the personal pronoun 'I', written ཧཱུྃ, transliterated as *HAM* and pronounced as *HUM*. It is white, in correspondence with the sexual fluid, which its visualization sets into psychic-activity. The brain psychic-centre is conceived as the place whence the sexual functions are directed; and, therefore, the *HAM* is to be visualized as in the *chakra* called the *Sahasrāra-Padma*, or Thousand-Petalled Lotus. The *HAM* symbolizes the masculine aspect of the mystic psychic fire-force; and, as a result of its union with that of the feminine aspect, symbolized by the short-*A*, the Secret Psychic-Heat is born. The Goddess Kuṇḍalinī is roused from her age-long slumber to ascend to her Lord in the pericarp of the Thousand-Petalled Lotus. She first ascends, like a flame, to the *Maṇipūra-chakra*, of which the navel is the hub; and the lower half of the body is filled with the mystic fire. Thence she continues her ascent; and in union with her Lord, the Divine One, the whole body is filled, even to the tips of the fingers and toes, with the Secret Psychic-Heat. In the passages which follow, the process is detailed.

of the median-nerve, in a bluish stream.[1] Actually, however, the breath hath its exit through the nostrils.

(77) Having arrived at mental concentration upon these visualizations, then, in a second course of exercises, holding to the same manner of breathing, think that, from the hair-like short-*A*, a flame of fire, half a finger in length and very sharp-pointed, flareth up.

(78) Think that the flame is endowed with the four characteristics, [of the median-nerve as visualized, namely, perpendicularity, transparent brightness, redness, and vacuity] ; and that it resembleth a revolving spindle.[2]

(79) Think that with each such breathing the flame riseth up half a finger higher ; and that by eight such breathings it reacheth the navel nerve-centre.

(80) With ten such breathings, all the petals of the psychic-nerves of the navel nerve-centre will have been filled with psychic-fire.

(81) With ten more breathings, the fire moveth downward and filleth all the lower parts of the body, even to the ends of the toes.

(82) From there, with ten more breathings, it burneth upward and filleth all the body up to the heart psychic-centre.

(83) With ten more breathings, the fire passeth up to the throat psychic-centre.

(84) With ten more breathings, it reacheth the crown of the head [i.e. the Thousand-Petalled Lotus].

(85) In this way meditate.

(86) It hath been said :

    ' Gradually milk the " Cow of the Heavens ".'[3]

---

[1] The bluish stream symbolizes a beneficial psychic influence apart from the psychic-force. Its visualization is here more in the nature of an elementary exercise ; but for the highly developed occultists it possesses great practical importance.

[2] This simile helps to illustrate the mystic motion of the awakened fire of the Serpent Power of the Goddess Kuṇḍalinī.

[3] Text : *Nam-mkhahi-ba* (pron. *Nam-khai-ba*) = ' Cow of the Heavens ', which is the secret name given to the Tibetan letter *HAM* when visualized as the masculine complement of the feminine half-*A*. It is so called because it is

(87) [In other words], with ten more breathings the visualized letter *HAM*, within the crown of the head, is dissolved by the psychic-fire into the secret vital-force of the transmuted 'moon-fluid',[1] and this filleth the psychic nerve-centre of the brain [i.e. the *Sahasrāra-chakra*, or Thousand-Petalled Lotus].

(88) With ten more breathings, it filleth the psychic-nerve centre of the throat.

(89) With ten more breathings, it filleth the psychic-nerve centre of the heart.

(90) With ten more breathings, it filleth the psychic-nerve centre of the navel.

(91) With ten more breathings, the whole body is filled to the tips of the fingers and toes.

(92) In thus learning the 'Milking Process', these 108 breathings constitute one course of exercises.

(93) At the outset, they are to be repeated six times during a day and night.

(94) Later on, reduce the number of repetitions to four, in keeping with the prolongation of the breathing-process.[2]

(95) Except when taking food and recuperative sleep, carry on the meditation incessantly.

(96) These processes, above described, which constitute the art of controlling the body, mind, and vitality, for the pro-

said to emit, as a cow does milk, the nectar of immortality, the *amrita* of the gods of Hindu mythology.

[1] Text : *byang-chub-hems* (pron. *chang-chub-sem* = '*Bodhisattvic*-mind'); an honorific term for the male generative-fluid, or 'moon-fluid'. In the present context it is symbolical of the transmuted sex-vitality, whereby the psychic-heat is produced, as are all occult psycho-physical powers. The generative-fluid, when rightly utilized, is the foundation of physical health and longevity. Only with a healthy and *yogically*-disciplined body and mind can there be true happiness and *Bodhisattvic* desire to lead all beings beyond Sorrow, beyond the *Sangsāra*; and these considerations give rise to this peculiar Tibetan idiom.

[2] The time of the duration of the breathing-process is gradually extended, so that after about thirty days, and in some *yogins* much sooner, it shows almost fifty per cent. of increase, due to the increase in lung expansion through deep-breathing. By constant practice, the duration can be extended this much in about one week. When this reduction in the number of breathings is attained, the number of the repetitions of the course of exercises is to be reduced accordingly.

ducing of the Psychic-Heat, are called 'The Executive Psychic Heat Processes'.[1]

## [FUNDAMENTAL PRACTICE 2: PSYCHIC-HEAT EXPERIENCES]

(97) The second of the Fundamental Practices, namely, Psychic-Heat Experiences, consisteth of two parts : Normal, and Supernormal Experiences.

### [NORMAL EXPERIENCES]

(98) Of the first, Normal Experiences, it hath been said :

' By retaining [or storing] in the psychic-centres the vital-
force,
Something akin to heat is produced at first ;
Secondly, blissfulness is experienced ;
Thirdly, the mind assumeth its natural state ;
Then the forming of thoughts ceaseth automatically,
And phenomena, appearing like smoke, mirage, and fire-
flies,
And something resembling the light of dawn,
And something resembling a cloudless sky are seen.'

(99) Comments upon this quotation now follow.

(100) The expiration being delayed by conscious effort, the psychic-force is retained in its own place [i.e. the psychic-centres] ; and this process is called 'Retention'.

(101) In virtue of the 'Retention' the number of breathings is reduced.   This is called 'Retention of the Motion' [of the breath].

(102) The shortening of the expiration is called 'Retention of the Length'.

(103) The lessening of the force of the expiration is called 'Retention of the Force'.

(104) The knowing of the colour of the breath is called 'Retention of the Colour'.[2]

---

[1] The Psychic-Heat is regarded as being in function the Executive, because through its agency are executed or carried into effect the occult practices dependent upon *yogic* mastery of the psycho-physical body.

[2] The colour refers to the purity of the inhaled air, and the impurity of the exhaled air. As in *The Epitome of The Great Symbol*, this knowledge implies concentration of mind to the end of attuning the breathing-process and tranquillizing the current of the thought-process.   (See p. 126, §§ 39. 40.)

(105) The absorbing of the power of the different elements is called 'Retention of the Power'.[1]

(106) The vital-force being retained thus, the waves of the Psychic-Heat are made stable.

(107) Thereupon, the mind and the vital-force being tranquillized [or made to assume their natural condition of primordial quiescence], heat is produced.

(108) That openeth out the apertures of the psychic-nerves, into which the psychic-force leadeth the 'moon-fluid';[2] and, as a result, there ariseth pain in the psychic-nerves.

(109) Then seminal pain ariseth.

(110) Then dawneth the experiencing of the conditions of existence in each of the Six *Lokas*;[3] and this, which cometh of the first stage of the transmuting of the seminal-fluid, is called 'The Time of Pain', or 'The Time of Warmth'.

(111) Then, the atrophied psychic-nerves becoming rejuvenated by the psychic-force and by the seminal-fluid, which continueth to increase and ripen [in its transmuted condition], one experienceth innumerable conditions of blissfulness of an exhaustible sort.[4] This is called 'The Second Stage', or 'The Time of Blissfulness'.

[1] As will be explained by the text itself, under Supernormal Experiences, on pp. 197-9 following, from each of the five elements the *yogin* derives a particular *yogic* power. Briefly stated, the essential property of the element earth is solidity; of water, fluidity; of fire, heat; of air, transparency and motion; and of ether, non-resistance. Each of these properties, when *yogically* transmuted, has its transcendental aspect or power.

[2] Here the text contains the ordinary Tibetan word for the male generative-fluid, namely, *thiglē* (pron. *tiglē*), corresponding to the Sanskrit *dhātu*, meaning 'seed'.

[3] The *yogin* feels as though he were out of the body and traversing, one after another, the five non-human states of *sangsāric* being. He experiences sufferings in the various after-death states of *karmic* retribution. He feels, with sympathetic consciousness, the unhappiness of existence in sub-human states. Again, he suffers as do the *pretas*, or unhappy ghosts, in their world. He realizes the joyfulness of life in the worlds of the *devas*; and the stern sorrowfulness of the ungodly *asuras*, or titans, in the *Asura-Loka*. With this greater sensitiveness to sorrow and to joy in their manifold aspects—which is a direct result of his *yogic* training—he arrives at right understanding of the human state, which, with the other five states, constitute the Six *Lokas*, or conditions of Transitory Existence. In other words, the *yogin* has attuned himself to the One Life, which pulsates in all existing things.

[4] This sort of blissfulness being psycho-physical is, like the body upon which

(112) Then, the mind being attuned by this internal bliss, one looketh upon all external nature with joyfulness. This is called ' The Experiencing of Bliss '.

(113) The poison of the unceasing current of thought-formation is thereby neutralized and the mind attaineth its natural condition, the True State of Abiding Quiescence, or the tranquil state of *samādhi*. This is called ' The Third Stage ' or ' The State of Non-Cognition ' [of the phenomena of the external world], the third degree of proficiency reached in the training.

(114) The state of quiescence thus realized is not a state devoid of all sensuous experiences; for phenomena appearing like smoke, and mirage, and fire-flies, and dull light, like that of a lamp, or the glimmer of twilight, and a cloudless sky, and other phenomena, too numerous to be enumerated, illumine it in a supernormal manner.

(115) During this third stage of the transmuting of the seminal-fluid, the *yogin* who is experiencing it should not ignore any of the signs or omens which may thus phenomenally appear. Nor should he seek after those which do not appear, but he should keep on producing the Executive Psychic-Heat in the normal way.

(116) The vital-force becoming efficacious, the *yogin* becometh immune from diseases, ageing, and other ordinary causes of physical deterioration; and he acquireth the five-fold supernormal knowledge of the exhaustible sort, and innumerable other virtues.[1]

### [SUPERNORMAL EXPERIENCES]

(117) Of the second part of Psychic-Heat Experiences namely, Supernormal Experiences, it hath been said :

' By that secondary cause,

it depends, transitory. *Nirvāṇic* blissfulness, not being psycho-physical, but a purely spiritual experience of the True State, independent of the physical body, is inexhaustible.

[1] This fivefold supernormal knowledge is of past, present, and future events, of thoughts in the minds of others, and of one's own occult limitations or shortcomings. It is exhaustible, because, like the physical body upon which it depends, it is *saṅgsāric* and transitory, even as is all knowledge of worldly or created things.

At the place where the three principal psychic-nerves meet,
Enter the vital-forces.'

(118) And, it hath also been said :

'Moreover, the Five Signs and the Eight Virtues dawn.'

(119) Comments upon these quotations now follow.

(120) The entering of the vital-force into the median-nerve
during the time of the normal experiences is spoken of as
the entering of the vital-force into the median-nerve by means
of vital effort.

(121) Hence it is known as the entering of the vital-force
into the median-nerve by the *yogin*'s own power; in other
words, the external and the internal vital-force unite and become one body of vitality shaped like a tube.[1]

(122) Entering the median-nerve, at the navel nerve-centre
from the region of the perineum, the vital-force moveth
through the middle of the four psychic-nerve centres, and,
becoming the fire-force of the Wisdom of the Psychic-Heat,
permeateth all the seminal nerve-channels, and thus untieth
the nerve-centres.[2]

(123) In virtue of this untying, the Five Supernormal Signs
appear.

(124) These Signs are the Flaring, the Moon, the Sun,
Saturn, and the Lightning.

(125) The Flaring will appear as yellow radiance ; the
Moon, as white ; the Sun, as red ; Saturn, as blue ; and the
Lightning, as pink.

(126) Within each of these radiances, in turn, one's own
body will be enhaloed.[3]

---

[1] The *prāṇa*, or psychic-force, retained in the right and left psychic-nerves
after an expiration and that brought into them by an inspiration, unite and
enter the median-nerve as transmuted vital-force in the form of one body of
vitality. This process is the uniting of the internal and external vital-force.
Inside the junction of the three chief psychic-nerves, about four inches below
the aperture where the psychic-forces enter, there is said to be a tube-like
space in which the psychic-force, or vitality, collects ; and this gives the one
body of vitality its shape. The next paragraph further elucidates this, and
indicates how the vital-force permeates all the psychic-nerve centres.

[2] This untying refers to its setting the psychic-nerve centres into functioning
activity, or, in other words, to its arousing them from their state of latency.

[3] These visions of coloured radiances, appearing like haloes, correspond to
different stages in the psychic development. The Lightning, like pink radiance,

(127) And one will have visible signs of having acquired the Eight Virtues, which are as followeth.

(128) By virtue of the element earth [of the body], one obtaineth strength like that of Nārāyana.[1]

(129) By virtue of the element water [of the body], one obtaineth bodily suppleness and smoothness, and immunity to harm by fire.

(130) By virtue of the element fire [of the body], one obtaineth ability to transmute and disperse all substances, and immunity to sinking in water.

(131) By virtue of the element air [of the body], one obtaineth fleetness of foot and lightness of body, like unto cotton-wool.

(132) By virtue of the element ether [of the body], one obtaineth power of flight, and immunity to being impeded either by earth or water.

(133) By virtue of the Moon-channel [of the psychic-force],[2] one's body becometh transparent and casteth no shadow.

(134) By virtue of the Sun-channel, all the gross matter of

arises from the flowing and transmuting of the seminal-fluid; and the others relate to the four chief psychic-centres.

[1] Text : *Sred-med-kyi-bu* (pron. *Sed-med-kyi-bu*) = 'Son of the Desireless', or 'the Desireless One' : Skt. Nārāyana, a form of the Hindu deity Vishnu, the Preserver of Creation. The superhuman strength of Nārāyana is, in mytho-logical terms, calculated thus : The strength of ten men equals that of one horse, the strength of ten horses equals that of one elephant, the strength of ten elephants that of one earth-guardian divine elephant, the strength of ten earth-guardian divine elephants equals that of one incense-exhaling divine elephant, the strength of ten incense-exhaling divine elephants equals that of one of the god Indra's elephants, and the strength of ten of these equals the strength of Nārāyana. This paragraph thus refers to the obtaining of the *siddhic*, or *yogic*, endowment of supernormal strength. Paragraph 129, which follows, refers to the obtaining of the *siddhic* endowment of perennial youth ; 130, to that of transmuting matter, or changing solids into gases or water, or *vice versa* ; 131, to that of levitation, and ability to traverse the air with the speed of an arrow in the fleshly body, or with the speed of thought in the 'astral' (or subtle) body ; and 132, to that of ability to traverse the ether, and to pass through any solid material bodies or substances in the 'astral' body. The other two paragraphs, 133 and 134, are self-explanatory.

[2] The channel of the Moon, or of the 'moon-fluid', is symbolized by the letter *Ham*, which represents the male *devatā*, enthroned in the pericarp of the Thousand-Petalled Lotus, wherein the Goddess Kundalinī, personification of the female divine power of the body, and symbolized as the half-*A*, or the Sun-channel, attains to the mystic at-one-ment.

the body is made pure, and one's body is transmuted into a body of vari-coloured radiances like unto those of a rainbow, and becometh invisible to others.

(135) By virtue of all these *yogic* powers being realized, the nine doors of the body[1] are closed, the four doors of the speech[2] are closed, the two doors of the mind[3] are opened; and thus great blissfulness ariseth within oneself.

(136) Thereby one experienceth, in every condition of conscious being, the unbroken current of *samādhi*, called ' The Ecstatic State of Quiescence.'[4]

### [FUNDAMENTAL PRACTICE 3: TRANSCENDENTAL PSYCHIC-HEAT]

(137) Of the third of the Fundamental Practices, namely, Transcendental Psychic-Heat, it hath been said :

' The Uncreated, Primordial Mind, the Simultaneously-born, Is the abode of inexhaustible *samādhi.*'

(138) To this quotation may be added the comments which now follow.

(139) The vital-force of the Five Aggregates,[5] in its real nature, pertaineth to the masculine aspect of the Buddha-principle manifesting through the left psychic-nerve.

(140) The vital-force of the Five Elements,[6] in its real nature, pertaineth to the feminine aspect of the Buddha-principle manifesting through the right psychic-nerve.

(141) As the vital-force, with these two aspects of it in

---

[1] These are, the two orifices of the eyes, the two apertures of the ears, the two nostril openings, the mouth, the anus, and the aperture of the organ of generation, all of which must be tranquillized, i.e. closed to external stimuli.

[2] These are the throat, tongue, palate, and the two lips ; or, in other words, they are the four instruments for the producing of vocal sound,, or speech, which, like the mind and body, must be tranquillized in realizing *samādhic* quiescence.          [3] These are volition and memory.

[4] This state implies complete tranquillization, or *yogic* disciplining, of body, speech, and mind. Then, with the awakening of the Saturn force, which is the afflorescence or complement of the virtues of the Moon and Sun forces, and of which the median-nerve is the channel, the climax of the supernormal experiences, resulting from the producing of the psychic-heat, is attained.

[5] Text : *Phung-po* (pron. *Phung-po*) : Skt. *Skandha*. This has reference to the body as being composed of the Five Aggregates.  (See p. 356[2].)

[6] These are, as above, earth, water, fire, air, and ether.

union, descendeth into the median-nerve, gradually there
cometh the realization of the Wisdom of the Simultaneously-
born [1]—the primordial state of the Pure Mind, inseparable from
the Voidness, and endowed with ever-present inexhaustible
Great Bliss.

(142) Within the navel psychic-centre abideth the *karmic*
principle which maketh *karmic* results to equal *karmic* actions;
within the heart psychic-centre abideth the *karmic* principle
which causeth *karmic* results to ripen; within the throat
psychic-centre abideth the principle which increaseth *karmic*
propensities; and within the brain psychic-centre abideth the
*karmic* principle which emancipateth from all *karmic* results.

(143) The 'moon-fluid', in moving upward through the
nerve-centres, awakeneth these *karmic* principles into activity,
and the upper extremity of the median-nerve is set into overwhelming vibration [of a blissful nature].

(144) And thus is produced the invisible psychic protuberance on the crown of the head.[2]

(145) When the protuberance becometh filled with the vital-
force of the transmuted seminal-fluid, one attaineth the transcendental boon of the Great Symbol, and realizeth the State
of the Great Vajra-Dhāra.[3]

(146) Simultaneously with this realization, the white-fluid
issueth in an intensified manner from the base of the organ of
generation and floweth upward to the crown of the head and
permeateth it completely; and the red-fluid issueth in an
intensified manner from the crown of the head and floweth

---

[1] For elucidation of this term, see pp. 115[1], 153[1].

[2] Many images of the Buddha show a protruding outgrowth on the crown of
the head, sometimes in the form of an ornament. This protuberance (shown in
the Illustration facing p. 57) symbolizes an invisible secondary psychic brain-
centre, a psycho-physical outgrowth of the ordinary brain, or a highly-special-
ized, *yogically*-induced, psychic organ through which functions the Divine or
*Bodhic*, Consciousness. In this connexion, it is perhaps worth noting that
phrenology localizes the so-called bump of sublime power in the same place,
i.e. the crown of the head, to which the *Bodhic* protuberance is assigned; and
the latter might, therefore, be regarded, phrenologically speaking, as the fully
evolved bump of sublimity.

[3] *Vajra-Dhāra* (Tib. *Dorje-Chang*), the Wielder of the Thunderbolt, here
symbolizes that Mystic Power which he telepathically confers upon the initiates
of the School of *The Great Symbol* and of *The Six Doctrines*.

downward till it permeateth all the body, even to the ends of the toes.[1]

[Here endeth Part II: the Three Fundamental Practices.]

## [PART III: THE PRACTICAL APPLICATION]

(147) The Third Part of the Psychic-Heat Doctrine, namely, the Practical Application, consisteth of two practices: Obtaining the Benefit of the Warmth; and Obtaining the Benefit of the Bliss.

### [APPLIED PRACTICE I: OBTAINING THE BENEFIT OF THE WARMTH]

(148) The First, Obtaining the Benefit of the Warmth, hath three divisions: From the Art of Posturing the Body; From the Art of Breathing; From the Art of Visualizing.

#### [OBTAINING WARMTH FROM THE ART OF POSTURING THE BODY]

(149) To obtain the benefit of the warmth from the Art of Posturing the Body, proceed as followeth:

Assume the squatting cross-legged posture [the calves and thighs resting on the feet, the knees above the toes, the left leg innermost]. Into the two cavities [formed by the bended legs] pass the hands, first crossing the arms if they be long, and grasp [the under part of the thighs]; or, if the arms be short, grasp in the manner most suitable.[2] Then whirl the stomach from right to left thrice and then from left to right thrice. Then agitate the stomach with a churning motion as forcibly as possible. Finally, shake the body just as a spirited horse shaketh itself and causeth each of its hairs to vibrate. At the same time perform one small bounce [by rising on the crossed legs and then letting the body drop back on to the meditation-cushion].

[1] Here we observe part of the process of the transmutation of the two aspects of the vital-force, the white-fluid, or the 'moon-fluid', representing the masculine, and the red-fluid, the feminine aspect, respectively visualized above as the letter *HAM* and the half-*A*.

[2] The grasping of the thighs is for the purpose of bracing the upper part of the body preparatory to the bouncing exercise which follows. Hence, one with short arms may secure the same effect by grasping the calves without crossing the arms.

(150) After having repeated this series of exercises thrice, perform a forcible bounce, which marketh the completion of one course of this practice of the posturing.[1]

[OBTAINING WARMTH FROM THE ART OF BREATHING]

(151) To obtain the benefit of the warmth from the Art of Breathing, one must press down the inhalation to the bottom of the lungs and then contract the diaphragm below the lungs so as to form the ' Pot-shaped '.

[OBTAINING WARMTH FROM THE ART OF VISUALIZING]

(152) To obtain the benefit of the warmth from the Art of Visualizing, proceed according to the directions which now follow.

(153) Visualize thyself as being the vacuous form of Vajra-Yogini, with the three chief psychic-nerves and the four chief nerve-centres and the half-*A* all most vividly visualized.

(154) While in that state of visualization, imagine at the centre of each of the two palms of the hands, and at the centre of each of the two soles of the feet, a sun ; and then place these suns one against the other.[2]

(155) Then visualize in the tri-junction of the three chief psychic-nerves [below the navel nerve-centre, in the perineum, at the base of the organ of generation], a sun.

(156) By the rubbing together of the suns of the hands and feet, fire flareth up.

(157) This fire striketh the sun below the navel [in the tri-junction].

(158) A fire flareth up from there and striketh the half-*A*.

(159) A fire flareth up from the half-*A* and permeateth the body.

(160) Then, as the expiration is going out, visualize the whole world as being permeated with fire in its true nature [as invisible psychic-heat, or psychic-fire].

---

[1] These exercises are intended to arouse the body and the whole psychic-nerve system to greater functioning activity. The bouncing itself has a very marked effect if done with full mental concentration on its purpose.

[2] Or, literally rendered, ' place these suns mouth to mouth '.

(161) Perform twenty-one forcible bounces during one period of these visualization exercises.[1]

(162) By meditating thus, for seven days, one will undoubtedly become able to endure [the most extreme cold] with only a cotton cloth on the body.

### [APPLIED PRACTICE 2 : OBTAINING THE BENEFIT OF THE BLISS]

(163) The second practice in the Practical Application, namely, Obtaining the Benefit of the Bliss, hath three divisions: the Preliminary Practice, which consisteth of Visualizing the Spiritual Consort of One's Mind ;[2] the Fundamental Practice, which consisteth of the Burning and Dropping Process; and the Conclusion, which consisteth of the Physical Drill.

### [VISUALIZING THE SPIRITUAL CONSORT OF ONE'S MIND]

(164) The Preliminary Practice, Visualizing the Spiritual Consort of One's Mind, is as followeth :

In front of thee visualize a human female form, endowed with all the signs of perfect beauty and so attractive as to fascinate thy mind.[3]

### [THE BURNING AND DROPPING PROCESS]

(165) The Fundamental Practice, the Burning and Dropping Process, dependeth upon the Art of the Six Physical Exercises for producing Psychic-Heat, the four combined processes of the Art of Breathing, and the Art of Visualizing.[4]

(166) Now visualize, clearly as before, thyself as being

---

[1] This implies the performing of the three-fold exercise, described above in paragraphs 149 and 150, twenty-one times, during the time occupied with the visualizations. And while so visualizing, one is to retain the cross-legged posture and the 'Pot-shaped', with such modifications as are necessary for the placing and rubbing together of the suns on the palms of the hands and soles of the feet.

[2] Text : *Yid-rig* = *Yid-kyi-rig-ma*, meaning, 'spiritual consort of the mind', that is to say, the mind in its negative or female aspect, personified by the Goddess Vajra-Yoginī.

[3] This visualization is particularly intended to excite the 'moon-fluid' through arousing desire, and thus accelerate the mystic melting of the visualized letter *HAM*, the symbol of the masculine aspect of the mind.

[4] Success at this stage depends, of course, upon mastery of all the preceding practices relating to the production of psychic-heat. See especially the exposi-

Sambhāra-chakra,[1] hollow like a blue filmy silk tent, and at the centre of the vacuity the three chief psychic-nerves, the four chief psychic-nerve centres [or *chakra*], the half-*A*, and the letter *HAM* as vividly defined as above.

(167) The vital-force setteth the half-*A* aflame ; and, by the heat thus engendered, the letter *HAM* is melted and the drops of it fall on the half-*A*.

(168) With a crackling sound, the flame quickly moveth downward ; and then, with increased burning force, it reacheth the navel nerve-centre.

(169) The letter *HAM* being very much melted, the drops of it falling downward, cause the flame to increase in intensity till it reacheth the heart nerve-centre, then the throat nerve-centre, and then the brain nerve-centre.

(170) Finally, the flow of the completely melted letter *HAM* descendeth to the nerve-centre of the throat and completely permeateth it ; and thereby is experienced ' Bliss of Delight ', or physical blissfulness.[2]

(171) Then momentarily dawn the various experiences.[3]

tion of the physical exercises contained under paragraph 180, below ; and then, concerning the breathing and visualizing processes, paragraphs 51-96, above.

[1] Text : *Hkhor-lo-Sdom-pa* (pron. *Khor-lo-Dom-pa*) : Skt. *Sambhāra-chakra* : ' Wheel of the All-restrained (or All-combined) '.  He is here the male aspect, while the Vajra-Yoginī of our text is the female aspect, of the mind.  His blue colour symbolizes, like the blue sky, immutability, or eternity.  According to this *maṇḍala*, or method, Sambhāra-chakra is a Tantric form of the Buddha-principle of Enlightenment.

[2] This state is to be differentiated from that of the super-physical blissfulness of *samādhi*.  The various degrees of blissfulness which the *yogin* experiences are classified as follows : Bliss of Delight ; Transcendental Bliss ; Wonderful Bliss ; Simultaneously-born Bliss.  The first three (which are psycho-physical, and distinguishable from the purely supra-mundane bliss of the Simultaneously-born State of *Nirvāṇa*) are otherwise known, in their due order, as Normal Bliss, Ecstatic Bliss, and Supreme Bliss.

[3] This seems to refer to a sort of panoramic vision which endures but for a moment, in which there is reviewed one's human experiences, analogous to the panoramic vision of the past events of a lifetime which a number of persons, resuscitated after having been drowned, report as having experienced in the process of drowning.  In this *yogically* induced vision, the *yogin* experiences momentarily one pair of opposite physical or mental states after another.  Pain blends with pleasure ; anger with love ; perturbation with quiescence ; and so on, with the result that opposites are realized to be unities and all of them a single unity.

(172) Abide in the equilibrium of the Voidness.

(173) By this nectar, dropping from the molten letter *HAM*, permeating the heart nerve-centre, one experienceth 'Transcendental Bliss', and attaineth consciousness of the faculty which ripeneth *karma*,[1] and realizeth the State of the Vastly Void.[2]

(174) By its permeating the navel nerve-centre, one experienceth 'Wonderful Bliss', and a thrilling, or vibratory sensation, throughout the body, and realizeth the State of the Great Voidness.

(175) Finally, by this vital-fire descending to the base of the reproductive organ [in the Root-Support, or *Mūladhāra-chakra*, the seat of the Serpent Power], one experienceth 'Simultaneously-born Bliss'.

(176) Then one hath the power to recognize the minutest conceivable fraction of time which in the normal state of consciousness is beyond cognition.

(177) And the Clear Light of the All-Voidness[3] being

---

[1] See paragraph 142.

[2] Text: *Shin-tu-stong-pa* (pron. *Shin-tu-tong-pa*) = 'Vastly (or Great) Void'. Northern Buddhism enumerates eighteen degrees of the Voidness (Skt. *Shūn-yatā*): (1) Internal Voidness, as of sensory response to stimuli; (2) External Voidness, as of external stimuli; (3) Internal and External Voidness in union; (4) Voidness of Voidance itself; (5) Great Voidness, as of space; (6) Real Voidness, as of the realization of *Nirvāna*; (7) Compounded Voidness, as of the Universe, or *Sangsāra*; (8) Uncompounded Voidness, as of the Uncreated, Unmanifested *Nirvāna*; (9) Boundless Voidness, as of infinity; (10) Voidness of Beginninglessness and Endlessness, as of eternity; (11) Remainderless Voidness, as of mathematical zero; (12) Natural Voidness, as of all objective things; (13) Voidness of Phenomena, (14) of Predications, (15) of Non-Thought, (16) of Immateriality, (17) of Reality, and (18) of the Non-Substantiality of Reality. There are in Tibetan voluminous works and commentaries devoted wholly to the expounding of these eighteen degrees of the Voidness. It would, therefore, be quite beyond the scope of our present treatise to attempt their detailed explication. We may here briefly state that this doctrine of the Void-ness aims at classifying the various aspects in which Reality is realizable, partially as in most instances, and completely in the state of *Nirvāna*. The Vastly Void appears to be a modified realization of the Great Voidness, the fifth degree of the Voidness, mentioned in the next paragraph.

[3] The All-Voidness corresponds to that transcendental visual state of *yogic* insight into the illusory nature of all component things wherein the Clear Light of Reality is realized. It is represented by the thirteenth degree of the Voidness.

realized, one becometh immersed in a condition of consciousness unaffected by all worldly [or external] stimuli.

(178) Practice recognizing these degrees of bliss, from the normal physical bliss, up to the 'Simultaneously-born Bliss', as they arise, one after the other, in virtue of the vital-fire permeating, in due order, the brain, the throat, the heart, and the navel nerve-centres.

### [THE CONCLUDING PORTION : THE PHYSICAL DRILL]

(179) The Concluding Portion, the Physical Drill, consisteth of the fundamental physical drill called 'Naropa's Exercises—the Six, Twenty, and Fifty', which are to be practised.[1]

### [*The Six Fundamental Physical Exercises of Naropa*]
### *Namo Mahā-Mūdrāya !* [2]

(180) The Six Fundamental Physical Exercises of Naropa are as followeth :

(1) Rest the fists on the knees, with the feet in the *Bodhisattvic-* [or Buddha-] Posture ; then whirl the waist round and round, from right to left and from left to right.[3] This practice

---

[1] Here the text of the Psychic-Heat Doctrine ends. The matter that follows, up to the Doctrine of the Illusory Body, has been interpolated from a very occult Tibetan work which was in the possession of the translator, who received it from his late *Guru* Norbu, in Bhutan. The title of the work is *Rdo-rje lüs kyi hkhrül-hkhor bde-chen nye-lam las yan-lag lnga-sbyong sogs rtsa-tshig-gi gzhyung-hgah bzhügs-so* (pron. *Do-rje lü kyi htül-khor de-chen nye-lam lay yan-lag nga-jong so tsa-tshi-gi zhyung-ga zhü-so*), meaning, 'Herein Lieth Some of the General Practices of the Root-Words of the Training of the Five Limbs, from " The Short Path [to] Great Bliss: the Physical Exercises of [or for acquiring] a *Vajra* [i.e. Perfect] Body ".' The term 'Root-Words' of this rendering refers to the essential teachings intended for the 'Training of the Five Limbs', which are the two legs and the two arms, and the trunk of the body inclusive of the neck and head. Our English rendering from this work, of the most essential of Naropa's Exercises, called 'The Six', is here presented to the serious student with the permission of the late Lāma Kazi Dawa-Samdup, who was himself an initiate of the Kargyütpa School to which they chiefly appertain. It was his most earnest desire that these hitherto secretly-guarded exercises be used only for the purpose intended and with due homage to the Great *Gurus* in whom they have origin.

[2] This salutation, or obeisance, to the *Mahā-Mūdra*, or 'Great Symbol', indicates that the Six Exercises, like the Six Doctrines, are a part of the teachings of the Great Symbol School.

[3] The whole body, supported by the fists on the knees, is to be held rigid, and the region of the waist, including the stomach, rotated with a churning-like

dispelleth the disorders of the region of the navel and untieth [i.e setteth into healthful functioning] the navel nerve-knot [or psychic-centre].    (2) Then [in the same posture] turn the neck round and round, and bend it backward and forward.    Thus the nerve-knots of the crown of the head and throat are untied.    (3) [With the hands open and held palms downward over the bended knees, and the body in all other respects postured as in the first exercise], twist the upper part of the body from right to left and left to right alternately.[1]    Diseases of the upper part of the body are thereby dispelled, and its nerve-knots are untied.    (4) The extending and contracting of the limbs [i.e. the arms and hands, and the legs and feet], which dispel the diseases of the limbs and liberate [or untie] the nerve-knots, are to be performed first with the two hands and arms.[2]    Then, placing the two hands on the ground [or meditation-cushion] behind thee, rest the buttocks on the ground [or meditation-cushion], and, extending the legs,

motion. Ordinarily, throughout these Six Exercises of Naropa, each single exercise and then each of two alternating exercises, as given here, are to be performed thrice; and each period of three performances of an exercise, whether single or double in its entirety, is to be marked by a forcible bounce, as previously prescribed in the text of the Psychic-Heat Doctrine.

[1] While holding the lower part of the body below the waist rigid, the upper part is to be turned in a twisting manner, with the head and neck and trunk held together as a unit of rigidity.

[2] Here the textual directions are chiefly suggestive; for the *guru* is expected to supply the details, which the translator, acting as the editor's *guru*, expounded as follows : 'The first part of this exercise, the extending, consists of the following processes : The right arm unbended is to be extended straight out in front of one, with the hand open, fingers touching, and palm turned downward horizontally.    Then, with a rapid motion, the open left hand, with palm downward, is to be passed over the upper surface of the extended right arm from the shoulder to the finger-tips and thence underneath and across the palm and along the under surface of the arm, and, then, with a sharp bang, into the armpit. Do this thrice.    Then do likewise with the left arm and right hand, thrice. Then perform one forcible bounce.    Then thrice similarly treat the right and left leg, using the left and right hand.    Then perform another forcible bounce, which completes one course of the extending part of the exercise.

' The contracting is to be done thus : Bend each arm from the elbow so that the forearm rests against the front of the breast and the upper part of the arm close against the side, the hands fisted; and then forcibly flap the two arms, thus postured, against the ribs thrice.    Then perform one forcible bounce. This completes one course of the contracting part of the exercise.    The remaining part of the exercise is self-explanatory.'

vigorously shake the feet in the air. (5) By bouncing upward and dropping downward [in the cross-legged posture, the hands resting on the knees, raising the body and letting it drop back forcibly on to the meditation-cushion] [1] the nerve-knots of the whole body will be untied. And at every bounce, twist the body to the right and to the left ; and, with the hands held against the knees, shake [or vibrate] the body vigorously. (6) Shake [or vibrate] the body [placed in a stooping posture with the hands, on the meditation-cushion, bracing the body]. Then utter *Uh*,[2] and rub and massage the body all over. Thus all the nerves will be calmed, each in its own place.

[Here endeth The Doctrine of the Pyschic-Heat.]

## [CHAPTER II: THE DOCTRINE OF THE ILLU-SORY BODY]

(1) The second doctrine, the Illusory Body, consisteth of three parts : Realizing the Impure Illusory Body to be *Māyā*, Realizing the Pure Illusory Body to be *Māyā*, Realizing All Things to be *Māyā*.[3]

### [*PART I: REALIZING THE IMPURE ILLUSORY BODY TO BE* MĀYĀ]

(2) Of the first, Realizing the Impure Illusory Body to be *Māyā*, it hath been said :

'Of ripened *karma* is the illusory body born.'

(3) In a mirror, attached either to a stake or to some other support in front of thee, let thy body be mirrored.

(4) Inasmuch as applying to the mirrored body such pleasing things as honour, fame, and adulation affecteth it pleasurably, and depriving it of some of its belongings and applying to it deprecatory and displeasing epithets affecteth

---

[1] Cf. the similar exercise and posture as expounded in paragraph 149, above.

[2] The uttering of *Uh* is the ejecting of the breath forcibly.

[3] Text : *Sgyūma* (pron. *Gyūma*) : Skt. *Māyā* : 'Illusion', with reference to all things of Nature as being no more real than the things which a clever Hindu magician causes his audience to see, as apparently real, but which are merely visualizations in his own mind telepathically impressed upon the minds of the hypnotically influenced onlookers. The 'Impure Illusory Body' refers to the human body, and the 'Pure Illusory Body' to the visualization of the body of a deity.

it adversely, therefore, visualizing it as being between thyself and the mirror, apply these pleasant and unpleasant things to it.[1]

(5) Then, regarding thyself as in no way unlike that mirrored form, apply to it the Sixteen Similes ;[2] thereby habituating the mind to regard one's own body as being *māyā*, and, therefore, unreal.

## [PART II: REALIZING THE PURE ILLUSORY BODY TO BE MĀYĀ]

(6) The second part, Realizing the Pure Illusory Body to be *Māyā*, consisteth of two divisions: the *Māyā* of the Visualizing State, and the *Māyā* of the Perfected State.

### [THE MĀYĀ OF THE VISUALIZING STATE]

(7) Of the first, the *Māyā* of the Visualizing State, it hath been said :

'It should resemble the mirrored form
Of a well-drawn likeness of Vajra-Sattva,
Seen on the surface of an unsullied mirror
During the mystic conferring of power.'[3]

[1] In the original, this passage is more or less ironical, the practice being intended to lead the disciple to see for himself the foolishness of his own egoism, upon which the *māyā* of his bodily form entirely depends. In the mirror he can see himself as others see him, and secretly observe the different purely human and monkey-like responses to the various pleasing and displeasing thought-stimuli applied, as they spread over his countenance. If the practice be seriously meditated upon, there can be but one result, namely, disgust with one's egotistical sense of self-importance, or false pride. The thought that one is wiser, or holier, or in any respect worthy of being differentiated from sentient beings, regarded as a whole, is incompatible with progress on the Path of Selflessness.

[2] These are sixteen similes illustrating the illusory nature of the physical body, such as : It is like a mirage, like clouds, like the moon reflected in water, like the illusions produced by magic, like the substance of dreams, like the reflection seen in a mirror, and so on.

[3] During the mystic initiation, here called the mystic conferring of power, there is employed a mirror, symbolical of the Mirror of *Karma*, in which all good and evil deeds of the neophyte are said to be mystically reflected ; and, also, a well-made likeness, usually painted in colours, of Vajra-Sattva ('The Indestructible-Minded One'), one of the two *Bodhisat* reflexes of the *Dhyānī* Buddha Akṣhobhya, with Whom the Mirror-like Wisdom is associated. This stanza of four verses is addressed to the disciple who is being made ready to

(8) Accordingly, either the figure of Vajra-Sattva, or of any other tutelary deity, having been drawn, let its superficial form be reflected in a mirror.[1]

(9) By looking at that mirrored form with fixity of gaze and mind, and meditating upon it, the figure will come to appear as if animated.

(10) Visualize it thus as being between the mirror and thyself.

(11) Next visualize thine own body as being like that reflected body of the deity; and should the visualization become substantial enough to touch,[2] proceed to visualize any other body thou happenest to see, as also being the deity's body; and should this visualization similarly become life-like, then visualize all visible forms as being the body of the tutelary deity.

(12) By so doing, all phenomenally-appearing things will dawn upon thee as being the sport [i.e. the manifold manifestations] of the deity.

receive his first initiation, which extends over a number of days; and, preparatory to the solemn ceremonial of his new birth, as a Child of Wisdom, he is directed to practise this rite of the Illusory Body.

[1] The picture is to be held, or preferably attached to a stake, in such manner that the *yogin* as he sits meditating can see it reflected in the mirror.

[2] This is the standard test applied to *yogic* visualizations. If the *yogin's* practising be successful, the visualization will appear to him substantial. or life-like. Remarkable, well-authenticated instances are reported from Tibet of *yogically*-induced visualizations becoming palpable and objective, and endowed by their creators with fictitious consciousness and volition, life-like functioning activity, and individualized existence. The 'spirit-medium' of the Occident commonly attributes similar materializations to forces apart from herself, unaware that their true origin is to be found in thoughts projected as visualizations from her own mental content, either consciously or unconsciously, and sometimes, possibly, through response to telepathic impulses communicated from sources apart from herself, which may be incarnate or discarnate centres of consciousness. The transmission of thought artificially, as in wireless telegraphy, is now a matter of common knowledge to the European races, as telepathy, or the transmission of thought naturally, i.e. without the cumbrous mechanism of Western science, has been for unknown ages to the *yogin*. There yet remains for physicists the discovery of mechanical means to materialize, or give objectivity to, thoughts, in the same way as the *yogin* does by natural means. A further step will be for the scientist to invent a method not only thus to integrate matter around a certain thought model, but to disintegrate any material object, and, in its electronic, invisible form, transmit it from one place to another and then reconstitute its objectivity, or aspect as a solid.

(13) This is called 'The Realizing of the Thatness of the Deity'; also 'The Illusory Visualization', or 'The Transmutation of all Objective Things into a God and a Goddess'.[1]

### [THE *MĀYĀ* OF THE PERFECTED STATE]

(14) Of the second, the *Māyā* of the Perfected State, it hath been said:

'The root of the All-Knowledge it is;
By entering into it, the Goal becometh nearer.'

(15) Accordingly, assume the seven postures associated with Vairochana,[2] whereby are understood all psycho-physical processes.

(16) Do not permit the mind to analyse the track of the past; do not anticipate the future; give no shape to the present; and fix the gaze one-pointedly on the empty space of the sky.

(17) Then the power of mind, along with the vital-force, enter the median-nerve; and the thought-process becometh tranquillized.

(18) This condition maketh one to see the Five Signs, which are the apparitional smoke and the other phenomena [mentioned above, in paragraph 123 of the Psychic-Heat Doctrine].

(19) In particular, one should have a vision of the Form of the Buddha outlined against a cloudless sky, like unto the moon's reflected form seen in water.[3]

---

[1] The god and goddess symbolize the two aspects of the Thatness,—the positive, or male, and the negative, or female,—as being ever in at-one-ment, or union (Tib. *yab-yum*). In other words, the *yogin* glimpses the unity of all things, or the One Reality, which is Primordial Mind. (Cf. pp. 146[3], 147[2].)

[2] Each of these postures is explained in the text of *The Epitome of the Great Symbol*; see p. 116. Another, and more detailed, description of them is contained in the Psychic-Heat Doctrine, above, §§ 49–50. *Yogins* refer to them as being the seven postures for realizing all psycho-physical and spiritual things. Hence there is associated with them the first of the Five Dhyānī Buddhas, Vairochana, the Manifester, 'He Who in Shapes Makes Visible [the Universe of Matter]'. Vairochana symbolizes the All-Pervading Wisdom, or the All-Knowledge, which is born of the Voidness. In virtue of these seven postures all spiritual intuitions become consciously cognizable, and the Goal is brought nearer.

[3] This is a further standard whereby one may measure success in visualiza-

(20) Or one seeth, as a form reflected in a mirror is seen, the unobscured, radiant *Nirmāṇa-Kāya* [i.e. the pure, illusory body in which a Buddha incarnates on Earth], endowed with the signs of perfect beauty and gracefulness.[1]

(21) Then dawneth the *Sambhoga-Kāya* [i.e. the invisible, super-physical body-aggregate of the perfect spiritual attributes of a Buddha], experienced as sound.[2]

(22) Of this, Ārya Deva,[3] hath said :

'All apparent phenomena are like dreams and magical illusions,

As all followers of the Buddha assert ;

But those [of the Southern School] who oppose the practice of inducing " gift-wave " conference on oneself,[4]

See not by actual realization this dream-like and illusory nature of things.'

tion. If the vision is not experienced, the practice has not been perfect. In a way, this vision is like visions seen in the after-death state called the *Bardo*, in that it is dependent upon the mental-content of the percipient, and has no existence apart from the mind. A non-Buddhist would need first to fix the mental impress of the Form of the Buddha upon his mind while in the normal state to be able thus to pattern the visualization and project it.

[1] This is not only a still higher standard of efficiency in visualization, but, also, a standard to measure the cultural ability of the disciple as regards beauty. (See the Form of the Glorified Buddha, facing p. 57.)

[2] This experience is highly occult. The sound refers to a sort of perfect melody born of the sixty vocal perfections of Brahmā or of a Buddha. As form, the *Sambhoga-Kāya* is mentally inconceivable, as sound it is not wholly beyond mental comprehension.

[3] Ārya Deva is one of the six most illustrious patriarchs of the *Mahāyāna* School of Buddhist philosophy. He was a disciple under the personal direction of the Great Sage Nāgārjuna.

[4] This refers to the practice common to Northern Buddhists, in Tibet, China, Mongolia, and Japan, and opposed by Southern Buddhists, of Ceylon, Burmah, and Siam, of employing rituals which imply a direct appeal or prayer to deities, either regarded as being imaginary, as in the visualizations contained in the various texts comprising this volume, or as real divine impersonal forces, as symbolized by the *Dharma-Kāya*. There are some, but very few, amongst Northern Buddhists who, in this matter, side with the Southern Buddhists. The 'gift-waves', or spiritual power telepathically transmitted from the super-human *gurus* to the *gurus* on Earth and thence to the disciples, are evoked in virtue of a *yogic* process akin to auto-suggestion. In other words, the *yogin* aims at making known his desire for divine guidance by consciously projecting perceptible waves of psychic influence to the superhuman realms wherein

*[PART III: REALIZING ALL THINGS TO BE* MĀYĀ]

(23) Of the third part, Realizing All Things to be *Māyā*, it hath been said :

'Everything, the " Moving " and the " Non-moving ",[1] of the Three Universes,[2]

Is, in its completeness, realized as a Unity.'

(24) The meaning of this quotation may be expounded as followeth :

When one hath attained mastery of the tranquil state of

exist the Great Teachers, Who are no longer incarnate. To this end he makes use of mental concentration upon rituals and visualizations of deities, either purely imaginary or relatively real. European critics of *yoga* have thought that such practices induce a sort of self-hypnotization. If, in some degree, this criticism be well founded, we must, nevertheless, take into account the fact that hypnotization by one's own efforts has a far different result, in so far as experimental knowledge is concerned, than hypnotization by another person. In self-hypnotization, the *yogin* is wholly the master of himself, whereas in hypnotic trance induced in one person by another the hypnotized subject loses mastery of himself and is more or less enslaved to the will of the hypnotizer, and upon being released from hypnosis has little or no conscious memory of the nature of the hypnotic state or of the character of the mind's reaction to the external stimuli inducing that state. On the contrary, the *yogin* enters the state fully conscious of what he is doing, and, while in it, trains his mind to retain memory of what is therein perceived or experienced. Hypnotization itself offers a vast and as yet little known field for psychological research ; and we are satisfied that the *yogin* knows far more that is worth knowing about the hypnotic state *per se* than any of our amateur psychologists of Europe and America. They, like our pathologists, prefer to experiment and theorize at second hand, by using the brains and bodies of animals or of other human beings, rather than, like the *yogin*, to know at first hand psychological facts by experimenting upon their own brains and bodies. The Southern Buddhists, in Ārya Deva's view, are in their opposition to these Northern Buddhist *yogic* practices, much like the psychologist who seeks knowledge at second hand, or from external sources, rather than from within himself. The essential teaching of our Mahāyāna texts is that the Divine Wisdom, the All-Knowledge, is innate, or internal ; in the Christian sense, that the Kingdom of Heaven lies within.

[1] The ' Moving ' is the *Sangsāra*, or the Cosmic Creation, as it appears to us in our state of unenlightenment ; the ' Non-Moving ' is *Nirvāṇa*, as we conceive *Nirvāṇa*. Both, however, to the Fully Enlightened, are inseparably One. Their apparent differentiation exists only in the mind of the *yogin* not Completely Enlightened, who looks upon them as two different states of consciousness.

[2] The Three Universes are of Desire (Skt. *Kāma*), of Form (Skt. *Rūpa*), and of Non-Form (Skt. *Arūpa*). (Cf. p. 94[1-3].)

*samādhi*, then, by adding the actual realization of the Voidness to the understanding already attained, and viewing all things accordingly, the *Sangsāra* and *Nirvāṇa*, which seem to be separable states, are together transmuted into the Wisdom of Non-Duality; and the Apparent Truths are understood to be *samādhic* illusion.[1]

(25) By keeping the mind concentrated upon this understanding, and retaining the state of perfect quiescence, the Wisdom thus attained deepeneth into the Clear Light of the Full Realization of the [Final] Truth.[2]

[Here endeth The Doctrine of the Illusory Body.]

## [CHAPTER III: THE DOCTRINE OF THE DREAM-STATE]

(1) The third doctrine, concerning the Dream-State, consisteth of four parts: Comprehending; Transmuting; Realizing the Dream-State to be *Māyā*; and Meditating upon the Thatness of the Dream-State.

### [PART I: COMPREHENDING THE NATURE OF THE DREAM-STATE]

(2) The first part, Comprehending [the Nature of the Dream-State] compriseth three practices: Comprehending It by the Power of Resolution, Comprehending It by the Power of Breath, and Comprehending It by the Power of Visualization.

---

[1] The Apparent Truths symbolize the partial realization, clouded by a certain degree of illusion, which results from all but the highest state of *samādhi*. For instance, natural facts, such as the existence of the Sun and stars, or of heat and cold, appear to be final, but are really phenomenal, or apparent, for they result from an underlying, fundamental noumenal cause which is non-apparent. Similarly, the law of duality, as seen in nature, is apparently, but not ultimately, true; the wisdom that all dualities are merely aspects of the One Unity underlying all things is the Final Truth.

[2] Just as when one has solved a great problem, the knowledge resulting changes little by little into a feeling of most complete satisfaction, so herein the realization that all phenomenal appearances are illusory, deepens into the State of the Clear Light, which is a visual condition in which the *yogin* realizes Truth in its undimmed completeness. In other words, where there has been realized the illusory nature of apparent truths, and the mind, in the tranquillity of the highest *samādhi*, is fixed upon this realization, the relative truth is transmuted into the absolute or final truth.

[PRACTICE 1: COMPREHENDING IT BY THE POWER OF
RESOLUTION]

(3) With respect to the first, Comprehending It by the
Power of Resolution, that which hath been called 'the initial
comprehending of the dream', referreth to resolving to maintain unbroken continuity of consciousness [throughout both
the waking-state and the dream-state].

(4) In other words, under all conditions during the day [or
waking-state] hold to the concept that all things are of the
substance of dreams and that thou must realize their true
nature.

(5) Then, at night, when about to sleep, pray to the *guru*
that thou mayest be enabled to comprehend the dream-state;
and firmly resolve that thou wilt comprehend it. By meditating thus, one is certain to comprehend it.

(6) It hath furthermore been said [in this connexion]:

'All things are the results of causes;
They depend wholly upon resolutions [or motives].'

[PRACTICE 2: COMPREHENDING IT BY THE POWER
OF BREATH]

(7) In the second practice, Comprehending It by the Power
of Breath, the methods are: Sleep on the right side, as
a lion doth. With the thumb and ring-finger of the right
hand press the pulsation of the throat-arteries; stop the
nostrils with the fingers [of the left hand]; and let the saliva
collect in the throat.[1]

---

[1] As a result of these methods, the *yogin* enjoys as vivid consciousness in the
dream-state as in the waking-state; and in passing from one state to another
experiences no break in the continuity of memory. Thereby the content of the
dream-state is found to be quite the same as that of the waking-state, in that it
is wholly phenomenal and, therefore, illusory. All the multitudinous forms,
both inorganic and organic, existing in nature, including the forms of men and
of gods, are found to be purely phenomenal, and thus, in themselves, non-real.
So dream-experiences and waking-experiences alike are discovered to be like
mirage or like the image of the Moon seen reflected in water. The *yogin*'s
aim is to attain to the causal or noumenal state wherein alone can there be
realization of Reality. Then, indeed, he ecstatically understands the illusory

## [PRACTICE 3: COMPREHENDING IT BY THE POWER OF VISUALIZATION]

(8) The third practice, Comprehending It by the Power of Visualization, consisteth of these processes : the Visualization Itself ; Deriving the Greatest Benefit from the Visualization ; and Preventing the Spreading-out of the Dream-Content.[1]

### [THE VISUALIZATION ITSELF]

(9) In the first, the Visualization Itself, the method is as followeth :

Thinking that thou art thyself the deity Vajra-Yoginī, visualize in the throat psychic-centre the syllable $\check{A}H$, red of colour and vividly radiant, as being the real embodiment of Divine Speech.[2]

(10) By mentally concentrating upon the radiance of the $\check{A}H$, and recognizing every phenomenal thing to be in essence like forms reflected in a mirror, which, though apparent, have no real existence of themselves, one comprehendeth the dream.[3]

### [DERIVING THE GREATEST BENEFIT FROM THE VISUALIZATION]

(11) In the second, for Deriving the Greatest Benefit from the Visualization, the method is as followeth :

At nightfall, [strive to] comprehend the nature of the dream-state by means of the visualization just described above. At dawn, practise ' pot-shaped ' breathing seven times. Resolve

---

character of all component things ; like a child that has outgrown its play-things, no longer is he enamoured of the worldly life ; thenceforth he seeks only the True State of the Uncreated, Unborn, Unmade.

[1] This last process refers to overcoming the tendency of dreams to lose their coherence, or to be lost to memory upon awaking.

[2] Midway between the heart psychic-centre and that of the throat, in a space about four inches long, a tube-like psychic-organ is said to exist. If the vital-force be quiescent within it, sleep ensues ; and if the vital-force be in motion within it, dreams occur. Hence this visualization chiefly concerns the throat psychic-centre. (Cf. p. 127[1].)

[3] In visualizing the syllable $\check{A}H$ as emitting radiance, the *yogin* is to imagine that the radiance illuminates and so makes visible all phenomenal things and shows them to be essentially transitory and non-real. Thus he comes to comprehend that the dream-phenomena, too, are of like character.

[or try] eleven times to comprehend the nature of the dream-state. Then concentrate the mind upon a dot, like unto a bony substance, white of colour, situated between the eyebrows.[1]

(12) If one be of plethoric temperament, the dot is to be visualized as being red of colour; if one be of nervous temperament, the dot is to be visualized as being green of colour.

(13) If by these means the nature of the dream-state be not comprehended, then proceed as followeth:

At nightfall meditate upon the dot. In the morning practise twenty-one 'pot-shaped' breathings. Make twenty-one resolves [or efforts] to comprehend the nature of the dream-state. Then, by concentrating the mind on a black dot, the size of an ordinary pill, as being situated at the base of the generative organ, one will be enabled to comprehend the nature of the dream-state.[2]

### [PREVENTING THE SPREADING-OUT OF THE DREAM-CONTENT]

(14) Preventing the Spreading-out of the Dream-Content hath four divisions: the Spreading-out into the Waking-State, the Spreading-out because of Fatigue [from the Exercises], the Spreading-out because of Physical or Mental Affliction, and the Spreading-out into Negativeness.

(15) The Spreading-out into the Waking-State occurreth when one is about to comprehend the dream, in virtue of thinking that it must be comprehended, and then waketh up.[3]

(16) The antidote for this is to eat nutritious food and to perform bodily work [or exercise] until fatigued. Thereby sleep becometh deeper; and that cureth it.

(17) The Spreading-out because of Fatigue occurreth when a dream recurreth frequently without any change of content.

---

[1] This has correspondence with the third eye of Vajra-Yoginī. (See p. 173[b].) The visualization of the dot (Tib. *thiglé*) is, in this practice, chiefly for the purpose of attaining mental concentration, or one-pointedness of mind.

[2] When the disciple is unable to attain to one-pointedness of mind because of nervous excitation, or for any other not unusual cause, the *guru* commonly prescribes this colour visualization in order to help the disciple to gain mental quiescence.

[3] In other words, the waking from sleep while one is trying to grasp the character of the dream-state is called the spreading-out of the dream-content into the waking-state.

(18) The antidote here is to meditate often upon that dream and to resolve most firmly to comprehend its essential nature; amalgamating in the process the 'Pot-shaped' breathing-exercise with the visualization of the dot between the eyebrows.[1]

(19) The Spreading-out because of Physical or Mental Affliction occurreth when one dreameth many dreams and recollecteth nothing of them upon awaking.

(20) The antidote here is to avoid pollutions and impurities,[2] to take the Initiation of *Samādhi*,[3] and to visualize the dot as being inside the root of the organ of generation. Thereby this spreading-out will be cured.

(21) The Spreading-out into Negativeness is the disinclination of dreams to come.

(22) To overcome this, vizualize, whilst meditating upon the 'Pot-shaped', the dot as being in the root of the generative organ ; and, in particular, worship with propitiatory offerings the *Vīras* and the *Ḍākinīs*.[4]

---

[1] The purpose of this combination of exercises is to gain better control of the mind, for indomitable mental control prevents and cures all the various spreadings-out of the content of dreams.

[2] These pollutions and impurities are such as arise from being in a place where a death or birth, or a battle or murder is occurring, or a law-suit is being tried and stirring up evil passions, or a smithy is forging death-dealing weapons like swords, arrows, spears, and fire-arms ; or from taking food of a person inimically disposed towards one.

[3] This initiatory rite, known in Tibetan as the 'Conferring of Power' or 'Initiatory Empowerment' (*Rig-pahi-rtsal-dvang*—pron. *Rig-pai-tsal-wang*), is for the purpose of developing the higher intellectual faculties. It is conferred only upon disciples who have been long on probation and found worthy of it. In modern Tibet, as was said of ancient classical Greece, ' Many are the wand-bearers ; few the chosen.'

[4] It is held by learned *gurus* that at this stage, or under this circumstance, elementals, comparable to the elementals of medieval mystics, and similar non-human entities, try to prevent the *yogin* from acquiring *siddhic*, or super-normal, powers, which are essential in this *yoga*. Consequently, before the *yogin* can establish himself securely on the 'astral' plane and be quite free of all such interference, he must make friends with its inhabitants, the elementals, called in Sanskrit *Vīras* ('Heroes') and *Ḍākinīs* ('Fairies'). When a traveller from a far country enters into a new and unexplored country peopled by uncouth savages, he first appeases them by simple gifts. Similarly, in the view of the *guru*, the inhabitants of the strange realm into which the *yogin* hopes to enter and make exploration must first be propitiated. The ritual offerings are of food, whence the 'Heroes' and 'Fairies' extract the invisible spiritual essences, upon

[*PART II: TRANSMUTING THE DREAM-CONTENT*]

(23) In the second part, the Transmuting, as it is called, the process is as followeth :

If, for example, the dream be about fire, think, 'What fear can there be of fire which occurreth in a dream!' Holding to this thought, trample upon the fire. In like manner, tread under foot whatever be dreamt.

(24) After having gained proficiency in this, then turn the thought to the various Buddha Realms [thinking that they are attainable].

(25) Accordingly, when about to sleep, visualize a red dot as being within the throat psychic-centre, and firmly believe that thereby thou shalt see whichever of these Realms thou desirest to see, with all its characteristics, most vividly.

(26) By concentrating the mind thus, one beholdeth the Buddha Realm which one hath wished to behold—the Tuṣhita Heaven,[1] or the Happy Western Realm,[2] or that called 'Happy to Know',[3] or any other of the Realms.

(27) This practice serveth as a test of efficiency [in the art of transmuting dreams].[4]

---

which they feed. This modern Tibetan, and also Hindu, practice, parallels that of the ancient and highly cultured Greeks of sacrificing to the daemons, believing that daemons enjoy the odour of burnt offerings. The use of incense, now adopted in Christian rituals, had originally, and still has, in the Orient, a similar propitiatory and exorcising purpose. And the Gaelic peasant, on November Night, still makes food-offerings to the 'good people', 'pucks', 'leprechauns', and other fairy folk, as the Breton peasant does to the spirits of the dead, that these dwellers in the Celtic Otherworld may be friendly rather than inimical, and so bless the hearth and family and cause increase of the flocks and bountiful harvest during the year to come.

[1] Text: *Dgah-ldan* (pron. *Gah-dan*): Skt. *Tuṣhita*, the paradise wherein dwell the *Bodhisattvas* prior to their final incarnation on Earth to become Buddhas. Maitreya, the Buddha next to come, is now in the Tuṣhita Realm, awaiting the destined hour of his descent among men.

[2] Text: *Bdeva-chān* (pron. *Dewa-chān*): Skt. *Sukhāvatī*, or 'Happy Land' ; the Happy Western Realm of the Dhyāni Buddha Amitābha. (See p. 339[9].)

[3] Text: *Mngon-par-dgah-va* (pron. *Ngon-par-gah-wa*). This is the paradise of Vajra-Sattva, the 'Adamantine' or 'Everlasting One', an esoteric reflex of the Dhyānī Buddha Akṣhobhya, the 'Unagitated One', assigned to the Eastern Direction ; or, according to its Tibetan name, the 'Happy-to-Know' Realm.

[4] The aim of this practice is to enable the disciple to realize of himself that all phenomenal things of the *Saṅgsāra*, or Cosmic Creation, even these sensuous

*[PART III: REALIZING THE DREAM-STATE, OR
DREAM-CONTENT, TO BE* MĀYĀ]

(28) The third part, Realizing the Dream-State [or Dream-Content] to be *Māyā*, hath been expounded as followeth:

'At the outset, in the process of realizing it to be *māyā*,
    abandon all feeling of fear [or dread];
And, if the dream be of fire, transform the fire into water,
    the antidote of fire.
And if the dream be of minute objects, transform them into
    large objects;
Or if the dream be of large objects, transform them into
    small objects:
Thereby one comprehendeth the nature of dimensions.
And if the dream be of a single thing, transform it into
    many things;
Or if the dream be of many things, transform them into
    a single thing:
[Thereby one comprehendeth the nature of plurality and
    of unity.]
Continue such practices until thoroughly proficient in
    them.'[1]

paradises (which are within the Universes of Desire, Form, and Formlessness, wherein existence is still individualized and personal, as in the Semitic Heaven), are, like the human body, and the content of both the waking- and the dream-state, *māyā*. Once this mighty truth is realized, the disciple is ready for further advance on the Path, the Goal of which is the Dreamless State (free from the illusoriness of both the waking and sleeping condition)—the Desireless State, the State beyond both Form and Non-Form—*Nirvāṇa*. The gods themselves and their heavens, like all sentient beings possessing form and a place of existence, are, in the last analysis of the Fully Enlightened Mind, of the stuff of which dreams are made. The seeing by the *yogin* of the realm upon which his mind is concentrated is the proof of his efficiency and success in the practice. The red dot serves somewhat like the eye-piece of a spiritual telescope, through which, in virtue of the visualization, the realm is said to be actually seen, or experienced, while out of the body in sleep. The practice in this respect partakes of the nature of that expounded in the last of the Six Doctrines, and again in Book IV, following, namely, that of the transference of consciousness from realm to realm or from one state of existence to another.

[1] By such practices the *yogin* is taught to realize that matter, or form in its dimensional aspects, large or small, and in its numerical aspects, of plurality and unity, is entirely subject to one's will when the mental powers have been efficiently developed by *yoga*. In other words, the *yogin* learns by actual experience, resulting from psychic experimentation, that the character of any

(29) Then by visualizing one's own body as seen in the dream-state, and all other bodies similarly seen, as being *māyā*-like bodies of deities, they will be realized to be so.[1]

## [PART IV: MEDITATING UPON THE THATNESS OF THE DREAM-STATE]

(30) The fourth part, Meditating upon the Thatness of the Dream-State, is, as hath been said, 'to meditate upon the real essence of the Thatness'; and thereby, the dream propensities, whence arise whatever is seen in dreams as appearances of deities, are purified.

(31) By concentrating the mind upon the forms of the deities seen in the dream-state, and by keeping the mind free of thoughts, in the quiescent condition, the forms of the deities are attuned to the non-thought condition of mind; and thereby dawneth the Clear Light, of which the essence is of the Voidness.

dream can be changed or transformed by willing that it shall be. A step further and he learns that form, in the dream-state, and all the multitudinous content of dreams, are merely playthings of mind, and, therefore, as unstable as mirage. A further step leads him to the knowledge that the essential nature of form and of all things perceived by the senses in the waking-state are equally as unreal as their reflexes in the dream-state, both states alike being *sangsāric*. The final step leads to the Great Realization, that nothing within the *Sangsāra* is or can be other than unreal like dreams. The Universal Creation, with its many mansions of existence, from the lowest to the highest Buddha paradise, and every phenomenal thing therein, organic and inorganic, matter, or form, in its innumerable physical aspects, as gases, solids, heat, cold, radiations, colours, energies, electronic elements, are but the content of the Supreme Dream. With the dawning of this Divine Wisdom, the microcosmic aspect of the Macrocosm becomes fully awakened; the dew-drop slips back into the Shining Sea, in *Nirvānic* Blissfulness and At-one-ment, possessed of All Possessions, Knower of the All-Knowledge, Creator of All Creations—the One Mind, Reality Itself.

[1] The student should here refer back to Part II of the Doctrine of the Illusory Body, §§ 11–13. The *yogin* is taught that there is a real at-one-ment between gods and men; for both alike find a common Unity in the Thatness. It is the illusory form, which each alike temporarily possesses, that gives them individualized and objective existence. And these forms, of even the highest of the gods, such as Indra and the Rulers of Planetary Forces, are like the forms seen reflected in a mirror, non-real. But behind all forms, behind all phenomenal appearances, behind all *māyā*, there is Reality. To have realized this by *yogic* experimentation is to understand the Thatness of all things, to know oneself, and to have reached the Goal, which is *Nirvānic* Enlightenment while still in the *Sangsāra*.

(32) If one attain mastery of this process, then, whether in the sleeping-state or in the waking-state, one realizeth both states to be illusory [in so far as their content are concerned] ; and all phenomena will be known to be born of the Clear Light [which is the noumenal reality sustaining the *māyā*], and phenomena and mind [or noumena] [1] will blend.

[Here endeth The Doctrine of Dreams.]

## [CHAPTER IV: THE DOCTRINE OF THE CLEAR LIGHT]

(1) The fourth doctrine, the Clear Light, consisteth of three parts : the Fundamental Clear Light, [2] the Clear Light on the Path, [3] and the Resultant Clear Light. [4]

### [*PART I: THE FUNDAMENTAL CLEAR LIGHT*]

(2) The first, the Fundamental Clear Light, hath been spoken of thus :

'That this select teaching for the recognizing of the Clear Light
Is the Foundation, the Path, and the Fruit, know thou full well, O disciple.' [5]

(3) It hath been said that the True State of the mind, the Thatness of all things, inseparable from the Voidness, beyond

---

[1] Without mind (or consciousness), as a noumenal source, there can be no phenomena, no illusory states, such as man experiences so long as he is man. Unenlightened mind, robed in matter, looks out upon the phenomena of Nature as being something apart from itself. The unconscious mind of man, of which the normal mind is a reflection, like the reflection of the body seen in a mirror, or like the body seen in the dream-state, is a ray of the Universal Mind, wherein gleams the Clear Light of Reality, the Light that illuminates every living creature and sustains or gives coherence, or unity, to all objectively existing things. It is the Inner Light of the mystics, and the Guiding Star of the Magi, which indicates the divine incarnation of a *Christos* on Earth.

[2] Text : *gzhi-hi-höd-gsal* (pron. *zhi-yi-wö-sal*) = 'Fundamental [or Primal] Clear Light'.

[3] Text : *lam-gyi-höd-gsal* (pron. *lam-gyi-wö-sal*) = 'Clear Light on [or of] the Path'.

[4] Text : *hbras-bu-hi-höd-gsal* (pron. *day-bu-yi-wö-sal*) = 'Resultant Clear Light'.

[5] That incomprehensible, omnipresent, transcendent Divine Radiance, that illumines the All-Mind, and glows in the heart of all living things, is the Clear Light. In its glory the *Bodhic* Path ends.

the domain of phenomena, while experiencing the thought-transcending Great Bliss, is the Primal [or Fundamental] Clear Light.[1]

## [*PART II: THE CLEAR LIGHT ON THE PATH*]

(4) The second part, the Clear Light on the Path, con-sisteth of three practices [or processes]: Blending the Nature of the Clear Light with the Path during the Day-Time [i.e. while experiencing the waking-state]; Blending the Nature of the Clear Light with the Path during the Night-Time [i.e. while experiencing the sleeping-state]; Blending the Nature of the Clear Light with the Path during the After-Death State [i.e. while experiencing the *Bardo*, intervening between death and rebirth].[2]

## [PRACTICE 1: BLENDING THE NATURE OF THE CLEAR LIGHT WITH THE PATH DURING THE DAY-TIME]

(5) The first practice, Blending the Nature of the Clear Light with the Path during the Day-Time, is known as ' The Five Doctrines '. For whatever be the stage reached in the Knowledge of the Thatness, in virtue of the power of the well-purified Three Wisdoms, one cometh to comprehend the actual progress made in the attainment of Perfection.[3]

---

[1] The Primal, or Fundamental, Clear Light symbolizes the visual condition of the mind in the primordial or true state, unsullied, i.e. unruffled, by the process of the *sangsāric* thought-process, and thus experiencing, as a natural result of *yoga*, inexpressible spiritual blissfulness, which is inseparable from the realizing of the Voidness, the Thatness of all that is.

[2] The *guru* comments upon these three *yogic* practices as follows : ' The blend-ing by day results in the Ignition ; by night, in the Light ; at sunset, or the rest-time, in the Attainment ; by twilight, in the Clear Light ; and at all times, in the Knowledge of the Thatness, or Knowledge of the Progress on the Path.' (Cf. §§ 5, 8, following.)

[3] If the *guru* upon probationally accepting a disciple wishes to ascertain how much, if any, spiritual progress the disciple has made, he asks him what stage he has attained in recognizing the Clear Light, or what degree of the Knowledge of the Thatness he has realized. The Three Wisdoms are the Offspring Clear Light (realizable by practising the Six Rules of Tilopa, as contained in the next section) ; the Mother Clear Light (realizable in the interval between two thought-processes), which is the Fundamental Clear Light; and the United Clear Light, which symbolizes the wisdom attained from the realizing of the Offspring and Mother Clear Light. The 'Five Doctrines' are, accordingly,

(6) What is the first step to be taken? To enter into communion with the *guru*.[1]

(7) A babe just delivered from the womb of the mother serveth as the simile [in the exposition of the *yogic* process which is to follow].[2]

(8) What defineth the limits? The Light, the Ignition, and the Attainment; these define it.[3]

(9) The identification [or realization of the Clear Light] is to be attained in the interval between the cessation of one thought and the birth of the next thought.

(10) The Clear Light is made use of on the Path by practising the Six Rules of Tilopa. They are:

'Imagine not, think not, analyse not,
Meditate not, reflect not, keep in the Natural State.'
['*Mi-no, mi-sam, mi-chad-ching,*
*Mi-gom, mi-sem, rang-bab-zhag.*'][4]

(11) By meditating thus, that which dawneth, as the Void-

---

(1) the Knowledge of the Thatness, (2) the Degree of the Clear Light, (3) the Three Wisdoms, (4) the Progress in Perfection, and (5) the Understanding of the Progress.

[1] If literally rendered, this passage would be, 'What goeth first? The *guru* goeth first.' In this instance (which is here presented in illustration), as in similar instances, where a purely literal translation of the Tibetan would be ambiguous, the late Lāma Kazi Dawa-Samdup preferred the freer rendering, which conveys unmistakably the meaning intended.

[2] The Mother, or Primal, Clear Light, the first to be experienced, gives birth to the Offspring Clear Light, as will be observed; and this process explains the use of the simile.

[3] In other words, the duration of the ecstatic experiencing of the Clear Light, the Ignition (or the psychic illumination which results from the experiencing), and the Attainment (or the acquiring of the permanent knowledge derived from the experiencing), when taken together, define the limits (or degree) of the realizing of the Clear Light.

[4] We have incorporated here the phonetic equivalent of the Tibetan original of this foundation doctrine of the Kargyūtpa School. Its transliterated form is,
'*Mi-mno, mib-sam, mid-pyad-ching,*
*Mib-sgom, mi-sems, rang-babs-bzhag.*'
This stanza serves to illustrate the most commonly used verse-form of the Tibetan language, namely, the verse of seven phonetic syllables, with the rhythmic accentuation falling on each second and on the seventh syllable. This sevenfold measure, being based on the sacred number seven, is said to be particularly appropriate in connexion with religious teachings. We have given an alternate rendering of these two verses in *The Epitome of the Great Symbol*, on p. 119, § 16. (Cf. p. 150, § 120.)

ness and Phenomenal Appearances [the two aspects of a duality which in its true nature is a unity], is the Offspring Clear Light.

(12) The unobscured, primordial condition of the mind, which shineth in the interval between the cessation of one thought-formation and the birth of the next, is the Mother Clear Light.

(13) The recognition of that is the Blending of the Mother and Offspring Clear Light ; and it is called ' Blending of the Nature of the Clear Light and the Path into Oneness '.

[PRACTICE 2 : BLENDING THE NATURE OF THE CLEAR LIGHT WITH THE PATH DURING THE NIGHT-TIME]

(14) The second practice, Blending the Nature of the Clear Light with the Path during the Night-Time, hath been spoken of as followeth :

' Having caused the Lotus of the Heart to open,
   Then, within its four petals and pericarp,
   Visualize the syllables, ĂH, NŬ, TĂ, RĂ, HŪM,' [1]

(15) It hath also been spoken of as followeth :

' Into the Aggregates,[2] the Constitution,[3] and the sense
      faculties,
   Concentrate now all the powers of the twofold ' Knower '.[4]

---

[1] As the text itself will proceed to explain, these five syllables are to be visualized, each in a particular part of the lotus, the *HŪM* in the centre of the pericarp, and each of the others on one of the four petals. In the Tibetan these five syllablic forms are as follows :

ཨཱཿ (*ĂH*, the phonetic equivalent of the letter *Ă*) ; ནུ (*NŬ*) ; ཏ (*TĂ*) ;

ར (*RĂ*) ; ཧཱུཾ (*HŪM*).

Taken together, the first four compose the Sanskrit word *Anuttara*, meaning ' highest [state]', or ' above which there is nothing '. The *HŪM*, to which attach various meanings, in accordance with the context or usage, here suggests the True State, the mind in its primordial condition, unmodified by the process of thought, to which state the *yogin* aspires.

[2] The Aggregates are the Five Aggregates (Skt. *Skandha*). (See p. 356².)

[3] The Constitution refers to the body of man as being constituted of the five elements—earth, water, fire, air, and ether. (Cf. 126⁴.)

[4] The ' Knower ' in its twofold aspect, as here, refers to the cognizing mind in its twofold *sangsāric* states, which are the waking-state and the sleeping (or dream)-state.

'To him who sleepeth, after having transmuted these into
     Great Voidness,[1]
Dreams will come, in virtue of the breathing-exercises.'

(16) When first falling asleep, one sleepeth soundly. This
state of sleeping is symbolized by the unruffled surface of an
ocean. Its limits are defined by the Light, the Ignition, and
the Attainment.[2]

(17) The recognizing of the Clear Light is achieved in the
interval between the cessation of the waking-state experiences
and the beginning of the sleeping-state experiences.

(18) The Clear Light is utilized on the Path by means of
the application of the selected teachings concerning the
blending of the state of *dhyāna* [i.e. profound meditation] and
the state of sleep.

(19) In this [i.e. the process of the blending of the state of
*dhyāna* and the state of sleep], supplication is to be made to
the *Gurus*, to the end that one may be able to recognize the
Clear Light. Then firmly resolve that thou wilt recognize it.

(20) When lying down to sleep, lie so as to sleep with the
right side downward, in accordance with the lying-posture of
a lion.

(21) Then, imagining one's own body to be that of the
tutelary deity, within the heart visualize a four-petalled lotus,
having at the centre of the upper surface of its pericarp the
syllable *HŪM*; on the upper surface of the front petal, the
syllable *ĂH*; on the upper surface of the right petal, the syllable *NŬ*; on the upper surface of the rear petal, the syllable
*TĂ*; and on the upper surface of the left petal, the syllable
*RĂ*; each syllable vividly defined.[3]

----

[1] This is the fifth degree of the Voidness, as shown in our category above,
on p. 206[2].

[2] Text: *Snang*(pron. *Nang*) = 'Light'; *Mched*(pron. *Ched*) = 'Ignition'; *Thob*
(pron. *Thob*) = 'Attainment', or 'Results'. In this context, the Light is not the
Clear Light. These three technical terms of *yoga* refer to three stages of spiritual
progress on the Path. The Light is the dawning of the ecstatic experience;
the Ignition is the duration of this experience and its enlightening effect; and
the Attainment is the sum total of the results, progressively considered, obtained
from the experience.

[3] In order to have the visualized lotus properly orientated, the *yogin* should

(22) Then, while subsiding into sleep, let all visible and audible things subside into thyself.

(23) Then, let thyself subside into the four-petalled lotus.

(24) Then, when sleep is overpowering thee, let all these experiences subside into the front *ĂH*; then that into the right *NŬ*; then that into the rear *TĂ*; then that into the left *RĂ*; then that into the *HŪM* at the centre; then the vowel-sign of the *HŪM* into the *HĀ* parts of the *HŪM*; then these into the surmounting crescent-sign of the *HŪM*; then that into the circle [or dot] above it; and then that into the flame-like flourish above the circle [or dot].[1]

(25) When cognition of this visualization is fading, then think that thou art profoundly sleeping in the state of the Clear Light. By so doing one entereth into the state of the *yoga* of the retrospective analysis [or meditation].[2]

(26) Or one may concentrate the mind upon the series of syllables taken together—*ĂH, NŬ, TĂ, RĂ, HŪM*—which is called the Complete Cognition.

(27) While thus meditating, in the interval between the

face the North. Thus the *HŪM* will be at the Centre; the *ĂH*, to the North; the *NŬ*, to the East; the *TĂ*, to the South; and the *RĂ* to the West.

[1] In order to understand these directions, an analysis should be made of the syllable *HŪM*, written in Tibetan in its long form as above, or as depicted, greatly enlarged, in the Illustration facing p. 334. The vowel-sign, resembling a numeral 6 slightly tilted to the left, is at the bottom. The *Ha* parts are those between the vowel-sign and the surmounting crescent-sign. Above the crescent-sign is the small circle (or dot) with its flame-like flourish, whence the visualization dissolves into the Voidness. Each of these divisions of the syllable symbolize different esoteric principles and teachings, as Book VI, following, makes clear. This practice is intended to attune the *yogin* to an exalted state of mind in which to enter into the dream-state.

Should the Occidental student in the application of these *yogic* teachings prefer to employ the transliterated, or anglicized, forms, of the syllabic visualizations prescribed, he may here visualize the three letters of the *HŪM* as being arranged in a perpendicular line, the *H* uppermost, the *Ū* underneath the *H*, and the *M* at the bottom, and above the *H* a crescent, and above the crescent an acuminated circle (or dot) tapering into flame. Then he is to apply the textual directions accordingly, so that the *M* is absorbed into the *Ū*, then that into the *H*, then that into the crescent, then that into the circle (or dot), and then that into the flame-like flourish. (See p. 340³.)

[2] The *yogin*'s aim is to be able to pass from the waking-state to the sleeping-state, or vice versa, with unbroken continuity of consciousness, so that he will be fully self-conscious and enjoy complete memory of everything seen and experienced in both states while in either state.

waking-state and the sleeping-state, one experienceth the Light.[1]

(28) The state of being overcome with sleep is known as the Ignition.

(29) The state of falling asleep is known as the Attainment.[2]

(30) The dawning of the Clear Light in deep sleep is the Mother Clear Light.

(31) By making the process of the gradual subsidence into sleep the basis [of the practice], while keeping the mind free of thought (in which mental condition the gradual subsidence appeareth as the Voidness), the Offspring Clear Light dawneth.[3]

(32) The recognizing of the Fundamental [or Mother] Clear Light by that method, being like the recognizing of a person whom one had previously known, is called 'Blending of the Clear Light of the Mother and Son '.[4]

[PRACTICE 3: BLENDING THE NATURE OF THE CLEAR LIGHT WITH THE PATH DURING THE AFTER-DEATH STATE]

(33) The third practice, Blending the Nature of the Clear Light with the Path during the After-Death State, is ex-

---

[1] Here, again, a literal rendering (e. g. ' In that way, the non-sleeping-state [is] the Light,') would be for English readers, unacquainted with the *guru*'s amplifications of the text, ambiguous, if not meaningless. This non-sleeping-state is that state which demarcates the world of waking-experiences from that of sleeping- (or dream)-experiences, wherein, if the meditation be successful, the *yogin* realizes an ecstatic clearness of perception called the Light. It dawns only when the *yogin* has succeeded in maintaining continuity of consciousness throughout the waking- and sleeping-states and the state intervening between them.

[2] The Light is the dawning of the dream-state ; the Ignition, the continuance of the dream-state ; and the Attainment, the result, or dream, attained.

[3] Here, as compared with the passage above, the psychic process is reversed, and the dawning of the Offspring Clear Light precedes that of the Mother Clear Light. It is in the condition when one is gradually passing into the sleep-state that the Offspring Light is realized, and the Mother Clear Light dawns as one is merging into deep sleep as stated in the preceding paragraph.

[4] This recognizing is the third stage in the *yogic* results to be attained ; and in the *Bardo* Doctrine, which follows, in the next Chapter, it is classified as the Fourth Clear Light, because it normally dawns after death in a fourth condition, or dimension.

pounded in the Doctrine of the After-Death State, which followeth.

### [PART III: THE RESULTANT CLEAR LIGHT]

(34) Of the third part, the Resultant Clear Light, it hath been said :

'The pure illusory body,[1] endowed with the knowledge of the Clear Light, which springeth forth from the State of the Clear Light like unto a fish leaping forth from water, or the Form of Vajra-Dhāra,[2] which riseth up as one doth upon awakening from sleep, symbolizeth the blending of the Clear Light of the Mother and Son, resulting from training, which hath as foundation the teachings and the student who studieth the teachings'.[3]

[1] This pure illusory body is that of the *yogin's* tutelary deity. The number of deities from which the *yogin* may make choice in selecting his protecting deity is very great. But, as a rule, he will have chosen one belonging to the sect or school in which he has been reared, very much after the manner of one of the early Christian *yogins* who dwelt in the deserts of Egypt and looked to some saint renowned for sanctity to serve as the tutelary, or spiritual protector, like unto a guardian angel.

[2] Vajra-Dhāra, the Divine *Guru*, the Celestial Buddha, in Whom the Esoteric Lore contained in these Six Doctrines is believed to have had origin, is sometimes chosen as the tutelary, especially by a *yogin* who aspires to the Highest Goal.

[3] A parallel passage, which helps to elucidate our own passage, occurs in the very occult Tibetan treatise entitled *Bsre-hpho* (pron. *Se-pho*), on the second half of folio 60, which belonged to the late Lāma Kazi Dawa-Samdup, as follows :

'Even as from the surface of a clear pool
There suddenly springeth forth a fish,
So also from the All-Voidness and Clearness
Cometh forth the Web of Miraculous Illusion,
The comprehending of which is *Nirvāṇa* ;
And to attain this comprehension the disciple hath striven.'

In some of the esoteric lore of Tibet the human body is likened to an earthen-pot ; and the Ray of the Eternal within, that innate consciousness of Reality, 'the true Light, which lighteth every man that cometh into the world', the Light on the Path, is called the Clear Light. And the *guru's* efforts are said to be directed to the one end of shattering the earthen-pot so that there shall remain only the Clear Light shining in the Voidness.

The conscious realization of the Mother and Son Clear Lights, as here referred to in our text, results from the state of *dhyāna* having been rightly attained, in accordance with the *yogic* instructions given. The perceiving in-

(35) This realization marketh the degree of spiritual perfection attained, called, among the Twelve Degrees, the Greatly Rejoicing[1] Degree, of which it hath been said :

'When illusory forms contact the Formless, Knowledge dawneth,[2]

And one gaineth understanding of the Pervading and of the Real,[3]

And mastery of the Very Bright and of the Enduring,[4] and of the *Siddhi* of Transformation ;[5]

---

tellect, the awakened ' Knower', which thereby springs forth, symbolizes the amalgamation of the two Lights, and is the result of having trodden this part of the Path successfully.

[1] Text : *Sa-rab-tu-dgah-va* (pron. *Sa-rab-tu-ga-wa*): Skt. *Pramudita* : ' Greatly Rejoicing ', referring to a state of blissfulness resulting from mental illumination as to the nature of Reality; and from it no relapse into the unenlightened view concerning man and the Universe is possible. It is thus the ' Greatly Rejoicing', because all wrong knowledge about mind and matter has been for ever transcended. According to the Buddhist *Sūtras*, there are ten degrees of perfection, and the Buddha Shākya Muni has gone beyond all of them. According to the Buddhist *Tantras*, there are sixteen degrees, or six more, and the Buddha Shākya Muni is now in the sixteenth. Samanta Bhadra (Tib. *Künto-zang-po*), the Ādi-Buddha of the Ñingmapas (otherwise known as the ' Red Caps ') is also in the sixteenth; and the Buddha Vajra-Dhāra, in the thirteenth. The first ten of these degrees of perfection, or stages attained on the Path, have been enumerated by the late Csoma de Körös (in his Sanskrit-Tibetan-English Vocabulary, i. 11) as follows : (1) the Greatly Rejoicing [of Great Joy] : Skt. *Pramudita* ; (2) the Immaculate : Skt. *Vimala*; (3) Making [or Causing] Light : Skt. *Prabhākara*; (4) Light [or Ray] Diffusing : Skt. *Archishmatī*; (5) Very Difficult to Practise [or conquer]: Skt. *Sudurjaya* ; (6) Eminent [or Excellent] : Skt. *Abhimukhin* ; (7) Far Advanced : Skt. *Dūrangama* ; (8) Immovable : Skt. *Achala* ; (9) Upright Understanding [or Fine Discerning Mind] : Skt. *Sādhumati*; and (10) Cloud of Virtue : Skt. *Dharmamegha*.

[2] This contacting of the Formless by illusory forms implies that they themselves become the Formless; Form (Skt. *Rūpa*) becomes Non-Form (Skt. *Arūpa*), and the *yogin* attains to the first degree of Right Knowledge, in virtue of actually realizing the unsubstantiality of all things shaped and formed.

[3] The Pervading is *Karma*, which is so called because it pervades, or governs, each of the Six States of Existence. The Real is Real Knowledge, or *Nirvāṇa* ; It emancipates from all states of *sangsāric* existence and from all *karmic* propensities and attachments, which are the causes of rebirth.

[4] The Very Bright is the Clear Light ; and the Enduring is the Eternal, or Mind.

[5] *Siddhi* literally means 'accomplishment' or ' fruition of *yogic* meditation ' ; but here it more particularly refers to the *yogically*-acquired supernormal powers of assuming any shape or form, large or small, visible or invisible.

And these are known as the Eight Supreme Endowments.'[1]

(36) Of such is the state of the perfect Buddhahood of the
Great Dorje-Chang [or Vajra-Dhāra], which resulteth from the
Untaught Wisdom, wherein the teaching and the taught end
[the Goal having been attained].

(37) Of this it hath been said :

' The enjoyment of the full power of the Principles of the
    Divine Body, of the Divine Speech,
And of the Divine Mind, and of the *Siddhi* of Transformation,
As they, all alike, manifest themselves in the " Moving "
    and the " Non-Moving ",
Satisfying every desire, and endowed with all virtues,
Constitute the Eight Almighty Powers, which are the Fruit
    of *Yoga.*'[2]

[Here endeth The Doctrine of the Clear Light.]

## [CHAPTER V: THE DOCTRINE OF THE AFTER-DEATH STATE]

(1) The fifth doctrine, the *Bardo*, consisteth of these three
parts : first, Realizing[3] the State of the Clear Light of the

---

[1] Upon analysis of these four abstruse verses, we find that the Eight Supreme
Endowments are : (1) the Merging of Form into Non-Form, by illusory forms
contacting the Formless ; (2) the resultant Knowledge of the non-reality ot
objectivity ; (3) Understanding of the Pervading, or *Karma*, thereby attaining
freedom from worldly existence ; (4) Understanding of the Real, or *Nirvāṇa* ;
(5) Realization of the Very Bright, or Clear Light ; (6) Realization of the
Enduring, or Eternal, as Mind ; (7) the mastery over this state of realization ;
and (8) the *Siddhi* of Transformation.

[2] The matter of these five verses in the original Tibetan is so excessively
elliptical and enigmatical that a very free rendering was found necessary. The
Tibetan of the parallel stanza of paragraph 35 is similarly abstruse. To aid in
producing an intelligible rendering of them, similar passages were consulted in
the *Se-pho*.

Here, again, analysis of the verses shows the Eight Almighty Powers, which
are the Fruit of *Yoga*, to be : (1) the Power of the Divine, or *Bodhic*, Body,
(2) of the Divine Speech and (3) Mind, (4) of the *Siddhi* of Transformation,
(5) of the manifestation of these in the ' Moving' as the moving force of the
*Sangsāra*, and (6) of their manifestation in the 'Non-Moving ', or *Nirvāṇa*, as the
antithesis of the *Sangsāra* ; (7) the satisfying, or quenching, of every *sangsāric*
desire; and (8) the endowment with all divine virtues.

[3] In this context ' realizing' implies, in addition to its ordinary meaning, the

*Dharma-Kāya* [or Divine Body of Truth] while in the *Bardo*; second, Realizing the State of the *Sambhoga-Kāya* [or Divine Body of Perfect Endowment] while in the *Bardo*; third, Realizing the State of the *Nirmāṇa-Kāya* [or Divine Body of Incarnation] while in the *Bardo*,[1] [or the Taking Birth as a *Tulku*].[2]

[*PART I: REALIZING THE STATE OF THE CLEAR LIGHT OF THE* DHARMA-KĀYA *WHILE IN THE* BARDO]

(2) The first, Realizing the State of the Clear Light of the *Dharma-Kāya* while in the *Bardo*, hath been spoken of as followeth :

'Light subsideth and the Gross subsideth,[3]
Thoughts subside and the Subtle [4] subsideth ;
After the subsidence cometh the at-homeness.

making right use of such *yogic* training as the deceased may have had in the human world prior to death.

[1] For the ordinary, not fully enlightened *yogin*, the first of these after-death realizations consists of an ecstatic glimpse of the Ultimate Truth ; the second, of a limited experiencing of *Bodhisattvic* blissfulness ; the third, of the attaining of a divinely endowed rebirth on Earth.

[2] Text : *Bsprul-sku* (pron. *Tul-ku*), i.e. one divinely incarnated, like the Dalai Lāma, who is the *Tulku* of Chenräzi (Skt. *Avalokiteshvara*, 'The One Looking Down [in Pity]', the embodiment of mercy, or compassion, known as 'The Great Pitier') ; or like the Tashi Lāma, who is the *Tulku* of Wodpagmed (Skt. *Amitābha*, 'He of Boundless Light'), the Buddha Who Illuminates, or Enlightens. The esoteric interpretation of the word *Avalokiteshvara*, as given by my friend Mr. E. T. Sturdy (see Preface, p. ix), is as follows : '*Avalokita* = seen, and *Īshvara* = Lord ; so that *Avalokiteshvara* is the Lord Who is seen [within]. This rendering is more in keeping with what the Sanskrit implies than the more popular rendering given above'. *Avalokiteshvara* is, in this sense, synonymous with the *Christos* within.

[3] The Light here is the ordinary light of the world which fades from perception at the time of death. The Gross is the physical body and its breathing.

[4] The Subtle is the human consciousness which temporarily ceases to function, there being in the case of the normal person, or of one who has not been *yogically* developed before dying, a period of unconsciousness, lasting for about three and one-half (or four) days, immediately after the completion of the death-process. When the deceased recovers consciousness, at the expiration of this period, he begins to feel at home in the *Bardo*, having passed through, while unconscious, the state preceding birth into the after-death world, which parallels the embryonic state preceding birth from the *Bardo* into the human world.

Then the Primal Clear Light dawneth,
And after that dawn the Two Bodies as One.[1]

'Of the Taught and Untaught Knowledge,
The Merging of the Taught into the Untaught
Hath been called the Attaining of the Fruit.'

(3) Death precedeth the *Bardo.*

(4) An unclouded sky of autumn symbolizeth the *Bardo.*

(5) The Light, the Ignition, and the Attainment at the moment of death define the bounds of the *Bardo.*[2]

(6) The recognizing of the Clear Light is to be accomplished in the interval between the cessation of consciousness in this world and the arising of consciousness in the after-death state; and the Clear Light to be utilized on the Path by applying the select teachings for combining into one the Path and the True State of the mind.[3]

---

[1] The Mother and Offspring Clear Light merge as One, in the Divine Body of Perfect Endowment, the *Sambhoga-Kāya*, which symbolizes their at-one-ment.

[2] The Light symbolizes the super-normal clearness of visual power which comes as the first conscious experience of the after-death state; the duration of this initial experience is called the Ignition, for it symbolizes the igniting, or arousing, of the innate divine consciousness by the Light; and the Attainment refers to the spiritual benefit attained by experiencing death. The degree of the Attainment depends wholly upon the *karma* of the deceased. The serious reader should not fail to refer to *The Tibetan Book of the Dead*, which contains a comprehensive and authoritative commentary on our present text.

[3] The spiritual development of the *yogin* should have been so directed by the *guru*'s select teachings that at the moment of death he will possess the *yogic* power to pass from this world to the after-death state without break in the continuity of his consciousness. By this means, escaping the unconsciousness experienced by the person who dies without such *yogic* training, he will be enabled to combine the True State of the mind, as experienced in the *samādhic* quiescence (to which he had become accustomed while in the body and in which he abides as he is dying) with the True State of the mind as it is likewise ecstatically experienced by the master of *yoga* in the condition of realizing the Clear Light in the *Bardo*. In virtue of this great accomplishment, he will be able to know, as a matter of actual super-normal realization, that both the state of incarnate existence in the human world and the state of discarnate existence in the *Bardo* world are essentially alike, both being transitory and illusory; and that the True State of the mind, being independent of both the two *sangsāric* states, is, unlike them, neither transitory nor illusory, and that it is the State of the Abiding, the Real, the Unmade *Nirvāṇa*. To attain to this supreme realization is to attain to Buddhahood.

[THE *BARDO* OF THE MOMENTS OF DEATH]

(7) In other words, when the vital-force of the five senses, including sight, sinketh inwards, concomitantly the cognition of form and all of objective things sinketh inwards. This is known as the Sinking of the Light [1] [or of the Perception of Things seen in the Light of this World].

(8) Then earth sinketh into water: the body loseth its prop [or power of coherence as a unit of organic matter].

(9) Then water sinketh into fire: the mouth and nose become dry and parched.

(10) Then fire sinketh into air [as vital-force]: warmth disappeareth [from the body].

. (11) Then air [as vital-force] sinketh into consciousness [or ether].[2]

(12) Thereupon, those of evil *karma* experience the pangs of the moment of death.

(13) And those who have performed good deeds, the *devas* and *gurus* and the *ḍākinīs* come to welcome.[3]

(14) With the cessation of the last expiration cometh the subsidence of the Gross.

(15) Then during the first part of the time of the duration [i.e. between the cessation of the breathing and the passing out of the consciousness] of the internal breath [or vitality] cometh the stages of the subsidence of cognition. The signs

---

[1] Text: *snang-va* (pron. *nang-wa*) = 'light', also 'that seen in the light'. In Tibetan there is but this one word to express similar yet different concepts, such as (a) light in its ordinary aspect, (b) things seen by means of the light, and (c) things mentally seen by the mind's eye. The atmosphere, too, as the medium of the transmission of light, is known as *nangwa*. For the Clear Light itself there is the technical term *Hod-gsal* (*Öd-sal*).

[2] These passages further illustrate the well-known philosophical conception common to India, as to classical Greece, that the human body is a combination of the five elements, as named. In our present text, earth represents the fleshly parts of the body and the bones; water, the blood and other fluids; fire, the animal heat; air, the vital-forces; and ether, the consciousness. (Cf. pp. 126[4], 347.)

[3] The divine, or superhuman, *gurus* have the power of so directing the after-death progression of the disciple, who happens not to be sufficiently developed spiritually to direct it himself, that he is enabled to take birth without undue delay in a family which will afford him the conditions suitable for continuing his treading of the Path from the point where it was stopped by death.

externally perceived [by the dying person] resemble the
shining of the Moon ; those internally perceived resemble
[mentally obscuring] smokiness. This is the time of the
dawning of the light [of the moment of death].[1]

(16) These signs merge into the Ignition [i.e. the period of
the duration of the experiences of the moment of death]. The
thirty-three impulses of anger [2] cease; the external sign of this
being like the shining of the Sun, the internal sign being like
apparitional fire-flies. This is the time of the Ignition.

(17) The time of the Ignition sinketh into the time of the
Immediate Attainment. The forty impulses of desire cease ;
the external sign of this being like a streak of darkness or
*Rāhu* [3] [eclipsing the Sun], the internal sign being like the
light of a lamp enclosed in a semi-opaque vessel. These
apparitional appearances signify the [stage of the moment of
death known as the] Immediate Attainment.

(18) The state of the Immediate Attainment mergeth into
the state of the Clear Light. The seven impulses of Ignorance [4]
cease. Then cometh the subsiding of the Subtle. The external
signs resemble the glimmer of twilight ; the internal signs
resemble an autumn sky without a cloud. This is the fourth
period of the Clear Light.[5]

(19) The initial experiences coincident with the process of

---

[1] The dying person perceives the external signs as a white moonlight-like
radiance round about him. Some Europeans of more than average spirituality
are recorded as having uttered before the final consummation of the death-
process such ecstatic exclamations as, ' Light ! ' ' More Light ! ', ' Now the
Light dawns ! ' and some, as a consequence, not knowing the nature of the
Light, have thought themselves entering into Heaven. This phenomenon arises
from the psycho-physical changes in the faculty of sight brought about by the
death-process. Similarly, the internal signs, the mentally beclouding or smoky
apparitional appearances, are produced by the same psycho-physical changes
affecting the mentality.

[2] These, and the forty impulses mentioned below, represent the various
aspects into which anger and desire are divided by the philosophy of the Great
Perfectionist School of Padma Sambhava.

[3] *Rāhu* (or the Dragon's Head) is a mythological representation of the Moon
when causing an eclipse of the Sun.

[4] That is, mentally obscuring ignorance, known in Sanskrit as *Avidyā*.

[5] Little by little, through four stages, the Clear Light has been approached ;
and this makes our present *Bardo* Doctrine a continuation of the Doctrine of
the Clear Light.

death being the foremost experiences at the beginning of the *Bardo*, those who have practised the select teachings call the stage now reached the First *Bardo* [otherwise known as the *Chikhai Bardo*, or the *Bardo* of the Moments of Death].

## [THE *YOGIC* ART OF DYING]

(20) The practices at this stage are those which follow.

(21) When about to die, cut off all entangling attachments [to the world and to worldly possessions], along with hatred [for any enemy or other person left behind].

(22) By allowing the mind to rest free of thought-forming during the stages of the subsiding-process, the experiences of the subsiding-process accordingly merge into the natural state of quiescence as soon as they have dawned. Thereby dawneth the Offspring Clear Light.

(23) Then, as a secondary result, there dawneth the Mother Clear Light, the fourth Clear Light.[1]

(24) The intellectual recognition of these two aspects of the Clear Light, being like the recognition resulting from meeting an old acquaintance [since death hath been previously experienced many times], is known as the Blending of the Mother and Son Clear Light.

(25) By abiding in the state of the Clear Light as long as desired and then rising out of it in the body of the Divine United Clear Lights, in virtue of the threefold reversive process,[2] and transferring the consciousness through the Aperture

---

[1] As a mother is not a mother until she has given birth to a child, so the Mother Clear Light logically dawns after that of the Offspring. It is otherwise known as the fourth degree of the Voidness of the Clear Light.

[2] This very difficult *yogic* process may be described as follows: At the moment immediately preceding death, as the text has explained, there shines a white light like moonlight, then a [red] light like sunlight, then darkness comes. In the reverse order of their appearing, the *yogin* must mentally dispel one after the other—darkness, the red light, and the white light. Concomitantly there must be traced backwards by conscious effort, in a post-mortem panoramic review of the process of death, each of the states experienced during the subsidence. These are : (1) the fourth Clear Light state ; (2) the subsiding of the Subtle, and (3) of the Gross. While in each of these states, as reviewed in this reverse order, the *yogin* is to hold a corresponding thought. Thus, in the first, the thought should be, ' Where am I ? ' ; in the second, ' What am I ? ' ; in the third, ' What is this condition in which I am ? ' Then, having mastered this

of Brahmā, on the crown of the head, one who is adept [in the *yoga* of consciousness-transference] passeth into the Buddha State [of Complete Enlightenment]. One who is weaker in the practice becometh a Holder of the *Dorje* in some one of the tenth-degree states [1] [of the highest celestial *Bodhisattvas*].

### [PART II: REALIZING THE STATE OF THE SAMBHOGA-KĀYA *WHILE IN THE* BARDO]

(26) The second part, Realizing the State of the Divine Body of Perfect Endowment while in the *Bardo*, hath been spoken of thus:

'Visibly produced [is the Body], with shape like that of the physical existence [on Earth],

Possessed of all sense-faculties, yet endowed with [power of] unimpeded motion,

And *karmic* miraculous powers of transformation and illusion.[2]

*yogic* process, he proceeds to employ the *yoga* of consciousness-transference, called in Tibetan *Pho-wa*, which is the subject of our next Book. If he be an adept in *Pho-wa*, the consciousness departs from the body through the Aperture of Brahma (Skt. *Brahmarandhra*), which forms the exit of the median-nerve, rather than through one of the nine external apertures of the body, described in the annotation to paragraph 30 following. By this means the master of *yoga* attains to Buddhahood.

[1] Text: *Chös-kyi-sprin* (pron. *Chö-kyi-tin*): Skt. *Dharma-Megha*: 'Cloud of Truth', the name given to the tenth-degree states of the highest *sangsāric* heaven known in Tibetan as *'Og-min*, meaning 'No-down', the realm whence there is no fall. (See p. 250.) The term 'Holder of the *Dorje*', the mystic symbol of super-normal power, has reference primarily, as here, to a Spiritual Originator, or Divine Inspirer, of a Tantric doctrine teaching the way to Emancipation.

[2] Another version of this quotation, from a Tantric work, is given in *The Tibetan Book of the Dead*, on p. 156. The miraculous powers are the *siddhi* of shape-shifting and producing illusory forms and phenomena, which can be exercised by the master of *yoga* in the after-death state as in this world. In the *Sidpa Bardo*, as contained in *The Tibetan Book of the Dead*, p. 159, there is this warning concerning them, addressed to the deceased: 'These various powers of illusion and of shape-shifting desire not, desire not.' Undisciplined use of such powers impedes true spiritual progress, just as does attachment to worldly pleasures. Being the result of one's having come into existence in the *Bardo* world, where they are as natural as walking is in the human world, these powers are called *karmic*. As a caterpillar after having made for itself

### [*KARMIC* RESULTS OF INABILITY TO RECOGNIZE THE CLEAR LIGHT]

(27) Through inability to recognize the Clear Light, the seven impulses which come from Ignorance arise; the resultant light [1] dawneth; the Greatly Void [or vastness of the Voidness] is experienced.

(28) Then arise the forty impulses born of Avarice [or [Attachment]; the Ignition stage dawneth; the Very Void [or intensity of the Voidness] is experienced.

(29) Then arise the thirty-three impulses born of Hatred [or Anger]; the stage called the Light dawneth; the Voidness [itself] is experienced.

(30) Then, by a concentrated effort of the all-pervading vital-force, the consciousness is transferred from the old body through any of the nine ' doors ',[2] and shapeth the new body of the *Bardo* existence.[3]

---

a cocoon emerges from it as a free-flying butterfly, so by the breaking of the cocoon of the human body its maker comes forth possessed of unimpeded motion.

[1] This resultant light symbolizes a visual condition much inferior to that symbolized by the Clear Light; the Clear Light itself being obscured, as by a heavy cloud, because of the lack of spiritual enlightenment.

[2] See p. 200[1]. In the case of a person dying *yogically* untrained, the departure of the consciousness ordinarily takes place through some one of these ' doors ', each ' door ' leading to birth in that non-human state to which it corresponds, as paragraph 31, following, suggests. For instance, the departure through the ' door ' of one of the ears leads to birth in the world of the Gandharvas (fairy-like celestial musicians), wherein musical sound is the prevailing quality of existence. It is through the Aperture of Brahmā that the consciousness of a Great *Yogin* quits the human form and passes on to the highest of the paradises or attains the state of the Supreme Awakening.

[3] Herein, from paragraph 26 to 30, is contained the exposition of the reverse process mentioned in paragraph 25. Thus, paragraph 27 refers to a third degree of the *Shūnyatā*, or Voidness, the Greatly Void, which is experienced first; paragraph 28, to the Very Void, which corresponds to a second degree; and paragraph 29, to the Voidness in its first degree. Then comes the consciousness-transference as the culmination of the reversive process of the dawning of the three lights, which the three degrees of the Voidness symbolize. The dawning of the various impulses corresponds to the panoramic after-death review of life's experiences such as persons who have died through drowning and then been resuscitated have commonly reported. The impulses are those of the Three Vices : Ignorance (Skt. *Moha*, or *Avidyā*); Avarice (Skt. *Lobha*); and Hatred (Skt. *Dvesha*). The lights are the psychic resultants of the arising

[DESCRIPTION OF THE AFTER-DEATH EXISTENCE]

(31) The *Bardo* body is a desire-body, endowed with all sense faculties, and possessed of the form appropriate to the plane of existence whereon one is to take birth.[1]

(32) It is unimpeded in its movements everywhere, except that it cannot enter into the mother's womb.

(33) It hath the miraculous power of traversing the Third-Void Universe[2] as quickly as thought.

(34) Those on the *Bardo* plane of the same level of knowledge or spiritual development see each other.[3]

(35) Thus those who are destined to be born in the world of the *devas*[4] see each other with *deva* vision.

of these impulses. Ignorance leads to a state of mental obscuration or deep sleep (Skt. *suṣupti*) with respect to the True State of Knowledge; and in this state of sleep, resulting from Ignorance, there dawns the Greatly Void, consciously perceivable for a moment by all human beings at the all-determining time of death. In the body, while in deep *samādhi*, a similar but less vivid experience of it is possible. And likewise is it with respect to the other impulses and their psychic resultants.

[1] This taking birth refers to passing on to that state of after-death existence to which *karma* destines the deceased. Such birth may take place in some paradise realm, or in the world of unhappy ghosts, or in a state of purgation. No such state is of eternal duration ; and thence the deceased passes on to the womb-state and to rebirth on Earth.

[2] The first degree of the Voidness of the Cosmic Whole corresponds to one system of nebulae and suns and planets, such as astronomers see through their telescopes, even to the most distant star ; the second degree consists of one thousand, and the third degree consists of one million such systems. Even then, so the Lāmas declare, the Voidness is but partially classified, there being Third Voids upon Third Voids, without conceivable end.

[3] Beings of like nature, development, inclination, and destination exist together consciously on the *Bardo* plane, just as human beings do in this world. Other orders of beings exist there, in that fourth dimension, invisibly to dissimilar orders, just as invisible races, like fairies, exist invisibly to man.

[4] Mrs. Rhys Davids rightly objects to the ordinary translation of the word *devas* as 'gods', because gods, for the most part unlike *devas*, are conceived as having 'if not perhaps creative power, at least informing influence, controlling force, some sort of cult and votaries, some power to bestow or withhold, aid or harm, reward or punish'. She distinguishes, too, between *devas* and *devatās*, the latter being the lower divinities of the common folk ; and of *devas* she says : 'The *devas* who now and then pay or receive visits, on earth, at home, are nothing more than so many ladies and gentlemen, pleasant, courteous, respectful to great earth-teachers or earnest disciples. They have, it is true, their governors, but these, too, are not immortal, but have been, and will probably

(36) The dwellers on the *Bardo* plane feed on odours [or the essences of material things].[1]

(37) The radiance of the Sun and Moon not being visible on the *Bardo* plane, there is neither light nor darkness there; the light of the *Bardo* world is light-darkness [or a twilight].

(38) The principle of consciousness remaineth in a state of unconsciousness [or swoon] for a period of three and one-half days [after death on the Earth plane].

(39) Thereafter, the deceased coming to know that he is dead, feeleth great sadness [or regret at having died].

(40) And at that time, one can know the *Bardo* world as it really is.

(41) Ordinarily, however, one fainteth off [into another state of consciousness] before being able thus to know the *Bardo* world.

(42) Misleading ideas becoming very powerful after that time [for recognizing the *Bardo*], that time is called 'the Stage of the Time' [i.e. the psychological moment for action], because of the need of remembering then the teachings concerning the *Bardo* [which one received while in the human world].

[THE AFTER-DEATH ATTAINING OF ENLIGHTENMENT]

(43) The carrying on to the Path after death the consciousness of having died, and of being in the *Bardo* state, hath been spoken of thus:

'After that stage, while in the *Bardo* of taking rebirth [or the *Sidpa Bardo*],
By assuming the *māyā*-like form of the United Divine Bodies,
One attaineth the Body of Perfect Endowment [or the *Sambhoga-Kāya*].'[2]

---

again be, denizens of earth. No, Buddhist *devas* are not gods. And one way to understand Buddhist doctrine is to cease calling them so.' (Cf. C. A. F. Rhys Davids, *Buddhist Psychology*, Supplementary Chapters, London, 1924, pp. 251-2.)

[1] See p. 219[4].

[2] This great attainment implies, of course, that the deceased died *yogically*, and that he is able to exercise the power of adeptship in *yoga* in the after-death state.

(44) Upon becoming conscious of having died, visualize thy body as being the body of a deity;[1] then, by the retrospective observation process, or by the Complete Comprehension,[2] place thyself in the state of the Clear Light.

(45) Then, with the practice of the three lights [or radiances] in their reverse order serving as the cause, there is obtained, as the result, the rising up into the United State of Dorje-Chang,[3] whereby one attaineth Perfect Enlightenment.

## [PART III: REALIZING THE STATE OF THE NIRMĀṆA-KĀYA WHILE IN THE BARDO]

(46) The third part consisteth of realizing the State of the *Nirmāṇa-Kāya* [or the taking rebirth as a divine incarnation] while in the *Bardo*.

### [THE BARDO OF SEEKING REBIRTH]

(47) If one findeth not the Path during the Second *Bardo* [i.e. during the *Chönyid Bardo*],[4] the four sounds called 'awe-inspiring sounds' are heard: from the vital-force of the earth-element, a sound like the crumbling down of a mountain; from the vital-force of the water-element, a sound like the breaking of ocean-waves; from the vital-force of the fire-

---

[1] As a result of this *yogic* practice there is rapid advancement in the after-death state; whereas without the guidance afforded by means of this visualization the dweller on the *Bardo* plane is quite likely to fall into the common error of assuming the ghost body of a *preta* and thus be retarded indefinitely, especially if he be called up in spirit evocations by his relatives or friends still on Earth. (See *The Tibetan Book of the Dead*, p. 170.)

[2] This refers to the visualization-process touching both the external and internal principles of personality, as the Complete Comprehension of the *ĀH-NŪ-TĀ-RĀ-HŪM* Mantra. (See p. 228, § 26.)

[3] This state of Dorje-Chang (Skt. Vajra-Dhāra), the Supreme Divine *Guru* of the White Dynasty of *Gurus* of the Kargyütpa School, is called United, because in it are united Compassion and the Voidness.

[4] In other words, if the deceased has failed to attain to the divine state of Dorje-Chang—and none save masters of *yoga* do attain to it—he must wander on in the after-death state from the Second *Bardo*, or the *Bardo* of the Experiencing of Reality, called in Tibetan the *Chönyid Bardo*, into the *Bardo* of Seeking Rebirth, called the *Sidpa Bardo*. In *The Tibetan Book of the Dead*, wherein the full text of the *Bardo* teachings are contained, the *Bardo* of the Moments of Death, the First *Bardo*, called the *Chikhai Bardo*, is divided into two stages, so that the *Chönyid Bardo* is classified as the Third *Bardo*.

element, a sound as of a jungle afire; from the vital-force of the air-element, a sound like a thousand thunders reverberating simultaneously.[1]

(48) The place one getteth into, in fleeing from these sounds, is the womb.

(49) The three terrifying Precipices [which obstruct the way of one fleeing from the sounds] are the White, Red, and Black Deep Precipices; to fall over any one of them is to fall into a womb.[2]

(50) The Five Radiant Paths, including the Path of White Radiance, are for the well-taught ones to understand. To tread any of them is to re-enter into *sangsāric* existence.[3]

(51) Other phenomena, too, appear, such as globular masses of dazzling light, along with radiant sparks; the being pursued by a terrific downpour of rain; the coming of wrathful male and female figures to menace one; the being led by the Executioner [of Dharma Rāja's judgement, after the testing by the Mirror of *Karma*]; and the being placed in a house of iron, which symbolizeth the Hell-state.[4]

---

[1] These phenomena are the psychic resultants of the disintegrating process called death, as affecting the four grosser elements of which the human body aggregate is composed. The ether-element is not named, because in that element alone—i.e. in the ethereal, or *Bardo*-body—the principle of consciousness continues to exist. (Cf. p. 337.)

[2] Any sort of *sangsāric* birth is regarded as undesirable, especially for one who has set out on the *Nirvāṇic* Path; and such birth is herein symbolized by the falling over one of the three Precipices. To fall over the White Precipice is to take birth as a *deva*; or over the Red, as a *preta*; or over the Black, as a dweller in Hell-like conditions of purgation. In *The Tibetan Book of the Dead*, p. 162, it is explained that the Precipices are Anger, Lust, and Stupidity, the three evil passions which cause rebirth.

[3] These paths are the white light-path leading to the worlds of the *devas*, the smoke-coloured light-path leading to the hell worlds of purgation, the yellow light-path leading to the human world, the red light-path leading to the world of the *pretas* (or unhappy ghosts), and the green light-path leading to the world of the *asuras* (or titans). They also have esoteric significance in relation to the Five Radiances of Wisdom. (See *The Tibetan Book of the Dead*, pp. 127-9.) It is for the well-taught ones, i.e. adepts in *yoga*, not to tread any of these paths, if they wish to avoid return to *sangsāric* existence.

[4] Here, again, a voluminous and detailed commentary is afforded by *The Tibetan Book of the Dead*. Dharma Rāja, the King of Truth, and Lord of Death, before whom the dead come for the Great Judgement, personifies the conscience in its stern aspect of impartiality, and love of righteousness; and the Mirror,

(52) The taking shelter in the hollows of trees and in cavities and crevices of the earth is to enter into the world of unhappy ghosts or into the brute world.[1]

(53) The sinking into a lake adorned with swans floating thereon is to be born in the Eastern Continent.[2]

(54) The sinking into a lake adorned with cattle grazing on its shores is to be born in the Western Continent.[3]

into which the Judge looks in order to pronounce judgement, is memory, wherein every good and evil deed done in the human world is vividly reflected. The good is balanced against the evil in the scale of justice ; and, in accordance therewith, the deceased is sentenced to meet his just *karmic* deserts. As, in *The Tibetan Book of the Dead*, p. 167, the *Bardo Thödol* makes it clear that ' Apart from one's own hallucinations, in reality there are no such things existing outside oneself as Lord of Death, or god, or demon '.

[1] The popular, but not the right, doctrine of rebirth, supports the erroneous theory, arising from Ignorance and false analogies, that the human principle of consciousness can take embodiment in sub-human forms. The esoteric rather than the vulgar, or exoteric, interpretation should be followed in studying the *Bardo Thödol*, upon which our present text is based. There must, too, be taken into account a certain amount of corruption, due to the influence of this vulgar interpretation, which has crept into the text. Mrs. Rhys Davids, with her vast knowledge of the Pāli canon, says, ' Outside folk-lore and the garrulous Commentaries, no actual cáses of a rebirth as animal recognized by a teacher's supernormal insight have I as yet met with. The Buddha is made to affirm in a few *Suttas* (e.g. *Majjhima*, iii. 167) that some classes of wrongdoers will meet with such a fate, but the *Suttas*, so far as I know, contain no other special illustrations of it.' (Cf. Mrs. Rhys Davids, *op. cit.*, p. 256.) As we have made clear in *The Tibetan Book of the Dead* (pp. 49–60) all such references to rebirth of the human into sub-human forms need not necessarily be interpreted literally. On the contrary, there is overwhelming evidence in support of interpreting them symbolically. In this context, too, one should remember that the Buddha had no part in the writing down of any of the scriptural teachings attributed to Him. It was only long after He had departed from the human world that they were placed on record. His advice to accept nothing not *yogically* proved to be true, even though it be found recorded in Scriptures, is as applicable now in this age of science as it was when uttered. The Buddhist, or Hindu, or even Christian who departs from this sound standpoint of the Enlightened One appears to prefer untested theories rather than scientific fact.

[2] Text : *Shar-gling* (pron. *Shar-ling*) ' Eastern "Continent".' The fuller form, *Shar-lüs-hpags-po* (pron. *Shar-lü-pa-po*), means, 'Eastern [" Continent "] of Great Size '. Though endowed with bliss and ease, it being a world wherein religion does not predominate, the deceased is warned not to take birth in it. (See p. 303[5].)

[3] Text : *Nub-ba-glang-spyöd* (pron. *Nub-ba-lang-chöd*) ' Western "Continent",' a human-like world to the west of Mt. Meru, wherein there are said to be vast herds of beautiful cattle. For one desirous of Liberation from all *sangsāric* states, it also is undesirable as a place in which to be born. (See p. 304[5].)

(55) The sinking into a lake adorned with horses grazing on its shores is to be born in the Northern Continent.[1]

(56) The seeing of grand mansions and parents therein in the sexual act is to be born in the Southern Continent of Jambudvīpa.[2]

(57) The seeing of celestial mansions of vast dimensions and entering any of them is the sign of taking birth as a *deva*.

(58) The misleading ideas [due to *karmic* propensities] being very influential [at this stage], one seeketh a womb; and, therefore, this period is called 'the time wherein the odour-eater [i.e. the dweller on the after-death plane] seeketh a womb for rebirth'.

### [THE *YOGIC* ART OF CHOOSING A WOMB]

(59) Of the practical application [of the select teachings concerning the art of choosing a womb for rebirth] it hath been said :

'Abandoning all feelings of attraction or repulsion,[3]

With memory's heedfulness restraining the roving tendency of the mind :[4]

[1] Text : *Byang-sgra-mi-snyan* (pron. *Chang-da-mi-nyan*), 'Northern 'Continent ",' the world to the north of Mt. Meru, wherein there are vast herds of beautiful horses. It, too, like all the non-human states, is undesirable as a place for rebirth. (See p. 305 [2].)

[2] Text : *Ndzam-bu-gling* (pron. *Jam-bu-ling*) 'Southern "Continent ",' which is our Planet Earth. (See p. 304[3].)

[3] In other words, the aim must be to attain to a state of quiescence dominated by supreme indifference to all *karmic* predilections for likes and dislikes. As stated in *The Tibetan Book of the Dead*, p. 191, 'Even though a womb may appear good, do not be attracted; if it appear bad, have no repulsion towards it. To be free from repulsion and attraction, or from the wish to take or to avoid—to enter in the mood of complete impartiality—is the most profound of arts. Excepting only for the few who have had some practical experience [in psychic development], it is difficult to get rid of the remnants of the disease of evil propensities.'

[4] The mind must be kept under strict control by exercising its memory of *yogic* disciplining acquired while in the human state, with the result that there is thereby bridged, by unbroken continuity of consciousness, the disembodied state preceding birth, including the embryonic state, while in the womb, and that to follow birth. Thus one is born fully aware of the process of choosing the womb and of birth therefrom, in the same way as one should be aware of the process of death, retaining continuity of consciousness from the pre-death state to the post-death state.

Apply thyself to the choosing of the womb-door.
Then, by performing the transference of the Happy-to-
   Know,[1]
One will attain birth in whatever place be desired.'

(6c) By one's knowing that all the apparitional sounds and
terrifying forms [seen while in the *Bardo* of Taking Rebirth]
are illusory, undesirable wombs are closed [to one's entry].

(61) Also by one's recollecting the Voidness [in accordance
with the select teachings which one hath had] and keeping
in mind one's human *guru* and tutelary deity [or Divine
*Guru*], undesirable wombs are likewise closed.

(62) Then, the choosing of a desirable womb in a family of
high caste, of exalted position, and possessed of wealth,—and
thus offering the advantages for following a religious career,—
being thought of, the coming to birth accordingly is called
taking rebirth as a divine incarnation [or *tulku*].

(63) He who hath been well trained in *yoga*, although
unable to realize the Clear Light, will become a *Bodhisattva*
of the order that no longer reincarnates on Earth, by being
born in any of the Pure Realms, such as the Realm Endowed
with Happiness,[2] or the Happy-to-Know Realm,[3] or some
similar Pure Realm.[4]

[Here endeth The Doctrine of the After-Death State.]

## [CHAPTER VI: THE DOCTRINE OF CONSCIOUS-NESS-TRANSFERENCE]

### [*PART I.   THE THREE TRANSFERENCES*]

(1) The sixth doctrine, *Pho-wa*, consisteth of three trans-
ferences: the Best, or the Transference into the *Dharma-*

---

[1] The transference refers to the *yogic* transference of the consciousness, while
in the after-death state, to the prenatal womb-state, in the same manner as
to the paradise realm called ' Happy-to-Know '.

[2] This is the high heaven known in Tibetan as Devachān (pron. Dewachān).
(See p. 220 [2].)

[3] See p. 220 [3].

[4] In other words, a great master of *yoga* will have the option of passing into
one of the Realms of the *Bodhisattvas*, if his hour has come to do so, or of
taking birth on Earth as a Divine Teacher.

*Kāya*; the Middling, or the Transference into the *Sambhoga-Kāya*; and the Last, or the Transference into the *Nirmāṇa-Kāya* [or the Taking of Divine Rebirth].

(2) The first, the Best, or the Transference into the *Dharma-Kāya*, consisteth of realizing the Clear Light during the first stage of the *Bardo*.

(3) The second, the Middling, or the Transference into the *Sambhoga-Kāya*, consisteth of the rising up in the United Divine Body [1] during the *Bardo*.

(4) The third, the Last, or the Transference into the *Nirmāṇa-Kāya*, consisteth of taking Divine Rebirth.

(5) Although these may be looked upon as being three differing results, nevertheless the selected teachings for guidance on the Path [by which these three results are attained] are not three different teachings [but one and the same system of teachings]

[*PART II. THE TRANSFERENCE OF THE CONSCIOUSNESS BY MEDITATING UPON THE* GURU]

(6) The *Pho- wa* called the Transference of the Consciousness by Meditating upon the *Guru*, is now to follow.

(7) It hath been described thus :

' Having first formed the " Pot-shaped "
By means of twenty-one breathings,
Forcibly draw from its place the consciousness,
Up through the lotuses of the spinal column,
By visualizing twenty-one *chakra*.[2]

---

[1] This is the Divine Body of the United State above mentioned, wherein Compassion and the Voidness (or True Wisdom) are in union, as in the body of a *Bodhisattva*.

[2] These *chakra*, or ' wheels ', are to be visualized as if strung upon the spinal column (consisting of thirty-four vertebrae) equidistant from one another. Or the spinal column may be regarded as being like an axle extending through the hubs of twenty-one wheels. (See the similar simile contained in sections 66–8 of the Doctrine of the Psychic-Heat, pp. 190–1, above.) And each of the *chakra* is to be visualized as being a centre of psychic-force, by means of which, in virtue of the meditation, the principle of consciousness is drawn from its place, in the heart-centre, and led, little by little, through the median-nerve, at the centre of the spinal cord, to the exit at the Aperture of Brahmā.

Let the process be *chakra* by *chakra*,
Both in the up-going and the down-going of the *mantra* syllables.
The syllables to be used are the one-syllable and the half-syllable.[1]
By uttering the sounds of the syllable loudly,
Direct the " Knower " towards Devachān.
Then, when the right moment cometh, the transference is accomplished.'

(8) There are two parts, the [mere] Practising, and the Practical Application.


## [THE PRACTISING]

(9) In the first, the Practising, resolve to attain to Buddhahood.

(10) Then visualize thyself as the Divine Lady [Vajra-Yoginī] in the vacuous form. At the very centre of the body visualize the median-nerve, as being like the central supporting pillar of an empty house, with its lower extremity closed, and its upper extremity open like unto an open skylight. Above this opening, visualize the Divine *Guru*, Dorje-Chang, as also having a vacuous body ; and, at the centre of His body, visualize the Median-Nerve of Wisdom ; and visualize it as being joined with thine own median-nerve [so as to form one continuous passage-way from thine own heart to the *Guru*'s heart].[2]

(11) Then visualize a syllable $H\bar{U}M$ in outline as fine as a hair, blue of colour, in the *Guru*'s heart, and another such

---

[1] In the up-going, the *mantra* syllable *HEEG* ( 𑖮 𑖅 ) is used ; and in the down-going, the *mantra* half-syllable *KĂ* ( 𑖎 ), pronounced as *KĂH*. In the up-going, the consciousness is led upwards, and in the down-going it is led back to its place. Until the *yogin* feels quite confident of success, the actual projection of the consciousness is not attempted ; he merely practises the up-going and the down-going repeatedly until the right moment comes.

[2] The *Guru*'s median-nerve is the Pathway of Wisdom, by means of which the disciple reaches the *Guru*'s own divine state, as the remainder of the passage indicates.

*HŪM*, in thine own heart, regarding this *HŪM* as the real essence of thine own principle of consciousness.[1]

(12) [Having performed these visualizations], then meditate upon the breath formed into the ' Pot-shaped '.

(13) Then visualize that from the syllable *HŪM* inside the *Guru*'s heart the vowel-sign [at the bottom of the *HŪM*] prolongeth itself downwards and entwineth itself with the symbol of the essence of consciousness in thine own heart ; and think that this [i.e. the *HŪM* as the symbol of one's own essence of consciousness] is being drawn upwards [by the *HŪM* in the *Guru*'s heart].[2]

(14) Meanwhile, as each breath is expired, utter the sound *HEEG* as loudly as if frightened and calling for aid ;[3] and practise this exercise twenty-one times [or *chakra* by *chakra*].

(15) Then think that the *HŪM* hath reached the crown of the head.

(16) Then cause the *HŪM* to descend [to the heart-centre through the median-nerve] by uttering the *KĂ*.

(17) Utter the *KĂ* [in the manner of uttering the *HEEG*

---

[1] In this practice, the blue *HŪM* symbolizes the essence of the Divine Wisdom of the Buddhas, or the Essence of Being. The *yogin* is to imagine, when inspiring the *HŪM*, that he is inspiring, or drawing into himself along with it, this essence of the Divine Wisdom, thereby filling his body with the Divine Vital-Force and Light. When the *HŪM* is at rest within, during the retention of the breath, it changes the syllable *ĀH*, which is to be visualized in the throat-centre, into an *ĀH* of dazzling red colour, symbolizing the life-principle. Then, when the breath is going out, carrying with it the visualized syllable *AŪM*, white of colour, the *yogin* is to imagine that the expired breath is radiant and transmitting its beneficial rays to all sentient beings throughout the Universe. (See pp. 127[1], 179[1].)

[2] In the parallel visualization set forth in Part II of Book IV, following, the

*HŪM* in its short form ( ![symbol] ) is employed. If in the present visualization the transliterated form of the *HŪM* is preferred, it may be imagined that its three letters are arranged in a perpendicular line, as above suggested (p. 228[1]), and that the right foot of the *M* of the *HŪM* in the *Guru*'s heart is crooked like a hook and prolongs itself downwards and entwines itself with the other *HŪM*.

[3] This is merely figurative to describe the method of loudly uttering the *HEEG*. Actual fear must, of course, not be present ; for, if it were, the practice would be unsuccessful.

for twenty-one times], all the while imagining that thereby the *HŪM* is descending [*chakra* by *chakra*].

(18) Practise thus till thou hast attained mastery [or the signs of proficiency in the practice].


### [THE PRACTICAL APPLICATION]

(19) In the second part, the Practical Application, the *HŪM* [in the disciple's heart] is absorbed into the *HŪM* in the *Guru*'s heart;[1] and then the *Guru* goeth to the Realm whence there is no falling again into rebirth,[2] and abideth in the State which is not mentally conceivable.

[Here endeth The Doctrine of Consciousness-Transference.]


### [THE COLOPHON]

[In our block-print text (which consists of thirteen folios, printed on both sides, each measuring nineteen and one-half inches in length and three and one-half inches in width), there next comes, in the form of a Colophon, the interesting history of the compilation of the text as follows.]

At the [mountain hermitage], Summit of the Essence of

---

[1] It must be understood that by exercise of *yogic* power of mind by a master *yogin*, even though outwardly the *yoga* practices appear as mere mental exercises of visualization, all things, according to the secret philosophy of Tibet and India, are possible. Even the Occidental thinkers have paid tribute to this doctrine ; and, as a result, we observe the infiltrations, directly originating in the Orient, in such systems of European and American thought as Christian Science, Auto-Suggestion, and the New Psychology of Mind. Thus, in virtue of the visualization and the final absorption of the symbolic *HŪM* in the heart of the disciple into that in the heart of the Divine *Guru*, the mystic at-one-ment is attained and the consciousness of the earth-dweller is transferred to the state beyond the need of further incarnation in human bodies.

[2] Text : *Hog-min* (pron. *Wog-min*, or '*Og-min*) : Skt. *Akaniṣṭha*, the Heaven of the Ādi-Buddha, the highest state attainable within the *Saṅgsāra*, the Vestibule to the non-*saṅgsāric* State of *Nirvāṇa*. From 'Og-min there is no longer *karmic* necessity to assume human rebirth. As a Divine Teacher, however, a *Bodhisattva* dwelling in 'Ogmin can reincarnate thence, or, as is more usual, inspire the Superior Ones already incarnated on Earth. The Ādi-Buddha has renounced the right to pass completely out of the *Saṅgsāra* and so remains in 'Og-min in order that *saṅgsāric* beings may be divinely guided to Freedom, as He, in inconceivably past aeons, once was guided by a preceding Buddha.

Perfection,[1] in Kuri[2] [Tibet], at the request of the noble
princely priest of Ngari Zangkar,[3] [named] Zhanphan Zang-
po,[4] this [Book] hath been compiled by the learned Bhikṣhu
Padma-Karpo.[5]

### *May It Be Auspicious!*[6]

This Guide, composed of divine words arranged in Six
Doctrines, is the Path whereby the Lāmas of the Divinely
Inspired Dynasty have realized Buddhahood.

In order that this profound treatise by Padma-Karpo
should be committed to printing, Namgyal-Paljor[7] made the
copy; the nephew of the Peerless Devotee [Padma-Karpo],
named Nyalrong-Panchen,[8] did the revising; and the donor

---

[1] Text: *Byang-chub-snying-pohi-spo* (pron. *Chang-chub-nying-poi-po*). (Cf.
p. 154[5].)

[2] Kuri is in Tibet in the Province of Lhobrak, which borders on Bhutan.

[3] Text: *Mngah-ris Zangs-dkar* (pron. *Nga-ri Zang-kar*). Ngari is a place name,
referring to the priest's origin in the westernmost province of Tibet. Zangkar
is a Tibetan name for a portion of Kashmir and Ladāk; it means 'white
copper'.

[4] Cf. p. 154[2]. In the present Colophon the King of Zangkar is represented
as having renounced his kingship and become a *bhikṣhu*, in imitation of the
Royal Prince of the Shākyas Who became the Buddha Gautama.

[5] Text: *Npadma-Dkar-po* (pron. *Padma-Karpo*), meaning, 'White Lotus'.
His fuller name, which is not contained in the text, is *Kun-mkhyen-Npadma-
Dkar-po* (pron. *Kun-khyen-Padma-Karpo*), meaning, 'Omniscient White Lotus'.
He was a native-born Tibetan. From Tibet he entered Bhutan during the
seventeenth century A.D. as a religious reformer, and established what is now
the predominant form of Buddhism in Bhutan, known as the Southern Branch
of the Kargyūpta School of the White Dynasty of *Gurus*, of which Marpa and
his illustrious successor Milarepa were the founders in Tibet about five centuries previously. See the Colophon of *The Epitome of the Great Symbol*, which
was compiled by Padma-Karpo as a companion treatise to this work, pp. 153-4.
It should also be noted in this context that the editor has followed herein a
Bhutanese tradition which assigns Padma-Karpo to the seventeenth century,
but fails to give the exact time in which he flourished or the date of his advent
in Bhutan.

[6] Here the text contains the Sanskrit-Tibetan form, *Swasti*, meaning, 'Let
this Book be auspicious!' or, in other words, 'May this Book be of good omen
to all to whom it shall come!'

[7] Text: *Rnam-rgyal-dpal-hbyor* (pron. *Nam-gyal-Pal-jor*), meaning, 'Wealthy
Victorious [One]'.

[8] Text: *Gnyal-rong-pan-chen* (pron. *Nyal-rong-Pan-chen*), meaning, 'Great
Pundit of Nyal-rong', in Tibet.

and the carver of the blocks was the illustrious artist Chö-kyong-Dorje,[1] exalted both in faith and in wealth.

In virtue of the perfect merit resulting from having performed these duties exceedingly well, may all sentient beings, all of whom have been mothers,[2] led by the donor, speedily attain to the state of Dorje-Chang in this very lifetime.

[Here endeth the Book, *The Epitome of the Abridged Six Doctrines.*]

---

[1] Text : *Chös-skyong-rdo-rje* (pron. *Chö-kyong-Do-rje*), meaning, 'Faith-Protecting [One] of the *Dorje*'.

[2] See p. 68 [1], 122 [5].

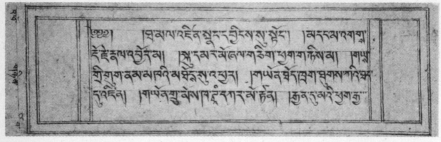

FOLIOS 1ᵇ, 2ᵃ, 2ᵇ, 3ᵃ OF THE *PHO-WA* MS.

Described on page xx

# BOOK IV

# THE PATH OF TRANSFERENCE: THE *YOGA* OF CONSCIOUSNESS-TRANS-FERENCE[1]

## THE INTRODUCTION

### I. *PHO-WA* AND ITS MASTERY

THE version of the *Pho-wa* herein presented forms an integral part of the *Bardo Thödol* cycle of doctrines, as reference to *The Tibetan Book of the Dead* will show. The first part, intended for the personal use of the devotee, is, as the text itself makes clear, like all secret doctrines which have been committed to writing, suggestive rather than detailed and complete. This is equally true of the complementary version comprising the last of the Six Doctrines. The second part, chiefly intended for the use of Lāmas who perform the death-bed or funeral rites, is, however, sufficiently complete to be comprehended and applied, on behalf of a dying person, when no Lāma is available, by any *yogin* or layman who has had sound instruction from a *guru* in the manner of its practical application.

Mastery of the Art of *Pho-wa* primarily confers the *yogic* power to bring about in oneself, at will, essentially the same process as that which under normal conditions is called

---

[1] The twofold Tibetan manuscript upon which our translation is based, bears the following titles: (1) *SNYAN RGYÜD GSANG-VAHI MTHAR-THUG LAS ZAB LAM HPHO-VAHI GDAMPA SNYINGI THIGLÉ BZHÜGS-SO* (pron. *NYAN GYÜD SANG-WAI THAR-THUG LAY ZAB LAM PHO-WAI DAMPA NYINGI TIGLÉ ZHÜ-SO*), meaning, 'Herein lieth the Profound Path of the Doctrine of [Consciousness-]Transference, "The Seed of the Heart", from the Final Secrets of the Ear-[whispered] *Tantras*'. (2) *GSANG-LAM HPHO-VAHI GDAMS-PA LAS TSHE HDAS RNAM-SHES SPAR-VAHI DMIGS-PA BZHÜGS-SO* (pron. *SANG-LAM PHO-WAI DAM-PA LAY TSHE DAY NAM-SHÉ PAR-WAI MÍ-PA ZHÜ-SO*), meaning 'Herein lieth the Visualization for the Transference of the Consciousness of One Deceased, from the Teachings concerning the Secret Path of Transference'.

death, there being the difference that in natural death the principle of consciousness departs from the human form permanently, whereas in *yogically*-induced death the departure may be but temporary. Secondarily, it confers the *yogic* power to direct the departure of the principle of consciousness of another person, or to influence the principle of consciousness of a person not long deceased, in ˙such manner as to afford it spiritual guidance in the after-death state and in the choosing of the womb at the time of its rebirth.

All Tibetan *gurus* who are familiar with *Pho-wa*, either theoretically or practically, are agreed that, because in practice it may readily be abused by unprincipled and faithless disciples, its applied technique ought never to be taught to any save those who have been long on probation and been found worthy. Accordingly, it is assumed that all recorded teachings concerning *Pho-wa*, such as these contained in our own texts, will be studied and put to the test of practice only under the personal guidance of a living *guru* who has already mastered them and is qualified, in virtue of having received the appropriate initiations, to supply their necessary amplifications and detailed explication.

## II. THE RELATED DOCTRINE OF *TRONGJUG*[1]

According to tradition, about nine hundred years ago, from super-human sources, there was revealed, to a select few of the most saintly Tibetan and Indian *gurus*, a divine secret science called by the Tibetans *Trongjug*, meaning 'Transference and Inspiration'. By means of this *yogic* art, it is believed that the principles of consciousness of two human beings can be mutually exchanged, or, in other words, that the consciousness which animates, or inspires, one human body can be transferred to and made to animate another human body; and, also, that the animal vitality and instinctive intelligence can be dissociated from the human elements of consciousness and temporarily infused into subhuman forms and directed by the overshadowing *manas* of

[1] Tib. *Grong-ḥjug* (pron. *Trong-jug*, or, as in *Tibet's Great* Yogi *Milarepa*, pp. 145-7, *Drong-jug*).

the discarnate personality. An adept of *Trongjug* is thus said to be able to discard his own body and assume the body of another human being, either by consent or by forcible dispossession of the latter ; and to enter into and resuscitate, and, thereafter, possess the body of a person who has just died. To forcibly dispossess one of one's own body is, of course, an act of black magic, only done by a *yogin* following the path of darkness.

### III. THE *YOGIC* TALE TOLD BY THE *GURUS*

The following story, current in varying versions among the *gurus*, helps to illustrate how *Trongjug* is capable of being abused. The *gurus* frequently narrate it to help explain their stern refusal to divulge occult teachings indiscriminately.

The story concerns a prince and the son of a prime minister who were most intimate friends, and adept in *Trongjug*. One day, while walking out together, they came across a bird's nest containing a number of fledglings newly hatched, and saw, as they were looking at them, the mother-bird killed by a hawk. Out of compassion, the prince resolved to practise the secret art, and so he said to his companion, 'Please guard my body while I resuscitate the mother-bird's body and cause it to fly to the little birds and feed them'. While guarding the apparently lifeless form of the prince, the prime minister's son was overcome with temptation, and, quitting his own body, entered the body of the prince, for it was afterwards proved that he had long been secretly in love with the prince's wife. The prince had no choice but to occupy the discarded body of his false friend ; and it is said that several years elapsed before the prime minister's son could be persuaded to surrender the prince's body and re-enter his own.

Owing to such abuse as this, *Trongjug* came to be kept so secret that the rule was instituted to impart it only to the one very carefully tested disciple who is chosen to become a *guru* in an apostolic succession of *gurus*, and then only just before the death of the chief *guru* by whom it is to be imparted.

### IV. THE *YOGIC* TALE CONCERNING TIPHOO

Marpa, having been favoured with this unique initiation into *Trongjug*, was advised by his own initiator and *guru*, Naropa, to transmit the teaching to Milarepa, Marpa's greatest disciple. Instead of following this wise advice, Marpa transmitted it to his own son, Doday-Bum, a *yogin* of exceptional ability. But, as Naropa had foreseen, Marpa's plan for the succession miscarried. Doday-Bum met with such sudden and unexpected death that there was no human body immediately available into which to transfer his consciousness ; and he was compelled to make transitional use of the body of a pigeon which had just died. Thereupon, as soon as the *Trongjug* had been applied, Marpa *yogically* directed the pigeon, so that it flew direct to a place of cremation in India, where, upon a funeral-pyre, lay the dead body of a Brāhmin boy. Before the fire could be set to the pyre, the pigeon had settled upon the corpse, and, after cooing thrice, dropped dead. At the same moment the boy revived and was carried home amid loud rejoicings, and his parents renamed him Tiphoo, which means ' Pigeon '. The lad grew up strong and healthy and became a very famous Indian philosopher and *yogin*. History now knows him as the great Buddhist Tantric Saint Tiphoo.

### V. THE SECRET LORE AND ITS SURVIVAL

The *Trongjug* appears to be the most transcendental aspect of the secret lore concerning consciousness-transference, of which our two texts, entitled *Pho-wa*, are faithfully representative. As explained in our annotations to the text of *Tibet's Great* Yogī *Milarepa*, on p. 146, *Pho-wa* treats of the *yogic* transference of the mundane (or *sangsāric*) consciousness within the *Sangsāra*, whereas the *Trongjug*, in its most recondite character, seems to treat of the *yogic* transmutation of the mundane consciousness into the supra-mundane consciousness, wherein all component things are realized to be *māyā*, or illusion. Accordingly, *Trongjug*, in its most transcendental scope, probably implies translation of the transmuted consciousness, freed of Ignorance, to *Nirvāṇa*—the Unbecome, Unformed, Unmade, beyond the *Sangsāra*.

To this day, as our texts seem to suggest, the secret art of transferring the human consciousness, either while in life or at the moment of death, still survives, both in Hindustan and in Tibet; and its adepts still hold fast to the strict rule governing its transmission. Among Hindus, as among Mahāyāna Buddhists, there is much occult lore and strange tales concerning its practical application. Thus, as another example of such tales, there is the rather well-known account of how Shankarāchārya, the famed expounder of the Vedāntic Philosophy, in order to avoid using his own *yogically* purified and highly disciplined body for the purpose of making experimental study of the science of sensual love, animated the body of an Indian king named Amaruka who had just died, and how, after the necessary knowledge had been acquired, returned to his own body, which all the while had been lying in the trance state of suspended animation guarded by his disciples.

Supplemented by the necessary personal guidance of one who has attained proficiency in *Pho-wa* or *Trongjug*, if perchance the disciple proves himself a worthy vessel for the secret science and is endowed with the good *karma* to find the right *guru*, our texts should prove to be faithful to the ancient tradition, although lacking in details, as they purposely are. But without such guidance, or without the thorough *yogic* preparation implied by the texts, the *yogin* should under no circumstances attempt to experiment in any way with these practices of consciousness-transference. If the question be asked, Why not? the answer is as follows.

As stated above, this *yoga* is no less than the art of producing at will, on the part of an adept in it, the same effect as comes naturally in the process called death. To project the consciousness-principle in the subtle (or 'astral') body is of all *yogic* practices the most dangerous. The text itself suggests that the very practising of this art tends to weaken the fleshly body's power of resistance to dissolution, so that compensatory *yogic* practices are necessary.

Should misfortune befall the *yogin* while practising *Pho-wa*, he may find himself unable to repossess his vacated Earth-plane body, either because of some unexpected break in the magnetic connexion between the two bodies, in which event death ensues; or because of some other entity, human or non-human, having taken possession of it. The first of the *yogic* tales narrated above helps to illustrate this latter danger.

On the other hand, when the *yogin* is performing the rite of *Pho-wa* on behalf of one who is dead, he may, in extra-ordinary circumstances of need, project his own conscious-ness-principle, embodied in the 'astral' form, in order to influence the 'astrally' embodied consciousness-principle of the deceased. This results in awakening the deceased if he be—as he is most likely to be—in the somnolent condition which immediately follows the death-process in the case of all persons save those who are masters of *yoga*. Upon thus being awakened on the *Bardo* (or 'astral') plane the deceased is made to comprehend the need of exercising his own *yogic* powers if, luckily, he has developed any prior to his decease.

More ordinarily, however, the *yogin* who performs the death-bed or funeral rites, in accordance with the *Bardo Thödol*, does not so project his consciousness. He aims to act from the human plane directly upon the consciousness-principle of the person dying or just deceased. If the person be dying, the *yogin* employs a sort of *yogic* suggestion, in-tended to guide the dying person through the death-process and thence onwards through the state intervening between death and rebirth. When death has already occurred, the *yogin* directs the progress of the consciousness-principle in the *Bardo* world by means of telepathy.

From the standpoint of psychical research, *Pho-wa* seems to have direct bearing upon what are known as phantasms. For the master of *Pho-wa* would doubtless tell us that all phantasms are explicable under two categories : (1) as visuali-zations unconsciously projected by the percipient as hallu-cinations, in response to stimuli produced telepathically by

an external agency, human or non-human, incarnate or discarnate; or (2) as actual 'astral' projections of the so-called
dead or living.[1]

Such then, are, in outline, the traditional teachings and lore,
the practices, and the *guru*'s interpretation of and warning
concerning this *yoga*.

---

[1] Much, if not all, of the evidence concerning phantasms which has been
recorded in the Occident is capable of explanation in accordance with this
Oriental view.    See S. J. Muldoon and H. Carrington, *The Projection of the
Astral Body* (London, 1929); E. Gurney, F. W. H. Myers, and F. Podmore,
*Phantasms of the Living* (London, 1886); F. Guyot, *Yoga for the West* (London,
n.d.), pp. 157-74.

## PRECEPTS FROM THE TIBETAN CANON

'Again and again seeking existence, they again and again enter the womb; beings come and go; to one state of existence succeedeth another.

\* \* \*

'The wise man through earnestness, virtue, and purity, maketh himself an island which no flood can submerge.

\* \* \*

'Arise, commence a new life, turn towards the Doctrine of the Buddha; trample down the hosts of the Lord of Death as an elephant doth a house of mud.

\* \* \*

'The best knowledge is that which enableth one to put an end to birth and death and to attain freedom from the world.

\* \* \*

'Even as the water of the Ganges floweth swiftly on and emptieth into the sea, so shall he who walketh in the even way of perfect understanding arrive at the cessation of death.

\* \* \*

'He who possesseth not steadfastness of mind cannot comprehend the Holy Law; he who is fickle of faith cannot attain the Perfect Wisdom.

\* \* \*

'The wise, who possess perfected memory, diligence, discrimination, and understanding, by means of their wisdom free their mind of all error.'

From the *Udānavarga*

(based upon W. W. Rockhill's translation.)

# [THE PATH OF TRANSFERENCE: THE *YOGA* OF CONSCIOUSNESS-TRANS-FERENCE]

## [PART I: THE MOST PROFOUND PATH OF CON-SCIOUSNESS-TRANSFERENCE: 'THE SEED OF THE HEART']

### [THE REFUGE]

(1) First cometh the Refuge:

' In the Divine *Guru*, the embodiment of all Protection,
From now till the Essence of Perfection be attained do I
  take refuge.
O ye *sangsāric* beings, innumerable in number,[1]
Dedicate your mind to the Divine Path of Good-Wishes for
  entering into Perfection.'

### [The Visualizing of Vajra-Yoginī and the *Gurus*]

(2) The mental imagery for one's use is as followeth:

Let the idea commonly held concerning the body[2] fade away into the voidness of space; and let the unobstructed radiance of thy consciousness shine forth as Vajra-Yoginī, her body red, with one face and two hands, the right hand held aloft overhead flourishing a curved knife, the left holding a blood-filled skull against her heart; leaning against a white staff held in the bend of her left arm; adorned with the five symbolic emblems and various ornaments; standing on a lotus-throne surmounted by the solar disk, upon which lieth a human corpse; gracefully postured, the body vacuous, though apparent, enhaloed with Flames of Wisdom.[3]

---

[1] Literally, 'having no centre or circumference'.

[2] This refers to the idea that the body is a solid substantial thing. By visualizing the body as being vacuous, in accordance with the directions contained in *The Six Doctrines*, the consciousness shines forth embodied in the divine illusory body, the *Nirmāṇa-Kāya*. (Cf. p 175, § 14.)

[3] For detailed explanation of this visualization see pp. 173-5. The lotus-throne, which is here described, symbolizes unsullied purity, with reference to pure, or divine, incarnation. The solar disk symbolizes development of the Radiance (or Flames) of Wisdom; and the corpse, the destruction of egoism.

(3) Then visualize, high above thee in the sky, seated on a lotus-throne surmounted by a lunar disk, the Root-*Guru*, the Supreme Protector, the body blue of colour, having one face and two hands, fully robed in the glorious robes of the Perfectly Endowed Ones, holding a *dorje* and a bell in His hands crossed over His heart.[1]

(4) Directly over thy head, in the space of the arched glory of a five-hued rainbow, visualize thy Lords, the *Gurus* of the Line of the Profound Path of Consciousness-Transference, sitting [in the Buddha-Posture], one above the head of another [in a perpendicular line].[2]

## [THE PRAYER TO THE *GURUS*]

(5) The Prayer [which cometh next] is :

' Unto Thee, of the pure and holy Realm of Truth,[3] whence
  there is no more fall into generation,
O Lord, Thou Wielder of the Divine Sceptre,[4] the very self
  of the Sixth Dhyānī Buddha,
I, thy son, pray in earnest faith and humility.
Vouchsafe me perfected practice on the Path of Conscious-
  ness-Transference ;
And, in the glorious and heavenly Divine Realm,
May I attain the Immutable State of the primordial *Dharma-
  Kāya*.

' Unto you of the Holy Paradise Realm,
O Lords Tilopa, Naropa, and Marpa, Father and Sons,[5]

---

[1] The coloured frontispiece of *Tibet's Great* Yogi *Milarepa* depicts the Root-*Guru*, the Celestial Buddha Dorje-Chang. His posture, robes, and the mystic significance of the *dorje* and bell are described in the same book, on pp. xv–xvi. The lotus-throne surmounted by the lunar disk (symbolical of the dispelling of the gloom of Ignorance) is commonly depicted, as in that frontispiece, resting upon a lion-throne, which symbolizes spiritual fearlessness.

[2] See pp. 274–6, following.

[3] Or the *Dharma-Dhātu*, here equivalent to '*Og-min*. (See pp. 250[2], 335.)

[4] Or *Dorje-Chang* (Skt. *Vajra-Dhāra*), 'Wielder of the *Dorje* (the Divine, or Mystic, Sceptre)'. Being the first of the Celestial Buddhas and, therefore, the Over-Lord of the Five Dhyānī Buddhas, Dorje-Chang is also called the Sixth of the Five Dhyānī Buddhas.

[5] Tilopa, as the human founder of the Kargyütpa Succession of *Gurus*, is called the Spiritual Father ; and Naropa and Marpa, and their successors, are known as the Spiritual Sons.

I, your son, pray in earnest faith and humility.
Vouchsafe me perfected practice on the Path of Conscious-
ness-Transference ;
And, in the glorious and heavenly Divine Realm,
May I attain the Immutable State of the primordial *Dharma-
Kāya.*

' Unto thee, of the Self-Emanated Rays of the Realization of
the Non-reality of Phenomenal Appearances,
O thou, the Venerable, Agèd Milarepa, whose graciousness
can never be repaid,
I, thy son, pray in earnest faith and humility.
Vouchsafe me perfected practice on the Path of Conscious-
ness-Transference ;
And, in the glorious and heavenly Divine Realm,
May I attain the Immutable State of the primordial *Dharma-
Kāya.*

' Unto thee, of the Self-Emanated Rays of the Primal Truth,
the Foundation of all Foundations,—Mind,
O thou, Shākya-Shrī, the untrammelled manifestation of the
power of mind,[1]
I, thy son, pray in earnest faith and humility.
Vouchsafe me perfected practice on the Path of Conscious-
ness-Transference ;
And, in the glorious and heavenly Divine Realm,
May I attain the Immutable State of the primordial *Dharma-
Kāya.*

' Unto Thee, seated on a lotus-throne surmounted by the
lunar disk, above the crown of my head,
O Thou Root-*Guru,* whose graciousness can never be
repaid,
I, thy son, pray in earnest faith and humility.

---

[1] Shākya-Shrī, one of the Kargyütpa Line of *Gurus,* was renowned for his
saintliness and mastery of *yoga.* Through him was made manifest on Earth the
power of mind over matter. He is said to have been born in Kashmir. In
or about A.D. 1202 he went to Tibet, and appears to have passed the rest of his
life there, practising *yoga* and helping the Lāmas to translate Indian religious
treatises into Tibetan.

Vouchsafe me perfected practice on the Path of Consciousness-Transference;

And, in the glorious and heavenly Divine Realm,

May I attain the Immutable State of the primordial *Dharma-
Kāya.*

' Being moved by my sincere faith and humility,

May the Line of *Gurus*, above my head, finally be dissolved
into light,

And become the Lord Himself, Dorje-Chang, the Root-
*Guru.*'

### [THE PRAYER TO THE ROOT-*GURU*]

(6) Then, with great earnestness, pray unto the Root-*Guru*
as followeth :

' Obeisance to all the Conquerors in the One Body of At-
one-ment !

' O Thou, the True Embodiment of all Protectors,

The Lord of the Great Mystic Faith in its entirety,

The Holy Lord of all that constituteth my Refuge, now
and hereafter,

O Thou, whose graciousness can never be repaid,

Thou knowest, O Thou Root-*Guru* of surpassing kindness,

Thou knowest, that I pray unto Thee from the very depths
of my heart

That I may speedily attain to Perfection on the Profound
Path of Consciousness-Transference.

O Thou, in the Akaniṣhṭha Heaven, the emanation of the
Pure Realm of the *Dharma-Kāya,*

Vouchsafe me Thy "gift-waves" [1] that Self-Knowledge, the
Immutable State of the *Dharma-Kāya,* may be attained.'

### [THE MEDITATION UPON THE *GURU*]

(7) Having thus prayed most earnestly, again and again,
create this mental imagery :

---

[1] 'Gift-waves' here, too, refer to helpful influences of a psychic nature telepathically transmitted from the Root-*Guru*, in the Akaniṣhṭha Heaven, to the
worthy disciple on Earth. In a somewhat similar frame of mind the Christian
*yogin* prays for the divine grace of the Father in Heaven.

Firstly, think, ' I shall lead all sentient beings, as in-numerable as is space boundless, to the State of the Highest Perfection ; and to that end I shall meditate upon the Pro-found Path of Consciousness-Transference.'

(8) The meditation to accompany this thought is as followeth :

' My *Guru*, the True Embodiment of the Threefold Refuge,[1] is present before me in the firmament. All sentient beings, as innumerable as is space boundless, and myself, are taking refuge in Him, until each of us shall have realized the Essence of Perfection. We shall so act as to lead every living creature of the four kinds of birth [2] to the attainment of the Highest Path.'

(9) After having thus meditated, conclude by absorbing the visualized form of the *Guru* into thyself.

[THE VISUALIZING OF VAJRA-ḌĀKINĪ AND THE *GURUS*]

(10) Then think that thine own body is transmuted into vacuousness, in the state of non-thought ; and that from the unobstructed, self-emitted radiance of the radiant, yet vacuous [intellect] there ariseth, suddenly, Vajra-Ḍākinī,[3] red of colour, with ornaments and attire clearly defined.

(11) Visualize, as extending through the centre of her body, the median-nerve, the size of an ordinary arrow-reed, white without and red within, endowed with the four characteristics [i.e. redness, brightness, straightness, and hollowness], the lower end closed and terminating four fingers [or, about three to four inches] below the navel [i.e. in the perineum, at the base of the generative organ], and the upper end opening out-

---

[1] Namely, the Buddha, the *Dharma* (or Scriptures), and the *Sangha* (or Priesthood).

[2] As taught in *The Tibetan Book of the Dead*, or *Bardo-Thödol*, p. 178, 'There are four kinds of birth : birth by egg, birth by womb, supernormal birth, and birth by heat and moisture. Among these four, birth by egg and birth by womb agree in character.' Supernormal birth takes place by transferring the consciousness from one state of existence to another. Birth by heat and moisture refers to the germination of seeds and spores, or the process of birth in the vegetable kingdom.

[3] Vajra-Ḍākinī is, as a visualization, herein equivalent to the Vajra-Yoginī visualization of *The Six Doctrines*, above.

wardly from the crown of the head [at the Aperture of Brahmā].

(12) [Visualize the median-nerve] as extending through the heart ; and, on the pericarp of a four-petaled lotus, within the heart, visualize a dot, which is, in reality, the symbolical embodiment of the breath and mind inseparably united, white in colour, with a reddish tint, and buoyant [or with a tendency to rise up].

(13) Let these visualizations be very vivid.

(14) Then, as overshadowing the crown of the head [of thy body visualized as Vajra-Ḍākinī], vividly visualize thine own root-*guru* as being the Form of Vajra-Dhāra ; and above that Form, seated, one above the head of another, the *Gurus* of the Consciousness-Transference Doctrine [from thine own human *guru*] up to Vajra-Dhāra Himself.[1]

(15) Manifest thy humble fervent faith till the very hairs of thy body stand on end and tears course down thy cheeks ; and, in that mood, recite the Prayer to the Line of *Gurus* [beginning as above], ' Unto Thee, of the pure and holy Realm of Truth '.

(16) Then, when the Prayer hath been said, imagine that all the Lāmas of the Succession of *Gurus* [i.e. those of the Line who were or are Superior Ones on Earth] gradually dissolve into radiance, which finally mergeth into the Root-*Guru*.

(17) Towards the Root-*Guru*, embodying the true protection, exert the most fervent and humble faith, in the ' Thou knowest ' mood, and pray earnestly [to Him] as many times as thou canst.

---

[1] The Line of *Gurus*, of the Kargyütpa Apostolic Succession, is said both to begin and end in Vajra-Dhāra (Dorje-Chang). Accordingly, He is to be visualized as being seated, in the Buddha-Posture, on a lion-throne, and as hovering over the disciple's head directly above the Aperture of Brahmā, through which the median-nerve has its exit. Above Vajra-Dhāra's head, in the same posture and corresponding position, the human *guru* is to be visualized. Above the human *guru*'s head, in the same posture and corresponding position, the *Guru* of the Line who is still on Earth is to be visualized, and, correspondingly one above another in a perpendicular line and each in due order of precedence, the discarnate *Gurus* of the Line are to be visualized, Tilopa being topmost. And above Tilopa is to be visualized the Root-*Guru*, Vajra-Dhāra, mystically overshadowing the whole perpendicular Line of visualized *Gurus* as, at the bottom of the visualization, He overshadows, in reflex form, the human disciple (himself visualized as being Vajra-Ḍākinī).

(18) Then, when the praying hath been accomplished, visualize in the heart of the *Guru* a syllable *HŪM̐*, embodying the real essence of the Mind of all the Conquerors [or Buddhas], blue in colour,[1] emitting the radiance of the Five Wisdoms.[2]

(19) Having visualized this vividly, then, while retaining the visualization, utter the sound *HEEG* loudly, imagining, at the same moment, the dot in the heart [of Vajra-Ḍākinī] to be rising up into the *Guru's* heart.

(20) Then, allowing the dot to blend with the *HŪM̐* in the *Guru's* heart, in the state of at-one-ment, abide in that state for awhile.

(21) Then utter *KĂ*, and let the dot fall back into its own place, [i.e. in the heart of Vajra-Ḍākinī].

(22) By repeatedly practising this exercise, the most advanced *yogin* ought most certainly to be able to produce signs of proficiency after twenty-one *HEEGS*; a *yogin* of middling ability, within one period of prayer [i.e. within one and one-half hours]; and even a *yogin* of the least ability, within a day's practice.

(23) These signs are as followeth : a swelling-up of the flesh on the crown of the head [around the Aperture of Brahmā] and the issuing from there of blood and yellowish watery secretions ; and the ability to pierce the swelling with a stalk of grass [i.e. to enter a thin stalk of grass into the Aperture of Brahmā, whence the consciousness is to be projected].

(24) Having obtained these signs, there is no need to continue the practice.

(25) Then, upon successful completion of the period of exercise, visualize Vajra-Dhāra, the Root-*Guru*, as having

---

[1] Here the *HŪM̐* is blue, in correspondence with the blue body of the Root-*Guru*, the blue symbolizing, like the blue of the sky, immutability and eternity. When the visualization is of the *yogin's* own body as Vajra-Ḍākinī (or Vajra Yoginī), or of the body of a person deceased, as in the second part of our present manuscript, the *HŪM̐* is red, in correspondence with the body of the Goddess.

[2] See Book VI, following, which expounds the Five Wisdoms in their correlation with the Five Dhyānī Buddhas. Here in this context, and on page 271, paragraph 7, the Five Wisdoms are correlated with all Buddhas.

been transformed into Amitāyus,[1] holding in his hands the Urn of Life, whence ambrosia is flowing and filling thine own body, and its psychic-centres of speech and mind, to fullest capacity; and think that thus the boon of Illimitable Life hath been attained.

(26) Repeatedly recite the essence *mantra* of Amitāyus [2] and visualize Him as being transformed into an orb of radiance, which is then absorbed into thyself.

(27) Then [in the mood of divine exaltation], rising up, as a god riseth up (which is, in itself, self-liberating), or as doth a bird in flight which leaveth no track, thou shouldst continue in the State of the Reality of the Incomprehensible *Dharma-Kāya*; and pray that thou shalt realize this Highest State.

(28) And the devotee on the Path of the Consciousness-Transference should persevere in the acquiring of longevity of life.[3]

(29) Such is that part of the Doctrine of the Transference of the Consciousness which is permissible to be committed to writing.[4]

## [THE COLOPHON]

[There now follows a brief account of the super-normal origin of this first part of the Consciousness-Transference Doctrine by the *yogin* who composed the text.]

---

[1] Text: *Tshe-dpag-med* (pron. *Tshe-pag-med*): Skt. *Amitāyus* = 'He of Illimitable Life' or 'The Eternal', a reflex of Amitābha, the Buddha of Infinite Light.

[2] This *mantra* is: *AŪM-AH-MA-RĀ-NI-JĪ-VAN-TI-YE-SVAH-HAH*! meaning, '*Aūm*! May Immortal Life be vouchsafed! *Svah-Hah*!'

[3] The continuous practising of these exercises tends to shorten life, for it rapidly ripens the physical body for death. Thus, as an antidote, or counteracting influence, longevity of life should be aimed at by indomitable resolve to live long, aided by supplication to the Buddha of Ever-Enduring Life, Amitāyus.

[4] The more technical and practical parts of this esoteric teaching are to be orally taught to the *yogin* by the *guru*. Some matter not contained in this treatise is supplied by that of *The Six Doctrines*. The present exercises, as given, are intended for preliminary practice, whereas those of the Transference in *The Six Doctrines* are, more or less, complete and complementary, although very condensed. The second part of this Book IV, treating of the Transference as applied to a person on the point of death, should also be carefully studied in order to gain a comprehensive idea of the Transference Doctrine as a whole.

Whilst passing my time in close devotional retreat I enjoyed many interviews, in the State of the Clear Light, with the Reverend Lord Milarepa ; and, in the mood of exalted love and faith, I received many profoundly mystic teachings from that Saintly One.

At last, an aged woman, with reddish-yellow eyebrows and a growth of hair on her upper lip, appeared, and said to me, ' My brother, I request of thee the teachings concerning the Transference of the Consciousness ' ; and then she vanished as vanisheth a rainbow.[1]

And at that time, at the request of the *Avatāra* [or *Tulku*] from the North, the Teacher of Beings, this mad mendicant, Shākya-Shrī,[2] composed whatever dawned, [as if by divine inspiration,] in his mind.

May this treatise be auspicious.

## [PART II : THE TRANSFERENCE OF THE CONSCIOUSNESS OF ONE DECEASED]

(1) The Visualization for the Transference of the Consciousness of One Deceased, from the Teachings concerning the Secret Path of Consciousness-Transference, is herein given.[3]

---

[1] The aged woman was a *ḍākinī* in disguise ; that is to say, she was one of the order of fairy-like beings who are said to impart to sincere *yogins* supernormal powers and spiritual insight.　(Cf pp. 45[1], 301[2].)

[2] It is uncertain whether the Shākya-Shrī mentioned here, and in the Colophon of the second half of this text, is the Great *Guru* of the Kargyütpa Line referred to above, in the Prayer, or is some succeeding *yogin* who assumed the name, believing himself to have been inspired by the Great *Guru* to compose this treatise or to have been his *tulku*, or reincarnation. We learn from the other Colophon that the *Avatāra* from the North was the chief disciple of the ' mad mendicant ', a euphemistic expression such as *yogins* like to apply to themselves. The statement that the request for the teachings was conveyed by the *ḍākinī* may be merely a metaphorical usage to imply that the request was telepathically transmitted to the ' mad mendicant '.

[3] As explained in *The Tibetan Book of the Dead*, pp. 86-7, this ritual should be used by a qualified Lāma for the purpose of setting free the consciousness of a person at the point of death, and thus making unnecessary the reading of the *Bardo Thödol* : ' If the Transference hath been effectually employed, there is no need to read this [*Bardo*] Thödol.'

[THE VISUALIZATIONS FOR DEVOTEES OF LOWER DEGREE]

(2) Devotees on the Path below the stage of the absence of thought-forming [1] should employ the visualizations which follow.

(3) Having repeated the Refuge and Resolution [2] over and over again, then regard the physical corpse of the one deceased as being non-existent, by transcending the thought that forms are real.

(4) Then, vividly visualizing the apparent, yet vacuous and illusory body of Vajra-Ḍākinī, imagine as extending through its centre the median-nerve, externally white and internally red of colour, the size of an arrow-reed, the lower end set down level below the navel, the upper end like an open sky-light.

(5) Then visualize a buoyant, very finely depicted syllable *HŪM*, red of colour, as being the actual embodiment of the consciousness-principle of the deceased, within the median-nerve at the place where the heart should be.

(6) Over the crown of the head [directly above the Aperture of Brahmā] of the deceased, visualize a lotus-throne surmounted by a lunar disk upon which is seated, and enhaloed

---

[1] Text: *Sprös-bral* (pron. *Tö-dal*), 'absence of thought-forming'. This corresponds to one of the higher stages on the Path, as described in *The Epitome of the Great Symbol*, p. 149. All Lāmas (or *bhikshus*) and *yogins* who have completed their novitiate and received the preliminary initiation are regarded as devotees on the Path. Those of them who have not made sufficient progress in *yoga* to inhibit the process of thought-forming are to employ the elementary visualizations which follow, up to the end of paragraph 11. In employing this ritual, the Lāma or *yogin*, acting as the officiant must depend upon his *yogic* ability to set up real telepathic communion with the Root-*Guru* in the super-human realm. To that end, he employs prayers and visualizations of a *yogic* character, such as are given or referred to in this part of the *Pho-wa*. He believes that if success attends his efforts the Root-*Guru* will telepathically transmit the divine power, symbolized as Rays of Wisdom, in such manner that the consciousness of the person dying or already deceased will be spiritually attuned to the State of the Clear Light and so be brought into at-one-ment with the transcendental consciousness of the Root-*Guru* and attain Enlightenment.

[2] As given on p. 261, where the Refuge and Resolution are combined into one formula. Or, if preferred, the Refuge and Resolution in the longer form, as set forth on p. 116[1], may be employed.

by a five-coloured rainbow, the Divine Deliverer, the Root-
*Guru*, in reality the Embodiment of all the Congregation of
Refuges,[1] all-embracing like the ocean, in appearance Vajra-
Dhāra, blue of colour, with one face, two hands crossed over
His heart, the right hand holding a *dorje*, the left hand a bell,
arrayed in various robes of silk and adorned with various
ornaments of precious gems, the legs crossed in the *Dorje*-
Posture.

(7) Then visualize a syllable *HŪM*, blue of colour, upon
a lunar disk, within the *Guru*'s heart ; it being, in reality, the
Embodiment of the Five Wisdoms of all the Conquerors ;
and pray earnestly, with profound faith and humility, in order
to produce response [telepathically] in the minds of thine own
*Gurus* of the Inspired [or Telepathic] Line.[2]

(8) Finally, think that simultaneously with the oral utterance of the syllable *HEEG* the u-vowel-sign of the blue
*HŪM* within the *Guru*'s heart elongateth itself downwards
and catcheth hold of the circle of the M-sign of the red *HŪM*
within the heart of the deceased and beginneth to draw the red
*HŪM* upwards ; and, then, that with a second performing of
the practice, the red *HŪM* reacheth the throat [of the de-
ceased], with a third, the crown of the head, and with a
fourth, it blendeth with the blue *HŪM* in the *Guru*'s heart.[3]

---

[1] The Congregation of Refuges refers to the Divine At-one-ment of all the
Buddhas, personified in the one form of the Root-*Guru*, Vajra-Dhāra. The
Communion of Saints of the Christian Faith refers to a like indescribable state
of spiritual at-one-ness.

[2] *Yogic* prayer should always be of this character, namely, telepathic, whereby
direct spiritual communication is established between the devotee on Earth and
the Celestial *Gurus*. This ideal of prayer has been lost by exoteric faiths of the
Occident.

[3] Comparison should here be made with the version of the Transference
Doctrine as given above in *The Six Doctrines*, pp. 246-50. In that, as in this

version, the u-vowel-sign at the bottom of the Tibetan letter *HŪM*,

namely, the ﾑ, of the upper *HŪM*, elongates itself and catches hold of, or
entwines, the m-sign, namely the O, or circle, at the top of the lower *HŪM*.
Then by the drawing-up process, the lower *HŪM* is amalgamated with the
upper *HŪM*  In the version in *The Six Doctrines*, which is employed by the
living *yogin* for performing the Transference on his own behalf rather than, as
in the present version, for a deceased person, the process is somewhat different,

(9) Then, concluding with a loud exclamatory utterance of
*PHAṬ!* the *Guru* Himself [in His illusory form, as visualized,
is to be thought of as being transferred] to the *Dharma-
Dhātu* State in the Akanishṭha Heaven and there absorbed
into the heart of Vajra-Dhāra [in His true form].[1]

(10) Abide in that condition of spiritual exaltation for a
time.

(11) Then perform the rites of dedication,[2] and recite the
Paths [or Prayers] of Good-Wishes[3] over and over again.

[THE APPLICATION OF THE TRANSFERENCE BY DEVOTEES OF
HIGHER DEGREE]

(12) Those devotees who have realized the at-one-ment of
mind and phenomena should perform the rite of consciousness-transference on behalf of a deceased person as followeth :

(13) First recite the Refuge and the Resolution, in the
state [of mental quiescence] devoid of thought-forming, and
pray repeatedly to the Inspired Line of *Gurus*, Who are the

being dependent upon the breath of the living body ; and therein the *HEEG* and
*KĀ* are used as the interjectory utterances instead of the *PHAṬ!* of the
paragraph which now follows. *Phaṭ* ཕཊ྄ is regarded by all Tibetan masters
of *yoga* as being psychically very powerful and efficacious when rightly employed
as an ejaculatory expression in connexion with *mantras*, or words of power,
especially in neutralizing or controlling evil influences, or spiritual entities
inimical to the success in *yogic* practices and rituals.  Milarepa is quoted as
having expounded it, as follows : ' Outwardly, *phat* is the condensation of
the items of Discriminative Perception, or the amalgamation when those
items have been too minutely subdivided and scattered ; inwardly, *phaṭ* is
the revival of one's sinking consciousness ; rationally, *phaṭ* is the classification
of things according to their primary nature.' (Cf. Rai Sarat Chandra Dās,
*Tibetan-English Dictionary*, Calcutta. 1902 ; also p. 302[2], following.)

[1] As suggested by the text, and as made clearer by the annotation on p. 266,
the form of the Root-*Guru* as at first visualized is merely a visualization intended to help in the process of the consciousness-transference.  The final
at-one-ment is with the Root-*Guru* in actuality, when the consciousness has
been transferred.

[2] The rites of dedication refer to dedicating all merit, which may accrue
from having successfully performed the Transference on behalf of one deceased
or on behalf of oneself, unreservedly to the end that all beings may be led to
Freedom.

[3] These Prayers are given in full, in translation, in *The Tibetan Book of the
Dead*, pp. 197–208.

very embodiment of all the Conquerors and the manifestation of the inseparable union of mind and phenomena.

(14) Then cause the consciousness of the deceased to blend with thine own consciousness in the state of at-one-ment.

(15) Then blend thine own consciousness with the consciousness of Vajra-Dhāra by uttering *PHAṬ!* and remain for a long time in the realm of the *Dharma-Dhātu* Voidness.

(16) Finally, the sealing of the rite with prayer and dedication, while immersed in the state devoid of thought-forming, is of great importance.

### [THE STATE OF THE HIGHEST DEVOTEES]

(17) Those Highest Devotees whose minds have attained to peace in the state wherein is realized the *Dharma-Dhātu* Voidness have transcended the need of differentiating that which is to be transferred and the one who doeth the transferring.

(18) On the attainment of peace, in the realization of the Clear Light of the Foundationless Mind, which is the embodiment of All Who have passed into Blissfulness, in the Clear Void State of Non-Thought, wherein appearances and the one who seeth the appearances are non-existent, for Them both the object of protection and the Protector are indistinguishable.

(19) For Them the concepts concerning the *Sangsāra* and *Nirvāṇa* as being two [states of being] are like unto forms depicted on the atmosphere, which disappear of themselves without leaving any trace, and are understood as soon as seen to be illusory and without reality.

(20) They are beyond conceiving birth and death, and for Them the self, as something apart from all other selves, hath no existence.

(21) Therefore, for Them there existeth no thing to which the Transference can be applied.[1]

---

[1] For those Highest Devotees, or Masters of *Yoga*, Who have transcended Ignorance, the concept of transferring the consciousness is meaningless, there really being nothing which can be separated from the Whole, nor any place to which anything can be transferred. For They exist in the non-conditioned

(22) The devotee who hath comprehended the Incomprehensible and the Unmeditatable, by whispering [these mystic truths] into the ear of the deceased, will thereby have closed for the deceased the doors of birth of the Six *Lokas*,[1] and will be assured of having conferred upon the deceased the boon of the *Anāgamī* State.[2]

## [THE COLOPHON]

This manual of visualization for the transference of the consciousness of one deceased was written by the *Yogin* of Etherial Space, Shākya-Shrī, who is beyond the need of such transference, at intervals [during his devotional retreat], at the request of his chief disciple, the *Avatāra Yogin* of the Northern Hills.

May the merit, born of his having written it, aid all sentient beings, as innumerable as the sky is all pervading, to attain to the *Anāgamī* State.

## [PART III: THE DESCRIPTION OF THE LINE OF THE GURUS]

(1) The Line of the *Gurus*, seated perpendicularly, one above another, is now described.

(2) Above the head of one's Root-*Guru*, as Dorje-Chang [or Vajra-Dhāra] on a lotus-lunar-throne,[3] is [to be visualized] Jetsün Milarepa, light-blue of colour, his right hand placed

---

state of the Primordial Mind, in rapt ecstatic contemplation, fully enlightened as to the Final Truth. And thus, for Them, Who are in divine at-one-ment with the One Mind and Consciousness, time and space have no existence, nor is there any immortal personal self (or soul), nor, in reality, any states of individualized *sangsāric* being,—heavens, hells, and worlds. The *Sangsāra* and *Nirvāṇa* are for Them, Who have attained the Supreme Awakening, one and inseparable.

[1] See pp. 90[2], 196[3].

[2] Text: *Phy-ir-mi-ldog-pa* (pron. *Chir-mi-dok-pa*): Skt. *Anāgamī*, meaning 'One who will not return [to *sangsāric* birth]' except it be as a *Tulku*, or Divine Incarnation, for the purpose of dissipating Ignorance. (Cf. p. 94[4].)

[3] That is to say, a lotus-throne surmounted by a lunar disk. (See p. 262[1]; the description of Illustrations III, IX, pp. xix, xxi; and the Illustrations themselves.)

against his right cheek in the *dorje-mudrā* posture,[1] his left
hand [placed in his lap] in the posture of equilibrium,[2] and
holding a human skull filled with nectar,[3] his feet in the
*Bodhisattvic* posture,[4] [his body] robed in white silk.

(3) Above him [is to be visualized] Marpa, of reddish-
brown colour, stout of body, in *lāmaic* robes, his legs crossed
under him, his hands [placed one above another] in equilibrium posture and holding a human skull filled with nectar,
his eyes turned heavenwards.

(4) Above him [is to be visualized] Naropa, of light-blue
colour, his hair knotted on the crown of his head [after the
fashion of an Indian *yogin*], wearing, as a head-dress, a tiara
of human skulls,[5] and adorned with the six bone ornaments,[6]
his loins clad in the loin-cloth as worn in India,[7] his right
hand holding an antelope's-horn trumpet,[8] his left hand, in the
menacing *mudrā*,[9] resting on the dais behind him, his feet in
the pose of a smithy.[10]

[1] Thus:

[2] As commonly seen in images of the Buddha, or as in the Illustration facing
p. 57.

[3] The nectar, which symbolizes the highest spiritual boon of Enlightenment,
and, also, *yogic* ability to confer super-normal powers (or *siddhi*), is sometimes displaced by blood, which symbolizes, along with the human skull, utter
renunciation of human, or worldly, life.

[4] In this posture the *yogin* is to be seated, with his right leg bent and outside
the left leg, which is also to be bent, in such manner that its toes touch the
calf of the right leg.

[5] This tiara is usually depicted as being composed of five miniature skulls,
which symbolize that Naropa has realized the Five Wisdoms, described in
Book VI, following.

[6] These, like the similar adornments of Vajra-Yoginī, symbolize the Six
*Pāramitā*. (See p. 174[6].)        [7] This indicates Naropa's Hindu origin.

[8] The antelope was often pictured on ancient Buddhist temples and monas-
taries as emblematical of peacefulness, and probably the antelope's-horn trumpet
(which is sometimes replaced by a ram's-horn trumpet), apart from its significance
as sounding the glory of the Bodhic Order of *Gurus*, may. as herein, symbolize
*yogic* quiescence, or the peacefulness of the True State of mind.

[9] The menacing *mudrā* is similar to that commonly used in the worldly life,
the index finger pointing and the other fingers closed against the palm, with
the thumb folded against the second finger.

[10] This refers to the easy sitting-posture of an Indian blacksmith, who works
in primitive fashion with a crude bellows and charcoal fire.

(5) Above him [is to be visualized] the Great and Glorious Tilopa, of brown colour, with a somewhat angry yet smiling mien of countenance, with his hair done up into a knot on the top of his head and surmounted by a gem,[1] with a tiara of white lotus blossoms, wearing loosely a meditation-band, his body brightly adorned with human-bone ornaments, and clad in a tiger-skin[2] fashioned like an apron round his loins, his feet in an easy posture, his right hand upraised and holding a large golden fish,[3] his left hand in the equilibrium posture and holding a human skull filled with nectar.

(6) Above him [is to be visualized] the Conqueror Vajra-Dhāra, blue of colour, arrayed in the full robes of a *Sambhoga-Kāya* deity,[4] His two hands crossed over the breast, the right hand holding a *dorje* and the left a bell.

(7) Each of the *Gurus* [is to be visualized] as being seated within the halo of a five-hued rainbow.

May this Book be auspicious!

[Here endeth the threefold manuscript of the Consciousness-Transference Doctrine, of Book IV.]

---

[1] This suggests the *Bodhic* protuberance, or phrenological bump of spiritual insight, as commonly shown on the head of a Buddha. (Cf. p. 201[2].)

[2] The tiger-skin apron (commonly displaced, in the case of present-day *yogins* of India, by a loose hanging apron of leopard skin) symbolizes, for the Tibetan *yogin*, the suppression of the erroneous belief in the existence of an ego (or self) capable of eternal personal existence apart from the Whole.

[3] The fish, as being golden, symbolizes the preciousness of *sangsāric* beings, who are to be freed from Ignorance. The fish itself symbolizes all sentient beings, who, like fish in an infinite sea, are immersed in the *Sangsāra*; and it suggests Tilopa's power to lead them to Freedom. The fish symbol as adopted by the early Christians, probably from Oriental sources, conveys similar significance with respect to the *Christos* as the Saviour of Mankind.

[4] In modern Tibetan art, this garb is modelled after the full royal dress of an Indian prince. Here, as throughout this description of the Kargyütpa *Gurus*, the reader should refer to the coloured frontispiece of these *Gurus*, with its accompanying explanation, in *Tibet's Great* Yogi *Milarepa*. In some unimportant details the descriptions as given in the present manual vary from those given therein.

FOLIOS 3ᵃ, 3ᵇ, 4ᵃ, 4ᵇ, 5ᵃ OF THE *CHÖD* MS.

Described on page xx

# BOOK V

## THE PATH OF THE MYSTIC SACRIFICE: THE *YOGA* OF SUBDUING THE LOWER SELF [1]

### THE INTRODUCTION

#### I. THE HISTORY OF THE DOCTRINE OF NON-EGO

THIS Book introduces the reader to one of the most marvellous of Tibetan doctrines, called, as pronounced, *Chöd* (written in the original as *Gchöd*), which here means 'cutting [off]', with reference to egoism, as represented by the human fleshly form together with all its passions and *karmically*-inherited predispositions constituting the personality.

Whereas the four preceding treatises had origin in the Kargyütpa School, this treatise has come down to us through the Ñingmapa School of Padma Sambhava. It is, nevertheless, as the reader will discover, more or less representative of the pre-Buddhistic Bön Faith, which was dominant in Tibet at the time of the coming of the 'Precious *Guru*'. And inasmuch as this treatise illustrates the manner in which the early animism of the Tibetans lent itself to reshaping and adaptation by the 'Old Style Ones', it is of special historical and anthropological value.

Our own two manuscript texts of *Chöd* belong to one of a series of occult treatises collectively entitled *Fundamental Essence of the Subtle Truth*, or more literally rendered, *Heart-Drops from the Great Space*, forming part of *The Great Perfection System* as compiled by Long-Chen Rab-jampa. Rab-jampa, being a *lāmaic* degree somewhat comparable to the European degree of Doctor of Divinity, indicates that Long-

---

[1] The Tibetan manuscript, upon which our translation is based, bears the following title: *GCHÖD-YUL MKHAH-HGRO-HI GAD-RGYANG* (pron. *CHÖD-YUL KHAH DO YI GAD-YANG*), meaning, 'The Method of Eradicating [the Lower Self], called "The Divine Mirth of the *Ḍākinīs*".'

Chen was a learned teacher of saintly character. His followers regard him as having been an incarnation of the Great *Guru* Padma Sambhava, who during the year 747 of our era arrived in Tibet and began to introduce among the Tibetans the Tantric (or deeply esoteric) aspect of Buddhism. Long-Chen himself seems to have flourished about five hundred years later.

The late Lāma Kazi Dawa-Samdup was of opinion that the literary matter contained in the numerous Tibetan works which form *The Great Perfection System* would probably equal that contained in *The Encyclopaedia Britannica*. Being a compilation of the secret doctrines of the Ñingmapas, or ' Old Style Ones ', of the Primitive Church of Tibetan Buddhism, *The Great Perfection System* is expounded and taught in practical manner only by authorized initiates, of whom Long-Chen was one of the greatest.

## II.  THE TIBETAN VERSIFICATION

The subject of Tibetan versification, arising in connexion with our two manuscript texts of the *Chöd* Rite, both of which are written mostly in verse, is somewhat difficult, inasmuch as it has received scant attention outside of Tibet, although very much of Tibet's vast literature, like that of India, is recorded in poetical form. The late Lāma Kazi Dawa-Samdup, who was himself somewhat of a poet and probably more conversant with Tibetan poetry than any other English-speaking Tibetan scholar of this epoch, stated, when I once discussed Tibetan poetry with him, that the number of its metres and its verse and stanza structure are, in a general way, comparable to those employed in European poetry. There is, too, in the philosophical and religious poetry of the Tibetans, as in that of the ancient Greeks, no rhyme, except in some few instances.

But, for the most part, as Csoma de Körös observes, there exists little difference between Tibetan verse and prose ; and ' since there is no distinction of vowels into short and long, accented and emphatic, consequently there are no [true] poetical feet measured by short and long syllables '.

'Although several poetical works (as the *Kavyādarsha*, by Dandi) have been translated by the Tibetans, they have not adopted the metrical feet used in Sanskrit versification. The several poetical pieces (or verses) occurring in the *Kah-gyur* and *Stan-gyur*, and in other works derived from India, have been rendered by the Tibetans in blank verse, consisting, generally, of four lines each of seven syllables. But in the invocations and benedictions, at the beginning and end of some treatises or works, a few verses or stanzas, of four lines, are sometimes introduced, consisting each of nine, eleven, thirteen, or more syllables.'[1] As the late Lāma Kazi Dawa-Samdup added, there are also verses of nineteen syllables.

The Tibetan text of the *Chöd* Rite is, at least in its first part (reproduced as the frontispiece of this Book V), more truly poetical by structure and by metre than the blank verse of the canonical literature thus referred to by Csoma de Körös. It consists of a kind of unrhymed or blank verse, somewhat like that which Shakespeare and Milton developed under the influence of the classical poetry of Greece and Rome. Although the number of feet to a verse varies in our Tibetan text, there is maintained throughout it a remarkable poetical balance of one stanza with another. This harmony of composition is suggested even by our English rendering of 'The Dance of the Five Directions' in which, however, no attempt has been made to make the verse structure syllabically conform to the Tibetan original. It has been my aim to convey the real meaning of the original text as literally as is compatible with good English, rather than to produce a highly laboured metrical imitation.

The prevailing type of this blank verse of the Tibetan text consists of nine syllables, or four and one-half feet to a verse, in place of five feet as in *Paradise Lost*. But in both works alike the stress falls upon the second, fourth, sixth, and eighth syllables ; and, in the former work, on the ninth syllable, forming the half-foot, instead of, as in the latter work, on a tenth syllable. The first half of the second stanza of the *Chöd*,

---

[1] Cf. A. Csoma de Körös, *Grammar of the Tibetan Language* (Calcutta, 1834), p. 115.

transliterated phonetically, illustrates this common Tibetan type of blank verse, as follows:

> '*Jig-me tul-shu chöd-pai nal-jor ngai,*
> *Khor-da nyam-par gdal-vai gong-chöd kyi,*
> *Dag-zin lha-dai teng-tu dau-cig dung,*
> *Nyee-zin khor-wai nam-tog dul-tu log.*'

The name given to this type of shloka is in Tibetan *Kang-pa-che-dang-nga-pai.* An example of the seven-syllable verse is contained in Book III, above, p. 225. The renderings from our other *Chöd* manuscript, as set forth in the Addendum, appear much more prosaic in their English form than those forming the main body of this Book V. Nevertheless, it was deemed advisable to record them in that manner, which is more or less in conformity with their original verse structure, rather than in prose.

### III. THE PRACTITIONERS OF THE *CHOD* RITE

The venerable Ñingmapa *yogin*, from whom the editor obtained the two texts of the *Chöd*, had, like many of his fellow-countrymen of Tibet, practised the rite for many years. Similar *yogins*, freed from all wordly possessions and ties, devote the greater part of their life to making pilgrimages to solitary and sacred places, often going into hermitage there during fixed periods, for the sole purpose of celebrating the *Chöd* amidst the most psychically favourable environments. Throughout Tibet, Bhutan, Sikkim, Nepal, and India, and even into Mongolia and China, they wander, undaunted by dangers and hardships such as few Occidentals could endure, in the hope of eventually attaining self-conquest.

As their *Gurus* make clear to them, they go forth into the world on the greatest of all great adventures. And, then, the supreme test coming, perhaps when the *yogin* is alone in the wilderness with no other aid at hand than his own *yogic* power, he must face the strange elemental beings which the ritual evokes and dominate them; or, failing, risk an unbalancing of mind and psychic constitution, possibly leading to madness or even death.

As in all *yoga*, so in this, the *yogin* seeks to outstrip the normal, and, to him, over-slow and tedious process of spiritual unfoldment ; and, *karma* permitting, win Freedom, as Tibet's Great *Yogin* Milarepa did, in one lifetime. The *Chöd* is thus one of the many Tibetan rites pertaining to the ' Secret Path ', also called the ' Short (or Direct) Path ', of attaining *Nirvāṇa*, or deliverance from all *karmic* necessity of further re-birth. In virtue of the mystic sacrifice of his own body, the successful *yogin* breaks asunder the fetters of personality, of passion, of separateness, and of all *māyā*, or illusion ; and, transcending Ignorance, of which these are the sources, attains to *yogic* insight into the true nature of human existence. Once having realized the illusory character of all phenomenal appearances, which the unenlightened hold to be real and external and separate, and classify as animate and inanimate, including the innumerable kinds of creatures of the six realms of sensuous being, visible and invisible, throughout the Cosmos, the *yogin* sees the many as the One, and the One as all, and knows that the sole reality is Mind.

## IV. THE ESSENTIAL TEACHINGS

In this way, our present text teaches, as do our other texts, that the body of man and of every phenomenally-appearing form and thing of the *Sangsāra* are mind-made. Some are merely visualizations, or thought-forms, consciously or unconsciously projected into nature and thus given illusive existence by their creator. Of such character are probably most of the materializations created by ' spirit ' mediums. As man, impelled by *karmic* necessity, unconsciously creates the physical form he wears, similarly the master of *yoga*, consciously and at will, can create any number of equally unreal bodies, of human and non-human shape, and give to them illusive separate existence. He may even make them physically as ' real ' as his own body, and, infusing into them a portion of his animal vitality, direct them as though they were living creatures. Many a weird tale is current in Tibet concerning this art, of which the Occidental scientist knows nothing by practical application.

Collectively considered, the *Sangsāra* itself is for the *yogin* merely a complex thought-form, which has emanated from and is being sustained by the One Mind. In the language of the Master *Yogins* of ancient India, it is, as has been more fully explained above, the Dream of Brahmā. For those still immersed in the *māyā* of nature, there are gods and demons, men and beasts, ghosts and the different classes of invisible beings that may affect one another for good or ill. But the adept in *Chöd* would tell us, as does *The Tibetan Book of the Dead* (page 167), that ' Apart from one's own hallucinations, in reality there are no such things existing outside oneself, as Lord of Death, or god, or demon '. Herein, then, is summarized the essential teaching underlying the whole of our present Book, concerning the *Yoga* of Non-Ego. And in connexion with this teaching the student should carefully re-read Sections III and IV of our Introduction to Book III, pp. 161–6.

### V. THE *CHÖD* RITE AS A MYSTIC DRAMA

Like the Tibetan Mystery-Play, which we shall presently consider in this connexion, the *Chöd* Rite is, first of all, a mystic drama, performed by a single human actor, assisted by numerous spiritual beings, visualized, or imagined, as being present in response to his magic invocation. Its stage setting is in some wild awe-inspiring locality, often in the midst of the snowy fastnesses of the Tibetan Himālayas, twelve to fifteen or more thousand feet about sea-level. Commonly by preference it is in a place where corpses are chopped to bits and given to the wolves and vultures. In the lower altitudes of Bhutan and Sikkim, a densely wooded jungle solitude may be chosen ; but in countries wherein corpses are cremated, such as Nepal and India, a cremation-ground is favoured. Cemeteries or localities believed to be haunted by malignant and demoniacal spirits are always suitable.

Long probationary periods of careful preparation under a master of *Chöd* are required before the novice is deemed fit or is allowed to perform the psychically dangerous rite. The ritual must be committed to memory ; the steps of the dance in relation to the various geometrical dancing-arenas must be mastered, along with the proper intonation of the *mantric* syllables, as well as the rhythmic beating of the small drum, called the *damaru*, and the sounding of the spirit-evoking trumpet, called the *kangling*, made of a human thigh-bone. The right way of pitching the symbolic tent, and of employing the *dorje*, the bell, and the various supplementary objects described in the second of the texts, must also be well known.

The dance itself, apart from its ritual significance, is looked upon by the *gurus* as a gymnastic exercise; for, according to them, celibacy, which is essential to success in all *yogas*, cannot be practised and health maintained without physical exercise. There is, for instance, another sort of dance which novices in training for *yogic* development are required to dance before the *guru*, called *Tül-khor* (written *Hkhrül-hkhor*), chiefly for the purpose of bodily development.

At the outset, the celebrant of the *Chöd* Rite is directed to visualize himself as being the Goddess of the All-Fulfilling (or All-Performing) Wisdom, by whose occult will he is mystically empowered ; and then, as he sounds the thigh-bone trumpet, invoking the *gurus* and the different orders of spiritual beings, he begins the ritual dance, with mind and energy entirely devoted to the one supreme end of realizing, as the Mahāyāna teaches, that *Nirvāṇa* and the *Sangsāra* are, in reality, an inseparable unity.

Stanzas three to seven inclusive suggest the profound symbolism underlying the ritual; and this symbolism, as will be seen, is dependent upon the Five Directions, the corresponding Five 'Continents' of the *lāmaic* cosmography with their geometrical shapes, the Five Passions (hatred, pride, lust, jealousy, stupidity) which the *yogin* triumphantly treads under foot in the form of demons, and the Five Wisdoms, the antidotes of the Five Passions. In their association with the Five Dhyānī Buddhas, the Five Wisdoms are explained in the Introduction to Book VI which follows. Then, in the ninth stanza, comes the dramatic spearing of the Elementals of Self with the spears of the Five Orders of *Ḍākinīs*.

As the Mystery proceeds, and the *yogin* prepares for the mystic sacrifice of his own fleshly form, there is revealed the real significance of the *Chöd*, or 'cutting-off'. Of the desire for sensuousness, for separateness, leading to egoism, the physical body, dominated by passion and Ignorance, is the *karmic* fruit. Not until all desire for *sangsāric* existence is overcome can the True State be attained. In the words of the text, it is 'This body which createth the distinction [which, too, is illusory] between the *Sangsāra* and *Nirvāna*'.

In the Addendum, complementary matter from the second of the *Chöd* manuscripts has been placed on record, describing the objects, the place, and the mental imagery needed for practising the rite ; and, also, how the various sacrificial offerings may be applied so as to make of the rite the Mixed, the Red, or the Black Feast. The Meditation to accompany the sacrifice is also given. Then there follow sections concerning the resulting psychic phenomena, the time for the celebration, the importance of the mental imagery, the visualizing of the human skeleton and of the Wrathful *Dākinī*, the state of mind required, the successful application, and the final meditation. This Addendum, combined with the copious annotations throughout the Book, will, it is hoped, guide the reader to a comprehensive understanding of the ritual as a whole.

## VI. THE COMPARISON WITH THE TIBETAN MYSTERY-PLAY

Among the various doctrines set forth in this volume, the *Chöd* is undoubtedly the most Tibetan in character; and although it has been reshaped by primitive Lāmaism, as our two texts indicate, the pre-Buddhistic origin is unmistakable. Viewed anthropologically, it appears to have had sources in animistic cults, relating to sacrifice and exorcism, which antedate even the ancient Bön Faith, whence the Lāmas adopted it. That this may be seen more clearly, we shall presently proceed to examine, in some detail, the very similar ritual connected with the Tibetan Mystery-Play, which, likewise, Lāmaism appears to have taken over from the Bönpas.

Originally, the Mystery-Play was probably little more than

a ritual dance of sacrificial exorcism. The Tibetan peasantry still call it 'The Dance of the Red-Tiger Devil', a Bön deity, which clearly suggests pre-Buddhistic history. In this aspect, it is comparable to the *Bali* Ceremony, also of very primitive origin, which has survived in like manner amongst the Buddhists of Ceylon, as a sacrificial exorcism employed to cure human maladies, wherein the chief actors are devil-dancers.

In its present highly developed form, the Mystery-Play has long been performed for the purpose of expelling the old year with its demons of ill-luck, through winning the aid of the deities by means of human sacrifice (nowadays made in effigy), and thus safeguarding the crops and cattle and assuring divine protection for the state and triumph over all enemies, both human and spiritual. Primitively, a sacramental eating of the flesh and drinking of the blood of the sacrificed one was probably associated with the rite. With the coming of Buddhism, the human victim was replaced by an anthropomorphic effigy, made of dough. According to tradition, this substitution became general during the latter half of the eighth century of our era, and is credited to Padma Sambhava.

### VII. THE ORIGIN OF DISEASE ACCORDING TO THE LĀMAS

Inasmuch as the Mystery-Play, like certain aspects of the *Chöd* Rite, presented more particularly by the second of the two manuscripts, thus appears to be fundamentally a ritual for the driving out of demons and evil influences and the consequent curing of ills both in man individually and in man collectively as the State, it is of importance at this point to consider how Lāmaism views disease.

The Lāmas maintain that there are three chief sources of disease, namely, lack of harmony in the functioning of the nervous system, in the flow of bile, and in the circulation of the phlegm or 'airs' (which are the vital-forces constituting by their measure of distribution in the body the various temperaments). The Lāmas also hold that external stimuli, emanating from spiritual beings, especially in relation to planetary and other astrological influences, can affect a human being, an animal or crops, as well as the nation, for good or ill, because all sentient creatures are, like the stars and planets, Sun and Moon, inseparably related and, in reality, an indivisible unity. Hence, whatever affects the individual affects the whole. Astrology is, therefore, for the Tibetans, as for all peoples of the Orient, and for a growing number of its adherents throughout the Occident, a subject of profound study, upon right understanding of which depends the prosperity of human society.[1]

---

[1] That Indian astrology is not without some scientific value, especially when utilized by *yogically*-trained masters of it, has been suggested by their astonishing accuracy in foretelling the great earthquake which in January of this year (1934) caused such appalling loss of life and property in Bengal, Bihar, and other parts of Northern India, as in Nepal. For some weeks prior to the day upon which it had been calculated the earthquake would occur, and did occur, religious ceremonies, some of occult character, were performed by the Hindu astrologers and priests to mitigate, so far as might be humanly possible, the impending disaster. Professor Amaranātha Jha, son of the former Chancellor of the Allahabad University, India, who confirms this account, which was published on the basis of telegraphic advice in the European press, told me, when he was recently in Oxford, that the astrological prediction of the earthquake was published about a year previous to its occurrence in the *Panchānga*, in Benares. The time was therein given as the afternoon of the fifteenth of January, and it came at 2.41 p.m. at Allahabad. This time varied by a few minutes in other parts of the area affected. *The Hindustani Times* (Delhi, Jan. 18, 1934, p. 15) published the following report from Lucknow : 'It is curious that the earthquake was apparently expected by the local astrologers, as many of them were offering prayers in certain local temples at the time the shock occurred. Their calculations were based on the reading of signs of the Zodiac, and the reasons for their apprehensions were that no less than seven planets were at present gathered together in the house of Capricorn. This unusual phenomenon, it is said, was last observed at the time of the *Mahābhārata*.' Professor Amaranātha Jha also stated that the exact hour and minute of his own birth, in Darbhanga, Bihar, was foretold by his family astrologer. All of this suggests that our own men of science in Europe and America, who are quite unable to foretell such events, especially earthquakes, might acquire a certain amount of purely utilitarian knowledge from an unprejudiced study of the astrology and occult sciences of the Orient. In this connexion it is well to remember that for years one patiently read in the English press ponderous 'scientific' denials of water-divining, and now there is a Society of Water-Diviners, members of which are employed by the British Government.

## VIII. THE COMPARISON WITH THE *BALI* CEREMONY OF CEYLON

The Buddhist priests of Ceylon, who give patronage and, therefore, sanction to the *Bali* Ceremony, propound a parallel theory. And the *Bali* Ceremony is itself more completely astrological than the Mystery-Play, being dependent for its efficacy as a curative exorcism upon successfully invoking the aid of the gods connected with the nine planets. These gods, who are imaged in anthropomorphic effigies made of clay, painted in symbolical colours, are : (1) *Ravi* (the Sun), who causes headache, eye-diseases, fever, and poverty ; (2) *Chandra* (the Moon), who causes fever and ringworm ; (3) *Kuja* (Mars), who causes almost all venereal diseases, and makes friends and relatives to become enemies ; (4) *Budha* (Mercury), who causes accidents leading to broken limbs, and, also, danger from wild beasts ; (5) *Guru* (Jupiter), who causes all external and internal diseases of the head and neck ; (6) *Shukra* (Venus), who causes bodily weakness, short-sightedness, and diseases accompanied by high temperature ; (7) *Shani* (Saturn), who causes anaemia, tuberculosis, decrease of wealth, mental disorders, heart-disease, and all sorts of misfortune, and, in certain position, death ; (8) *Rāhu* (the Dragon's Head), who causes boils, ulcers, wounds, joint-diseases, rheumatism, all crippling maladies, and also heart-disease, and tuberculosis; (9) *Ketu* (the Dragon's Tail), who causes bowel disorders, dysentery, and diarrhoea, diseases of the limbs, and death. Since it is only when the planets are in unfavourable position that their influence is evil, and spirits inimical to man can in conjunction therewith harm man, any rite of exorcism, such as the *Bali* Ceremony, or the Mystery-Play, depends for its successful application upon an astrologer choosing, as he invariably does, the auspicious time for its performance.

## IX. THE ART OF EXORCISM

The Lāmas explain how in nature all things influence one another, and that in man's constitution there are elements, forces, passions, and mental powers, in constant activity, similar to those in invisible non-human beings, whereby the

latter, unconsciously to man, influence man and bring about
disease and misfortune. The practical aim of all exorcizing
rites is to neutralize the disharmony in nature and in man's
body and mind, which inimical influences, howsoever arising,
have caused. Accordingly, in all historic ages, propitiatory
offerings have been made to spiritual beings to win their
harmonious co-operation with man; and, in the case of evil
spirits who refuse to be appeased by such means, exorcism
has been employed, as it still is in all countries, and by all
the chief churches of Christendom.

The Founder of Christianity Himself also believed that
obsessing evil spirits can produce disease and madness in
mankind. This is illustrated by His healing of the maniac by
driving out from him a legion of devils and allowing them to
enter into a herd of swine; as by other instances of His use
of exorcism.[1] 'And', as St. Matthew (x. 1) tells us, ' when
He had called unto Him His twelve disciples, He gave them
power against unclean spirits, to cast them out, and to heal
all manner of sickness and all manner of disease '.

Throughout the Orient, particularly in China, demon-obses-
sion is still a commonly recognized disorder, and numerous
sorts of exorcism are employed to cure it. In Tibet there is
a widespread belief that a King Spirit, that is to say, a discarnate Lāma, who had practised black-magic while on Earth,
can, by projecting his malignity into an incarnate human
being, produce insanity in him. Similarly, as in the Sinhalese
astrological belief, other species of spirits, aided by unfavourable conditions, produce other disorders in man. Thus,
abscesses and sores, and also gall- and bladder-stone, are said
to be due to the evil influences of Serpent Spirits, vulgarly,
but not in an esoteric sense, confused with *Nāgas*. *Danabs*,
a species of elementals like the Salamanders of Medieval
Philosophy, who inhabit the element fire, can produce sharp
pains in the pulmonary passages and high fevers; and one of
the lower orders of *Devas*, who are habituated to an existence
of purely sensuous delights, if offended by a human being,

---

[1] Cf. *St. Mark* v. 1-20; *St. Luke* iv. 33-6, x. 17.

may take revenge by bringing upon him epileptic fits or apoplexy. In all such spirit-produced diseases the Tibetans regard exorcism as being the only panacea.

## X. THE PERFORMANCE OF THE MYSTERY-PLAY [1]

The Mystery-Play, in slightly differing versions, is nowadays annually celebrated by all sects of Lāmas, either, as is more common and in keeping with pre-Buddhistic usage, at the end of the year, or, by many of the Ñingma Orders, on St. Padma Sambhava's birthday, in the early summer, as in Ladāk. When performed at the end of the year, it forms a very important part of the ceremony known as ' the sacrificial body of the dead year '.

The performance is held in the temple courtyard. The notification of the commencement of the Play is given by a loud bugle like sounding of a human thigh-bone trumpet, precisely as in the opening of the *Chöd* Rite. The *lāmaic* orchestra strikes up a weird wailing sort of air, accompanied by a low chant on the part of the musicians, and then there appear a number of black-mitred priests, representative of the pre-Buddhistic Bön Faith. They make the mystic Bön sign of ' The Three ', and dance to slow, solemn music. After their exit, hosts of demons enter. As these move round in their ritual dance, the officiating Lāmas make propitiatory offerings to them and to all the beings of the Six States of *sangsāric* existence. There appear next, group after group, representatives of the demoniacal beings of the invisible realms, many of them animal-headed, very similar to those described in *The Tibetan Book of the Dead*. The Lāmas appease and exorcize one group after another until St. Padma

---

[1] Our observations made herein concerning the Tibetan Mystery-Play are based upon that version of it which is acted by the monks of the Unreformed Church at the Himis Monastery in Ladāk, Kashmir ; for these monks have preserved its ancient pre-Buddhistic elements better than have the monks of the Reformed Church. Moreover, the Ladāk Mystery-Play corresponds in all essentials to the Mystery-Play performed by other Ñingma monastic orders throughout Tibet, Bhutan, and Sikkim, and is well known, having been witnessed and reported by a number of competent Europeans. (See L. A. Waddell, *The Buddhism of Tibet or Lāmaism*, London, 1895, chap. xx.)

Sambhava himself appears, whereupon all the demons make
obeisance to him and disappear, in symbol of the triumph of
Buddhism over the indigenous Shamanism of the Bönpas.

Similarity with the *Chöd* Rite, as a sacrificial exorcism,
also appears in the service chanted by the priest who personifies St. Padma Sambhava. Being wholly a demon-ex-
pelling rite, in which are invoked the officiant's tutelary deity
and the tutelary deity's spiritual attendants, comparable to
the Goddess of the All-Fulfilling Wisdom and the *Ḍākinīs*
of the *Chöd* Rite, the service is entitled 'The Expelling
Oblation of the Hidden Fierce Ones'. Through the aid of
these 'Fierce Ones', as through the aid of the Goddess of
the All-Fulfilling Wisdom and the *Ḍākinīs* in the *Chöd* Rite,
the exorcizing or dominating of the demon hosts is accomplished. The invisible demons to be exorcized are made to
enter into an effigy of a sacrificial victim, after which the
officiant chants the following exorcism for keeping them at
bay :

'*Hūṃ!* Through the blessing of the blood-drinking Fierce
One, may the injuring demons and evil spirits be kept at
bay. I pierce their hearts with this hook; I bind their
hands with this snare of rope ; I bind their bodies with
this powerful chain ; I keep them down with the tinkling
bell. Now, O! blood-drinking Wrathful One [Chief of
the Fierce Ones], take thy sublime seat upon them.'

Then the chief of the Fierce Ones is requested to 'tear out
the hearts of the injuring evil spirits and utterly exterminate
them'. The sacrificial effigy, which is visualized as being in
actuality a corpse, is symbolically dipped in the blood of the
demons and offered up to the Fierce Ones to the accompani-
ment of the following chant :

'*Hūṃ!* O! ye hosts of gods of the magic circle! Open your
mouths as wide as the earth and sky, clench your fangs
like rocky mountains, and prepare to devour in their
entirety the bones, the blood, and the entrails of all the
injuring evil spirits.' [1]

---

[1] Cf. L. A. Waddell, *op. cit.*, pp. 531-2.

The Mystery-Play moves onwards to its dramatic climax, which on the first day consists of the spearing and on the second day of the stabbing of the Enemy; and in the *Chöd* Rite this is paralleled by the spearing of the Demon of Egoism by the *Ḍākinīs*. The Enemy, a collective personification of the innumerable hosts of evil that afflict the people of Tibet and oppose Lāmaism, is represented by the effigy of a human body.

' Some days previous to the commencement of the Play, an image of a young lad is made of dough, in most elaborate fashion and as life-like as possible. Organs representing the heart, lungs, liver, brain, stomach, intestines, &c., are inserted into it, and the heart and large blood-vessels and limbs are filled with a red-coloured fluid to represent blood.' [1]

Four cemetery ghouls carry in the effigy and place it in the centre of the monastic court-yard. Then demons, representing skeletons, dance round it with upraised spears and freely spear it. The Lāmas now exercise their occult power, and, as the ghouls fall back at their approach, draw round the effigy a magic triangle and retire. Troups of ghosts and death-demons rush in and frantically try to snatch away or injure the effigy; but the surrounding triangle, aided by the chanting and the clouds of incense from censers swung to and fro by holy men in mitred and purple copes, prevents them from doing so.

The first day's performance usually ends with the coming of a Saint, apparently an incarnation of the Buddha, who subdues the demons and shows mercy upon them by giving each a little flour, as a food-offering, and a drink of holy-water.

On the following day comes the stabbing of the Enemy by the magic dagger (known in Tibetan as the *phurba*). As before, four cemetery ghouls bring in an effigy, now wrapped in black cloth. They dance round it; and then, raising the cloth, disclose a human-shaped figure made like the effigy used on the first day.

Next enter the demon chiefs, followed by hosts of demons

[1] Cf. L. A. Waddell, *op. cit.*, p. 527.

and a group of black-hat devil-dancers (representative of the Bön priests), and then the God of Wealth, accompanied by other deities, both male and female, with their retinues. Lastly, there appears the Holy King of Religion, whose head is like that of a bull with long outspread horns, attended by many followers. He is a form of Yama, the God of the Underworld, in wrathful aspect, otherwise known as the Bull-headed Spirit of Death. With his attendants he dances round the effigy, holding in his right hand a *phurba* and a noose, and in his left hand a human heart (in effigy). He, too, makes the sign, or *mudrā*, of ' The Three ' with the dagger. Presently he stabs the Enemy over the region of the heart and in the arms and legs with the dagger, and binds its feet with the noose. Then, after ringing a *lāmaic* hand-bell, in the manner of the *yogin* in the *Chöd* Rite, he seizes a sword and cuts off the limbs, slits open the breast and extracts the bleeding heart, lungs, and intestines of the Enemy. There now rush in a number of monstrous beings having heads with horns like deer and yak. These gore the remains and scatter the fragments in all directions.[1]

Attendant fiends now gather together the fragments into a huge silver basin shaped like a human skull, comparable to the huge skull-cauldron into which are collected the fragments of the *yogin*'s body in the *Chöd* Rite.[2]

[1] The Lāmas of the Reformed Church have arbitrarily modified this part of the Play so as to make these goring demons symbolical of the Lāma Pal-dorje who, about the beginning of the tenth century A.D., assassinated Lang-Darma, the Tibetan King who, because of his apostasy from Buddhism and subsequent persecution of the Lāmas, has been called the Julian of Lāmaism. The character of the King of Religion has also been changed in such manner as to make him represent the god Mahākāla, who is believed to have delivered Lang-Darma into the Lāma's hands; while the graveyard ghouls are made to represent the scavengers who carried off Lang-Darma's corpse. (Cf. L. A. Waddell, *op. cit.*, p. 531[1].)

[2] We seem here to see survivals of a secret initiatory rite surprisingly like that of the Orphic Mysteries, in which Dionysus-Zagreus, the divinity born of the union of Zeus and Persephone, who became the Great Lord presiding over death and regeneration, is slain out of jealousy by his Titan brethren. They cut his body into pieces and throw the pieces into a cauldron. Pallas Athene saves the heart and carries it to Zeus, who, to avenge the evil deed, slays the murderers with his thunderbolts. Apollo is charged by Zeus to gather together the scattered parts of the body of the martyred Zagreus. It was this

In a pompous procession, in which the black-hat devil-dancers take part, four of the attendants carry the basin, heaped-up with the sacrificial remains, to the King of Religion. The King seizes the bleeding fragments and, after eating a morsel of them, throws the remainder up into the air. Thereupon they are caught and fought for by the other demons. These throw the pieces about in a most frantic manner, until, at last, the pieces are scattered amongst the crowd, who now take part in the orgy. There ensues a wild scramble by the crowd for bits of the broken body, which are either sacramentally eaten at once or treasured as holy relics, efficacious against human ills and misfortunes.

In the next scene, the King makes a burnt sacrifice of a miniature paper image of a man placed inside a skull and consumed in a cauldron of flaming oil. Thereby all evils are overcome and destroyed.

Following this rite there comes a procession of monks, preceded by maskers and followed by laity, bearing a three-headed human image made of dough, which is ceremoniously abandoned, somewhat in the manner that a Jewish scapegoat is abandoned. Then the laity, rushing upon the abandoned effigy, tear it to pieces and fiercely compete with one another for the fragments, which, as in the previous scene, are treasured as talismans.

myth that the Orphic priests dramatized in their own Mystery-Play, which was enacted only before neophytes and initiates. In the Omophagic Rites, the myth was represented by the sacrifice of a man and the dismemberment of his body. The devotees tore the flesh to bits, and, eating it, participated in the divine nature of Zagreus. By the end of the third century B.C. this sacramental rite, as then celebrated in Rome and Italy, had so degenerated that, finally, it led to the enactment of the famous *De Bacchanalibus* Edict, which banished the Mysteries from the whole of the Italian Peninsula. Speaking of this edict, Pliny (*Hist. Nat.*, xxx. 1) tells us that 'it was regarded as a supreme act of religion to slay a man and as a most salutary act to eat his body'. In the Egyptian Mysteries a similar rite was dramatized and enacted, representing the death of Osiris, as slain by his brother Typhon and Typhon's companions. The body was cut up into twenty-six pieces. These were cast into the Sacred River Nile and afterwards collected, with the exception of one, by the Goddess Isis. (Cf. Baring-Gould, *Origin and Development of Religious Belief*, London, 1869, i. 405–7). Similar parallels exist in the religious records of many other peoples, throughout the New as throughout the Old World.

Meanwhile, the Lāmas return in procession to the temple and celebrate a special service. Finally, with a ritual dance by the black-hat devil-dancers followed by the appearance of the Chinese priest entitled Hwashang, whom Padma Sambhava expelled from Tibet, the Mystery-Play ends.

### XI. THE KINCHINJUNGA WAR-DANCE

There is a Sikkimese adaptation of the Mystery-Play said to have been established by Chagdor Namgyal, the sixth Mahārāja of Sikkhim. It is a mystic war-dance in worship of the spirit of Kinchinjunga, Sikkim's mighty five-peaked sacred mountain, whose altitude is but slightly less than that of Mount Everest. By invitation of the present Mahārāja, I was privileged to be his only European guest to witness its annual celebration in the courtyard of his palace in Gangtok, during the two days of its performance, on the 19th and 20th of December 1919.

Popularly known as the Snowy-Range Dance, this festival is essentially a religious rite of purification, being performed by the Sikkimese Lāmas, under the personal supervision of the Mahārāja, for the purpose of exorcizing all evil from the State. In the older Mystery-Play of Ladāk and Tibet, this evil, as we have seen, is personified by demon actors and a human effigy called the Enemy. In the Sikkimese War-Dance, too, an effigy, having similar significance, is brought in and placed prostrate in the centre of the palace court-yard and danced around by two skeletons. The other dancers close in on the effigy; and then, with piercing war cries, raise their bared swords and plunge them thrice into the effigy, scattering in all directions the floury substance of which it is made. On the second day of the Dance, unlike its Ladāk prototype, there is only a paper effigy. This is burnt to symbolize the utter destruction of all evil afflicting man and beast, crops, and the State.

Both in the Snowy-Range Dance and in the Mystery-Play, the destruction of the Enemy esoterically symbolizes the destruction of Ignorance, just as the mystic renunciation of personality and the consequent destruction of egoism does in the *Chöd* Rite.

The food-offerings made to the deities associated with the worship of Kinchinjunga in the War-Dance consist of small triangular cone-shaped cereal cakes called *tourma*, which means 'that strewn [to all]'. According to the Sikkimese Lāmas, these are symbolical of the threefold offering (the body, speech, and mind of every sentient being) to the Buddhas. This, too, is paralleled in the *Chöd* Rite. The sacrificial *tourmas* are finally set on fire in a triangular cone made of dry grass and foliage and reduced to ashes. Thereby the offering is transmuted into Voidness, which in this ritual signifies the Divine Essence infused in all *sangsāric* things. Of like significance is the transmutation of the *yogin's* body into divine ambrosia in virtue of the renunciation, or 'cutting-off', of egoism, in the celebration of the *Chöd* Rite.

## XII. THE ANTHROPOLOGICAL INTERPRETATION

In the *Chöd* Rite, as in the Tibetan Mystery-Play and Sikkimese War-Dance, the anthropologist will discern much valuable data appertaining to the age-long history of human sacrifice, from the time when human sacrifice was performed in reality, and not as nowadays in Tibet and elsewhere in effigy, right up to to-day, when human sacrifice has been sublimated into a highly symbolic form of sacramentalism as illustrated by the doctrine of transubstantiation. The sacramental eating of the flesh and drinking of the blood of the god appears to have found expression in almost all known epochs and conditions of human society, from the lowest savagery to the high culture of the ancient Greeks.

Prior to the coming of Buddhism, the Tibetans under the Bönpas, and no doubt long prior to Bönism, were accustomed not only to human and animal sacrifice, but, according to trustworthy evidence, practised cannibalism, possibly of a religious and sacramental character, as have many of the ancestral stocks of the present European races, including those of Great Britain and Ireland. Then, as shown by the Tibetan rituals, largely of pre-Buddhistic origin, which we have briefly reviewed, there came a cultural transition, parallel to that of the Occident, from sacrifice in effigy to transubstantiational sacrifice, employed as a transcendental form of exorcism intended to purify and sanctify the communicant spiritually.

An interesting illustration of one stage in this cultural transition is to be seen in the words of the ritual of the Kinchinjunga War-Dance which are spoken in the worship of the Spirit of Kinchinjunga by the Herald who represents Mahā-kāla, the Over-Lord of all the Sikkimese Faith-Guarding Deities :

'Arrows, spears, swords, and martial arms are turned towards the Enemy, flashing and glistening. Mountains of dead are consumed as food. Oceans of blood are drunk as draughts. The five senses are used as garlands of flowers. The organs of the senses are eaten as sweet-meats.'

Another stage is illustrated by the ritual which has come to be called 'The Eucharist of Lāmaism'. Therein the priestly officiant first mystically draws into his own heart the divine essence, by the intermediary of the image of the Buddha Amitāyus, the Buddha of Infinite Life, and then, taking an altar-vase filled with holy-water which has already been consecrated, sprinkles some of the sacred fluid on the food offered as a propitiatory sacrifice to the demons, chanting as he does so :

'I have purified it [i.e. the rice offerings] with [the *mantra*] *Svabhāva*, and converted it into an ocean of nectar within a precious *Bhum*-bowl.'

Having so appeased the forces of evil, the priest proceeds with the mass-like ceremony until, finally, the celestial Buddhas and *Bodhisattvas*, and other deities, having been invoked, transmute the holy-water into divine ambrosia. Then, to the music of cymbals, the priest intones the following chant :

'This vase is filled with the immortal ambrosia which the Five Orders of Celestial Beings have blessed with the best life. May life be permanent as adamant, victorious as the King's banner, strong like the eagle, and everlasting. May I be favoured with the gift of undying life and all my wishes be realized.'[1]

The mystical transmutation having been accomplished, each communicant receives from the priest, into the hollow of the hand, a little of the consecrated water, and then a drop of consecrated wine from a skull-cup. This wine having been upon the altar throughout the whole of the ceremony has been infused, like the water, with the immortality-conferring essence of the Divine Ones. The communicant also receives three holy pellets, from a plateful which has been sanctified by the priest's touch. These are made of flour, sugar, and butter. After all of the communicants have partaken of the water, the wine, and the pellets, there follows the *lāmaic* benediction by the laying on of hands by the priest, wherewith the service for the conferring of everlasting life ends.

### XIII. THE *BODHISATTVA*'S MYSTIC SACRIFICE

As a fitting conclusion to this outline exposition of sacramental sacrifice as it presents itself throughout its long historical development, chiefly in pre-Buddhistic Tibet, Kashmir, and Sikkim, we place before the reader what is perhaps the highest and most sublime aspect of the doctrine yet evolved by mankind. The matter used in illustration is derived from that remarkable compendium of Buddhist teachings known as the *Śiksha-Samaccaya*, compiled by Sāntideva, chiefly from early Mahāyāna *Sūtras*, and now translated from a Sanskrit manuscript brought from Nepal by the late Mr. Cecil Bendall, formerly Professor of Sanskrit in the University of Cambridge.[2]

In the *Nārāyaṇa-Paripṛcchā* it is said, 'The *Bodhisattva* must think thus: "I have devoted and abandoned my frame to all creatures; and much more so my outward possessions. Any being who shall require it for any purpose, it being

---

[1] Cf. L. A. Waddell, *op. cit.*, p. 447.

[2] Cf. *Śiksha-Samaccaya* as translated by C. Bendall and W. H. D. Rouse (London, 1922), pp. 23-8.

recognized for a good, I will give hand, foot, eye, flesh, blood, marrow, limbs great and small, and my head itself, to such as ask for them; not to mention external things—wealth, corn, gold, silver, gems, ornaments, horses, elephants, chariots, cars, villages, towns, markets, peoples, kingdoms, capital cities, menservants, maidservants, messengers, sons, daughters, and retinue." '

All things that the *Bodhisattva* possesses, even his own body, he vows to renounce 'without regret and without grudging, without waiting for merit to mature', and 'out of compassion and pity', in order that others, 'as by one who hath attained wisdom, may learn to know the Law'.

Likewise, in the *Akshayamati Sūtra*, the *Bodhisattva* says : 'I must wear out even this, my body, for the behests of all creatures.' And in the *Vajradhvaja Sūtra* we are told, 'So, indeed, [is] the *Bodhisattva* giving himself amongst all creatures by aiding all roots of good, regarding all creatures in their roots of good, offering himself as a lamp amongst all creatures, establishing himself amongst all creatures, as their happiness. Thus, indeed, if the *Bodhisattva* is asked for his tongue, he sitteth down and speaketh with lovable and friendly voice, prompted by friendly thoughts; and, seating him in a goodly couch fit for a king, he addresseth that suitor with pleasure. He becometh unangered in mind, unoffended, not vexed, with mind absorbed in magnanimity, with mind like that of the Buddha's race, with the chain of his thought unwavering in nature, full of strength and power, with mind not fixed upon his body, not devoted to talking, his body resting on the knees; putting all his body at the service of the suitor, he speaketh from his own mouth, uttering words that are affectionate, gentle, and gracious, a friendly service. "Take thou my tongue; do with it as seemeth thee good. Do so as pleaseth thee, that thou be pleased at heart and satisfied with thyself, contented and delighted with pleasure." With these words he sacrificeth his head, bringing about the highest knowledge which is the topmost head of all things, attaining the wisdom which is the head of the salvation of all creatures, craving incomparable knowledge which is the chiefest head of all the world, resolved to attain the kingship of knowledge, the headship of all regions, desirous of accomplishing the culmination of lordship over transcendent things, with a mind bursting with affection for an endless number of applicants.'

Only the Body of Truth, the *Dharma-Kāya* itself, does the *Bodhisattva* value : ' He cherisheth the idea of a body uncut, unbroken, undiminished, which consisteth in the Body of the Law, formed by Unobstructed Wisdom.' And 'attentively remembering that the body hath its end in the cemetery, regarding his body as food for wolves, jackals, and dogs, remembering that it is the share of others', the *Bodhisattva* 'applying his reflection to the Law', meditateth thus: ' " Whether I give from this body the intestines, liver, heart, or lungs to the suitor, or do not give them, this body, not being eternal, at the end of my life is owed to the cemetery." Thus he with nature content and satisfied, with knowledge of the Law, with resolve established in the idea of the good friend, at the instance of a suitor desirous of extracting the essence from this non-essential body, through love of the Law, even when he sacrificeth only a nail from his own flesh with the thought, " This is applied to the root of good ", thus renounceth his own body.'

Even so does the *yogin* in performing the mystic ' cutting-off' renounce all worldly things, even his own fleshly body, through love of the Law of Good. Then, when every attachment to *sangsāric* existence shall have been sundered thereby and the great Emancipation won, he, too, will take the vow of the *Bodhisattva* and enter upon the Higher Path.

# THE SCIENCE-TRANSCENDING WISDOM

' I entered, but I know not where,
And there I stood naught knowing,
All science transcending.'— St. John of the Cross,
*The Ecstasy of Contemplation* (David Lewis's translation).

'Let this be my prayer ; but do thou, dear Timothy, in the diligent exercise of mystical contemplation, leave behind thee the senses and the operations of the intellect, and all things sensible and intellectual, and all things in the world of being and non-being, that thou mayest arise, by Unknowing, towards the union, so far as is attainable, with Him who transcendeth all being and knowledge.

\*     \*     \*

'We pray that we may come unto this Darkness which is beyond Light, and, without seeing and without knowing, see and know that which is above vision and knowledge, through the realization that by not-seeing and by not-knowing we attain True Vision and True Knowledge.

\*     \*     \*

'For the higher we soar in contemplation the more limited becometh our expressions of that which is purely intelligible ; even as now, when plunging into the Darkness which is above the intellect, we pass not merely into brevity of speech, but even into Absolute Silence, of thoughts as well as of words.'— Dionysius the Areopagite, *The Mystical Theology* (Version by the Editors of the Shrine of Wisdom).

# [THE PATH OF THE MYSTIC SACRIFICE: THE *YOGA* OF SUBDUING THE LOWER SELF]

## *AUM!*

## [THE *YOGIC* DANCE WHICH DESTROYETH ERRONEOUS BELIEFS]

(1) Now visualize thyself as having become, instantaneously,[1]
The Goddess of the All-Fulfilling Wisdom,[2]
Possessed of the power of enlarging thyself to the vastness of the Universe,[3]
And endowed with all the beauties of perfection;
[Then] blow the human thigh-bone trumpet[4] loudly,

---

[1] There are two processes of mentally creating, or visualizing, as taught by the Tibetan *Gurus*: (1) the Gradual Process, by forming in the mind round some central idea as a nucleus, little by little, the visualization desired till it be sharply defined; and (2) the Instantaneous Process, as in this text, likened to a fish instantaneously leaping out of the element water into the element air.

[2] Text: *Yeshes-mkhah-hgro-ma* (pron. *Yeshĕ-khah-do-ma*), one of the higher order of the spiritual beings called by the Tibetans *khahdoma*, equivalent to the Sanskrit *ḍākinī*. They are believed to render divine assistance, especially in *yoga*, to whomsoever appeals to them when about to perform a difficult ritual like that now under consideration. The *yogin* while performing this ritual must visualize himself as being the Goddess herself; and his own body, about to be offered up in the mystic sacrifice in sign of his renunciation of the lower self, he is to look upon as something apart, as a mere conglomeration of flesh and bones, which he is abandoning for ever.

[3] The need of this visualization is particularly emphasized in 'The Visualization of the Corpse and Wrathful Goddess', which follows. A similar *yogic* practice is set forth in the text of the Doctrine of the Psychic-Heat, paragraph 15.

[4] Many of the symbolic adornments used by Tibetan and other Tantric *yogins*, such as necklaces, breastlets, rosaries, and objects like the thigh-bone trumpet, for use in rituals, are made of human bones to signify their possessors' utter renunciation of the world.

And dance the Dance which Destroyeth Erroneous Beliefs.[1]


*Phaṭ!* [2]

(2)  I, the *yogin*, who practise the Dauntless Courage,[3]
     Devoting my thought and energy wholly to the realiz-
     ing that *Nirvāṇa* and the *Sangsāra* are in-
     separable,
     Am dancing this measure on [the forms of] spiritual
     beings who personify the self; [4]
     May I [be able to] destroy the *sangsāric* view of
     duality.[5]


[1] Or the ' Dance of Devotional Zeal '.

[2] The Sanskrit word *Phaṭ!* (as an interjection) is onomatopoeic, somewhat like the English interjection Bang! and, as here, is expressive of the culmination of a psychic climax. It is placed throughout this text at the head of each stanza of the dance measure, and, in some instances, at the end of stanzas. The use of *Phaṭ!* according to the *gurus*, is three-fold : (1) Exoterically, for recalling a mentally distracted mind to one-pointedness, with respect to any *yogic* practice or meditation being undertaken ; (2) Internally, as in this ritual, to emphasize the seriousness of the offering of one's body to elemental beings ; and (3) Esoterically, for attaining spiritual insight of such intuitive character as will enable the *yogin* to analyse and synthesize all mental processes. (Cf. p. 272ᵇ.)

[3] In other words, the *yogin* practising this rite must be of dauntless, or indomitable, courage, and free even from the fear of death.

[4] The *yogin* must visualize as he dances that he is treading under foot the forms of *sangsāric*, or illusory, beings, which, throughout the *Chöd* Rite, are to be thought of as being human corpses. (Cf. p. 175².) This symbolizes the treading under foot of, or in other words the renunciation of, human life ; and shows that the *yogin*'s aim in the performing of the rite is to attain to freedom from the spiritually cramping belief in the personal self, as something independent of the physical organism. It is this Wrong Belief which must be destroyed by the realizing of Right Belief. If the weird dance happens to be performed, as it often is, in some place of cremation or locality where corpses are thrown to the wild beasts and birds of the air, as they are throughout most of Tibet, and the *yogin* sees there an uncremated or undevoured corpse, he will be likely to displace the visualization for the actuality. He thus follows his *guru*'s instructions to put to the severest of tests the ' Dauntless Courage '.

[5] So long as one is dominated by the belief in an ego, as being something separate and for ever distinct from all other egos, a dualistic view of life is inevitable. Even the Ultimate Duality, the *Sangsāra* and *Nirvāṇa* as the two poles of being, must, at last, be realized to be a Unity.

Come to the Dance, ye revered *Gurus* of the Root
Faith ; [1]

Come, ye Heroes and Heroines,[2] as innumerable as the
drops of the Ocean ;

Come to the Dance, ye Sky-Traversing Ones,[3] who
wander everywhere :

May this zealous devotion [of mine] be successful ;
vouchsafe your blessings upon it.


[THE *YOGIC* DANCE OF THE FIVE DIRECTIONS] [4]

*Phaṭ !*

(3)  When I beat this measure in the Eastern Continent of
Superior Physique,[5]

The Heroes and Heroines move round in a crescent-
shaped dancing-arena ; [6]

Their feet flash [as they dance] upon [the prostrate
forms of] King Spirits, who symbolize Hatred or
Wrath ; [7]

---

[1] These are the *Gurus* of the Apostolic Succession of the Ñingmapa School,
referred to here as of the Root (or Original) Faith.

[2] The Heroes and Heroines belong to an order of elementary spiritual beings
comparable to the *Vīras* of Hindu belief.

[3] These are the *Khahdoma* (Skt. *Ḍākinī*). (See p. 45[1].)

[4] These are the four cardinal directions and the centre.

[5] This refers to the Eastern 'Continent' called in Tibetan *Lüpah*, meaning
'Vast Body', and in Sanskrit *Virat-deha*. It is one of the four chief 'Continents' (i.e. Worlds), situated in the Four Directions of which Mt. Meru,
like a central sun, is the gravitational centre. Its inhabitants live four times as
long as human beings, are taller, and in every way superior to them in physique.
The symbolical colour white is assigned to it. Its diameter measures 9,000 miles.

[6] This symbolic shape of the dancing-arena is in correspondence with that of
*Lüpah*, which is shaped like a crescent moon.

[7] King Spirits, as explained in the Introduction to this Book V, are discarnate
Lāmas who when incarnate practised black magic. As such, they are very
powerful on the 'astral' plane, and cannot be exorcized save by priests of great
spiritual development. King Spirits, having been disappointed in their worldly
aims, are inclined to be very malignant towards human and all other embodied
beings. Hence they here symbolize Hatred or Wrath, which the *yogin* treads
under foot in his ecstatic dance.

They sound the Flute of the Mirror-like Wisdom.[1]

*Hūṃ.   Hūṃ.   Hūṃ.*[2]

*Phaṭ!*

(4)  When dancing in the Southern Continent, the Human
World,[3]
The Heroes and Heroines move round in a triangular
dancing-arena ;
Their feet flash [as they dance] upon the [prostrate]
Head of Pride, embodied in the Lord of Death.[4]
They drum upon the skull-drums of the Wisdom of
Equality, with a peculiar sharp tapping sound.

*Hūṃ.   Hūṃ.   Hūṃ.*

*Phaṭ!*

(5)  When dancing in the Western Continent, blessed with
cattle,[5]

---

[1] For detailed exposition of the Mirror-like Wisdom and of each of the other
of the Five Wisdoms, which are mentioned in the next four stanzas, reference
should be made to Book VI, following.   Here, and in the next three stanzas,
a musical note is associated with the first four of the Five Wisdoms, and the
fifth is symbolized by a tiara.   The esoteric meaning implied thereby is that the
*yogin*, by the treading under foot, destroys in himself the particular passion
named in each of the stanzas, namely, Hatred or Wrath, Pride, Lust, Jealousy,
and Stupidity or Slothfulness, which are the five chief obstacles at the beginning
of the Path leading to Spiritual Emancipation.   And with each passion its
antidote is given, as in this stanza, where the antidote for Hatred or Wrath is
the exorcizing note of the Flute of the Mirror-like Wisdom.

[2] Concerning the significance of this use of the *mantra Hūṃ*, see Book VI,
following, which is concerned entirely with the esotericism of the *Hūṃ* in its
long form.

[3] The Southern 'Continent' is our Planet Earth, called by the Tibetans
*Jambuling* (Skt. *Jambudvīpa*).   Its symbolic shape, to which the dancing-arena
mentioned in the following verse conforms, is sub-triangular, or rather pear-
shaped, like the faces of its inhabitants.   Blue is the colour assigned to it.
Being the smallest of the Four Continents, its diameter is said to be 7,000 miles.

[4] The Lord of Death, mythologically of Hindu origin, is Yama, known in
Tibetan as Shinje (*Shin-rje*), the Osiris-like judge of the Dead, and the Controller of Rebirth, who, being of proud and haughty, but righteous, demeanour,
here symbolizes Pride.   The treading of Yama under foot signifies that the
*yogin* is striving to overcome all *karmic* necessity for further incarnation in
*sangsāric* forms.

[5] The Western 'Continent' is known in Tibetan as *Balangchöd* and in
Sanskrit as *Godāna*, meaning 'Gift of Oxen'.   It is red of colour and round

The Heroes and Heroines move round in a circular
   dancing-arena ;[1]
Their feet flash [as they dance] upon the [prostrate]
   head of the Ogress of Lust ;
They tinkle the bells of the Discriminating Wisdom in
   sweet harmonious tones.
             *Hūṃ.  Hūṃ.  Hūṃ.*

             *Phaṭ !*

(6) When dancing in the Northern Continent of Unpleasant Sound,[2]
The Heroes and Heroines move round in a square
   dancing-arena ;[3]
Their feet flash [as they dance] upon the [prostrate]
   heads of the mischievous Sprites of Jealousy ;
The tiara of the All-Fulfilling Wisdom glisteneth
   brightly.[4]
             *Hūṃ.  Hūṃ.  Hūṃ.*

             *Phaṭ !*

(7) When dancing in the Centre of the Perfectly Endowed
   Spot,[5]

like the Sun. Its inhabitants, whose faces are likewise round, are said to be
very powerful physically and to be addicted to eating cattle. In diameter it is
8,000 miles.

   [1] The text here, and in the stanza second above, through error, due to
transposition, assigns to the dancing-arena of the Eastern 'Continent' the circular
shape of the Western 'Continent' and vice versa. In the translation the error
has been corrected.

   [2] The name of this 'Continent', in Tibetan *Daminyan*, is here translatable
as referring to a world of unpleasant sound. It is known in Sanskrit as
*Uttara-kuru*, meaning 'Northern Kuru'. It is of square shape and green colour.
Correspondingly, its inhabitants have squarish faces like those of horses. It is
the largest of the Four 'Continents', being 10,000 miles in diameter.

   [3] Here, too, the shape of the dancing-arena corresponds to the shape of the
'Continent'.

   [4] A tiara of human skulls is worn by the Goddess of the All-Fulfilling Wisdom,
of whom the *yogin* has become, in virtue of the visualization prescribed by the
first stanza of this ritual, the external yet illusory representative. (See p. 174[4].)

   [5] 'Perfectly Endowed Spot' (Tib. *Lhūndub-tse*) refers to a celestial region
wherein all things desired are immediately at hand as soon as desired, without
any effort of seeking or asking for them save the mental effort. Cosmologically,
it refers to Mt. Meru, the gravitational centre of the 'Continents'. Following

The arena for the dance of the Heroes and Heroines
  is blessed [with their divine influence];
Their feet flash [as they dance] upon the [prostrate]
  head of the Vampire of Stupidity;
The joyous songs of *Hūṃ*, of the Wisdom of the Real
  Essence,[1] sound melodiously.
    *Hūṃ. Hūṃ. Hūṃ.*

## [THE TRANSFIXING OF THE ELEMENTALS OF SELF]

(8) [Instructions to the *yogin*:] Think that now thou art
about to transfix the Elementals of Self with Spears.

*Phaṭ!*

(9)   The Divine *Ḍākinī* cometh from the East,
Carrying the Spear of All-embracing Love;
The Precious *Ḍākinī* cometh from the South,
Carrying the Spear of Great Compassion;
The Lotus *Ḍākinī* cometh from the West,
Carrying the Spear of Great Affection;
The *Karma Ḍākinī* cometh from the North,
Carrying the Spear of Great Impartiality;
The Buddha *Ḍākinī* cometh from the Centre,
Carrying the Spear of *Bodhisattvic* Mind:
Standing on the [prostrate] heads of the Elementals of
  Egoism,
And on their four limbs, in them they implant their
  Spears,

the symbolism of the Tibetan *Ch'orten,* which corresponds to the *Chaitya*
and *Stūpa* of Indian, and the *Dāgaba* of Sinhalese, Buddhism, the shapes
assigned to the five dancing-arenas convey the following significance: the
square typifies the solidity of the Earth upon which the *Ch'orten* rests, and thus
the Element Earth; the circle, like the corresponding shape of the water-drop,
symbolizes the Element Water; the triangle, shaped like a flame. symbolizes
the Element Fire; the crescent, like the inverted vault of the sky, symbolizes
the Element Air; and the Element Ether is symbolized by the Centre (parallel
to the acuminated circle tapering in flame into space) of the 'Perfectly Endowed
Spot'. (Cf. *Tibet's Great* Yogī *Milarepa,* facing p. 269.)

[1] Otherwise known as the All-Pervading Wisdom of the *Dharma-Dhātu*
('Seed, or Potentiality, of Truth'), or the Wisdom born of the Voidness, which
is all pervading.

Transfixing them immovably, and remain there motionless [at peace].[1]

*Phaṭ!*

(10) [Instructions to the *yogin* :] Having recognized the
Elementals [Hatred or Wrath, Pride, Lust, Jealousy, and
Stupidity, of which egoism is composed] now thou must
recognize the [sacrificial] gift of thy body.[2]

## [THE VISUALIZING OF THE *GURUS* AND DEITIES]

*Phaṭ!*

(11) In the Supreme Blissfulness of the Clear Light of
Primordial Consciousness,

[1] The *Ḍākinī* are here to be regarded as like mother-goddesses majestically
divine in appearance, possessed of spiritually purifying and exorcizing powers,
and as exercising functions similar to those of the angels of Christianity, or of
the daemons of Greek and Pagan mysticism. Each of the Five *Ḍākinī* herein
named is related to, and is the embodiment of the divine antidote of, one of the
Five Passions composing Egoism, which are above personified as Hatred (or
Wrath), Pride, Lust, Jealousy, and Stupidity. There is also a colour and a
characteristic assigned to each of them ; to the Divine (or *Vajra*) *Ḍākinī*, white
(sometimes blue) and peacefulness; to the Precious (or *Ratna*) *Ḍākinī*, yellow
and grandness ; to the Lotus (or *Padma*) *Ḍākinī*, red and fascination ; to the
*Karma Ḍākinī* (or *Ḍākinī* of Action), green and sternness; and to the Buddha
*Ḍākinī* (or *Ḍākinī* of Enlightenment), dark-blue and Knowledge of the Truth.
As in the text, the first four are endowed with one of the four kinds of Divine
Action, namely, Love, Compassion, Affection, and Impartiality (or Justice), all
of which are attributes of the *Bodhisattvic* Mind, wherewith, in its spiritual
completeness, the Buddha *Ḍākinī* is related. The divine antidote for Hatred is
Love ; for Pride, Compassion; for Lust, Altruistic Affection ; for Jealousy,
Impartiality ; and for Stupidity (or Ignorance : *Avidyā*) it is Enlightenment.
Furthermore, the Five *Ḍākinī* in this *yoga* of the 'cutting-off' are the active
agents of the Five Buddhas of Meditation, assigned to the Five Directions,
East, South, West, North, and the Centre. With reference to the Five Buddhas
of Meditation. see Book VI, which follows.

[2] Here a very free translation might be made to bring out the fuller meaning
implied : 'Having identified thyself with the nature of the Elementals and
annihilated them, now thou must undergo the ordeal of identifying thy lower
self with thy body and giving thy body in sacrifice.' At this stage, the *yogin*
must comprehend that it is the body which gives to him the illusion of a personal existence, separate and apart from all other living things, and that to
overcome this egoism he must renounce the body even as he renounced the
world, and strive for divine at-one-ment with the One-Reality, Primordial
Mind, as manifested in the Great Beings of Wisdom and Compassion called
*Bodhisattvas.*

> Of that state which transcendeth action, volition, and
>     *sangsāric* mind,[1]
> Thy Root-*Guru*, Vajra-Dhāra, the Sixth [Dhyānī
>     Buddha, as the Ādi-Buddha],
> And all the Line of the *Gurus* of the Telepathic,
>     Symbolic, and Ear-whispered Truths,[2]
> And the *Ḍākinīs* and the Truth-Guarding Ones,[3] both
>     Gods and Goddesses,
> Gathering together as numerously as storm-clouds, are
>     to be visualized vividly,
> Amidst a halo of rainbow hues and dazzling radiance.

(12) [Instructions to the *yogin*:] Here look upon these deities with deep faith, and rely wholly upon them.

## [THE *YOGIN'S* PRAYER]

### *Phaṭ!*

> (13) This Intellect [or Mind], which dawneth of Itself alone,
>     being the Uncreated,
> [By the unenlightened] is not realized to be the True
>     Protector;
> O may it come to pass that those who are submerged
>     in the Ocean of Sorrow[4]
> Shall be protected by the Mind of the Primordial
>     Trinity [or the *Tri-Kāya*].

(14) [Instructions to the *yogin*:] Recite thrice the above prayer and mentally concentrate upon it. [Then there cometh the resolution which followeth.]

---

[1] This, as a reflex of the *Nirvāṇic* State, corresponds to an ecstatic condition of profound intuitive insight into Reality, induced by the highest *samādhi*, into which, for the purpose of this visualization, the *yogin* must enter.

[2] See pp. 150[1], 171 § 4, 271 above.

[3] These belong to an order of daemons, whose function it is to safeguard Truth (Skt. *Dharma*), known in Tibet as *Ch'os-skyon* (Skt. *Dharma-pāla*).

[4] The 'Ocean of Sorrow' is the *Sangsāra*, or the phenomenal universe, wherein the unenlightened are fettered to the Wheel of Life, to the interminable round of death and rebirth, as a result of their own *karma*.

## [THE *YOGIN*'S RESOLUTION]

*Phaṭ!*

(15) O! the unenlightened mind, which looketh upon the
    apparent as being the Real,
    May it be thoroughly subdued [by me] in virtue of
      religious practices;
    And thus in order to master and thoroughly compre-
      hend the true nature of the Real,
    I resolve to free myself of all hope and of all fear.

(16) [Instructions to the *yogin*:] Now, in performing the
sacrifice,[1] imagine thy body to be constituted of every desirable [worldly] thing.[2]

## [THE DEDICATION OF THE ILLUSORY BODY IN SACRIFICE]

*Phaṭ!*

(17) This illusory body, which I have held to be so precious,
    I dedicate [in sacrifice] as a heaped-up offering,
    Without the least regard for it, to all the deities that
      constitute the visualized assembly;
    May the very root of self be cut asunder.

*Phaṭ!*

(18) [Directions to the *yogin*:] Next cometh the prayer to
the *Gurus*.

---

[1] This phrase in a more literal rendering would be, 'Then, in offering the
*maṇḍala*', the *maṇḍala* being the sacrificial offerings arranged so as to form a
symbolic geometrical figure. The *maṇḍala* in this context is the *yogin*'s own
fleshly body.

[2] These desirable things are all those purely mundane things, such as sensuous
pleasures, worldly pursuits, and ambitions, which for the unenlightened constitute life and bind mankind to physical existence. The mystic sacrifice must
be complete; it must include not only the physical body, but all the elements of
*sangsāric* sensuousness, and, thus, everything which comprises ego, or human
personality. As the ritual proceeds, the reader who happens to be somewhat
acquainted with occultism will readily discern within it more than a *yogic*
exercise designed to aid the *yogin* to attain selflessness, for it describes in
symbolic language, akin to that of the Mysteries of Antiquity, a great mystic
drama of initiation.

## [THE PRAYER TO THE *GURU*]

*Phaṭ!*

(19) In the indestructible Realm of the *Dharma-Kāya*,
In the midst of rainbow halo and dazzling radiances,
O Father Omniscient, Knower of Past, Present, and
Future, Thou Lotus-Born One,[1]
Appearing in the guise of a penance-practising *Heruka*,[2]
Accompanied by the *Mātrikās*[3] and innumerable
groups of *Ḍākinīs*,
Radiant with majestic beauty of form and gracefulness,
Proclaiming religious teachings in deep sonorous voice,
With thy mind ever tranquil in the Clear Light of the
Essence of Divine Wisdom,
I, thy son, in fervent faith and humility, pray unto thee.
Externally mine own thought-creations, which have
risen up against me as enemies in the shape of
deities and daemons,
Internally the concept of dualism, whence come hopes
and fears,
In the centre[4] the various illusory phenomena, which
are evil obstructions [on the Path],—

[1] The Lotus-Born One is the 'Precious *Guru*', Padma Sambhava. Before
his advent in Tibet, Padma Sambhava was a very illustrious professor of the
Occult Sciences in the far-famed Buddhistic University of Nālanda, which in
his day was probably the greatest seat of learning in the world.

[2] A *Heruka*, or 'Unclad [One]', is a purely Tantric personification of
Divine Powers. Esoterically, the term *Heruka* refers to a devotee of high rank,
who is 'unclad' or 'naked' with respect to all *sangsāric* things, of which he has
divested himself. (Cf. pp. 174⁷-5¹.)

[3] The *Mātrikās* (or *Mātris*) are the protecting Mother-Goddesses of the Hindu
pantheon. They are said to appear in repulsive guise, as does the great Mother-
Goddess Kāli; for so beautiful are they in their true form that if thus seen by
the unperfected *yogin* they would be apt to arouse in him uncontrollable sensual
desire.

[4] 'In the centre' refers to those distracting influences affecting *yogic* meditation which are caused by uncontrolled reflexes of such external phenomena as
sights, sounds, smells, and all the other stimuli of the five senses.

May all these be cut off [1] [from me] whilst I sit here
[in my *yogic* posture of devotion],[2]
In virtue of the enemy-eradicating power of this subtle
and deep doctrine.
O Holy Lord and Father, vouchsafe thy grace and
blessing,
That I may attain the Realm of the *Dharma-Kāya.*
*Phaṭ! Phaṭ! Phaṭ!*

(20) [Instructions to the *yogin :*] Keep thy mind in the
state of at-one-ment [or in *yogic* quiesence].

## [THE VISUALIZING OF THE CORPSE AND WRATHFUL GODDESS]

### *Phaṭ!*

(21) Then imagine this body, which is the result of thine
own *karmic* propensities,
To be a fat, luscious-looking corpse, huge [enough to
embrace the Universe],
Then [saying] *Phaṭ !* visualize the radiant Intellect,
which is within thee,
As being the Wrathful Goddess and as standing apart
[from thy body],
Having one face and two hands and holding a knife
and a skull.[3]
Think that she severeth the head from the corpse,

[1] There is here obvious corruption of text, probably attributable to the copyist, so that instead of ' may be cut off', which the context implies, the original is literally translatable as ' truth '.

[2] From the moment when the Elementals, personifying his own lower self, or Egoism, were fixed immovably to the earth with the spears of the *Ḍākinīs,* the *yogin* has been sitting in *yogic āsana,* absorbed in the subtle visualizing exercise which has now given place to the present prayer to, or meditation upon, the *Guru* Padma Sambhava.

[3] The *yogin* must visualize the Goddess as red of colour and as having, in addition to the two eyes, the third eye of wisdom, nude, except for the symbolic adornments (cf. p. 174[6]), and as dancing. She is another aspect of Vajra-Yoginī, known in Tibet as *To-ma,* ' The Wrathful She '.

And setteth it, as a skull [like an enormous cauldron],
    over three skulls placed like legs of a tripod
    embracing the Three Regions,[1]
And cutteth the corpse into bits and flingeth them
    inside the skull as offerings to the deities.
Then think that by [the mystic power of] the rays of
    the three-syllable *mantras, Aum, Ăh, Hūṃ,* and
    *Hā, Hō, Hrī,*[2]
The offerings are wholly transmuted into *amrita,*[3]
    sparkling and radiant.

(22) [Instructions to the *yogin* :] Repeat the above *mantras*
several times, and think that thereby the impurities [of the
body offered in the mystic sacrifice] have been purged away
and the offering as a whole hath been transmuted into *amrita*
and that the *amrita* hath been increased into universe-filling
quantities [for the good of all beings].

### [THE SUMMONS TO THE SACRIFICIAL FEAST]

*Phaṭ!*

(23) Ye objects of worship, the Trinity and the Faith-
    Guarding Deities,
And more especially ye Eight Orders of Spiritual
    Beings and Elementals,

---

[1] The Universe, according to the Buddhism of Tibet, comprises 'The Three
Regions' (Skt. *Trailokya* : Tib. *K'ams-gsum*). These are described above, on
p. 94[1-3].

[2] In employing these *mantras*, the *yogin* must use the proper intonation and
maintain concentration of mind upon the mystic process of the transmutation
which is to result.

[3] *Amrita* is the nectar of the gods, which when partaken of by mortals confers upon them the very great length of life, of hundreds of thousands of years,
enjoyed by the higher gods. Here the *yogin* is to visualize his consecrated body
as having been transmuted into this nectar of the gods, so that it will be pleasing to the various orders of spiritual beings whom he is about to visualize as his
invited guests come to partake of the sacrificial feast.

And ye hosts of evil spirits who are worthy of the charity [afforded by mine offering],[1]

Come ye all here where devotional penance is being observed.

This day, I the fearless *yogin*,

Am offering in sacrifice this illusory body of mine,

This body which createth the distinction between the *Sangsāra* and *Nirvāṇa*,

Having made the skull as vast as the Third-Void Universe [2]

And filled it with inexhaustible quantities of Elixir of Wisdom.

To all of you, enjoying the miraculous power of appearing in whatever shape desired,

This gift is offered most ungrudgingly and without the least feeling of regret.

O ye guests, come ye to this great feast.

The skull-drum, which is the best and rarest of drums, possesseth a clear sound ;

The plaid [or cloth] of human hide [upon which the feast is laid] is wondrous to behold ;

The human thigh-bone trumpet giveth forth a melodious tone ;

The bells, adorned with miniature bells, and the tiara, are fascinating.

As birds of prey [or vultures] flock round a dead body, come ye all here now.

*Phaṭ !*

(24) [Instructions to the *yogin* :] Then offer the feast and dedicate the act [of having offered it].

---

[1] The *yogin* has taken the vow to serve all beings, and therefore the evil spirits are as worthy of his charity as the good spirits ; his altruistic hope of assisting all living things to attain to Enlightenment admits of no partiality.

[2] This refers to the voidness of space as being vast enough to embrace the 'Three Regions' of the Universe ; and the *yogin* must visualize the skull as being correspondingly vast.

## [THE OFFERING OF THE SACRIFICIAL FEAST IN WORSHIP]

*Phaṭ!*

(25) To the Wise *Gurus* of the Three Orders,[1]
From the Primordial Lord [2] downwards,
And from my True *Guru* upwards ;
And to the Tutelary and Faith-Guarding Deities
and *Ḍākinīs*,
I offer, in worship, the Elixir of this Great Corpse.

May all beings, inclusive of myself, and more especially
the genii and evil spirits,
Acquire [as the result of this sacrificial rite] the Twofold Merit to cleanse them of the Twofold
obscuration.[3]

Having successfully carried out the purpose of this
ascetic practice [or penance],
And, in realizing phenomena [to be] illusion, may I
comprehend the Clear Light,
And attain Liberation in the *Dharma-Kāya*, freed
from all fear and awe ;
And vouchsafe [O ye *Gurus* and Deities] your blessing,
to the end that I, too, may become a *Heruka*.
*Phaṭ!*

---

[1] These are the *Gurus* who convey their teachings in the three ways—
namely, by telepathy, by symbols, and by ear-whispered, or secret, vocal
instruction.

[2] The Primordial Lord is the Ādi-Buddha Samanta-Bhadra (Tib. *Kün-tu-
zang-po*), Who is without Beginning or End, the Source of all Truth, and the
Head of all the Divine Hierarchies, according to the ' Great Perfection ', otherwise known as the *Ādi-Yoga*, School, of Padma Sambhava. (See p. vi.)

[3] The Twofold Merit are temporal and spiritual merits ; the former consisting
of such worldly advantages as health, beauty, wealth, and position ; and the
latter, of endowments conferring ability to comprehend the highest religious
truth, such as exalted intelligence, keen powers of discrimination, indomitable
faith, selfless humility, and all-embracing altruism, leading to Liberation. The
Twofold Obscuration are evil passions and habitual propensities born of evil
passions. (Cf. p. 97²⁻³.)

# [THE OFFERING OF THE SACRIFICIAL FEAST
## TO SPIRITUAL BEINGS]

*Phaṭ!*

(26) Be ye *sangsāric* or *non-sangsāric*, ye Eight Orders of
Spirits, ye elementals and non-human beings,

And ye mischievous and malignant hosts of flesh-
eating sprites who would mislead [the devotee],[1]

On the outspread human-hide, covering all the World
Systems,[2]

Heaped up flesh, blood, and bones have been laid out,
as a [sacrificial] offering.

If I consider these to be ' mine ' or as being ' I ', I will
thereby manifest weakness.

Ungrateful would ye all be should ye not enjoy the
offering most heartily.

If ye be in haste, bolt it down uncooked ;

If ye have leisure, cook and eat it, piece by piece ;

And leave not a bit the size of an atom behind.


# [THE DEDICATING OF THE ACT OF SACRIFICE]

*Phaṭ!*

(27) From countless ages in past *sangsāric* existences,
doubtless there are unsettled [*karmic*] accounts
due to flesh-eating.[3]

---

[1] Certain classes of malignant elementals are believed to take delight in distracting and impeding the devotee treading the Path to Liberation. (See p. 219⁴).
The *yogin*, in offering to them in the mystic sacrifice his own body, hopes not
merely to appease them, but to encourage and aid them to overcome their evil
nature and to seek the Holy *Dharma*. As has been set forth in other words in
our General Introduction, on pp. 10 to 14, the Buddhas of Compassion proclaimed
the Truth for the deliverance of all sentient beings—for those most deeply
immersed in the Morass of Ignorance as for those who have caught a glimpse of
the Light, for all species of spirits and elementals, for beings embodied on
Earth, or in sensuous paradises, or in the lowest hells.

[2] Text: *stong-gsum* (pron. *tong-sum*), referring to the Universe as composed
of world-systems, said to be one billion in number or, in other words,
innumerable.

[3] Although the question of a Buddhist's ethical right to eat flesh is nowadays

And to those of my guests for whom compassion is
   begotten by [this] chance [of my seeing them],
Who being weak and powerless [fail to get a share of
   the feast],[1] overlooking none—
To each and every one, satisfying all their desires—
I dedicate this [*maṇḍala*] as being an inexhaustible
   store of sustenance.
And may every being with whom I have [hereby and
   ever] been brought into contact attain to Buddha-
   hood ;
And may all [*karmic*] debts be paid and cleared.
   *Phaṭ !*


## [THE DEDICATING OF THE MERIT OF THE ACT OF SACRIFICE]

*Phaṭ !*

(28) Ah ! when one hath uncoiled, and become emancipated
   from, the concepts of ' pious ' and ' impious ',[2]

more or less controversial among Buddhists, both of the Southern School,
especially in Ceylon, and of the Northern School, in Tibet, there can be no
doubt that in the time of the Great Buddhist Emperor Ashoka, during the third
century B.C., as his surviving edicts on stone prove, the slaying of animals
either in sacrifice or for food was prohibited, in keeping with the Buddha's
teaching against the taking of life. Apparently in agreement with primitive
Buddhism in this matter, our text assumes that evil *karma* accrues from flesh-
eating ; and that this is carried down from the most prehistoric and pre-
Buddhist ages as *karmic* predisposition for the consuming of animal corpses.
In the strange ritual under examination, the *yogin*'s body, as offered in
sacrifice, is actually fleshly, and yet by a subtle mental effort it has been
visualized by him as having been transmuted into elixir. It would seem,
however, that the body appears to the elementals and other classes of unenlightened non-human beings in its natural or untransmuted condition, as so
much flesh, blood, and bones, described in the text above, of which they partake
because of their *karmically* acquired liking for animal or fleshly sacrifice.  In
this respect, they resemble the orders of genii and daemons of ancient India,
Greece, and Rome, to whom animals were offered up.

   [1] This refers to the weakness of *pretas*, or unhappy ghosts, whose hunger
and thirst are never satisfied.
   [2] By one of fully enlightened mind, such dualism as the *saṅgsāric* concepts of ' pious ' and ' impious ' suggest, has been transcended. Dualistic
concepts, being innate in the spiritually undeveloped mind, uncoil, or unfold, of
themselves, and should then be neutralized by Right Knowledge.

There should not remain the least trace of hopes and
    fears ; [1]

Yet, in accordance with the unerring working of the
    interdependent chain [of causes and effects],[2]

May the stream of the accumulation of merits be
    dedicated to the Realm of Truth and be in-
    exhaustible.[3]

*Phaṭ !*

(29) In virtue of the merits arising from this crude, illusory
    gift of mine own body,

May all accumulated *karmic* obligations and unpaid
    balances of the aeons be paid and cleared.

When the Real Truth of the *Dharma* illuminateth my
    nature,

May all of you [i.e. the unenlightened deities and
    elementals at the feast] be born [as humans] and
    become my first disciples.

Thereupon, may the Uncreated Essence of the Pure,
    Unborn Mind

Arise in the nature of the three,—deities, men, and
    elementals ;

And, avoiding the path of the misleading belief in the
    reality of the ' I ' [or Egoism],

May their principle of consciousness be thoroughly
    saturated with the moisture of Love and Com-
    passion.

As for myself, may I complete my ascetic practices
    successfully,

[1] The *yogin* should be selfless, without thought of hopes and fears concerning
his own deliverance or the merits arising from the sacrifice of the self of egoism.

[2] Seeing that effect follows cause unerringly, the stream of merit (as set forth
in the Twelve *Nidānas*, or Interdependent Causes of Rebirth), which has arisen
as a result of the sacrifice, should be dedicated to the good of all beings; for
without such altruistic dedication the merits would normally accrue to the *yogin*
alone. The Twelve *Nidānas* are given, in explanatory detail, in *Tibet's Great
Yogi Milarepa*, p 138[2]. (See, too, herein, pp. 347, 357[2].)

[3] The Realm of Truth, the *Dharma-Dhātu*, is here thought of as being like
an inexhaustible Ocean of Good, which is ever being fed by streams of merit
flowing into it in virtue of such selflessness as the *yogin* herein exhibits.

And [be enabled to] regard pleasure and pain with
equanimity,

And to realize the *Sangsāra* and *Nirvāṇa* as being
indistinguishable.[1]

Triumphing over all Directions,[2] may I be enabled to
serve every being with whom I have come into
contact.

Thus may my divine mission be crowned with success,
And may I attain to the Body of Glory.[3]

*Phaṭ !*

[Here endeth the Rite for Eradicating the *Sangsāric* Self.]


[THE COLOPHON]

[On the last page of the manuscript there is added the
following exhortation to make the best use of the great
opportunity afforded by having attained human birth.]

[1] This is in accordance with the Mahāyānic teachings already referred to in
various annotations above, and in the General Introduction.

[2] This refers to what may be called Psychic or Philosophical Directions,
which the Lāmas symbolically describe by making use of the geometrical figure
of a square, representing the 'Extremes of Belief'. The top of the square
represents the region or direction, of the assertion 'Is'; the bottom, the
opposing region of the assertion 'Is not'; the left-hand side, the region of the
assertion 'Exists'; and the right-hand side, the opposing region of the assertion 'Exists not'. (Cf. p. 143[1].) By triumphing over all such mentally limiting
concepts and dualism, the *yogin* reaches to the Realm of Truth, wherein there
is but Divine At-one-ment. And ever thereafter, so long as he remains in the
human state as a worker for social betterment, he exhibits that divine indifference (which Krishna proclaims in the *Bhagavad-Gītā*) to all the dualistic causes
of disagreement among the unenlightened multitude, such as arise from creeds,
castes, social distinctions, racial discriminations, and all worldly strivings and
ambitions. He looks on at the drama of life with sadness and compassion, as
his eyes behold mankind, like babes in knowledge, struggling for the baubles
and playthings of this world; and he prays that their minds, too, may be
illuminated with the Light of *Bodhic* Wisdom, and their playthings be speedily
outgrown.

[3] The 'Body of Glory', synonymous with the 'Rainbow Body' (referred to
on pp. 80[1], 183[n], 346, is said to be the highest body attainable by a *yogin* who is
still within the *Sangsāra*. It is comparable to the glorified body of the *Christos*,
as seen by the disciples on the Mount of Transfiguration. In the Body of Glory
the master of *yoga* is said to be able to exist for aeons, possessed with the
*siddhi* of appearing and disappearing at will in any of the many mansions of
existence throughout the Universe.

This is the opportunity [which cometh] of our having attained the blessed human state ;
But no certainty is there that death and change may not
overwhelm us at any moment.
In whatever state we may be, we ever meet with sorrow,
And good and evil *karma* inevitably result [and keep us
bound to the Wheel of Life].
Vouchsafe thy grace, O *Guru*, that I [and all beings] may
attain Liberation.

May it [i.e. this Book and its teachings] be auspicious.


## THE ADDENDUM

Herein there are placed on record, in their original textual
order, certain important explanatory directions which the
above version of the *Chöd* Rite lacks.  They are contained,
in the original Tibetan, in a parallel, but more detailed manuscript version of the *Chöd* entitled *Klong Schen Snyingi
Thiglē* (pron. *Long Chen Nyingi Tiglē*), meaning ' Fundamental Essence of the Subtle Truth ', or more literally,
' Heart-Drops from the Great Space '.  As stated in the
Introduction, this, is also the general title of a series of
similar treatises appertaining to the esoteric lore of the Unreformed, or Primitive, School of Tibetan Buddhism.  The
matter which follows thus serves to amplify and elucidate the
smaller, but complete, version of the *Chöd* Rite already set
forth.  In addition, it is of much value anthropologically in
helping to illustrate how the Lāmas have reshaped and given
Buddhistic interpretation to the primitive animism underlying the pre-Buddhistic religion of Tibet called Bön.  The
manuscript itself consists of seven folios, each measuring
fifteen inches in length and three and one-half inches in
width.  Being itself the copy of an older manuscript, its age
is not very great—probably about fifty years.

### I. THE OBJECTS NEEDED FOR PRACTISING THE RITE

Immediately after the ' Obeisance to the One Deeply
Versed in the Knowledge of the Space of Truth, the Great

Bliss-Conferring Lady, the Conqueress of the Lake',[1] and an
Introduction, composed of six verses, referring to the ' Doctrine of the Great Perfection', of *Guru* Padma Sambhava,
the things necessary for the *yogin* who would practise the
*Chöd* Rite are described as follows :

' For overpowering the proud [elementals] by one's being of
    majestic appearance,

A hide, with the claws intact, of a beast of prey ;

A miniature tent, to symbolize one's upward-tending aspira-
    tions ;[2]

A trident-staff, to symbolize one's upward-climbing aims ;

A human thigh-bone trumpet, for controlling genii and
    daemons ;

A *damaru*,[3] for overpowering apparitional beings ;

A bell, with miniature bells attached to it, for dominating
    the *Mātrikās* ;[4]

A bannerette, made of narrow strips of tiger and leopard
    skin and human-hair braid '.[5]

---

[1] Text : *Mtsho-rgyal-ma* (pron. *Tsho-gyal-ma*) : ' Conqueress of the Lake ', a
name, probably initiatory, of *Guru* Padma Sambhava's chief female disciple in
Tibet. Her disciples called her ' the Great Bliss-Conferring Lady ', in recognition of her *yogic* power to confer the Blissfulness of Enlightenment ; and the
Great *Guru* called her ' the One Deeply versed in the Knowledge of the Space
of Truth '. Another famous disciple of the *Guru* was a princess of the Punjab.
Thus, in Tibetan, as in Indian, Buddhism, there was no discrimination on
account of sex ; and woman shared with man the glory of the Faith and the
high privilege, if spiritually qualified, of aiding in its propagation.

[2] The tent is usually of cotton cloth, often ornamented with the *mantric*
syllables *AUM, ĀH, HŪM*, marked upon it in ink or paint, or, according to
Madame David-Neel, ' cut out in blue and red material and sewn on the three
closed sides '. (Cf. A. David-Neel, *With Mystics and Magicians in Tibet*, London,
1931, p. 159.)

[3] The Tibetan *damaru* is made of the upper portions of two human skulls
fastened together at their apex so as to form an hour-glass-shaped double-drum,
of which the sounding surfaces are human hide. The *damaru* is used, somewhat like a timbrel, by Lāmas and *yogins* in religious rites, especially in those
of esoteric and mystic significance ; for its parts are symbolical of the transitoriness of human existence. Knotted cords, which hang loosely from it, strike
against the sounding surfaces as it is twirled, and cause them to sound. Anothei
kind of *damaru*, made of non-human materials, is used by Hindus in rites
connected with the worship of Shiva.

[4] The *Mātrikās*, or Mother-Goddesses, here comprise numerous orders of
*Ḍākinīs* and female deities.

[5] This bannerette symbolizes the conquering of pride.

## II. THE PLACE AND THE MENTAL IMAGERY PRESCRIBED

'Then, in a [solitary], awe-inspiring place,
And free from fear of being overawed by the genii and
    daemons,
Or by any of the influences [or motives] of the Eight
    Worldly Ambitions,[1]
One should be imbued with the virtue of the Four Bound-
    less Wishes;[2]
[And thus] dominate every apparitional appearance [arising
    out of the mind].

'If at this stage one should fail to safeguard oneself by
    means of mental imagery [or visualization],
It would be like giving to the enemy the secret of one's
    strength.
Therefore energetically maintain clarity of intellect,
And uttering *Phat!* think that from within thy heart
A nine-pointed *dorje,* made of thunderbolt iron,
Unbreakable and equipoised, heavy and strong,
Emitting flame-like radiances,
Falleth with the might of a thunderbolt wheresoever one
    mentally projecteth it
Against the local genii and antagonistic spirits with their
    followers,
Rendering them powerless to flee or to be carried away.

---

[1] The Eight Worldly Ambitions are : Profit, and Avoidance of Loss ; Fame,
and Avoidance of Defamation ; Praise, and Avoidance of Disparagement ; Plea ·
sure, and Avoidance of Pain. This and the verse following represent purely
Buddhistic additions to an originally pre-Buddhistic cult.

[2] The Four Boundless Wishes, otherwise known as the Formula of Good-
Wishes, the virtue of which must so fill the nature of the *yogin* as to radiate
from him, as divine compassion, towards all the unenlightened genii, daemons,
and elementals, are as follows :

'May all sentient beings be endowed with happiness and the causes of
    happiness ;
May each of them be separated from pain and the causes of pain ;
May they ever enjoy supreme bliss unalloyed with sorrow ;
May they be freed from attachment and hatred ;
So that their Eight Worldly Ambitions shall be cut down and levelled [or
    overcome].'

Think that thus they are held and cowed down, their heroic
and dignified nature dominated.[1]

'Then, putting aside all conventional feelings of shame or
common hypocritical thoughts,
But holding to devotional confidence with zeal and energy,
Walk with the four exalted steps,
Walk with the vigorous gait [born] of unshakable faith in
the [Perfection] Doctrine.

'Then, summoning the genii and daemons of the invisible
realms,
And the malignant wandering spirits of the locality,
Drive them all before thee like a herd of sheep and
goats,
Compelling them powerlessly to go to the awe-inspiring
place.
And, as soon as they have arrived there,
With the gait of superabundant energy and force,
Catch hold of the legs of all of them,
And whirl them round thy head thrice,
And think that thou dashest them to the ground.
Whilst holding to this visualization,
Throw the hide and the miniature tent to the ground
forcibly.[2]

'[Thereby], howsoever great and influential the genii and
other spiritual beings may be,

---

[1] The primitive animism is herein made particularly prominent by the reference to the world-wide use of iron as an animistic taboo. As among the modern
Celtic peasantry and other peasantries of Europe who resort to bits of iron,
which may be placed in a babe's cradle, or tied to a cow, to ward off inimical
spiritual influences of 'good people' or 'pixies' or similar fairy beings, so in
Tibet, as throughout Asia, Polynesia, Africa, and both Americas, this strange
method of safeguarding against evilly disposed beings of the invisible realms is
common. Being a survival from the prehistoric ages of man's long history, it
suggests, too, that the one mind of man in its workings transcends the superficial barriers of clime, and race, and creed.

[2] To give greater vividness to the visualization, the hide and tent, which,
apparently, symbolize the herded spiritual creatures, and which all the while
the *yogin* has been holding in his hands, are whirled round his head thrice and
then thrown down, with great force, to the earth. (Cf. p. 330.)

They will most certainly be controlled and be made to
  remain passive.[1]
If, however, the devotional firmness of the *yogin* be weak,
He should practise this mental imagery by gradual steps,
  in accordance with his courage.'[2]

### III. DIRECTIONS TO THE *YOGIN*

After this point, the matter of the two manuscripts is
essentially the same.  Apart from a few orthographical variations, there appear no important differences between the two
texts save that in the larger manuscript the directions to the
*yogin* are more detailed and the Goddess of the All-Fulfilling
Wisdom is displaced by the Goddess of the Mysteries (Tib.:
*Sangwa-Yeshē-Khahdoma*).  Thus, in the manuscript now
being considered, just after the stanza describing the dance on
the head of the Vampire of Stupidity, there come the following directions:

' This having been done, then that called the beat of the
  dance is danced without any particular aim.[3]
Then cometh the pitching of the tent.[4]

[1] After the various orders of spiritual beings have been controlled and made
passive, or subject to discipline, they are then to be impelled to obey the commands of the magician-*yogin*, and so assist him.

[2] Quite apart from the psychic phenomena said to result from these *yogic*
practices, the weirdness of the place in which the 'cutting-off' is to be celebrated, and the character of the visualizations, are of themselves quite sufficient
to test the courage of the most fearless of *yogins*.  Accordingly, the *yogin* should
gradually familiarize himself, both mentally and physically, with the environment and the symbolical imagery before proceeding to the practical application
of the *Yoga* of Non-Ego itself.

[3] Ordinarily, a dance is danced for pleasure or to exhibit agility, but in this
religious dance worldliness has no place, and so the dance is said to be danced
without any particular, or worldly, aim.  And in the rest of the ritual, after the
rhythmic dance measure of the five stanzas of the Five Directions, the mode
appears to change or to be less regular and more aimless.  Buddhism itself
prohibits dancing, music, and all performances which are worldly.

[4] Whilst the tent is being pitched, the *yogin* must visualize it as though it
were a prostrate spirit (symbolizing his own physical body, the representative
of Egoism), and imagine that each peg, as he drives it into the ground, is a
thunderbolt (or mystic spear) of iron, driven through one of the legs or arms or
the head of the prostrate spirit and transfixing it immovably.  In the smaller
manuscript, it is the visualized *Ḍākinīs* who come with spears and transfix the
four limbs of the Elementals of Egoism.

And having flung prostrate on its back any of the malignant
   genii or spirits of the locality,
Think that through the five limbs [i.e. the two legs and
   arms and head] of its body
Thunderbolt spears are being driven and are transfixing the
   being.'

Then, after the transfixing, described in a succeeding stanza
of the manuscript, these directions are given :

'Having done so, of these three: human beings (including
   thyself), beneficent spirits, and malignant spirits,
Think not at all, but keep thy mind in a state of quiescence ;
Then, upon having recognized [or understood the nature of]
   the genii and other spiritual beings,
The [rite of] offering up thy body is to be performed.' [1]

## IV. THE VISUALIZING OF THE *MAṆḌALA*

Prior to the offering of the sacrifice there comes this
interesting visualization, which is lacking in the smaller manuscript :

'Then, in offering up the circle of offerings,
Imagine the central part [or spinal-column] of thy body to
   be Mt. Meru,
The four chief limbs to be the Four Continents,[2]
The minor limbs to be the Sub-Continents,[3]
The head to be the Worlds of the *Devas*,

---

[1] The rite is to be performed on behalf of the three classes of beings referred
to : (*a*) human beings, including the *yogin* ; (*b*) beneficent spiritual beings, or
gods, who should be thus worshipped with praise and offerings ; and (*c*) malignant spirits or elementals, who should be led out of their evil ways by the
love manifested in the ritual and turned from their enmity to friendship by
the gift of the fleshly body.

[2] These are named above, in the first four of the stanzas of the Dance of the
Five Directions, in the text of the smaller manuscript. The fifth of the
Directions, or the Centre, refers to the central point of the Cosmos, the centre
of gravitation, symbolized as Mt. Meru ; and here, in keeping with *Kuṇḍalinī
Yoga*, microcosmically represented by the spinal-column.

[3] To each of the Four 'Continents' are assigned two satellites, or Sub-
'Continents', making in all twelve, the number twelve being in this connexion
symbolical, probably like the cabalistic number twelve, which has reference to
the twelve signs of the Zodiac. See *The Tibetan Book of the Dead*, pp. 61-6.

The two eyes to be the Sun and Moon,
And that the five internal organs [1] constitute all objects of
wealth and enjoyment amongst gods and men.'

After the *maṇḍala* has been offered up in worship, the *yogin*
is directed as follows :

' Having done so, mentally absorb the [visualized] objects of
worship into thyself,
And keep thy mind in the equilibrium [or quiescence] of
the non-two state.' [2]

## V. THE MIXED, THE RED, AND THE BLACK FEAST

If incorporated in the smaller manuscript, which lacks them,
the following instructions, as to the various ways in which
the ritual can be applied, would come after the stanza therein
containing the three-syllable *mantras*. The smaller manuscript, however, having been written to expound only the
White-Feast Rite, has been, in essentials, shaped by the
high altruistic ideals of Mahāyānic Buddhism, whereas in
the larger manuscript the primitive animism appears to have
been much less modified.

' If [thou desire] to make a Mixed Feast of the ritual,
mentally produce, from the corpse,[3]
Parks and gardens, food and raiment, and medicaments,
In accordance with thy desires, and multiply them and
transmute them.[4]

---

[1] These are the heart, lungs, liver, kidneys, and spleen.

[2] After having mentally absorbed the circle of offerings, or the *maṇḍala*,
visualized as above directed, the *yogin* must remain in the non-two state, that
is, the state of *samādhi*, in which all dualism is realized as being in at-one-
ment. In other words, he must realize the All in One, and the One in All.

[3] It is over the body, visualized as a corpse, that the *mantras* are recited
and that thence this subsidiary visualization is produced. Sometimes, however,
an actual corpse is used as the basis for the visualization.

[4] The transmutation is to be either into *amrita* or celestial objects of enjoyment, which are then offered to the genii and daemons in order to propitiate
them and thereby gain their assistance in increasing merit. This rite is often
performed by worldly-minded Lāmas, either for their own benefit or for
that of laymen, to increase worldly prosperity. The popular belief concerning
it is that by thus dedicating the visualized ' parks and gardens, food and
raiment, and medicaments' to the gods, the one for whom the rite is performed
will eventually attain them in reality here on Earth.

' To employ the ritual as the Red Feast, imagine thyself as
being the Wrathful Black One,[1]

And that thou strippest the hide from off thy body, which
is the dregs of egoism,

And spreadest it out so that it covereth the Third-Void
Universe,[2]

Heaping up upon it the flesh and blood and bones of thy
body aggregate,

And that the hide then resembleth a butcher's shambles.[3]

' The ritual when employed as the Black Feast consisteth
[of heaping up the evil *karma*] of all sentient beings,
including thyself,

Of gathering together all the diseases and malignity caused
by evil spirits since beginningless time—

The sins and obscurations [of all sentient beings] being
[visualized] in the form of black clouds—

And of then absorbing the whole into thine own body ;

And then of thinking that thy body, upon being devoured
by the genii and evil spirits,

Changeth their bodies in colour to the blackness of charcoal.'[4]

---

[1] Text: *Htö-nag-ma* (pron. *Tö-nag-ma*) : 'Wrathful Black-One (or Goddess)'.
This Goddess, of the class of Wrathful Ones (Tib. *T'o-wo*), is qualified as
'black' because of her wrathful appearance. She is really red of colour, in
correspondence with *Vajra-Ḍākinī*, of whom she is the wrathful aspect ; all
deities of her Tantric Order having the two aspects, namely, the peaceful
aspect and the wrathful.

[2] The Universe as composed of ' The Three Regions '.

[3] This part of the visualization is for the purpose of making the mental
imagery as vivid and realistic as possible and, therefore, more effective ; for the
Red Feast is commonly employed to exorcise persons and places of evil
spirits.

[4] This remarkable rite of visualization, called the Black-Feast Rite, is employed for the absolving of evil *karma*, and also as an exorcism for the curing
of human maladies. In direct contrast with it, the White-Feast Rite, as contained in the smaller manuscript and given in full in the translation above, is
purely devotional, and practised, with no selfish or worldly end in view, for
the sole purpose of helping the *yogin* to realize the non-reality of the personal
self, or ego. At this point in the larger manuscript the pre-Buddhistic
animism, more or less of Bön shaping, is again very prominent. Upon the
genii and evil spirits, as upon a scapegoat, are imposed the sins and diseases of
all sentient beings accumulated throughout the aeons. (Cf. the rite of the

## VI. THE MEDITATION TO ACCOMPANY THE SACRIFICIAL OFFERING

Then, after this description of the Mixed, the Red, and the Black Feast, which is more or less parenthetical, there comes, about a folio further on, the Meditation to be employed when making the sacrificial offering. This, in relation to the White Feast, should follow the stanza on page 316 above, ending, ' And may all [*karmic*] debts be paid and cleared. *Phat!* '

' Having done so, then offer up the body without considera-
  tion of anything whatsoever,
Keeping thy mind quiescent and in the True State [or
  State of the Void].
If, at that time, thought of setting value upon thy [sacrificial]
  act,[1]
Or lack of sincerity or feeling of fear should arise,
[Meditate thus :] " The body hath been given to both the
  good and evil spirits and nothing of it is left.
The Mind hath no foundation and is separated from any
  root ;
And, being so, not even the Buddhas have seen it." [2]
By meditating in this manner, inspire thyself [with fear-
  lessness].

abandoning of the three-headed effigy, described above, on p. 293). This seemingly unjustifiable treatment of the genii and evil spirits was explained by
a Lāma as being no more than their *karmic* deserts. ' And to them in their own
turn ', as he added, ' will come the opportunity of transferring all such sins and
diseases, along with their own evil *karma*, to *Yama*, the Lord of the Lower
World, who consumes and thus destroys the Ignorance and Darkness of the
*Sangsāra*.' This appears to be a symbolic way of explaining that all living
things must eventually attain to Deliverance, and Evil be swallowed up in Good
—a doctrine thus apparently common both to the old Bön Faith and to Buddhism.
This is made clearer by the further reference to the Black-Feast Rite on
pp. 328 following.

[1] Any thought of selfishness destroys the virtue of the act.

[2] In other words, the Mind is the Uncreated, Unshaped, Unborn, to which
no concepts of the finite mind are applicable. As such, it is without foundation
or support and without root or origin ; and not even the Enlightened Ones
have ever been able to conceive it in terms of *sangsāric* experience. Here, in
this context, the manuscript transcends its original animistic background and
unmistakably shows Mahāyānic reshaping.

' Whatever [ideas or apparitions] appear to thee at this stage, analyse thoroughly :

A visible *māra*,[1] as an external cause of attraction or repulsion, like wild beasts, robbers or savages ;

An invisible *māra*, as an internal enemy, like joy, sorrow, or anger ;

The merriment-causing *māra*, like ambition, and love of pleasure, pomp, and ostentation ;

The fear-causing *māra*, like doubt and hypocrisy.

And eradicate each of them by uttering *Phaṭ !* '

### VII.  THE TIME FOR PERFORMING THE VARIOUS FEASTS

' As to the time, it is at dawn, for the sake of perfecting the the Twofold Merit,

That the White-Feast Rite of producing *amrita* should be performed.

' At noon, for the sake of repaying *karmic* debts or obligations of the past,

The Mixed-Feast Rite, in accordance with the occasion, should be performed.

' At night, for the sake of utilizing one's ascetical practices on the Path,

The Red-Feast Rite, in order to eradicate one's egoism, should be performed.

' In the evening twilight, for the sake of absolving one's evil *karma*,

The Black-Feast Rite, whereby all beings become capable of Emancipation, should be performed.'

---

[1] Text: *bdüd* (pron. *düt*) : Skt. *māra*; with reference, as the text explains, to anything capable of disturbing the mental quiescence of the *yogin* and arousing in him dualistic feelings of attraction or repulsion.  It may be an external physical object or phenomenon, or a thought, or a phenomenon internally, or mentally, perceived.  Temptations such as prevent the *yogin* from attaining Enlightenment and keep him dominated by Ignorance have been collectively personified by the Hindus as the Great God Māra.  And it was Māra who, after having exhausted all his arts of temptation, failed to overcome Gautama at the supreme moment when Gautama was sitting in meditation under the Bo-tree at Budh-Gayā about to attain Buddhahood.  As the Devil, Māra also tempted Jesus the *Christos*, and failed likewise.

## VIII. THE VISUALIZING OF THE HUMAN SKELETON AND WRATHFUL *ḌĀKINĪ*

' The most essential thing [in these rites] is the practice of
the mental imagery.

' If any supernormal phenomenon [or apparition] occur
while thus practising,

Overcome it by entering the fourth stage of *dhyāna*

And realizing thereby the true nature of phenomena.[1]

If, however, the devotee be one that hath practised meditation but little,

And thus cannot either incite the local genii and daemons
to produce phenomena

Or control phenomena if produced by them,

Or if the local genii and daemons, being too haughty, refuse
to be incited,

Then let him create the mental imagery of the human
skeleton.[2]

---

[1] The apparitional forms of spiritual or non-human beings are to the *yogin*
of enlightened mind no more real than any other forms perceivable in Nature,
all forms being equally illusory, or *māyā*, as explained in previous texts. It is
because of Ignorance that one attributes either good or evil to other beings.
In the fourth stage of *dhyāna* all such Ignorance is dissipated by Wisdom, and
no longer is there possible the erroneous belief that any thing or phenomenon
is separable from other things or phenomena—all dualities, including good and
evil, being realized to be parts of an Inseparable Whole.

The *yogic* character of the four stages of *dhyāna*, or meditative abstraction
from the world, as recognized by Buddhism, may be described as follows : The
first stage consists of *Vitarka*, analysis of one's thoughts ; *Vicāra*, reflection
upon the deductions derived from the analysis ; *Prīti*, fondness for this process
of analysis and reflection and for what may follow ; *Sukha*, transcendental
blissfulness derived from the state of abstraction ; and *Ekāgrata*, the one-
pointedness of mind attained. In the second stage the *yogin* is free from *Vitarka*
and *Vicāra*. In the third stage he is free also from excess of *Prīti* ; and, in
addition to *Sukha* and *Ekāgratā*, enjoys *Smriti* (Mindfulness) and *Upekshā*
(Equanimity). In the fourth stage he enjoys perfected *Smriti, Upekshā*, and
*Ekāgratā*, or true *Samādhi*, and attains a condition of unmodified consciousness,
free from all attachment to the world and to the three lower stages of *dhyāna*.
These four *dhyānas* represent four progressive degrees of *yogic* development,
related to which are the Four Brahmā Worlds wherein the successful *yogin*
progressively takes birth. (Cf. p. 92[7].)

[2] Two processes are fundamental in the practice of any of these rites :
(*a*) visualization, whereby the imaginative faculty is employed to produce certain
mental pictures or concepts, which have the effect of arousing definite psychic
powers in the *yogin* ; (*b*) mental quiescence, whereby all such visualizing is

' Uttering *Phaṭ!* visualize thyself as having become, instantaneously,

A radiant white skeleton of enormous size, whence issueth
flames,

So great that they fill the voidness of the Universe,

And consume, in particular, the habitations of the genii
and daemons ;

And that, finally, both skeleton and flames vanish as doth
a flash of light.

[All the while] keep thy mind quiescent.

This practice affordeth supreme protection against in-
fectious diseases.[1]


' If instantaneously-occurring phenomena come not at the
right moment,

Or if malignant spirits need to be brought to bay,

Thereupon visualize thyself as having been transformed
[instantaneously] into the Wrathful *Ḍākinī* ;[2]

And, [as before], that thou strippest the hide from thy
body (which is the dregs of thy egoism),

And spreadest it out so that it covereth the Third-Void
Universe,

And upon it heapest up all thy bones and flesh.

Then, when the malignant spirits are in the midst of enjoying the feast,

Imagine that the Wrathful *Ḍākinī* taketh the hide and
rolleth it up,

And, tying it together with serpents and intestines as
ropes,

Twirleth it around her head and dasheth it down forcibly,

Reducing it and all its contents to a mass of bony and
fleshly pulp,

---

brought to an end, the aim of it having been realized.  The first process is a
process of mental projection, the second of mental absorption, comparable to
the similar processes expounded in *The Six Doctrines* and therein linked with
the breathing-process.

[1] Here, again, is discernible in this visualization, which is employed as an
exorcism, the primitive animism underlying these rituals.

[2] This is another aspect of the Black Wrathful One mentioned above.

Upon which many mentally-produced wild beasts feed ;
And think that these leave not the smallest bit of it
undevoured.'

### IX. THE STATE OF MIND NECESSARY

' Put thy mind in the quiescent state by blending thine
intellect with the Voidness [of Intellect].
Thereby the instantaneously-occurring phenomena are
certain to come,
And vindictive and malicious spirits are certain to be
conquered.

' In all this, renounce every feeling of fondness for [or every
attachment to] life ;
It is of utmost importance for one to be inspired by the
assurance [born] of the highest realization of Truth.

' At this time, slowly produced phenomena resembling those
produced instantaneously,
And instantaneously-produced phenomena resembling those
produced slowly,
And phenomena of a mixed sort resembling both the other
sorts,
And hallucinations, due to habit-shaped memories, resembling the mixed phenomena [may occur].[1]

' Then having withstood successfully both classes of phenomena to the end,[2]
Thou shouldst analyse the experiences and signs and continue practising.[3]

---

[1] The Lāmas explain this somewhat as follows. A person having dread of
serpents may dwell in a locality where he sees serpents quite frequently, so
that each time he sees a serpent his fear of serpents augments until it becomes
habitual. Vernacularly speaking, the fear of serpents ' gets on his nerves '. As
a direct result, he may come to imagine that almost every stick or obstruction
in his path is a serpent ; and from this mental condition arise hallucinations of
serpents.

[2] The two classes of phenomena are those instantaneously and those slowly
produced. Those called ' mixed ' partake of both these two classes, and so they
are not classified apart from them.

[3] The experiences include all phenomenal appearances ; and the signs refer
to the indications concerning the *yogin*'s psychic development and progress.

'In short, the Doctrine of Eradicating [Egoism] hath been
 utilized on the Path
When thou hast comprehended the [Divine] Mind,
Which is that of the Great Mother, the Transcendental
 Wisdom,[1]
The Good Goddess, the [Personification of] Non-Ego.

'Upon this [ritual] hath been placed the triple seal of secrecy.'[2]


### X. THE FINAL MEDITATION

There now follows the Dedication of the Merit, born of the
art of sacrifice, to all sentient beings. This is in essence
the same as in the smaller manuscript, starting therein with the
stanza, numbered 28, beginning, 'Ah! when one hath uncoiled,
and become emancipated from, the concepts of "pious" and
"impious".' Then comes the Final Meditation followed by
the Good-Wishes and Benediction. These are lacking in the
text of the smaller manuscript, and if added to it would come
at the end, immediately preceding the Colophon.

The Final Meditation is as follows:—

'Having done this, then continue in the state of *dhyāna*, as
 long as possible;
And, filled with the divine feeling of Great Compassion,
Meditate upon the exchanging of joy for sorrow;
Thine own joy to be given to the spiritual beings and their
 sorrow assumed by thee.'

---

[1] Or the *Prajñā-Pāramitā*. As more fully explained in Book VII, following,
the *Prajñā-Pāramitā*, which is the transcendental, or metaphysical, part of the
Northern Buddhist Scriptures, corresponding to the *Abhidhamma Pitaka* of
Southern Buddhism, is personified as the Great Mother.

[2] In the original text there is the single word *Samaya*, a Tibetan transliteration from the Sanskrit. Literally, *samaya* means 'proper time', or 'proper
season', with respect to the giving of these teachings to the neophyte. The
translator, considering it to be one of the many secret code-words in use among
Tibetan *gurus* and initiators of this *yoga*, gives us the implied fuller meaning
which they would read into it. It might also be translated as 'No revealing
without proper authority'. It is with the direct sanction of the editor's *guru*,
in keeping with this injunction, that this heretofore esoteric ritual has been
translated into English.

### XI.  THE GOOD WISHES AND BENEDICTION

' Then offer [to them] the gift of the immaculate *Dharma*
[or Doctrine] in purity of heart, [saying]:
" All Truth cometh from the Cause and that Cause hath
been revealed by the Tathāgata ; [1]
And that which obstructeth the Cause hath also been
expounded by the Great Shramana.[2]
Abstain from doing evil ; ceaselessly do good ; keep pure
of heart ; this is the Doctrine of the Buddha.[3]

' " In virtue of these Good-Wishes may all those elemental
beings who have not as yet attained Liberation
Be permeated with the Essence of Compassion and Mutual
Love and speedily attain *Nirvāṇa*."

' The recital of these [five] concluding verses [above] constl-
tuteth the pronouncing of the Benediction.'

### XII.  THE CONCLUSION

' Mayest thou place every being with whom thou hast
established relationship, be it good or evil,
Upon the Path leading to Final Emancipation.'

---

[1] As here applied to the Buddha Gautama, the title Tathāgata, common to
both Northern and Southern Buddhism, being equally applicable to any of a
series of Buddhas preceding Gautama and to which He belongs, refers to One
Who has ' similarly gone ' before, and also to the need for another ' succeeding
(or coming) Buddha '. The coming Buddha, Who will come as Gautama's
successor, is Maitreya, ' The Loving One ', now in the Tushita Heaven awaiting
the hour for His incarnation among men, whom He will lead to Liberation
through the divine power of His All-Embracing Love and Compassion.

[2] The Great Shramana (or ' Conqueror of Passions ') is another title applied
to the Buddha. Herein, at the end of the larger manuscript, is discernible something of the method used by Northern Buddhism in adopting to its own purposes
preceding cults and beliefs, much after the manner employed by other religions.

[3] This stanza of three verses, composed of precepts familiar to all Buddhists,
is not given in full in the text, but as follows : ' All Truth cometh from the
Cause, &c. Abstain from doing evil, &c.' The next two verses are similarly
abbreviated, the scribe having assumed that all readers would fill out the
abbreviated forms, as has been done in translating them.

The larger manuscript ends with repeated reference to the esoteric character of these teachings followed by a *mantra*:

'Upon this hath been placed the triple seal of secrecy.'

'*MAMA KO-LING SAMANTA*'

[Here endeth Book V.]

### PRECEPTS FOR THE WISE

'Restless and Wavering is the mind
Hard both to guard and to restrain.
The man sagacious makes it straight.
As fletcher makes the arrow-shaft.

\*          \*          \*

'Just as a bee, not harming flower
In hue or fragrance, flies away,
The nectar taking, even so
The Sage should through the village go.

\*          \*          \*

'Like to a rock that's of one mass,
And by the wind unshook,
E'en so, by praise or blame,
Unmovèd are the wise.

\*          \*          \*

'Just like a lake deep, clear, serene,
Whenas they things in *Dharma* hear,
Wise men become serene, composed.'

From the *Dhammapada* of the Pāli
Cānon (Mrs. Rhys Davids's Translation).

THE ONE-FOLIO MS. OF THE LONG *HŪM*

Described on pages xx–xxi

# BOOK VI

# THE PATH OF THE FIVE WISDOMS: THE *YOGA* OF THE LONG *HŪM*[1]

## THE INTRODUCTION

### THE *YOGA* OF THE FIVE WISDOMS

THE matter of this Book, the smallest of the seven Books, is *yogically* similar to that of the *Chöd* Rite, in that the central theme concerns the transmuting of the Five Poisons, otherwise known as the Five Obscuring Passions, which are concomitant with Ignorance, into Right Knowledge (represented herein in its fivefold esoteric aspect as the Five Wisdoms), by means of the *yoga* of visualizing and spiritualizing. Thereby the successful *yogin* realizes Buddhahood. This doctrine is summed up in the last four verses preceding the concluding *mantra*.

The chief purpose of this brief introduction is, therefore, to expound, in epitomized manner, the Mahāyānic teachings concerning the Five Wisdoms, which, as the text itself and its annotations indicate, are esoterically a part of the teachings concerning the Five Dhyānī Buddhas; for upon understanding of the Five Wisdoms depends understanding of the *Mantra Yoga* of the Long *Hūm*.

As in *The Tibetan Book of the Dead*, to which serious readers should refer for further explication, the Essential, or Foundation, Wisdom is the All-Pervading Wisdom of the *Dharma-Dhātu* ('Seed, or Potentiality, of Truth'), or the Wisdom born of the *Dharma-Kāya* ('Divine Body of Truth') in its aspect as the All-Pervading Voidness. The *Dharma-Dhātu* is symbolized by the Aggregate of Matter, whence spring all physical forms, animate and inanimate, visible and invisible. The *Dharma-Dhātu*, being the Thatness consti-

---

[1] A photographic reproduction of the small Tibetan manuscript of one folio, upon which our translation is based, is presented herewith, as the frontispiece of this Book VI. We have rendered its title as follows: 'Herein Lieth [the Explanation of] the FiveFold Wisdom [Attribute] of the Long *Hūm*'.

tuting the *Dharma-Kāya*, is personified by the Chief of the Dhyāni Buddhas, Vairochana.

In this context, the Aggregate of Matter may be looked upon as being Nature, or the *Sangsāra*, characterized by interminable change, or transitoriness, wherein, as a result of *karmic* actions, man is enslaved by the incessant round of birth and death. When, in virtue of Right Knowledge, the fruit of *yoga*, man breaks his bondage to the *Sangsāra*, there shines forth in his inner consciousness the symbolic blue divine radiance of the *Dharma-Dhātu* Wisdom. Then, having conquered life itself, the *yogin* rejoices in utter Freedom, for he is nevermore to return to the Kingdom of Ignorance and Illusion save as a *Bodhisattva*, vowed to selflessness, to guide those who still dwell in the Darkness of the Cave to the Light of Day.

The Mirror-like Wisdom, personified by the Dhyāni Buddha Akshobhya, of whom the Dhyānī Buddha Vajra-Sattva is the *Sambhoga-Kāya* reflex, confers the *siddhi* (or *yogic* power) of seeing clairvoyantly the innate reality reflected, as in a mirror, in all phenomenal or apparent things, organic and inorganic. As with a telescope or microscope men of science study the Universe externally in its unreality, so with the *yogic* insight conferred by the Mirror-like Wisdom the master of this *yoga* studies the Universe internally in its True State. Through having realized the Wisdom of Equality, personified by the Dhyānī Buddha Ratna-Sambhava, the *yogin* sees all things with divine impartiality, in virtue of the *yoga* of equal-mindedness. The Discriminating Wisdom, personified by the Dhyānī Buddha Amitābha, confers the *yogic* power of knowing each thing by itself and, also, all things as the One. The fifth, the All-Perfecting Wisdom, personified by the Dhyānī Buddha Amogha-Siddhi, confers power of perseverance, essential to success in all *yogas*, and infallible judgement with consequent unerring action.

Whereas the *Dharma-Dhātu* Wisdom, following *The Tibetan Book of the Dead*, is symbolized by, or illusorily manifests itself as, the Aggregate of Matter, as Nature, producing all physical forms, the Mirror-like Wisdom is symbolized by the Element Water, whence originates the life-stream, represented by the sap in trees and plants and the blood in man and animals. The Wisdom of Equality, in like manner, manifests itself through the Element Earth, and thus produces the chief solid constituents of man's body and of organic and inorganic forms. The Discriminating Wisdom, by manifesting itself through the Element Fire, produces the vital heat of embodied human and lower animal beings; and the All-Performing Wisdom, using as its vehicle of manifestation the Element Air, is the source of the breath of life.

The Element Ether is not included in this category, for it symbolizes the sum-total of all the Wisdoms, namely, the the Supramundane Wisdom, which is purely *Nirvāṇic*, beyond the range of the mundane consciousness. Only a Fully Enlightened Buddha can comprehend it. Esoterically, the Element Ether is personified by the Dhyānī Buddha Vajra-Sattva, and related, in a comparative way, with the Mirror-like Wisdom. Its aggregate is the Aggregate of *Bodhic* Wisdom. Vajra-Sattva, in this esoteric relation, is synony-mous with Samanta-Bhadra, the *Ādi* (i.e. Primordial) Buddha, personification of the Unborn, Unshaped, Unmodified *Dharma-Kāya*, or *Nirvāṇa*. Samanta-Bhadra, in turn, is frequently per-sonified in Vairochana, the Chief of the Five Dhyānī Buddhas.

Again, as in *The Tibetan Book of the Dead*, with each of the Five Wisdoms there is related an obscuring passion, cor-responding to the Five Poisons of our text, and a *sangsāric* aggregate and world, and also a mystic colour, as follows:

With the *Dharma-Dhātu* Wisdom, Stupidity (or Sloth, or Delusion), the Aggregate of Matter, the *deva* world (or worlds), and the colour blue; with the Mirror-like Wisdom, Anger, the Aggregate of Consciousness, the hell world (or worlds), and the colour white; with the Wisdom of Equality, Egotism (or Pride, or, as in the quotation on the page facing the Pre-face herein, Selfishness), the Aggregate of Touch, the human world, and the colour yellow; with the Discriminating Wis-dom, Lust (or Greed), the Aggregate of Feelings (or Attach-ment), the ghost world, and the colour red; and with the All-Perfecting (or All-Performing) Wisdom, Jealousy, the Aggregate of Volition, the titan world, and the colour green.

The present treatise, though so brief, should convey to the well-instructed *yogin* the very essence of the Esoteric Lore; and upon it a very bulky volume of commentary might readily be written. For the Occidental student it should prove to be of great practical value if studied as a complement to the other *yogic* doctrines set forth in this volume.

# [THE PATH OF THE FIVE WISDOMS: THE *YOGA* OF THE LONG *HŪM*]

## [THE SYMBOLIC SIGNIFICANCE OF THE LONG *HŪM*]

(1) The Acuminated Circle [tapering in flame into Space, symbolizeth] Vairochana,[1] [as personifying] the *Dharma-Dhātu* Wisdom.[2]

(2) The Crescent [symbolizeth] Akshobhya,[3] [as personifying] the Mirror-like Wisdom.[4]

(3) The Top-Portion [5] [symbolizeth] Ratna-Sambhava,[6] [as personifying] the Wisdom of Equality.[7]

(4) The [Aspirated] *HA* [8] [symbolizeth] Amitābha,[9] [as personifying] the Discriminating Wisdom.[10]

[1] Text : *Rnam-par-snang-mzad* (pron. *Nam-par-nang-zad*) : Skt. Vairochana, the Dhyānī Buddha of the Centre (or Central Realm). Vairochana literally means, 'in shapes making visible'. He is, therefore, the Manifester of Phenomena, or the Noumenal Source of Phenomena.

[2] Text : *Chös-dvyings-yeshes* (pron. *Chö-ing-yeshē*). Here, as throughout this small treatise, reference should be made to the exposition of the Five Wisdoms in their close relationship with the Five Dhyānī Buddhas Who personify them or manifest their virtues, as contained in the Introduction immediately preceding this text.

[3] Text : *Mi-bskyöd-pa* (pron. *Mi-kyöd-pa*) : Skt. Akshobhya, meaning, the 'Unagitated' or 'Immovable [One]', the Dhyānī Buddha of the Eastern Direction. There being, in the Tibetan text, a transposition of the names of Akshobhya and Vairochana, we have corrected it in our translation.

[4] Text : *Melong-ltabu-hi-yeshes* (pron. *Melong-tabu-yi-yeshē*).

[5] 'The Top-Portion' is the single horizontal stroke, or line, upon which the Crescent rests.

[6] Text : *Rinchen-byung-ldan* (pron. *Rinchen-jung-dan*) : Skt. Ratna-Sambhava, meaning, 'Born of a Jewel', or the 'Jewel-born [One]'. He is thus the Beautifier, the Source of Preciousness and Beauty. As a Dhyānī Buddha, He presides over the Southern Direction.

[7] Text : *Mnyam-nyid-yeshes* (pron. *Nyam-nyid-yeshē*).

[8] The Aspirated *HA* is that portion of the Tibetan letter *HŪM* resembling a figure 5, between the Top-Portion (immediately below the Crescent) and the Silent *HA* ( ). The Silent *HA* is referred to in the next line, along with the Vowel-Sign, which is the remainder of the *HŪM* or the Bottom-Portion ( ).

[9] Text : *Snang-va-mthah-yas* (pron. *Nang-wa-tha-yay*) : Skt. Amitābha, meaning, '[He of] Boundless (or Incomprehensible) Light', the Dhyānī Buddha of the Western Direction.

[10] Text : *So-sor-rtogs-pahi-yeshes* (pron. *So-sor-tog-pai-yeshē*), meaning literally,

(5) The [Silent] *HA* together with the Vowel-Sign are Amogha-Siddhi,[1] [as personifying] the All-Perfecting Wisdom.[2]

(6) The *HŪM* [thus] compriseth [in its symbolism] the Nature [or Essence] of the Five Orders [of the Buddhas of Meditation].[3]

## [THE OBEISANCE AND MEDITATION]

(7) Obeisance to Vajra-Sattva![4] *Aum! Svasti!*

(8) The Mind of the Buddhas of the Three Times,[5] omit-
　　ting none,

　　Immaculate from beginningless time, perfect, and tran-
　　　scending concept and definition,

　　The Embodiment of the Five Wisdoms, void,[6] and
　　　radiant, and without impediment,

---

' Separately-Knowing Wisdom', or the Wisdom whereby each thing is known by itself.

[1] Text: *Dön-yöd-grub-pa* (pron. *Dön-yöd-rub-pa*) : Skt. Amogha-Siddhi, meaning, 'Almighty Conqueror [of *Saṅgsāric* Existence]', the Dhyānī Buddha of the Northern Direction.

[2] Text : *Bya-grub-yeshes* (pron. *Cha-dub-yeshē*). As in *The Tibetan Book of the Dead*, this is also called the All-Performing Wisdom, synonymous with the All-Fulfilling Wisdom of the *Chöd* Rite.

[3] In the *Shrī-Chakra-Sambhāra Tantra* (cf. Arthur Avalon, *Tantrik Texts*, vol. vii, pp. 4–6) there is set forth a similar analysis of the *HŪM*, as follows :

' Of this *HŪM*, the letter *Ū* standeth for the knowledge [or wisdom] which accomplisheth all works; the body of the letter *H*, for the knowledge which distinguisheth ; the top of the letter *H*, for the equalizing knowledge ; the Crescent [*Chandra*, the Moon], for the mirror-like knowledge ; and the *Bindu* [*Thiglē*, the Acuminated Circle], above that, for the changeless knowledge.

' Mental concentration upon these various parts of the *Mantra*, symbolizing Mind, is the means whereby mind [in its unenlightened condition] is fitted for pure [or true] experience, and enjoyeth that blissfulness which ariseth from contemplation on the Bliss of Divine [or Supramundane] Mind.'

[4] Text : *Rdo-rje-sems-dpah* (pron. *Do-rje-sem-pa*): Skt. Vajra-Sattva, the 'Triumphant One of Divine Heroic Mind', is the *Sambhoga-Kāya*, or glorified active reflex, of Akṣhobhyà. Vajra-Dhāra (Tib. Dorje-Chang), Who appears as the Root-*Guru* of the doctrines contained in Books III and IV, above, is the other of Akṣhobhya's two reflexes. Both are of fundamental importance in the secret lore of the *Mahā-Mudrā* and *Ādi-Yoga* Schools.

[5] Namely, of the Past, Present, and Future.

[6] That is to say, void in the sense implied by the Doctrine of the Void (the *Shūnyatā*), and, therefore, void of all *saṅgsāric* characteristics; for the Void-ness is beyond human concept or definition, being the Uncreated, Primordial Essence of all things.

Riseth up [or is made manifest] in the [symbolic] form of *HŪM*, vividly defined and complete in all its parts and functions.

(9) The Five Poisons freely transmute themselves into the naturally radiant Five Wisdoms,[1]

In virtue of practising this *Yoga* [or Path of the Union] of the Visualizing and Spiritualizing [of the *HŪM*].[2]

(10) And thus attaining the Four Bodies and the Five Wisdoms,

May the *Vajra* of the Heart [3] be realized in this life-time.

[THE CONCLUDING *MANTRA*]

(11) *SARVA SIDDHI KARISHYANTU.*[4]

*Shubham.*[5]

[Here endeth Book VI]

[1] By the alchemy of Right Knowledge, 'the Poisons Five, of Ignorance', as Milarepa calls them, which are set forth above, in the Introduction, are trans-muted into the Divine Wisdom in its fivefold aspects.

[2] This, of course, assumes that the *yogic* practices suggested rather than given in detail herein are to be applied through visualizing and meditating upon the symbolic significance of the various parts of the Long *Hūm*. In order better to bring out the abstruse sense of the teachings conveyed by this very concise text, a translation somewhat freer than that of our other manuscripts and block-prints has been preferred by the translator.

[3] The significance of the expression '*Vajra* of the Heart' is occult, and has reference to the realizing of Complete Enlightenment, or Buddhahood. It might otherwise be freely rendered as 'the Immortality of the Divine Mind of the Buddhas'.

[4] The meaning of this *Mantra* is, 'May all *yogic* accomplishments be realized'.

[5] *Shubham*, literally meaning 'good', is here equivalent to a concluding *Amen*.

## THIS FLEETING WORLD

'Thus shall ye think of all this fleeting world :
A star at dawn ; a bubble in a stream ;
A flash of lightning in a summer cloud ;
A flickering lamp ; a phantom ; and a dream.'

*Prajñā-Pāramitā Sūtra*
(Kenneth Saunders's Version).

THE *BODHISATTVA*, THE GREAT BEING, ĀRYA
AVALOKITESHVARA

Described on page xxi

# BOOK VII

## THE PATH OF THE TRANSCENDENTAL WISDOM: THE *YOGA* OF THE VOIDNESS[1]

### THE INTRODUCTION

I. THE *PRAJÑĀ-PĀRAMITĀ*: ITS HISTORY AND ESOTERICISM

HEREIN, in one very short *Sūtra*, there is epitomized the great *yogic* doctrine of the Voidness, known in Tibetan as the *Stong-pa-ñid* (pronounced *Tong-pa-ñid*), and in Sanskrit as the *Shūnyatā*, upon which the vast literature of the *Prajñā-Pāramitā*, or 'Transcendental Wisdom', is chiefly based.

The *Prajñā-Pāramitā* Scriptures, called by the Tibetans the *S'er-p'yin* (pronounced *Sher-chin*), form a part of the third division of the Tibetan canon of Northern Buddhism, which corresponds to the *Abidhamma* of the Pāli canon of Southern Buddhism. They are commonly divided into twenty-one books, which in block-print form fill one hundred volumes of about one thousand pages each.

In the original Sanskrit, the *Prajñā-Pāramitā* comprises more than 125,000 shlokas. By the followers of the Mādhyamika School, which has now come to imply the Mahāyāna as a whole, it is considered the most valuable and sacred of all canonical writings. In Chinese, Mongolian, Manchu, and Japanese, as in Tibetan, there are various abridgements of the *Prajñā-Pāramitā*, some canonical, some apocryphal. Among these belong our own text, which, being a part of the Tibetan canon, is one of the most popular and widely circulated of all Mahāyānic treatises.

[1] The Tibetan block-print upon which our translation is based bears the following title: *SHES-RAB SNYING-PO BZHŪGS-SO* (pron. *SHE-RAB NYING-PO ZHŪ-SO*), meaning, 'Herein lieth the Essence [of the Transcendental] Wisdom', or 'Essence of the *Prajñā-[Pāramitā]*'. An English rendering from a Chinese version of this *Sūtra*, made by S. Beal, appears in his *Catena of Buddhist Scriptures from the Chinese* (pp. 282-4), published in 1871. A later translation from a Sanskrit version, made by F. Max Müller, appeared in 1894 (see E. B. Cowell, *Buddhist Mahāyāna Texts*, Part II, Oxford, 1894, pp. 147-9).

The matter of the *Prajñā-Pāramitā* consists of discourses by the Buddha, mostly addressed to superhuman hearers and to His chief human disciples, delivered on the Vulture's Peak and elsewhere. It recognizes various gradations of celestial Buddhas and *Bodhisattvas*. Its style is profoundly metaphysical and symbolically mystical, in keeping with its original esotericism. Its chief theme is Reality.

Nāgārjuna, who flourished (or did his chief work in the world)[1] during the first half of the second century of our era, the thirteenth of the Buddhist Patriarchs (of whom Mahā-kāshyapa, the Buddha's senior disciple, was the first, and Ānanda, the Buddha's cousin, the second), is credited with having been the first to enunciate publicly the teachings concerning the Voidness. According to Nāgārjuna, the Buddha Shākya-Muni Himself composed and placed the teachings in the custody of the *Nāgas* (Serpent Deities), to be kept hidden in the depths of a vast lake or sea till such time as men should be fit to receive them. This seems to be a symbolic way of stating that the Buddha taught the teachings esoterically, and that since prehistoric times they had also been so taught by the Buddhas Who preceded Shākya-Muni, as by the *Bodhic* Order of Great Adepts of *Yoga*, the wisest of the Wise Men, who have long been symbolized by the *Nāgas*, or Serpent Demigods.[2] The lake or sea, representing the water-world, symbolizes the superhuman realm whence the teachings are believed to have originated. The tradition goes on to tell how the King of the *Nāgas* (i.e. the Chief of the Wise Ones) initiated Nāgārjuna into the Secret Lore of the Buddhas, in the ' Dragon's Palace ' under the sea.

The Lāmas, too, maintain, on the authority of an oral tradition, said to have been at first secretly transmitted by the Buddha's most intimate disciples, that the Buddha taught the *Prajñā-Pāramitā* sixteen years after His Enlightenment, or in the fifty-first year of His life, on the Vulture Peak, and

---

[1] See the *lāmaic* tradition concerning his birth and life as set forth above, on p. 120³.

[2] The same ancient symbolism was employed by the Christ, according to the Gospel of St Matthew (x. 16): ' Be ye therefore wise as serpents, and harmless as doves '.

at other of His favourite places of teaching; and that Mahā-kāshyapa, His most learned disciple and apostolic successor, secretly recorded it.[1] The Japanese also have a tradition that the Buddha taught esoterically to His disciples as well as exoterically to the multitude, and that the Pāli canon represents those of His exoteric teachings made public prior to the compilation of the Sanskrit Mahāyāna Scriptures, which records some of the originally esoteric teachings, as represented in the *Prajñā-Pāramitā*.[2]

It was very largely due to the doctrines expounded by Nāgārjuna, and put forth partly as justification for such traditions concerning an Esoteric Buddhism—which the Theravādins of Ceylon, Siam, and Burma reject as being heretical—that the schism between the Northern and Southern Schools widened. This was after Kanishka's Council of the first century had affirmed the orthodoxy and superiority of the Mahāyāna and published its Sanskrit Scriptures, now collected together in the Tibetan canon, which is much more voluminous than the Pāli Canon of the Theravādins.

According to Northern Buddhists, the interpretation of Buddhism which is presented by the *Prajñā-Pārmitā* avoids the two extreme views held in Nāgārjuna's day concerning *Nirvāṇa*. Hence it is known as the Mādhyamikā, or the System of the 'Middle Path'.

Nāgārjuna, known in Tibetan as Klu-grub (pron. *Lu-grub*), was probably a disciple of Ashvaghosha, the saintly author of that marvellous work entitled *The Awakening of Faith*, and the first of the Patriarchs to help establish the Mahāyāna on a sound philosophical foundation. Nāgārjuna is said to have worked in the world for three hundred years, and thereafter to have lived for another three hundred years in spiritual retreat. According to some *yogins*, he is still incarnate, for,

---

[1] Cf. Nalinaksha Dutt, *Aspects of Mahāyāna Buddhism and its Relation to Hīnayāna* (London, 1930), p. 62.

[2] The Tibetan Mahāyāna canon contains, according to the Tibetan Mahā-yānists, all that is essential to the exoteric understanding of the *Dharma*, or in essence all that is contained in the canon of the Theravādins; but, in addition, also contains esoteric teachings of the Buddha which are not contained in the latter.

having become a Master of *Yoga*, he transmuted his gross physical body into the body of radiant glory, otherwise called by the Tibetans the *jai-lüs*, or 'rainbow body', wherein one may become visible or invisible at will.

## II. TRANSLATIONS FROM AN APOCRYPHAL TEXT

An apochryphal treatise, very similar to the canonical treatise herein recorded, but somewhat longer, which appears to have been anonymously compiled in Tibet, probably during the eleventh century, and afterwards associated with Atīsha, expounds the Transcendental Wisdom in a positive style, in direct contrast with the negative style of all the canonical texts. This treatise, which the late Lāma Kazi Dawa-Samdup, assisted by the editor, also translated, bears the following title: ' Herein is Contained the Narrative of the Essence of the Epitome of the One Hundred Thousand [Shlokas of the *Prajñā-Pāramitā*] '.[1] The title shows that its unknown author based it upon the first twelve books of the canonical Tibetan version of the *Prajñā-Pāramitā* popularly called the ' *Boom* ', or according to the fuller Sanskrit name, the *Shata-Sahasrika*, meaning the ' One Hundred Thousand [Shlokas of Transcendental Wisdom] '.

The following extracts, in translation from it, will serve to illustrate its peculiar positive style, in contrast with the negative style of the canonical text which forms the chief matter of our present Book:

' The [Six Principles of Consciousness are the] eye-consciousness, the ear-consciousness, the nose-consciousness, the

---

[1] Text: *Hboom gyi Bsdüs-dön Snying-po Lorg-yüs Bzhügs-so* (pron. *Boom gyi Dü-dön Nyingo-po Long-yü Zhü-so*). The Colophon contains the following account of the history of the treatise: ' This [text] was given to Asu, the Newar [or Nepalese Buddhist], by the Rev. Lord [Atīsha], the Enlightener [Skt. of text: Dīpānkara], and the Newar put it into verse form. . . . The Rev. Lord Atīsha, having perused all the Scriptures for twelve years, found this Epitomized One Hundred Thousand [Shlokas] to be so useful that he made it his chief [text for] recitation.' Atīsha, whose proper Indian name is Dīpānkara (meaning the ' Enlightener') was a Bengali Buddhist, of royal birth (see p 99[2]). Atīsha's association with this treatise may possibly be due to no more than a literary device on the part of its anonymous author, intended to gain for it popular sanction.

tongue-consciousness, the body-consciousness, and the mind-consciousness.[1] The Contacts by Touch are the contact of the eye, of the ear, of the nose, of the tongue, of the body, and of the mind. The Sensations resulting from the Contacts are of the eye, of the ear, of the nose, of the tongue, of the body, and of the mind.

'The Six Elements are Earth, Water, Fire, Air, Ether, and Consciousness.

'The Twelve *Nidānas* are Ignorance, Conformations [of Thought], [Birth] Consciousness, Psychic and Physical Elements [Six] Sense-Faculties, Contact, Sensation, Craving, Grasping [or Enjoying], Existence [or Becoming], Birth, Age, and Death.'

Then, at the end, concerning the Divine Duties, or *Pāramitās*, it teaches: 'All the bodily divine duties precede the Wisdom and follow the Wisdom. All the divine duties of the Speech precede the Wisdom and follow the Wisdom. All the divine duties of the Mind precede the Wisdom and follow the Wisdom.' In other words, as the canonical *Prajñā-Pāramitā* also teaches, these Divine Duties of the *Bodhisattva* must be mastered, or fully discharged, before the Supreme Wisdom of *Bodhi* can be attained; and thereafter, as adornments of Buddhahood, they glorify It.

Although recognized as being apocryphal, this work is, nevertheless, highly esteemed and regarded by the laity as being almost as authoritative as the canonical epitomes themselves. The canonical stating of the *Prajñā-Pāramitā* corresponds to the negative aspect of the Doctrine of the Voidness, as denoted by the term *Shūnyatā*, while this non-canonical exposition corresponds to the positive aspect, as denoted by the term *Tathatā*.

### III. THE CANONICAL TEXTS AND COMMENTARIES

The 100,000 shlokas, contained in the first twelve volumes of the *Prajñā-Pāramitā* of the Tibetan canon, expound the whole of the Transcendental Wisdom, and the remaining

[1] Or, as the text itself explains, there are 'six sensory organs—the eye, ear, nose, tongue, body, and [mundane] mind'; and 'six objects' to which they are related, namely, 'form, sound, odour, taste, touch, and quality'. Thus arises mundane consciousness.

nine volumes are merely different abridgements or epitomes
of these twelve. Three of these last nine are called *Ñi-k'ri*
(pron. *Nyi-thi*), or ' The Twenty Thousand [Shlokas] ', which
are used for such monasteries or individuals as cannot study
or afford to purchase the fuller text. Another of the epitomes,
in a single volume, consists of 8,000 shlokas, and is intended
for the ordinary and younger monks. For the use of school-
boys and the laity there is an epitome about the size of our
own text, comprised in three or four leaflets, entitled ' Transcendental Wisdom in a Few Letters' (Tib. *Yige-Ñuṅ-du*:
Skt. *Alpākshara*). Mystically the whole of the *Prajñā-Pāramitā* is condensed into the letter *A*, which is said to be 'the
Mother of All Wisdom ', and, therefore, of all men of spiritual
power or genius, as well as of all *Bodhisattvas* and Buddhas ;
for *A* is the first element for forming syllables, words,
sentences, and a whole discourse, or an enlightening sermon.

Included in the *Prajñā-Pāramitā* cycle is the *Diamond
Sūtra*, or *Diamond-Cutter* (known in the Tibetan version as
the *Dorje-Schepa*), a booklet very popular with the laity
throughout the Mahāyānic world. In it there is attributed
to the Buddha, Who therein instructs the disciple Subhuti,
the following estimate of the *Prajñā-Pāramitā* teachings :
' Subhuti, the relative importance of this Scripture may be
summarily stated : its truth is infinite ; its worth incomparable ; and its merit interminable. The Lord Buddha
delivered this Scripture specifically for those who are entered
upon the Path which leadeth to *Nirvāṇa*, and for those who
are attaining the ultimate plane of *Bodhic* thought [or for
those of the Mahāyāna].' [1]

The full Tibetan text of the *Prajñā-Pāramitā* was translated out of the Sanskrit in the ninth century A.D., by two
Indian pundits, namely, Jina Mitra and Surendra Bodhi,
assisted by a Tibetan interpreter named Ye-s'es-sde.[2]

[1] Cf. W. Gemmell, *The Diamond Sūtra* (London, 1912), p. 62, an excellent
English rendering of the Chinese version, known as the *Chin-Kang-Ching*,
which, like the complete *Prajñā-Pāramitā*, was originally written in Sanskrit.
In addition to the Tibetan, there are also a Mongolian and a Manchu version.

[2] Cf. L. A. Waddell, *The Buddhism of Tibet or Lāmaism* (London, 1895),
p. 161.

A very important commentary on the *Prajñā-Pāramitā* is the *Mahā-Prajñā-Pāramitā Shāstra* by Nāgārjuna, in which he expounds in great philosophical detail the Doctrine of the Voidness, or *Shūnyatā*, literally meaning 'Vacuity'. And of the one hundred and thirty-six volumes of the *Sūtra* (Tib. *Dō*) class contained in the *Tanjur*, the Tibetan Commentary on the Tibetan canon, the first sixteen are commentaries on the *Prajñā-Pāramitā*. These are followed by several volumes explanatory of the Mādhyamikā Philosophy of Nāgārjuna, which is based, as we have observed, upon the *Prajñā-Pāramitā*.[1]

#### IV. THE DOCTRINE OF THE VOIDNESS VIEWED HISTORICALLY

Historically viewed, the Doctrine of the Voidness is a re-stating of the Doctrine of *Māyā* by the illustrious founders of the Mahāyāna School, beginning with Ashvaghosha, of the first century A.D., and followed by Nāgārjuna, who gave it definite Buddhistic shape.

As modern scholars have noted, those great thinkers of ancient India taught, as Kant did seventeen centuries afterwards, that the world is will and representation; for the Doctrine of *Shūnyatā* implies that True Knowledge is attainable only by the All-Enlightened Mind, freed of all Ignorance, of all Illusion, and transcendent over representation, or phenomenal appearances, born of the will-power of Mind.

'The Sage has gone down into the depths of his heart. He has seen there—and here he forestalls our critiques of pure reason—the external world, in the phenomenon of representation, taking shape and vanishing there. He has seen the dissolution of all that we call the ego, of the substantial soul, because Buddhism denies it, and of the phenomenal ego, because its fall is involved in that of the external world. In place of this world of moral suffering and material obstacles, of internal egoism and external adversity, an apparently bottomless gulf opens in the heart—a luminous and as it were submarine gulf, unfathomable, full of ineffable beauties,

---

[1] Cf. L. A. Waddell, *op. cit.*, p. 164.

of fleeting depths, and infinite transparencies. On the surface of this vacuity into which the eye plunges dazzled, the mirage of things plays in changing colours, but these things, as we know, "exist only as such "—*tathatā*—and, therefore, are as if they were not.

'And once this mirage is dispelled, behold—in the intimate contemplation of that bottomless and limitless depth, in that unrivalled purity of absolute vacuity—behold all virtualities arising, all power emerging. What can now check the heart? It has broken its bonds and dissipated the world. What can check the mind? It is freed not only from the world, but from itself. In destroying its own lie it has overcome itself. From the unfathomable gulf it now rises up victorious.'[1]

In terms of the Doctrine of *Shūnyatā*, as of the parallel Doctrine of *Māyā*, the sole reality is Mind, and Mind is the Cosmos. Matter is but the crystallization of thought; or, otherwise stated, the Universe is merely the materialization of thought-forms—the Idea which illusorily appears as objects of Nature. Hsüan-Tsang, the most learned of the early Chinese exponents of the Mahāyāna, who lived in the eighth century A.D., and studied under Sīlabhadra, then the illustrious head of the famous Mahāyānic Buddhist University of Nālanda, in India, has bequeathed to us this explanation: 'Because thought attacheth itself to itself, it developeth in the form of external things. This visible doth not exist; there is only thought.'[2]

The gist of Nāgārjuna's own teaching as contained in his famous philosophical treatise, the *Avatangsaka Sūtra*, has been summarized thus: 'The One True Essence is like a bright mirror, which is the basis of all phenomena. The Basis itself is permanent and real, the phenomena are evanescent and unreal. As the mirror, however, is capable of reflecting all images, so the True Essence embraceth all phenomena, and all things exist in and by it'.[3]

---

[1] Cf. R. Grousset, *In the Footsteps of the Buddha* (London. 1932), pp. 291–2, a work which has afforded us much assistance.

[2] Cf. R. Grousset, *op. cit.*, p. 301.

[3] Cf. S. Beal, *A Catena of Buddhist Scriptures from the Chinese* (London, 1871), p. 125.

### V. THE ABSOLUTE AS INHERENT IN PHENOMENA

The soul, or ego, is philosophically conceived by the same School as the perceiver of phenomena, the microcosmic aspect that the macrocosmic consciousness assumes in its own eyes, the play of an illusion on the surface of the Ocean of Mind. ' In reality ', says Hsüan-Tsang, ' soul and world do not exist with an absolute existence, but only with a relative truth.' [1]

Asanga, another of the Masters of the Mahāyāna, who lived in the fifth century A.D., propounds, as does the treatise concerning non-ego contained in our Book V, ' In the transcendent sense there is no distinction between the *Sangsāra* and *Nirvāna*.' [2] Thus the Doctrine of the *Shūnyatā*, underlying the whole of the *Prajñā-Pāramitā*, posits, as does the *Avatangsaka Sūtra*, an Absolute as inherent in phenomena, for the Absolute is the source and support of phenomena; and, in the last analysis of things, by the *Bodhi*-illuminated mind, freed of Ignorance, duality vanishes, and there remains but the One in All, the All in One. The phenomena are the Ocean of Mind conceived as waves of thought; the Absolute is the waves conceived as the Ocean. Finally, it may be said, in the words of Asanga, ' Thus the duality is present in appearance, but not in reality.' [2]

This supreme doctrine of Emancipation may be summarized by saying that all things are eternally immersed in *Nirvāna*, but that man, held in bondage by the hypnotic glamour of appearances, is wrapt in an unbroken Sleep of Ignorance, dreaming dreams which he thinks real. Not until man awakens from the illusion of self and the world can he realize that *Nirvāna* is here and now and everywhere, inherent in all things—as Perfect Quiescence, the Qualityless, the Unborn, the Uncreated. In the ecstatic trance state of the highest *samādhi* the Great *Yogin* attains this Undifferentiated Knowledge, the Transcendent Wisdom.

According to the *Prajñā-Pāramitā*, Emancipation is, however, to be attained only for the purpose of treading the

---

[1] Cf. R. Grousset, *op. cit.*, pp. 306, 313.
[2] Cf. R. Grousset, *op. cit.*, p. 302.

Higher Path, the sublime Path of the *Boddhisattva*. Of him who has conquered the Sleep of Ignorance, Asaṅga speaks thus : ' By a supreme mastery he hath conquered comprehension and hath brought under his sway again the world that was no longer in possession of itself. His only delight is to bring Emancipation to beings. He walketh among the Existences like a lion.' [1]

Thus it is that the *Prajñā-Pāramitā* is the Mother of the *Boddhisattvas*, for it brings them to birth and suckles them to Buddhahood. So regarded, as a personification of the Perfected Wisdom of *Yoga*, the *Prājña-Pāramitā* is the Divine *Shakti*, known to the Tibetans as Dolma, ' The Saviouress ', the Great Goddess of Mercy, and in Sanskrit as Tārā.[2]

## VI. THE PRACTISING OF THE *PRAJÑĀ-PĀRAMITĀ*

Rather than practised in accordance with the ordinary methods of *yoga*, the *Prajñā-Pāramitā* is to be meditated upon and its wisdom realized by ecstatic introspection. In this respect it is to be differentiated from the other five of the Six *Pāramitā*, which are to be observed by the devotee as ' Boundless Charity ' (*Dāna Pāramitā*), ' Boundless Morality ' (*Shīla-Pāramitā*), ' Boundless Patience ' (*Kshānti-Pāramitā*), ' Boundless Industry ' (*Vīrya-Pāramitā*), and ' Boundless Meditation ' (*Dhyāna-Pāramitā*). The ' Boundless (or Transcendental) Wisdom ', like *Nirvāṇa*, or Buddhahood, is really a condition of mental illumination of the most exalted character, to be acquired by the aid of all the Six *Pāramitā* combined with perfected *yogic* practices.

' A *Bodhisattva* may perfect himself in the *Dāna-Pāramitā*, but as there is every possibility of his forming a conception of the *Dāna-Pāramitā* as having a sort of existence (*svabhāva*), it may become for him an object of grasping (*grāhya*). He

---

[1] Cf. R. Grousset, *op. cit.*, 314.

[2] According to recent researches of Sj. Atal Bihari Ghosh, of Calcutta, who contributed important annotations to *The Tibetan Book of the Dead* and to *Tibet's Great Yogī Milarepa*, the *Shakti* of the *Prajñā-Pāramitā* is to be identified with the Goddess *Kuṇḍalinī*, the Divine Guardian of the ' Serpent Power '.

may also have a conception of the giver and the receiver and the thing given. It is to counteract all these conceptions, which are really misconceptions, that the *Prajñā-Pāramitā* steps in and makes the *Bodhisattva* try to develop a state of mind in which the *Dāna-Pāramitā* would appear to him as devoid of signs (*alakṣaṇa*), without any independent existence of its own; and, at the same time, eliminate from his mind any conception regarding the giver, the receiver, or the thing given. In short, the function of the *Prajñā-Pāramitā* is to convince a *Bodhisattva* that the *Dāna-Pāramitā*, or whatever it may be, is really formless, baseless, and is indistinguishable from *Shūnyatā*. It serves as a guard to the *Bodhisattva*, who has risen much above the average and has acquired various meritorious qualities, but still may cling to some idea or concept which in itself may be highly pure and meritorious, but, being an attachment, must be got rid of.'[1] Hence it is that the *Prajñā-Pāramitā* has been extolled over all the other *Pāramitā*; and has come to be regarded as the chief *Pāramitā*, whereby man, as in a boat, reaches the Wisdom of the Other Shore.

[1] Cf. Nalinaksha Dutt, *op. cit.*, pp. 334-5.

## THE TRUTH BEYOND DEMONSTRATION

' I and the Buddhas of the Universe
Alone can understand these things—
The Truth beyond demonstration,
The Truth beyond the realm of terms.'

The Buddha, *Saddharma Pundarīka Sūtra*
(W. E. Soothill's Translation).

# [THE PATH OF THE TRANSCENDENTAL WISDOM: THE *YOGA* OF THE VOIDNESS]

## [THE OBEISANCE]

### (1) OBEISANCE TO THE CONQUERESS, THE TRANSCENDENTAL WISDOM!

### [THE SANSKRIT AND TIBETAN TITLE]

(2) In the language of India ['The Conqueress, the Essence of the Transcendental Wisdom', is written], *Bhagavatī Prajñā-Pāramitā Hridaya*: in the language of Tibet, *Bchom-ldan-hdas-ma Shes-rab kyi Pha-rol-tu Phyin-pahi Snying-po.*[1]

(3) [It is] one section.[2]

## [THE QUESTION OF SHĀRI-PUTRA]

(4) Thus have I heard: Once upon a time the Conqueror, amidst the great congregation of the *Sangha*, composed of *Bhikṣhus* and *Bodhisattvas*, on the Vulture's Peak in Rāj-Griha,[3] was sitting immersed in that *Samādhi* called the Profound Illumination.

(5) And at the same time the *Bodhisattva*, the Great

---

[1] Pronounced *Chom-dan-day-ma She-rab kyi Pha-rol-tu Chin-pai Nying-po.* It is interesting here to catch a glimpse of the way in which much of the great Buddhist literature now preserved in the Tibetan was originally translated out of the Sanskrit, onwards from the time of Sambhota, who gave to Tibet its alphabet (based on the Sanskrit) during the latter half of the seventh century A. D. The *Prajñā-Pāramitā* is personified as the Great Mother of Divine Wisdom or, as herein, the *Bhagavatī* (*Chom-dan-day-ma*), the 'Conqueress', which indicates that She represents the negative, or female, aspect of the Emancipating Knowledge. There are also, in the Tibetan, treatises which, in contrast with our present treatise, expound the same doctrines from the positive aspect, as explained in our Introduction hereto.

[2] That is to say, one section, or part, of the very voluminous canonical *Prajñā-Pāramitā.*

[3] Most of the *Sūtras* and other recorded teachings attributed to the Buddha begin, as does this treatise, by showing the Buddha in the midst of His disciples gathered together on the Vulture's Peak in Rāj-Griha, in the Patna district, India, near Buddha-Gaya, the place where He attained Enlightenment.

Being, Ārya Avalokiteshvara,[1] sat meditating upon the deep doctrine of the *Prajñā-Pāramitā*, that the Five Aggregates [2] are of the nature of the Voidness.

(6) Thereupon, inspired by the power of the Buddha, the venerable Shāri-Putra [3] addressed the *Bodhisattva*, the Great Being, Ārya Avalokiteshvara, thus: 'How may any nobly-born one,[4] desirous of practising the profound teachings of the *Prajñā-Pāramitā* comprehend them?'

## [THE REPLY BY AVALOKITESHVARA]

(7) Upon this being asked, the *Bodhisattva*, the Great Being, Arya Avalokiteshvara, made reply and spake thus to the son of Shāri-Dvatī: [5]

(8) 'Shāri-Putra, any nobly-born one, [spiritual] son or daughter,[6] desirous of practising the profound teachings of the *Prajñā-Pāramitā* should comprehend them in the following manner :

(9) 'The Five Aggregates are to be comprehended as being naturally and wholly Voidness.

(10) 'Forms are Voidness and Voidness is Forms; nor are Forms and Voidness separable, or Forms other than Voidness.

(11) 'In the same way, Perception, Feeling, Volition, and Consciousness are Voidness.

(12) 'Thus, Shāri-Putra, are all things Voidness, without

---

[1] See Description of Illustrations, ix, p. xxi.

[2] The Five Aggregates, or Five *Skandhas*, of which the human body is composed, are : Body-Aggregate, Perception-Aggregate, Feelings-Aggregate, Thoughts-Aggregate, and Consciousness-Aggregate.

[3] Shāri-Putra, meaning 'Son of Shāri', is the name of one of the Buddha's most learned and famous disciples.

[4] This refers not to a person of noble birth, but to one nobly born to love of the Doctrine ; or, in other words, to a *yogin*, or devotee.

[5] The surname Shāri is here expanded to Shāri-Dvatī.

[6] In other words, the Path to Liberation is open to all beings irrespective of sex, the expression '[spiritual] son or daughter' having reference to a Brother or Sister of the Religious Order. It was the Buddha's own wife who became His first female disciple, and founded, with His permission, the first Buddhist Sisterhood.

characteristics, Unborn, Unimpeded, Unsullied, Unsulliable, Unsubtracted, Unfilled.[1]

(13) ' Shāri-Putra, such being so, Voidness hath no form, no perception, no feeling, no volition, no consciousness ; no eye, no ear, no nose, no tongue, no body, no mind, no form, no sound, no smell, no taste, no touch, no quality.

(14) ' Where there is no eye there is no desire ', and so on to,[2] ' there is no consciousness of desire.[3]

(15) ' There is no Ignorance ; there is no overcoming of Ignorance ' ; and so on to, ' there is no decay and no death ', and to, ' there is no overcoming of decay and death.[4]

(16) ' In the same way, there is no sorrow, there is no evil, there is no taking away, there is no Path, there is no Wisdom nor any attaining nor not-attaining.[5]

---

[1] In the rendering from the original Sanskrit by Max Müller, this passage has been rendered as follows : ' Thus, O Shāri-Putra, all things have the character of emptiness ; they have no beginning, no end ; they are faultless and not faultless ; they are perfect and not perfect.'

[2] The phrase, ' and so on to ', occurring here and in the next paragraph, indicates that our text is a greatly abbreviated version of the original text of the *Prajñā-Pāramitā*. The complete categories which it thus suggests belong to the categorical sequences of the Twelve *Nidānas*, or Interdependent-Causes, which keep the Wheel of Life revolving in its incessant rounds of birth and death.

[3] The eye's perception of an object results in consciousness of, and like or dislike for, the object. Thence arise volitional impulses which produce desire. Hence, where there is no eye, or sense of sight, or sensuousness, there can be no consciousness of desire.

[4] This abbreviated category, like all the other categories of our text, is dependent upon the Mahāyānic teaching that Mind is the sole reality, and that apart from Mind, which gives to the *Sangsāra*, to Nature, its illusory appearance of reality, nothing has independent existence. All objective appearances are evanescent phenomena, no more real than the content of a dream. Enwrapped in the *māyā* of the world, man sleeps and dreams. When the dreaming ends, he awakens possessed of supramundane insight. Transcending appearances, such an Awakened One passes beyond all dualities, and realizes that there is no Ignorance to overcome, nor any decay and death to overcome.

[5] The Awakened One also realizes, concomitantly with his Awakening, that all the other dualities, such as joy and sorrow, good and evil, adding to and taking away, are merely *sangsāric* hallucinations. So, too, for such an One there is no Path, nor any traverser of the Path, as the first Book of this volume likewise teaches. There is no Wisdom just as there is no Ignorance, nor any attaining or not-attaining of Wisdom. In short, there is nothing that the unilluminated mind may conceive which has other than an illusory, dualistic existence. (Cf. ' The Ten Figurative Expressions ', on pp. 96-7.)

(17) ' Shāri-Putra, such being so—for even the *Bodhisattvas* have nothing which is to be attained [1]—by relying upon the *Prajñā-Pāramitā*, and abiding in it, there is no mental obscuration [of the Truth] and, therefore, no fear ; and, passing far beyond erroneous paths [or doctrines], one successfully attaineth *Nirvāṇa*.

(18) ' All the Buddhas, too, Who abide in the Three Times, have attained the highest, the purest, and the most perfect Buddhahood by depending upon this *Prajñā-Pāramitā.*

## [THE *MANTRA* OF THE *PRAJÑĀ-PĀRAMITĀ*]

(19) ' Such being so, *Mantra* of the *Prajñā-Pāramitā*, the *Mantra* of the Great Logic,[2] the Highest *Mantra*, the *Mantra* which maketh one to equal That which cannot be equalled, the *Mantra* which assuageth all sorrow, and which not being false is known to be true, the *Mantra* of the *Prajña-Pāramitā*, is now uttered :

*TADYATHĀ GATE GATE PARA-GATE PARA-SAM-GATE BODHI SVA-HA.*[3]

(20) ' Shāri-Putra, a *Bodhisattva*, a Great Being, should comprehend the *Prajñā-Pāramitā* in that manner.'

## [THE BUDDHA'S APPROVAL]

(21) Then the Conqueror arose out of the *Samādhi*, and,

[1] The *Bodhisattvas* who have realized that there is neither *Nirvāṇa* nor not-*Nirvāṇa*, neither the *Sangsāra* nor the not-*Sangsāra*, have gone beyond desiring or seeking to attain anything.

[2] The *Mantra* being the concentrated essence of the whole of the *Prajñā-Pāramitā* equals the *Prajñā-Pāramitā* itself; for it suggests to one of *yogic* insight the complete categorical chain of the vast logical deductions contained in the supreme Doctrine of the *Voidness*, upon which the *Prajñā-Pāramitā* is based. The Doctrine is, however, regarded as being incomprehensible to all beings save Buddhas and highly developed *Bodhisattvas* like the Great Being, Avalokiteshvara, of our present text. Spiritually gifted men of lesser power may, nevertheless, comprehend it as the *Mantra* of the Great Logic by realizing, in profound meditation, that it transmits the full emancipating power of the Conqueress, the Transcendental Wisdom.

[3] This *Mantra* may be rendered into English as follows : ' O Wisdom, departed, departed, departed, to the Other Shore, disembarked on the Other Shore, *Sva-ha* !' Wisdom in this context may be taken as referring to the Buddha, Who has passed on beyond the *Sangsāra*, to the Other Shore, *Nirvāṇa*.

to the *Bodhisattva*, the Great Being, Ārya Avalokiteshvara, said, 'Well done. Well done. Well done.'

(22) And having thus expressed approval, [He added], 'That is so, O Nobly-born One; that is so. Even as thou hast shown, the profound *Prajñā-Pāramitā* should be comprehended. The *Tathāgatas*,[1] too, are satisfied [therewith].'

(23) The Conqueror thus having given utterance to His command, the venerable Shāri-Dvatī's son, and the *Bodhisattva*, the Great Being, Ārya Avalokiteshvara, and all beings there assembled—*devas*, men, *asuras*,[2] *ghandharvas*,[3] and the whole world—were gladdened, and praised the words of the Conqueror.

This completeth *The Essence of the Wondrous Transcendental Wisdom.*

## THE ADDENDUM

In amplification of the above brief treatise and of our introduction to it, we here add the following extracts, in their original textual sequence, as translated by the late Lāma Kazi Dawa-Samdup assisted by the editor, from chapter xvii of the Tibetan canonical *Prajñā-Pāramitā*, entitled *Dvagspo-Thar-rgyun* (pron. *Dagpo-Thar-gyun*), which is chiefly explanatory, and, therefore, especially valuable for our purpose. The chapter extends from the 120th to the 124th folio of our block-print text of it.

### I. THE SUPERIORITY OF THE *PRAJÑĀ-PĀRAMITĀ*

'Were a *Bodhisattva* to practise incessantly all the [Five] *Pāramitās*, *Dāna*, *Shīla*, *Kshānti*, *Vīrya*, and *Dhyāna*, and

---

[1] The *Tathāgatas* are the Buddhas, of Whom Gautama the Buddha is but one, in the Great Spiritual Succession of the Buddhas of the Three Times. (Cf. p. 333[1].)

[2] The *asuras* are titans, who having fallen from the estate of gods, through pride, seek the guidance of the Buddha that they, too, may be comforted and attain Enlightenment. Here, again, it is to be noted that Buddhism teaches that all sentient beings, even the lowest and the most fallen, will ultimately reach Liberation.

[3] The *gandharvas* are an angelic order of celestial musicians who sing the glories of the Great Ones.

failed to practise the sixth, namely, *Prajñā-Pāramitā*, he would be unable to attain the state of All-Knowledge. ... Therefore, in *The Transcendental Synopsis*,[1] it is said: " An eyeless multitude of many millions of blind folk knowing not the way would never arrive at the city they wished to reach. Without *Prajñā*, the other Five *Pāramitās* being eyeless, how could they touch the Realm of *Bodhi*! If, on the other hand, there should be one man with eyes among the multitude of blind folk, they would, undoubtedly, attain their destination." In like manner, the accumulation of other merits, if guided by *Prajñā*, leadeth to All-Knowledge. ...

' Now, if it be asked, what bondage would result should *Upaya* [or Method] and *Prajñā* [or Wisdom] be employed separately ?

' Any *Bodhisattva* having recourse to *Prajñā* apart from *Upaya* would be liable to be bound [or fettered] to the quiescent state of *Nirvāṇa* desired by the Srāvakas and would not attain the state of *Nirvāṇa* which is not fixed.[2] ...

---

[1] Text : *Hphags-pa Sdüd-pa* (pron. *Pha-pa Düd-pa*), meaning ' Transcendental Synopsis [or Summary] '.

[2] Or, as in Book II (p. 149[1]), ' the Unabiding State of *Nirvāṇa* ' — that state of *Bodhic* Enlightenment which is not a state of finality. The Mahāyānist regards the goal of the Srāvakas, with whom he classes the Theravādins of the Southern School, to be self-perfection like that of the Pratyeka Buddhas, and not the greater goal of those who tread the Path of Selfless Altruism of the *Bodhisattvas*. If the Srāvakas employ *Upāya* without *Prajñā* (born of the *Bodhisattvic* Ideal) they realize only that *Nirvāṇa* which is attainable by the *Arhat* while still in the fleshly body ; and, upon their final decease, they are liable to be fettered to the state of transcendental quiescence concomitant with such realization.

There are thus two stages, or degrees, of *Nirvāṇic* Enlightenment. The first arises in virtue of having transcended the *Sangsāra* and overcome all *karmic* need of further *sangsāric* being. The second is dependent upon realizing that this mighty accomplishment is but the stepping-stone to a higher evolution ; the conqueror must realize, once the conquest is made, that the conquest is not of itself enough, that it must be utilized as a means to a still mightier end and not merely enjoyed as by the Pratyeka Buddha. The Svrāvaka Buddhist mistakenly regards the first degree, as realized by him, to be the full realization of *Nirvāṇa*. He therefore makes no effort to progress beyond it, with the result that he becomes fettered to it. Had he employed *Upāya* united with *Prajñā* instead of *Upāya* alone, he would have attained the second degree, or *Nirvāṇa* in its completeness, and, like the Mahāyānist, would have escaped the last of all possible fetters and entered upon the Highway of the Supramundane Evolu-

'In the *Sūtra* called *The Questions of Akshshayamati*[1]
it is said: "*Prajñā* separated from *Upāya* fettereth one to
*Nirvāṇa*, and *Upāya* without *Prajñā* fettereth one to the
*Sangsāra*". Therefore the two should be in union. . . .

'Again, for illustration, just as one desirous of reaching
a certain city requireth the eyes for seeing and the feet for
traversing the way, so doth one desirous of reaching the City
of *Nirvāṇa* require the eyes of *Prajñā* and the feet of
*Upāya*.

'Furthermore, this *Prajñā* is neither produced nor born of
itself. For illustration, a small faggot of dry wood will not
produce a large fire nor burn for long, but a great pile of dry
wood will produce a great fire which will burn for a very long
time ; so, likewise, merely a small accumulation of merits will
not produce a great *Prajñā*. Great accumulations of *Dāna*
[or Charity] and of *Shīla* [or Morality] and of the rest [of the
Five *Paramitas*] alone will produce a great *Prajñā*, consuming
all impurities and obscurations. . . .

'The characteristic of *Prajñā* is to discern the nature of all
things. . . . What is *Prajñā*? It is the differentiating of all
things.'

## II. THE THREE KINDS OF *PRAJÑĀ*

'There are three kinds of *Prajñā*, namely, Worldly Wisdom,
Lower Transcendental Wisdom, and Higher Transcendental
Wisdom. They are differentiated as followeth : the first con-
sisteth of the four *vidyās* [or the four arts and sciences], which
are, Medicine or the Healing Art, Philosophy, Language or
Literature, Handicrafts. The *Prajñā* which is produced or
born from the practice and comprehension of these four
classes of worldly knowledge is called Worldly Wisdom.
The Lower Transcendental Wisdom compriseth that sort of
*Prajñā* which the Srāvakas and the Pratyeka Buddhas[2]

tion. The Mahāyānist recognizes a degree of *Nirvāṇic* Enlightenment which is
even lower than this first degree. It appears to be an imperfect realization or
rather a foretaste of *Nirvāṇa* ; for, as our text says, 'a being once attaining that
*Nirvāṇa* remaineth therein for 84,000 *mahā-kalpas*'.

[1] Text : *Blo-gros-mi-zad-pa* (pron. *Lo-do-mi-zad-pa*) : Skt. *Akshshayamati
Paripricchā*.

[2] See p. 94[5].

attain by hearing, pondering, and meditating [upon the *Dharma*]. It consisteth in realizing the physical body to be impure, transitory, and the source of sorrow, and that the physical body containeth no permanent [or unchanging] ego. The second kind of Transcendental Wisdom, called the Greater or Higher Transcendental Wisdom, is that which the Mahāyānist attaineth after having listened to, pondered over, and sat in meditation upon the Mahāyānic teachings. It consisteth in realizing all things as being by nature *Shūnyatā* [or Voidness], having in reality no birth, no foundation, and devoid of root. In the *Prajñā-Pāramitā Sapta-Shatika* [1] it is said : " To know that all things are unborn is *Prajñā-Pāramitā.*" . . .

### III.  THE PERSONAL EGO

'The term personal ego [Tib. *gang-zag* : Skt. *pudgala*], of which there are various interpretations by various Schools, is essentially the term applied to that which accompanieth *Chit* or *Buddhi*, and taketh births in the successive chains of physical shapes ; or it is that which persisteth in performing all classes of actions, appeareth to be conscious—the rogue who playeth every sort of trick. In the *Fragments* [2] it is said : " The continuous course or persistence [of *karmic* propensities] is called the *pudgala* ; that which exhibiteth all rogueries is that very thing." Believing the ego to be permanent and single [or separate], one becometh attached to it ; and that is [then] called the *ātmā*, or ego, of the selfish being, or individual. This bringeth on defilements ; the defilements breed bad *karma* ; the bad *karma* breedeth miseries ; and the source of these undesirable things is the ego [or self]. For it is said in the *Explanations* : [3] " The idea of ' I ' suggesteth ' others', and from this holding to the ' I ' come like and dislike. And together, these, in turn, breed all manner of evils."

[1] That is, the *Prajñā-Pāramitā in Seven Hundred Shlokas*, another of the epitomized versions.

[2] Text : *Sil-bu*, meaning, ' Fragments [or Particles]', apparently a Tibetan *sūtra* of collected Mahāyānic aphorisms.

[3] Text : *Rnam-hgrel* (pron. *Nam-del*), meaning, ' Explanations'.

'As to the "ego of *dharma*", why is it so called?

'Because it hath [or to it is attributed] characteristics; and it is said that whatever hath a characteristic is known as a "*dharma*". Hence the belief in the reality of external objects and of internal mind is called the "ego of *dharma*". These two kinds of belief, in an individualized "I" and in the universal reality of matter and [mundane] mind, are designated as the "Two Egos".'[1]

### IV. THE EXISTENCE OR NON-EXISTENCE OF ATOMS

There now follow two folios of argumentation refuting the belief in the 'Two Egos'. The most remarkable of the arguments concern the existence or non-existence of material atoms, of which the master minds of India had already conceived unknown centuries ago, long before the rise of European science.

'The Vaibhashīkas assert that atoms exist; that each of them, independently of another, hath a space in which to whirl; and that it is due to mind's activity that they have coherence. The Sautrāntikas assert that the atoms exist, that they have no space in which to whirl, but remain in close proximity to one another without actually being in contact with one another.'[2]

The text proceeds to expose the fallacy of both these theories, and also of the theory of a universe built up of atoms, inasmuch as all such theories, like all worldly wisdom, are *māyā*.

'If there be put the question, "But what then is this which existeth round about us—these vivid manifest phenomena, unquestionably obvious to our perceptual faculties?" the reply is, "They are but the outward reflection of our own mind. Or, in other words, they are but the hallucinations of the mind outwardly reflected as such."

'How are we to know that such is actually so?

---

[1] The *pudgala* ego is the erring 'I', the selfish self, which, by clinging to the *Buddhi*, impedes spiritual unfoldment. The ego of *dharma* consists of the erroneous belief that external phenomena and internal mind have real existence of themselves, as something apart from the One Mind.

[2] The Vaibhāshikas and Sautrāntikas represent early sects of Indian Buddhism.

'In virtue of that which hath been revealed by means of various similes and illustrations, and by our own reasoning [or realizing].'

In short, as this teaches, the *Prajñā-Pāramitā* represents a method of arriving at Right Knowledge, which, for the Great *Yogin* who has first put it to the test of successful application, in the transcendent realm of the Supreme Science of Internal Mind (the *Ātma-Vidyā* of the Vedāntists), is as scientific and rationalistic as any of the laboratory methods employed by our scientists of Europe and America. The latter experiment with *Māyā*, the Great *Yogin* analyses Reality, and, by the 'Short Path', attains the 'Boundless Wisdom' and reaches the Other Shore.

Here endeth the Seventh and last Book
of this Volume of *Yoga* Lore
of the *Gurus*.

# INDEX

Black-type figures indicate the chief references, most of which may be used as a Glossary.